1010

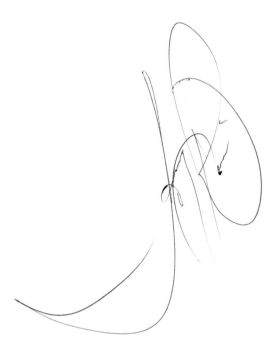

Still Inside

The Tony Rice Story

Tim Stafford & Caroline Wright

For Alison Krauss
with unfathomable love, respect and admiration.
—*Tony Rice*

For Daniel.
—*Tim Stafford*

For three dear men:
my father, Tony; my husband, Matt; and my son, Jay.
—*Caroline Wright*

STILL INSIDE: The Tony Rice Story

Word of Mouth Press, Inc.

Editorial director: Johnny Burton
Editor-in-chief: Tim Stafford
Project manager: Scarlett Smith
Design director: Bobby Starnes
Composition: ElectraGraphics, Inc.
Cover design: Bobby Starnes

Printed in the United States of America

1 2 3 4 5 6 7 8 9 10

ISBN 978-0-578-05113-0

Word of Mouth PRESS

About This Book

Welcome to the world of guitarist Tony Rice and his music.

Some of you are devoted acoustic music lovers who have waited years for this biography. Some of you are casual fans who are curious about Tony Rice. Still others will be completely unfamiliar with our subject and his music. We hope our presentation of Tony's story provides an informative, inspirational and entertaining experience for all.

In preparation for this book, we recorded hundreds of hours of interviews and countless outrageous, funny, heartbreaking, remarkable stories, enough to fill three books of this size. We also developed our own references to keep our project organized. These references are included at the very end of the book for quick access. A complete discography of the recorded music of Tony Rice may be found on page 298. On page 284, there's a detailed timeline of the milestones in Tony's life and career. We've provided a "Cast of Characters" on page 275, with a brief description of many of the individuals who are quoted or mentioned in this book. Fans who would like to read more about Tony will find a collection of select resources on page 306.

As you read, you will likely notice overlap and contradictions in some stories. All have been included intentionally. To the best of our ability, the anecdotes in this book have been faithfully transcribed in the natural voices of the people who shared them. Natural voices are sometimes profane, and this book does contain the occasional profanity. "Language like that is simply a way that musicians communicate with each other," says Tony. We have tried to reproduce their voices accurately. Therefore, we encourage parents to review this book to determine if it is appropriate for their children.

There are seven chapters in Tony's story, each with two parts. In the first, Tony tells his own story in his own words. In the second part, we hear the voices of his family, friends, and fans, adding their own memories and testimonials . . . joining in on the chorus, as it were. Extraordinary photographs appear throughout, providing reference points for the milestones in Tony's life.

In 2003 and again in 2005, Tim's co-author Caroline Wright visited Tony and his wife, Pam, in their small North Carolina town. Caroline stayed for several days with Tony's mother, "Aunt Lou" Rice, who generously shared her photos and most intimate family memories. She also traveled with Tony to some of his gigs, interviewing him for this book as they drove and documenting her experiences along the way. An installment of "On The Road with Tony Rice," excerpted from her journal, accompanies each chapter.

Chapter 7 addresses the very special subject of Tony's guitar, an instrument whose history and character are steeped in legend. It also includes a study of Tony's technique written by Tim Stafford, co-author and instigator of this book and a guitarist himself.

As his friends, fans and peers testify throughout the book, often with great passion, the presence of Tony's music in their lives has enriched, changed, and sometimes even redeemed them. In the bluegrass community, his fellow musicians are quick to describe him as the most generous of men, yet they also regard him as mysterious, even impenetrable. It is our wish that this book will underscore Tony's relevance as a groundbreaking American musical artist, and demystify an icon who often seems enigmatic even to those he calls his closest friends.

Table of Contents

Introduction
by Ricky Skaggs

Of all the bluegrass guitar players in the 20th and 21st centuries, Tony Rice has been the most influential.

The first time I saw Tony was in 1970. I was 16 years old, playing mandolin with Ralph Stanley. Tony was playing with the Bluegrass Alliance, a group from Louisville, Kentucky. I remember thinking what a great guitar player he was and also what a unique-sounding voice he had. We worked at some of the same bluegrass festivals but on different days, so years went by before we would officially get to meet.

The next year Tony left the Bluegrass Alliance, joined J.D. Crowe's band and moved to Lexington. A few years later I left Ralph Stanley's band and moved to Washington, D.C. to work with the Country Gentlemen. While I was there I became great friends with John Starling, a doctor at Walter Reed Army Hospital by day and a bluegrass musician and singer by night with the Seldom Scene. One day in 1974 John called me for a recording session. He was going to be producing an album called *California Autumn* for Tony Rice. I thought, "*Finally* I'm going to get to meet this guy!" Not only did I meet him, but I got to play and sing on his record. That started a friendship that's still going today. It was amazing how our voices blended the very first time we sang together. It wasn't Tony's first solo album, but his first record to use musicians other than J.D. Crowe's band. It was a way for him to play outside of his normal musical surroundings, stretching him a little bit in a new direction. It really showcased his versatility as a serious player and singer.

In the fall of that year, I got a phone call from Crowe, who said that Larry Rice, Tony's brother, was going to be leaving the band. He asked if I would be interested in taking the job. I told him I didn't know how long I could stay because I had plans to start a group with my childhood friend, Keith Whitley, who'd been in Ralph Stanley's band with me when we were kids. J.D. said, "Just come and stay as long as you can." One of the main reasons I accepted was I knew it would be a great opportunity for me to get to sing and play some more with Tony.

Working with Tony that year in the New South was a great thing for me. I learned so much about the groove, about playing in the pocket, something that he and J.D. owned! Also, getting to sing with Tony every night was a little bit of heaven. I loved it so much. It was a wonderful experience, but way too short-lived. In 1975 Tony left the New South, moved to California and went to work with the David Grisman Quintet, stretching his musicianship even more. That group made some of the freshest new acoustic instrumental music I'd ever heard. Tony's guitar playing was now becoming recognized around the world.

Today, he's the gold standard. Younger guitar players like Tim Stafford, Kenny Smith, Jim Hurst, David Grier, Bryan Sutton, Clay Hess, Cody Kilby and so many others grew up listening to him. These are all great players who are at the top of their game today. I think they can all look back and say that Tony Rice had a deep impact on their playing style. Even musicians known for playing other instruments and in other genres—including Alison Krauss, Béla Fleck, and Chris Thile—have been moved and inspired by his peerless taste, tone, and timing.

It's pretty amazing to see how Tony's seed has been sown into good soil, and now a great harvest of young guitar players are out in the marketplace influencing a whole new generation. I know for sure that I've been influenced by Tony's great playing. God bless you, Tony Rice. You are loved by so many of us. You keep playing, and the world will keep listening!

Ricky Skaggs & Tony Rice during the recording of Skaggs & Rice *in 1979.*
(Photo by Jon Sievert)

STILL INSIDE
The Tony Rice Story

Every once in a while, there are seminal figures. They don't come along even every five years. You might, by a fluke, get two of them in 20 years. Tony's one of those guys. He's literally changed the face of the guitar and how it's played in this music, and set the standard.

Béla Fleck, banjo legend, innovator

When *Now That I've Found You* went platinum, Denise [Stiff, Alison's manager] asked, "Well, do you want to send your awards to anybody?" I was like, "I really want to send one to Tony, but I can't just send it, I have to write something!"

And so I sat at the typewriter and I'm typing and crying, I don't even know how many drafts. "He doesn't want that record! He'll think it's stupid and I'm stupid!" I was just trying to write one line and I couldn't do it. I don't know how many pieces of paper I threw away. *[mock sobbing]* "You don't understand! There's no way I could write it down!"

I think it ended up saying, "Thank you for being nice to me." There were probably tears all over it. He's thinking, "What is this film on this note here?"

Alison Krauss, singer/fiddler/bandleader

Tony doesn't seem to have fans; they're more like disciples.

Raymond Fike, fan

Tony's an amazing player. There's just a handful of players who have achieved that level of virtuosity, and he's one of them. It's an astounding thing; like Pablo Casals or Yo Yo Ma. He's in that category. Those people are in a whole other universe by themselves.

Linda Ronstadt, legendary vocalist

One day I was listening to one of Tony's albums and Roy came to the front of the bus and asked what I was listening to, so I took the headphones off and put them on him. He wandered to the back of the bus. About ten minutes later he came up front and asked who it was that he was listening to. I told him Tony Rice. He said, "This guy is the best singer I ever heard."

And from that time on, Roy was Tony's biggest fan.

Benny Birchfield, longtime road manager, guitarist, close friend of Roy Orbison

I remember at the age of eight waking up and going to sleep to *Church Street Blues*. The music was so beautiful that I honestly cried at times, but not from sadness. The songs, the words, the melody . . . all moved me. Like most of Tony's fans, I play guitar. Most days as a child, my old Martin was in hand and Tony was in mind.

At age 12 I met Tony at the Ashland Kentucky Paramount Arts Center. Tony let me come backstage after the show. I remember his hands the most—he seemed to completely engulf my arm in those hands. At first I couldn't speak. What do the angels say to God? Mr. Rice was kind enough to say "So, you're a picker, son?" I told Tony how much I admired him, how I grew up listening to him, that he was my hero, and all I ever did was sit around and try to play like him. Tony's reply was, "I'm flattered, son. Keep pickin'." Needless to say, I never stopped.

At the age of 19 I joined the Army. It was the loneliest time of my life. I was sent to Bosnia while Kosovo was being bombarded. The jets flew by nightly and bombs blew men and women to hell. I heard it all. I can honestly say it changed me.

Through all of the adversities, all the trials, Mr. Rice and his guitar pulled me through. On lonely nights I sang "Summer Wages" while snow fell in the Balkans. When I was homesick and sad it was "Home from the Forest." Tony pulled me through all of it. To this day I always say "Thank God for Tony Rice." He was, is, and forever will be, my hero.

Brandon Lee Adams, fan

In 1991, during hunting season, I was very down and depressed, to a level I didn't even know I could sink to. I did not know what was wrong but I knew I could not go on living. I had a very good job with a Fortune 500 company but I just wanted to die. I had already arranged my suicide to look like an accident in the woods that day. I sat in my truck, waiting for daybreak. I had my radio on and they played a song that took me back to when I was a kid. I had not picked a guitar in over 15 years, but I had an overwhelming desire to find out who was playing that song and picking.

It was Tony Rice's "Church Street Blues." That day, I sought help. I found out that I had an illness called bipolar disorder. I take medication for this and I am fine now, and a good picker. I see Tony whenever he comes around because I credit him in a big way with being the person that saved my life. This is the first time I have ever told this to anyone. In a way, Tony with his hands took the gun from my hand early that morning.

Rick Campbell, fan

Tony Rice pretty much saved my childhood, saved me from going insane, because when my mom and dad split up, I leaned on him and his albums to get me through a lot of hard stuff. I could sit down in my room and play and get away from everything. He really helped.

> **Guitarist Clay Jones**

Tony is one of those musicians I can listen to and actually weep. When *Unit of Measure* came out, I was driving through Lexington, Kentucky and we had it on. "Shenandoah" came on, and I just started crying. I said, "Boy, that's his epitaph right there." "Shenandoah" sort of encapsulates everything about Tony's ability to communicate musically as anything else for me, really. And it certainly isn't a hot lick song. It's just a laid-out baring of emotions and feeling.

I don't think it makes any sense just to say, "Well, he's the best there ever was," because I really think there's never been a guitar player that had absolutely no barrier between his emotions and feelings and the music that flowed through him like Tony does. And to me, that's the beauty of music, because that's an infinite thing. Absolutely infinite.

> **Banjoist Dave Talbot**

My love and admiration for Tony goes back to what made me really want to play music. My whole concept of music itself came alive because of Tony. The singing and the playing are so shockingly beautiful, but for me, more than anything, it was Tony's production of the songs that he chose to sing, and the kind of person he portrayed, and portrays, himself to be in the choices he makes musically. His records are the textbooks for me. Tony is the epitome of the kind of things that I would want to be someday—that's my desire as a musician, to reach for that.

> **Alison Krauss, quoted in "Krauss & Rice: A Bluegrass Star and Her Hero" by Richard Harrington, Washington *Post*, May 11, 2007**

Tony is sort of like the Earl Scruggs of the guitar because his influence is just massive. People define flatpicking based on how many standard deviations it is away from the Tony Rice style.

One of the first times I ever sat down and watched Tony really play, I remember thinking he had a facility on the guitar that reminded me of the greatest guitar player I ever saw: Sabicas [*née* Agustín Castellón Campos, the great flamenco guitarist]. I saw Sabicas three times, the first when he was about 60 years old and at the absolute height of his powers. I remember staggering out of the concert hall, thinking, "In the war between man and guitar, this is the first man I've seen who is winning," [the first] who was actually in control of the instrument. And the first time I saw Tony, I thought the same thing about him: "Here is a guy who actually treats the guitar not as a sort of mountain to climb every day and doesn't quite get there—sort of like the myth of Sisyphus—but instead as an instrument he has *mastered*." It was really impressive.

Flatpicking legend Dan Crary

In my years of attending bluegrass festivals, band contests, and jam sessions, I have lost count of the players who were trying to be carbon copies of Tony Rice, even down to the type of guitar they were playing.

Barry Bales, bassist with Union Station & The Dan Tyminski Band

Charles Mingus once said, "If Bird [Charlie Parker] was a gunslinger, there'd be a lot of dead copycats!"

John McGann, multi-instrumentalist and composer

I've only played one of my many electric guitars once since I heard Tony several years ago. Guess I should get around to selling them.

Mark Harrison, fan

On the Road
with Tony Rice

By Caroline Wright

Charlotte, North Carolina

July 2003: Tony Rice picks me up at the airport in Charlotte. He lifts my suitcase into the tiny backseat of his Mustang Cobra and we make our way to his town, where I will stay in a home owned by his cousin, Jewell Penn. The place is a huge, wonderful old mansion filled with antiques.

Pamela Hodges Rice, Tony's wife, is there to welcome me. Pam, in her own way, is as fascinating and complex as her husband. She's a darkly exotic beauty, wilting a bit in the heavy midday heat. She has worked for several days to prepare the room in which I will be sleeping. The bed is an antique four-poster so tall that it requires a miniature staircase to climb into it. Pam is embarrassed because there is a problem with the bed's frame; it's not quite locked into place and she hasn't been able to fix it by herself. It is the sort of bed that probably once caused maids and housekeepers great consternation. We shake our heads helplessly for a moment or two.

Then Tony Rice coolly and efficiently gets down on his back on the old Persian carpet and lifts those Lucchese boots and kicks the frame, not too hard, not hard enough to leave a mark even, and he does it once and then again, and we all hear the satisfying *click* when it finally shifts into place.

Leaving North Carolina

The backseat of the Cobra is loaded with gear, its suede upholstery carefully protected by rubber floor mats Tony has placed there just for that purpose. His wife comes to my side of the car and tells me to be sure to keep an eye on the ties he wears. "He's colorblind, you know," she confides, "and sometimes he makes some really bad choices about what tie goes with what shirt . . ." She kisses him and beseeches him to call from the road. "I worry!" she says plaintively.

He *pshaws* and folds his lanky frame into the cockpit. The scent of his cologne, Alfred Sung for Men, fills the air, not unpleasantly. "Feed the dogs!" he growls. "They're about starving, all eight of 'em." And we are off.

Tony drives effortlessly, with one hand on the wheel. His eyes are hidden by his Maui Jim shades. We pass a sign that says EXCEEDING SAFE SPEED WHEN FLASHING, and he is indeed exceeding the posted speed limit, doing 60 mph in a 45 mph zone. The radar detector is silent.

Our chatter brushes against various topics: dogs, Vassar, marketing and junk mail, Rolls Royces . . . We pass Boones Mills, get on U.S. 220 North towards Roanoke, then we'll proceed on I-81 to eastern Pennsylvania. It's a road filled with trucks taking curves on two wheels. Tony smokes and dips coffee from the thermal cup that is always at his side when he drives.

We are at the edge of the Blue Ridge Mountains. There are signs that say BABY GOATS 4 SALE. More landmarks: Fork Mountain . . . Rigg River, the signs say. We pass a huge coach. "Hey, that looked like just Lonesome River Band's bus," exclaims Tony, poking fun at bluegrass acts with big buses. "And they're from right around here!"

Eventually we stop at a Cracker Barrel. It's very busy. We wait in the gift shop for a table, and with a wink, Tony points out the New South's landmark recording, known to serious bluegrass aficionados as Rounder 0044, now re-released on Cracker Barrel's own label and available for $12.53.

Finally we walk through the restaurant to our table. We seem to stand out in this crowd of typical Americans in transit. Tony is impeccably dressed, as always, in a burgundy silk shirt, pressed Levis, and fancy brown boots, his long ponytail trailing down his back, and he's almost alarmingly skinny. But as I am about to observe, he certainly likes to eat.

He orders the meatloaf dinner with pintos and refried beans and a chocolate milkshake in a big water cup. He cleans his plate completely and efficiently, swabs the gravy with his biscuit, downs his shake. All the while, he continues to discuss the Clintons, technical riders, and gas mileage in his vehicles (21 mpg in the old Cobra, 27 mpg in the new one). Then we are on the road again.

Somewhere in Virginia

Tony Rice is the ultimate seasoned road musician. There's a slim guitar case in the Mustang's trunk. It fits perfectly into the car's boot, and he's got another one just like it at home. He travels with a dark brown leather garment bag and a light brown leather travel bag (each of its corners has been used as a dog's chew toy at one time or another).

When he travels, seemingly wherever he goes, he wears silk shirts in a rainbow of exotic colors, all long-sleeved; a lot of narrow Levis (30Wx32L); various snakeskin belts and fancy boots. Narrow elastics pull his long hair into a neat ponytail. He is acutely conscious of his appearance. He likes to look good on the road, and he will lament, on more than one occasion, the sloppiness of travelers he sees on this trip.

We are still in Virginia, it is night, and traffic abruptly halts, the big trucks around us grinding gears to slow down. Suddenly, right behind us, a huge silver pickup truck flashes its high beams.

Tony is talking intently into the recorder, and I notice that the gap between us and the semi ahead of us has gotten very wide.

He twists his upper body around in the seat to glare at the truck's aggressive and impatient driver. The movement is unexpected and amazingly fast, and filled with a dark promise. "Mess with me," it seems to say, "at your peril."

Chapter 1
Hard Love
Origins: Birth–1970

We all need heroes that are human.

Captain Dayton F. Rogalski, USAF, Tony's fan

I think people are afraid to ask Tony why he does things the way he does. Usually I don't have to ask him why. We have been living under the same roof together since October 1987. So I just *know* . . . but then, I also knew the boy growing up. If you knew the boy, it is easier to know the man.

Pamela Hodges Rice, wife of Tony Rice

Chapter 1: Introduction

If you'd hung out backstage at any of the popular California folk and country concert halls in the 1960s, you would inevitably have encountered young Tony Rice.

He was a skinny, edgy, polite little kid, transplanted from the South, dressed in a cowboy shirt his mother had sewn for him, usually carrying a Martin guitar that was almost as big as he was. And he was usually with his brothers, in their matching shirts, who played with him in a band called, much to his embarrassment, the Haphazards.

As a member of a fairly popular child's novelty act, and son of a founding member of one of only two bluegrass bands in 1960s Southern California, Tony Rice heard an extraordinary variety of music. The Golden State Boys, comprised of his father and uncles, played old Stanley Brothers and Flatt & Scruggs tunes and took the boys along to their gigs—or at least, to the ones that weren't in saloons. When Tony and his brothers began performing as the Haphazards, they often rubbed elbows with big acts like Merle Travis, Chet Atkins, the Stonemans, Bill Monroe, Glen Campbell, Peter, Paul & Mary, and the Kingston Trio. Once Tony even got to play Travis' guitar.

The Haphazards sometimes shared the bill with the Country Boys, a young band that would soon change its name to the Kentucky Colonels to avoid confusion with Mac Wiseman's Country Boys. Tony made it a point to hang around with the band's guitar player whenever he could. The kid, whose name was Clarence White, could play his beat-up old D-28 in a way Tony already knew was special and different.

His learning methodology began to evolve. He picked up a few things from his Uncle Junior Poindexter, whose G-run he admired. He played his dad's Flatt & Scruggs records and watched with fascination as the needle dropped and the record turned and the music filled the room. He stood with his brothers on stages at Knott's Berry Farm, the Riverside Auditorium, and the Hollywood Palladium, observing every band that played. And he hung out with his friend Clarence, watching his hands move on that ragged-out old Martin. It was a priceless musical education.

It didn't stop when Tony left California with his family in 1965, but useful learning experiences were harder to come by. His father followed big welding projects all over the Southeast and the family never stayed in one place for long. Tony took his lessons wherever he could get them: from a guy in Texas who played fiddle tunes on the banjo; from an art teacher who shared the latest record from a fantastic Canadian singer/songwriter named Lightfoot; from a buddy whose little Martin 00-17 played like butter; from a rich girlfriend whose daddy let her borrow his convertible and an eight-track tape of something called *Take Five*.

He probably spent his most valuable formative learning hours in isolation. At 17, Tony finally chose to leave his family's turbulent home. He spent a lot of that summer at his Grandma Poindexter's, alone in a sweltering attic bedroom, searching up and down the neck of his guitar for the key to the door of his own vision and potential. He also lived for a time with the Smith family, kin of his Uncle Junior's wife. He flourished in their care, and advanced his playing to a new level in their home.

But he didn't discover the key by accident, and it wasn't something that was handed to him. He forged it himself, by playing until his fingers ached and bled.

Intense focus seemed to be a family trait; Tony had seen it burn in his own father. A complex man with little formal education but plenty of natural intelligence, Herb Rice was a musician whose influence and charm motivated his wife's brothers to move across a continent, a highly skilled welder whose expertise kept him working all over the United States. The things he taught Tony had little to do with music. Like many alcoholics, Herb often seemed to his family to be two men. One man was honest and wise and generous, a fine provider and involved parent, and the other was a domineering narcissist who alternately bullied and ignored his wife and children as he frittered away the family resources.

Like many sons raised by such men, Tony is vexed by his own memories. "When my father would drink and upset my mother and the family . . . yep, I would get angry about that, but there wasn't a lot I could do about it," he says. "Sometimes I talked to him about it when he was sober. And he would listen . . . and he would go do what he was gonna do anyway."

He laughs about that for a moment. "There's a lot of my father in me," he says finally. The love and pride in his voice are so strong you almost do not hear the pain.

Tony in the 10th grade,
Seminole County High School,
Dunellen, FL.
(Courtesy Louise Rice)

I don't remember anybody ever showing Tony anything on the guitar. He could just look at people play and then he could pick up a guitar and play the same thing. And it comes so easy.

Hal Poindexter, Jr., guitarist & Tony's uncle

There's another song I wrote on *'68 Sessions* called "Thank and Be Thankful." It's got a kickoff on there, Tony does it with a flatpick, and even today, I don't think a lot of flatpick players would be able to do that. It sounds like a three-finger banjo roll when he kicks off that song. And he was doing that then, at that age! It's incredible.

Frank Poindexter, resonator guitarist & Tony's uncle

I knew from Day One that he would end up a picker. He was *that interested* in it, even when he first started. You wouldn't have to tell him to pick up the guitar and practice or anything; he just did it on his own.

Louise Rice, Tony's mother

In His Own Words: Tony's Story

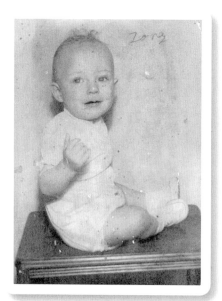

Tony at about nine months, Danville, VA, 1952.
(Courtesy Louise Rice)

The earliest thing I remember . . . I was a child in Los Angeles, by an open window, waiting for my father to come home. The reason I remember it is one time the window fell on my fingers.

By trade, he was a welder. Probably the most famous thing my father was ever a significant part of was the construction of the steamship *United States*, in Norfolk, Virginia. One year, all the employees got this elegant, high-detail framed print of the steamship *United States*. It was always on our wall in California.

I don't exactly remember when my father first moved the family out to California. I want to say it was in 1955 he bought a brand-new home there. Later my father had some land out in the desert, and rental properties. That was during the Eisenhower years, when a dollar would *buy* something. If you were a middle-class citizen, you could have a brand-new car, and a new four-bedroom house with two bathrooms, and two big yards, in a nice neighborhood, on a regular day job without going in debt.

Friendship was a very important part of my childhood. I would befriend anybody. It wouldn't matter—girls or boys—if it was somebody I thought I could converse with, it simply did not matter. I was fairly outgoing as a child. I got shy later on, in later grade school years.

My fascination with music really started not with the guitar, but of all things, a record my father had, a Columbia 78 of Lester Flatt and Earl Scruggs doing a tune called "You're Not a Drop in the Bucket." He brought this old record player out of nowhere—I'd never seen it before in my childhood, and then all of a sudden one day it was there. It was the kind you just opened the lid up on, and put the record on it. For me to see this record turning around like that, and have this music come out of this thing . . . I mean, I was *fascinated.* I'm not sure to this day that the tune was of any significance. The important part, back then, was that it was spinning around and around at this constant rate of speed on this machine.

I had caught the bug. From that mo-

Little T
(Courtesy Pam Rice)

ment on, it was as if the recorded form of bluegrass music had started to run in my veins. And it has never left me, and never will. Most bluegrass musicians of a generation before me, perhaps, would have had similar introductions to bluegrass, or music in general. I've heard a lot of them say that they were fascinated by the look of a radio, and then one day, they heard this music coming out of it, and it really just kinda grabbed them.

The standard rock 'n' roll era had just begun—you know, Bill Haley and the Comets. I didn't care any more for it then than I do now. I could go for hours about the shoddy musicianship that began in the rock 'n' roll era, and continues to this day. The pop entertainers that sold millions of records were serious musicians, and you had to be serious to be able to play that music. But rock 'n' roll, the only thing you needed to know how to do as a musician was to stand onstage and hold the guitar and put a bunch of grease in your hair. I mean, if you're somebody that can see the importance and validity of the musicianship of Jascha Heifetz, how in the hell can you simultaneously see any musical validity in Buddy Holly? As a kid, growing up, I liked listening to Flatt & Scruggs, and Bill Monroe, and Reno & Smiley, a million fold better than listening to the radio rock 'n' roll stations.

The notion of country AND western music back then was just a marketing thing.

That was a way to categorize the music—to call it country AND western. Like we've heard the term folk and bluegrass. They put those together in record stores. Back then, they did the same thing with country music. My father wasn't so much into the western part of it as the country part. The early music on the radio that influenced him to start playing was not bluegrass; it was country. Bluegrass was just another part of country music. There weren't any bluegrass radio stations on the air; there weren't any bluegrass record bins in stores.

He grew up listening to the Grand Ole Opry on the radio, and other little obscure stations that would play the Stanley Brothers. My father grew up on the music of the Monroe Brothers and the Louvin Brothers and the Delmore Brothers. And Reno and Smiley—my father was a Reno and Smiley *fanatic.*

Growing up, I loved baseball as much as any kid. My father used to take us regularly to see the Los Angeles Dodgers. I had

L-R: Tony, Ronnie, and Larry Rice in Los Angeles, mid-1950s. *(Photo by Louise Rice)*

all their baseball cards. I was on a Little League team, and I had to have the best bats, the best gloves, stuff like that. I played baseball whenever I could, but not in anything that had to do with school. I never liked P.E. I was the guy who had to forge a note every few days as to why I wasn't dressing. I would get some chick to do it or something, and the next week I'd write it with my left hand. After a while, I think every P.E. teacher I ever had got frustrated to the point where they just threw up their hands.

My brothers and I were close in a hard love kind of way. Larry was my hero. He was two years older. There was, and still is, a very deep, deep love between me and all my brothers. I don't think anything will ever diminish it. We had the normal frustrations. Sometimes we *really fought.* Me and my brothers would fight over weird shit. We'd slug it out, boy—I remember the bloody noses.

For years, one of the things I really loved to do with the neighborhood kids was marbles. We were marble fanatics! I mean, *tournament level* here. Ronnie came along and started getting kinda good at marbles. He'd have these little strokes of luck. He'd win the game and that would piss me and the other guys off real bad. So we'd fight over that, start sluggin' it out.

One time my father got so mad at Larry and I fighting that he yanked us up from out of the living room and said "I am tired of this! I want you to do it again in the backyard right now. You are gonna start slugging it out till one of you knocks the other one out. I want to put an end to this."

Larry and I started pretending like we were slugging it out, and we were both crying. I look out of the corner of my eye, Mom's over there snickering, my dad started laughing . . . Larry and I started laughing.

I read books for school—*Dick and Jane, see Spot run, see Spot play.* That's the way I learned to read, and I'm very proud of my education. I don't know that there was a better school system on the planet, than the Los Angeles County Public School System back in the early 1950s. I think they'd reached that happy medium of accommodation and education of the kids, and just the right amount of discipline, so the disciplinary process itself wouldn't create *more* psychological problems in the kids. They had paddles in the school, and if you were bad enough, if you had done the ultimate bad thing, no matter what it was, the principals at the school I went to had a paddle, and you'd get one whack on the butt.

I remember this: I was six years old, and it was the first time I ever kissed a member of the opposite sex. It was a birthday party for this girl. She had a crush on me, and I had a crush on her. Her name was Janelle LaCroix . . . I never will forget that name.

I adapted real easily. I could never understand why people would have so much trouble with that. When I was in L.A. I had established childhood friends for many years. Well, you know, they moved away, too. It's something many of us subconsciously get used to, early on: the fact that some friendships will not last forever. I don't know if there's anybody from L.A. I'm in contact with today, outside of musi-

cians . . . Chris Hillman, Don Parmley, the remaining Kentucky Colonels. I don't keep in touch with anybody from my early childhood, though there's quite a few I remember very well, kids from when I was five or six, just guys in the neighborhood.

In the year 1959, my family was involved in a horrible auto accident. I was sitting in the right place at the right time at the moment of impact. Everybody with the exception of myself was very badly injured. Multiple bones broken, multiple cuts. It was real traumatic. The other car was a big station wagon full of people that had just come from the fireman's ball, and the whole carload of 'em was drunk, and they ran a stop sign. There's no way my father could have seen them, so he broadsided 'em. I think they eventually got sued, or their insurance company got sued, by my father's lawyer. My family won the suit hands down.

Everybody was really tore up. My brother Larry had a couple lacerations that required a lot of stitches, and a mild concussion. He was treated and released. We went from one family member to the next, and the neighbors would help out, and we'd go to school. My father's mother had a broken arm from the collision, and was in a cast, but she was able to stay at the house, and be there for me and Larry.

There wasn't a house in that neighborhood, at least 50 houses, that didn't shower my family with toys and food. People would come when my mother and father couldn't do anything at all. They were in the hospital for weeks, in casts and braces.

My brother Ronnie was in traction for six months, through Christmas. People we didn't even know came to bring stuff.

I'm hesitant to use the word "normal," but we were quite normal as a family, in middle-class suburban Los Angeles. In my adulthood, I've come to realize that behind the door of every house in the world is a living drama of some kind. If somebody next door doesn't have a drunken father, then they've got a drunken mother. Or they have weird lewd sex habits or they're members of a nudist colony. Or they have terminal disease, or bankruptcy. In retrospect, I don't think my family would have been considered anything that would have deviated very far outside of the norm, if at all.

The neighbors loved my father because he was who he was. He just had a good

Herb Rice in Florida with his prized knife collection, circa 1982. (Courtesy Louise Rice)

soul. My father was a guy who would have showed up and mowed somebody's grass, if he thought they were unable to do it themselves. There's no doubt about it, he would become this other person at times when he drank—but not all of the time. Sometimes, when he drank, he was very happy, and he'd want to congregate with people, and he'd want to play with his kids. If I was around him and he was drunker than a shithouse rat, boy, if he was in a playful mood, shoot, yeah, you *bet* I liked it!

It could be the amount of Native American blood he had in him, which was a lot. Some people chemically react differently to consumption of alcoholic beverages than other people. There's speculation as to how it happens, and the physiology involved, but I'm not sure anybody knows why ten times a guy will get intoxicated and be happy-go-lucky and not cause any trouble at all, but the eleventh time, he'll be a total bastard. Or a woman, because they're not excluded.

My father was involved in the hobby of bluegrass music with my mother's brothers. They would get together to play and sing. And my father started a band because three of my uncles, my mother's younger brothers, came out from North Carolina, and my father taught them how to play. They went on the radio, and they had to be introduced as some sort of band. My mom said, "Hey, just call yourselves the Golden State Boys," because the milk we had was Golden State Milk.

At the time, there were maybe two bluegrass bands in the greater Los Angeles area, maybe even the southern half of California, *period:* the Country Boys, as they were called then—the White Brothers, Clarence and Roland and Eric, and Billy Ray Lathum and LeRoy Mack, the Dobro® player—and the Golden State Boys.

Those bands were there during the initial stages of the folk music revival—the Bob Dylans, and Joan Baezes, and Pete Seegers. If memory serves me right, Lester Flatt and Earl Scruggs were starting to become popular on virtually every college campus in the United States, even as far as California. Bluegrass music was becoming this thing that wasn't just for tobacco-chewin', moonshine-drunken hillbillies. It was a legitimate, valid art form.

My father had a Martin 000-18, and a Martin mandolin. He would occasionally, but rarely, drag them out and play them. Without those instruments being around, I may not have taken an interest in playing music. I didn't take an interest in wanting to play music just because I had heard Flatt & Scruggs on a 78-rpm record player. I took an interest because of the two things *combined:* hearing them on the record player, and knowing there was musical instruments in the house that played that music.

The first thing I fooled around with was the mandolin. And strangely, the first thing my brother Larry fooled around with was the guitar. I don't know how to play a mandolin, so obviously it didn't take us very long to make the switch. It was just something I did whenever I felt like it, which wasn't always as often as anybody would think.

One of my early heroes, maybe the very first hero I ever had as a guitar player, was my Uncle Junior. He was a real good rhythm player, and he had a real good G-run. He did it the right way! I'm not sure my father ever really showed me anything. I learned to make a "D" chord with the wrong three fingers, and he tried to correct me on that. He was partially successful, but I still make the chord the same way, to this day.

Once in a while, a couple of the kids at school would catch me in the act, strumming some chords, playing a bluegrass tune or something. They'd say, "Wow, that's something!" But I instinctively felt that if anybody knew I was playing this hillbilly music, I'd be the laughingstock of the school. I had a complex about that. I just kind of hid it from them.

Our band was called the Haphazards. I claim no part in naming that band. For one thing, phonetically, it sounds *stupid.* For another thing, I consider bluegrass to be a serious form of music, and to attach a cutesy-sounding name to it just seems preposterous.

Somewhere on my website is a picture of me when I was nine years old, standing in front of a microphone playing my D-18. That picture was made on the day I met Clarence

(Courtesy Tony Rice)

White and his D-28, and the first time I played on a stage, in the town of Compton, CA, at an indoor public performance that was broadcast over the radio on KFOX in Long Beach. I asked Clarence how old he was, and he said 16. It would have been the latter half of 1960. I went over there to sing this tune, "Under Your Spell Again." I don't know how my father arranged this, but anybody with any talent of any kind could get up and do a song.

I thought all Martin guitars were D-18s. Well, here was this big kid playing this guitar that I thought had to be a D-18. It wasn't. I heard him playing it, and when they quit momentarily, I had to ask him. I said, "That's a Martin, isn't it?" It didn't have a name on the headstock. He said, "Yeah, this is a Martin, but it's a D-28." I said, "A *what?*" He said, "A D-28." I'd never heard that term before, didn't know it existed.

So now I had this new number to work with. It came into my consciousness: the Martin guitar D-28. Boy, this one was ragged out, too, I gotta tell ya. It looked like somebody had left it outside in an active daycare center for a couple weeks! I asked him if I could play it, and he said, "Yeah."

He handed me the guitar and I sat on these steps and started playing. Then Clarence walked away. I didn't think there was anybody around. All of a sudden I heard this voice outta nowhere. It said, "HEY, BOY, PUT THAT GUITAR DOWN!" I was scared, you know? I thought the guy who said that had to have been the original boogeyman!

It turned out to be Billy Ray Lathum. I knew he was a good banjo player, but that's

all I knew. And in a soft voice, I said, "Well, Clarence said I could play it."

And he yelled back, "Well, all right then! Just don't *break* it."

Clarence and I saw each other a lot for quite a few years when we were kids. Our families befriended each other. Whenever that band played a gig where the Haphazards were playing, Clarence would always let me play that D-28. If he was there, he would just assume I would play it. He was kind to the world! I don't know if there was anything bad about Clarence White at all.

Bluegrass music was very limited and when the folk revival came in '61 or '62, it really almost gave bluegrass some validity. When I was 11 or 12, a promoter got together this diverse range of acoustic talent, all kinds of folksingers and bluegrass bands. My brothers and I ended up on this Hootenanny '63 thing developing in L.A. We played the standard bluegrass repertoire: Bill Monroe, Flatt & Scruggs. The Kingston Trio were popular, so we did a

Tony and Larry, date unknown. (Courtesy Tony Rice)

The Haphazards—Larry, Tony, and Ronnie Rice, and an unknown banjo player—with TV star Clint Walker (courtesy Tony Rice)

couple of their tunes: "Greenback Dollar," "Tom Dooley." I did a very limited amount of clean guitar playing. "Wildwood Flower," "Jimmy Brown The Newsboy." After that, somebody handed me an enormous amount of money—$20 or something.

There was a guy, Floyd Cecil, who used to travel around with boxes of new albums. This guy somehow managed to come up with every bluegrass album on any label. He would sell these things at gigs and radio shows, wherever we all ended up—Clarence, Roland, Herb Pedersen and Chris Hillman and Vern and Rex Gosdin and whoever was around. Anything that looked decent, my father would buy it for us, no matter what it was.

Man. What a day that was in my life, when a guy that played with my father's band brought Doc Watson's first Vanguard record over to the house, the one that had "Sittin' on Top of the World" and "Deep River Blues" and other stuff on it. I just died and melted to that music. I thought it was like God had come down and started playing a D-28.

By the time I got to the sixth grade, my brothers and I were on a regular Friday evening TV show on KCOP Channel 13 in Hollywood. The show was called *Country Music Time.* We ended up on there as Friday night regulars. The moment the whole school knew I was doing that, I was more or less a little underground celebrity. Even my teachers would constantly inquire about it: "Are you playing on the TV show tonight?"

Of course, the Kentucky Colonels were occasionally on the show, and my father's band. The Stoneman Family would be on after their arrival in California. There was a husband and wife team that later recorded a few albums for Columbia, Johnny and Joannie Mosby. Glen Campbell was a regular there; Merle Travis was another. Merle was this older guy who was a hero to me. I loved his D-28, and he let me play it on our portion of the show one night.

I remember talking to Clarence about rhythm guitar playing one night at the Ash Grove. This would have been about '63. I asked him point-blank, "Who's your favorite rhythm guitar player?" And he said, "Jimmy Martin." I put two and two together and realized that, aside from Clarence's syncopation, when he played a straight-ahead, driving rhythm, it was Martin's rhythm pattern, right down to the teeth. *The same identical thing.* You could hear it when you heard Clarence playing with Roland, Billy Ray, Scotty Stoneman and all of them. Boy, you listen to that rhythm guitar. It ain't Lester Flatt or Mac Wiseman, or Ed Mayfield. It's pure Jimmy Martin.

I don't want to paint a picture that's distorted in any way. From the time I started playing guitar at a very early age, my interest was *very* sporadic for many years. I had no idea when I was 10 or 12 that I would be a guitar player for a living. There were long periods after the family moved back East where I just did not have any interest in playing a guitar. I don't want people to be misled into thinking that, from the moment I started playing until the present day, my whole entire life has revolved around the guitar on a daily basis. That's not correct.

In retrospect, very young bluegrass bands now, the kids that are 10 or 11 years old, so many of them sound more technically proficient than some original bluegrass bands that started in the 1940s. Their musicianship, at age 11, is superior to that of somebody who played bluegrass music back then, at age 30. I have virtually no interest whatsoever in hearing any recording of anything I played at that age, because by the standards of today's 10- and 11-year-old musicians, it would be embarrassing. No doubt about it. And I wouldn't be able to derive any sort of pleasure out of it for its historic content, either. In other words, it was just *bad*. Period. I'm not speaking in this light to downplay or invalidate the growth process of my musicianship. I'm being realistic and saying that the music we created as kids was not worth a shit by today's standards. It just *wasn't*.

Realistically, my dad's musicianship was very crude. His guitar playing never developed outside rhythm, and his mandolin playing never progressed outside the early mandolin playing of Bill Monroe. He had all the basics. He had very good pitch; didn't have any tolerance for an out-of-tune guitar or mandolin. He had a naturally high tenor voice; he instinctively knew correct harmony without knowing the technical aspects. If he heard somebody sing a lead line, he knew the part above that, and he could sing without clashing, by instinct.

My father was a hard worker, took a lot of pride in his work, was one of the most well-respected men in his trade till the day he died. His work was known all over the United States by his fellow workers. He would show up on a job, and men he had never met would know him by reputation.

He ran the whole gamut, probably spanned all the versions of character defects that human beings can have, with equal amounts of kindness and compassion. He could be a bastard. And he could be really mean. My father had a very, very low tolerance for any kind of bullshit. *Any kind.* My father was a guy that prided himself on calling a spade a spade. He would size something up and see the reality of it instantly—not what he wanted to see, but what was *really there*. And if anybody threw him any bullshit, he didn't like it. He'd let 'em know it. Sometimes he'd *physically* let 'em know it. I was afraid of him, and I loved him.

In April of 1965, we moved from California to Florida. My father saw a change coming in Los Angeles that did not have anything to do with the reason he'd originally moved his family out there in the first place. He saw *that* California dwindling away—the California that was a growing, prosperous place, almost a separate land from the United States. You could be a hillbilly, or a Yankee; it didn't matter whether you were from Chicago, or Minnesota, or Florida, or New York . . . in California, back in the early 1950s, they loved you. It's a place you could move your family. People accepted you for what you were.

It may have been strictly work-related. Maybe he got wind of the technological advances that were taking place in the Southeast; there was a need for new hydroelectric plants at the time. There was a gazillion jobs. It could have been that. But knowing him, he was probably seeing things change around him in a way he didn't like. I think he was just tired of it. To make a long story short, he probably said, "I've had enough; I'm getting the fuck out." That's probably the simple story.

At the time, we were happy to move, because the only thing we'd heard about was this mysterious place on the other end of the continent called *Florida*. We drove with as much of our stuff as we could get in the car, and the rest we had sent. When we moved to Florida, we rented a nice house. My father never bought a house again after that. He would always rent whatever would be available and decent in whatever town we'd end up in. He was at this new level of his trade, working on nuclear and hydroelectric power plants. Whatever job he worked on was only gonna last so long.

After my father moved, my uncles started going back East, which kinda re-inforces the reason my father had done it. They wouldn't have left if there was a reason to stay. Everybody in the family started to slowly move back, with the exception of a few diehards that remained until just a few years ago.

My 8th grade school year was almost over; there were only a couple months left. We ended up in Safety Harbor, this little town near Tampa Bay. I went into the school there, and I don't know . . . I felt like I didn't belong in Florida. I had done extremely well until that point. I just smelled the vibe all over the place that I was a weirdo to them, and they were weirdos to me. And the school was backwards and dirty, and it stunk. It was like going to reform school, versus what I had just left.

The person who helped get us situated in Florida was one of my mother's brothers. He had a friend who had known Vassar Clements, who was from Florida, since a very early age. It was a very common thing in Tampa Bay for people to go fishing with a cast net. Everybody would occasionally get together for outdoor gatherings, what they would call fish fries. I used to call 'em mullet parties. It was at one of those that we met Vassar Clements. I didn't realize the importance of his musicianship at the time.

We spent the summer of 1965 in Clearwater Beach. By the end of that summer, my father's work took him further north in Florida, to a town called Dunellen, where I started high school. I don't remember that being particularly bad. But I had lost interest in school to the point where I didn't pursue any kind of studies. I was the guy that *never,* under any circumstances, took any kind of book home. If it wasn't something I could get my brain in gear for, sitting in that class, I wasn't gonna do it. But I passed. I finished out my freshman year in Florida, and then the family moved to a little town in southwestern Georgia, where I went to school for the school year, 1966 going into 1967, if you can call it going to school. I played hooky most of the time.

At some point in 1967 I found an old record player, and I got it up and running and went through the old stack of records we'd had in California. One of them I remembered from childhood days was the first Jimmy Martin album on Decca, *Good and Country,* with J.D. Crowe. I put it on, and for some reason, it sounded a hundred times better than when I'd heard it five years before. A couple cuts I would play over and over again, just to hear them in amazement. One was J.D. Crowe playing "Bear Tracks." Another was Jimmy Martin's version of "You Don't Know My Mind." I would play those tunes over and over again, in amazement, until the grooves were colored white from playing.

Go back and listen to the same record now, and it's still *amazing.* What's even more amazing is I knew it back then, when I was 16 years old, the significance and power of *that* banjo playing, and the way it differed from any banjo playing before. There was something special about anybody who could play like that. To this day, if I want to hear a powerful bluegrass instrumental, that's the record I'll grab.

I got really incredible grades in school, up to a point. My father and mother had to have noticed, because in Los Angeles this was a bright kid in the school system. All of my report cards were excellent. Now all of a sudden, here's this kid getting this report card in Florida and it's full of Cs and shit. They had to have known that something was wrong. From the moment I walked in a classroom back East, after being in Los Angeles County public schools all my life, it was never the same. I did not want anything to do with public school again as long as I lived. It's amazing I squeaked by as long as I did.

There was an exception: the last completed year of high school that meant anything to me was the tenth grade. I spent a school year with my family outside of Houston, in a town called Rosenberg. My father's work took him out there for a year that coincided with the start of the school year, and we stayed to the end of the school year. I liked that part of Texas; I liked my friends, I liked the school. I got along with my teachers.

I don't remember that I enjoyed one subject more than another, except for maybe science, and I was good at math. I was horrible in English. By the time I quit high school, I was still taking ninth-grade English. I did not particularly care for Spanish and typing, or a couple other things I ended up taking in junior high. I felt like I didn't have a choice. The first day of school, you show up in the rooms they point you to.

I never was that involved in school dances or any of that stuff. I was the guy who would occasionally get caught smoking in the bathroom, or something like that. I started smoking when I was 15 or 16.

When we lived in Texas for a year, Larry and I played some with two guys down there, Doc Hamilton and Floyd Jasper. That was another point when I started to get real serious about the guitar. Doc was amazing; he could play real good

Tony, Wyatt, Louise & Ronnie in Florida, 1968. (Courtesy Louise Rice)

Keith-style banjo, and good fiddle. And Floyd Jasper was a good Dobro player who lived out in Galveston. We'd get together a lot, Larry and I and Doc and Floyd. No band name; we just played. We'd go to an occasional juke joint.

We left Texas in '68 and moved back to Florida. I was in high school, dating and bumming around . . . That's when I left home and went out on my own, so to speak; I was staying with different friends and relatives. Occasionally I would stay some with my parents, wherever they happened to be living, and I would pay my mother and father some rent.

I became friends with a guy named Leroy Arnold. He was the only guy around with a Martin; it was an old 00-17. There were some Chet Atkins things he played fingerpick-style. I didn't have a guitar then; Leroy got me interested in playing again. I would go over to his place and play his

old 00-17. It was a smaller-bodied guitar, but it played so good it was unbelievable.

This teacher, Arthur Smith, was one of the underground folkies that ended up in Crystal River, FL, this little fishing village, teaching art in high school, just as a gig so he could make some money. I was a student, and he knew I knew how to play guitar. I went to his house one night, me and this other friend; this was in 1969. He said, "I just got an album I want you to hear." It was Gordon Lightfoot's first United Artists album.

For a period of at least five years, even though I would progress slightly as a guitar player, learn new things and so forth, it wasn't a day-to-day part of my life. If I could look back through the lens of history, I wouldn't be surprised to find out there were periods as long as a couple of months when I didn't look at a guitar. Maybe even longer.

By the time I quit school in 1969, my father and mother had separated. My mother, Ronnie, Wyatt and I went to North Carolina in the middle of the school year. That's when I started living with the Smiths. One of my mother's brothers who played in the Golden State Boys was Hal, or Junior. Junior's wife was a Smith and I knew all the Smith family. I was very fond of them. They wanted me to come over there and hang out, so I did.

For three months, I worked at a union job with Alton Smith, one of the Smith Brothers. I love the fellow dearly. I rode back and forth to work with him from Schlitz Brewery in Winston-Salem. I wasn't a pipefitter *per se,* but I was working with pipefitters as the hired help. My father got me the job and worked on it, too.

I had many good times at Ma Smith's. Probably my biggest leap forward, with the seeds being sown for what would be Tony Rice as a lead bluegrass guitar player, happened right there. I still had a D-28 my father got for me in Ocala. That was when I was frantically trying to search every avenue on the fretboard of the guitar for anything new and unique that sounded good. I made a lot of discoveries at Ma Smith's.

It was out in the middle of the country, I had a lot of free time and I started really getting serious about the guitar. I knew I had something to work on, and if I worked on it hard enough, it could become something lucrative; I could turn this into a living somehow. I started coming up with stuff on my own because I had time to noodle.

Before long, I knew this was probably what I was going to be doing until the day that I died. *I was gonna be a guitar player.*

I hadn't heard anybody else coming up with what I was playing, "Shenandoah Breakdown" and "Salt Creek" and stuff like that. Maybe Clarence played some of it, but to my knowledge, that stuff hadn't been played much. I'm not a melodic player anyway, so if I could imply the basic melody enough to state the tune, to me that was good enough. The rest was just improv. I never could play anything like Clarence White. I tried like crazy, but I just could not. I don't feel bad about it, because nobody else can either.

My uncle Frank Poindexter and I were playing with Bobby Atkins and Joe Stone on *The Stone and Atkins Show* on Channel 2, WFMY in Greensboro. In late '69 or early '70, we did a single, and then some stuff for this B-movie called *Preacher Man.* The album [*'68 Sessions*] ended up being a combination of stuff from the 45-rpm single and the movie soundtrack Bobby, Frank and I did. But it wasn't 1968, it was 1970. It says *'68 Sessions* on the cover, and when I first saw it, I thought, "*Wait a minute . . .* I lived in Texas in 1968!"

In 1969 I didn't resume the school year. I would have been 18. I hadn't got a draft notice yet, but I knew I would. I was talking to a couple guys about the Navy. I had to go register for the Selective Service, and the guys said, "If you *enlist* in the Navy, that's gonna be a feather in your cap, because the Navy's got musical programs. They're looking for guys with a good ear." They had me convinced that if I enlisted in the Navy, that might keep me off the front line of the infantry in the Army, in the event I got drafted. I failed the exam because I'm color-blind.

I remember telling my mother, "You know, Mom, I just really don't think that I can make myself go to school up here in North Carolina." She was disappointed, to say the least, but she knew it wouldn't do any good to tell me, "Well, you're going anyway."

I think my parents knew it would have been futile. The only option would have been for them to sit me down and to have said, "Okay, whether you like it or not, you're gonna go to every one of your classes, and you're never going to skip, and you're gonna make all good grades." Do you think I would have done it? No. They knew I wouldn't. I think deep in their souls, they knew I was a free-spirited kind of person that was going to do something else.

I suspect, by then, that they knew it was gonna be music.

Family, Friends & Fans

It was a real interesting music scene out here in California in the late '50s, early '60s. Not a huge amount of bluegrass players, but the ones that were around went on to other things.

Chris Hillman, original member of The Byrds

One time, Tony come in from school and he said, "Bluegrass music's the most unknown music I ever heard of!" He was probably 10 or 11. He was learning to play the guitar then, and he said the kids didn't know what bluegrass was.

Don Parmley, banjoist and former Golden State Boy

My favorite time was when the boys were old enough to play music as the Haphazards, and they'd play at the Troubadour, and the Palladium, and Knott's Berry Farm. That was our good times. Herb was proud of the boys, and I was, and together, we were a family.

Louise Rice, Tony's mother

Louise Rice (Tony's mother):

My maiden name was Dorothy Louise Poindexter, but I was always called by my middle name, Louise. I was born in a little town between here and my mom's: Ruffin, North Carolina, on October 17, 1929.

Dad was mostly a tobacco farmer. All the kids worked in tobacco. That is hard work. I think I was six or seven, walking into the fields and helping Dad, droppin' the plants in the planter. I remember taking him fresh water. As the other 14 kids came along, they had to do the same thing.

We all worked. We lived in a place for two or three years, and then moved to another place. A lot of people did that back then. And Dad was one of those people that liked to move around. Ruffin, Pelham, Yancyville, and all these other little places we lived, not a long distance apart. That was our life.

Louise Rice at home in 2007.
(Photo by Tim Stafford)

Frank Poindexter (Louise's youngest brother; Tony's uncle):

From a study my older brother Clarence did, he said Mom and Dad moved a total of 32 times! Daddy was a sharecropper; I'm the youngest son. When my brothers and sisters would get old enough to marry and move away from home and get away from farming, they would leave. We were extremely poor people, in a big family.

Dad, for his age—he was born in 1898—having an eighth-grade education was better than probably the majority of people he grew up with. You wouldn't have found a more honest and hard-working person anywhere.

Louise Rice:

I was Mom's helper, being the oldest. I learned at an early age to change diapers and cook. Of course, we didn't have electricity, so Dad bought a battery radio, and we'd come in from the field and turn the music on at dinnertime. That's the first place I heard bluegrass music. Charlie & Bill Monroe had a show in Greensboro at that time, and we'd be all gathering round the radio. I never dreamed I would grow up and have four boys that play music!

Mom and Dad didn't play, but they would sing; Dad would bounce his babies up and down on his knee, and he'd be singing "Ole Joe Clark" or something like that. My oldest brother Clarence was the first to have a guitar. The music really didn't start in our family until I met Herb Rice.

I got me a job. I was 14. Dad didn't want me to go, but he knew I needed to work. And I went to work in Dan River Mill. I had to tell them I was 16 to get the job. Dan River is a real famous cotton mill, with spinning and weaving, in Schoolfield [now Danville], VA. Me and two friends went together, and we all got jobs that day.

We asked my boss about a place where we could get a room, and he mentioned Mom Rice. Her name was Dossie, but everyone called her Mom Rice. The next day we found the house. When I walked in the living room, there was Herb and his dad. Mom Rice said she could take us in as her boarders. And that's how I met Herb. He was 15 at that time, and I was 15. He looked like a little kid to me. At that time, most all of Mom Rice's kids were married, with families of their own. Herb was the baby. He quit school at an early age, too. He went to work early. But later on, I think he got his GED when he went to work in Louisiana.

They were a musically-minded family. Papa Rice and Lillian and Julia, two of the daughters, were real good singers, and they played on the radio in Danville. Pop Rice could play the guitar a little bit, and Lillian could play. And Herb, at 15, he played guitar and was a good singer, so he would harmonize with them.

Herb had a girlfriend when I'd first met him. Her name was Reesie. He worked at Cousin's and Sam's Hardware in Danville. One day he came in and said he had broken up with Reesie and would I go to the movies with him sometime?

After I met Herb, I got a job in Burlington Mills, and then Mom and Dad moved to Ringgold, Virginia. Mom wanted me to come home, so I did, which was closer to Herb. We saw each other every weekend. He would ride a Greyhound bus and then walk to where we lived out in the country, carrying his guitar. The whole family would gather around and just listen. And they really became interested in the music then. We'd go for a walk and look for four-leaf clovers, and he'd be pickin' on the guitar and singing. The whole family loved him.

Hal Poindexter, Jr. (Louise's eldest brother; Tony's uncle):

When Herb Rice started dating my sister, he'd bring his guitar, and play and sing for us kids. That's when I started learning playing. They would take walks, and he'd leave his guitar on a bed, and I'd run for it and start trying to make chords. He played the guitar and knew a lot of Carter family songs, a lot of good songs.

I never did ask for lessons, but he did show me some chords. He played the mandolin and he said, "You know, if I had somebody to play guitar, it really would be nice!" And that's when I started really learning.

Frank Poindexter:

My uncle on my mother's side was the first musical person I remember in our family. He loved Django Reinhardt, and he played that slap style. We learned some of that stuff and we later got more interested in bluegrass.

My brothers Hal and Walter and Leon were able to get instruments. I don't know how they come up with the money. They would get together on the weekends and play, and they'd lay the instruments down and I'd run in there and grab one and try to learn something too. When Louise married Herb Rice, there was another musical person coming into the family.

Louise Rice:

I was working at Mack's Five and Dime in Danville when my husband and I married.

Dorothy Poindexter Weds Herbert H. Rice

On Wednesday morning, Dec. 24, at 9 o'clock, Miss Dorothy Louise Poindexter, daughter of Mr. and Mrs. H. W. Poindexter, of Route 1, Ringgold, and Herbert Hoover Rice, son of Mr. and Mrs. G. P. Rice, of Route 1, Danville, were united in marriage at the home of the groom's parents. Rev. S. B. Houghton, pastor of the groom, officiated.

The ceremony, witnessed by the immediate families and a few close friends, was performed before an improvised altar of greenery and cut flowers.

The bride wore a light blue tailored suit, with black accessories. She wore a shoulder corsage of gardenias.

Miss Estelle Harville, of Schoolfield, cousin of the groom, was the bridesmaid. Her dress was of pink alpaca, with lace trimming. She wore a bouquet of gardenias.

Eugene Rice served as best man for his brother.

Immediately after the ceremony a reception was held at the home of the bridegroom. The guests were invited into the dining room, where the table was beautifully covered with a lace cloth. Flowers in a crystal bowl centered the table. A two-tiered wedding cake and punch were served by a sister of the bridegroom to about 35 guests.

The couple left after the reception for a Southern wedding trip, and upon their return will make their home at Stokesland.

Mrs. Rice was educated at Ruffin High School and Mr. Rice attended Schoolfield High School.

Mom Rice and Louise Poindexter Rice in her wedding suit. (Courtesy Louise Rice)

He had asked me to marry him earlier, but I wasn't ready for marriage. Plus, his dad and my dad had to go with us to Chatham, which was the county seat, and even at 18, they had to sign for us to get married.

The wedding was December 24, 1947, Christmas Eve, in front of a Christmas tree, in Herb's home. I was a nervous wreck! My dad wouldn't come to my wedding. Me being the first one to get married . . . I think it hurt Dad. He had to get used to it.

Hal Poindexter, Jr.:

They were both only about 17. But they seemed much older than that, both of 'em. Somehow they just matured quicker than most people.

Louise Rice:

We lived with his parents for a while, and mine, until we could find a home that we could afford. We finally found a little place in Ruffin. That was in '47 before Larry was born. Mom Rice lived with us. We didn't even have electricity. We had to walk to the spring to get water. But we took it because we wanted to be on our own. Mom still worked in the mill, and she caught the Greyhound bus to go to work and back. We were real close.

There was a strike in Dan River Mills, and Mom Rice and Herb both walked through the picket lines and went to work. I was pregnant with Tony, and I had all new things that people had given me at the baby shower. The baby bed was in front of the window across the room. I think we had gone to my mom's to visit; she lived down the road. We lived real close to the railroad tracks. They had to have picked a time when a long freight train went by that cut out the noise, so that the people next door wouldn't hear. They broke every window in our house! The one by the baby bed shattered glass all in Tony's clothes. I had to wash everything. His little clothes, all that shattered glass. Because Herb and Mom Rice walked through the picket line, we were sure some of the people from the mill got mad at them, and that was their way of getting back at them.

Most of the time everything was good. And back then, Herb didn't drink or say bad language around me. One of his brothers blurted out something once in front of him, and he said, "You don't say things like that in front of my wife!" But once we left this area, he became a construction worker, and they're the worst, as far as language.

I don't like to talk about the drinking. It was years before he did that. He could take, at Christmas, a little drink, and that was it. He didn't drink when they got the band together, but the only place they could play was beer joints. There was nowhere else.

He'd have a beer or two, and then it just kept increasing until he had a problem with it. But sometimes he would stay for months without drinking anything. So it was good times . . . and bad times. But we loved each other, you know.

Frank Poindexter:

Herb impressed me as a very professional adult, family man, smart man . . . I had a lot of respect for him, and he handled himself well. And he was a very successful man. If he could have stayed off the alcohol, it would have created such a more *joyful* family. The alcohol ruined that whole thing. There were times when he poured gas over the house and was gonna set it on fire—all kinds of crazy things. Louise had to leave her house many, many times until he sobered up.

This went on and on, even when they moved from California. And the kids, they didn't want to be around him; they'd have to leave.

Louise Rice:

We made another move after Tony was born, to Newport News, Virginia, and Herb went to work in the shipyard. I think he left there in '54. He was a welder. It paid good money, and we had a nice apartment.

Larry was born in '49; Tony in '51. I knew with David Anthony, he'd be called Tony, and at that time, I liked Tony Curtis! Larry was named after a guy on a soap, Larry Noble. [The soap was *Backstage Wife,* a radio serial that aired from 1935–1955.] Prentis is from a doctor in Danville. Ronnie is named after Ronald Reagan. He was an actor, and I liked him. With Wyatt, we just liked the name Wyatt.

Tony was hyper where Larry was just laid back. I would put Tony in his crib and pull the side up, and he would bounce up and down. And he was the talker! I'd get my husband off to work, and I'd get the kids all dressed and comb their hair. I'd put them out by the picket fence in the yard and say, "Now, Larry, you keep an eye on Tony! If he tries to get out of the fence, come tell me." He'd run in the house: "Mom! Tony's over in somebody's yard, knocking on their door . . ." Tony was two and a half, something like that. He'd knock on the door and they'd come, and he'd say, *"Me Tony. Me a good boy."*

Tony, age 2, at Copeland Park, Newport News, VA. *(Courtesy Louise Rice)*

When we moved to California, we had to take him to have his tonsils out. The doctor found out his nose was broken; he'd broken it when he was a baby. He climbed on the kitchen table when my back was turned. He was just old enough to climb up in a chair and on the table, and he fell off! He was forever doing stuff like that. That was Tony. He broke his nose, and we didn't know it until we moved to California. He was just real hyper. The other three were sort of laid-back kids.

Hal Poindexter, Jr.:

I lived with Louise and Herb in Newport News in '52 and '53, and part of '54. I moved down with them for a while, probably to play music. Herb worked for the shipyard on some right famous ships, and I worked for an electrical supply company. We was in a little band in Newport News, Virginia, about 1953, called the Blue Steel Boys. Herb played mandolin, I played guitar, and we would sing a few duets. We played the radio station a few times, and I think we appeared on a TV station in Norfolk one or two times. It was just something we was doing for the fun of it.

Going way back, Herb always talked about moving to California for the job opportunities. Around 1954, he finally decided to go for it. He got my brother-in-law, Wesley Barrow, that married Betty, my sister, and they all moved out at the same time.

Louise Rice:

California was a dream. We just talked about it through the years, and we'd always wanted to go to. We were the first ones in the family to move out. Wesley and Herb went out together. They had to get a job and find a place. Then Betty and I flew out there a few months later. I was pregnant with Ronnie; he was the third one. We went out in October, and Ronnie was born in February. It was a hard trip. I just wanted to get there. It was rough to leave Mom and Dad and my sisters and brothers behind.

Frank Poindexter:

Around where we lived, you either worked in a tobacco field or you worked in a cotton mill. And neither one was a real appealing job. Herb had heard of some good work with the aircraft and aluminum companies in California. So they moved out there, and not long after that, my other brothers moved there, too.

Hal Poindexter, Jr.:

It was like going to another world. I found a good job right quick. We settled in, got a house, everything settled in place. And we started playing music as soon as I got out there.

Me, my brothers Leon and Floyd, and Herb actually started the band. We went to the Squeakin' Deacon show. On Sunday, this Squeakin' Deacon would have a talent show. Lee Casteen heard us on the radio. He drove over, and that same day we met at Herb's house and practiced. Lee played banjo with us until my younger brother Walter moved to California and started playing banjo.

Frank Poindexter:

It was always a real happy time, almost like Christmas, when Herb and Louise and the boys came home to visit. WOW! *You guys came all the way from California, and you're all the way back here in North Carolina . . .*

We messed with the guitar some, and we would sit there with it, and share some chords . . . At that point, it wasn't like we were heavily into it, but we did all have an interest in it. And it was pretty much just guitar. I don't remember Larry playing a lot of mandolin at that point.

Ronnie Rice (remastering consultant for *Time/Life*; Tony's younger brother):

When Dad died in 1983, I wound up with the old tapes, a form of communication for our family and the rest of the Poindexters in California at the time. They would make a reel-to-reel tape and mail it back to North Carolina. There's a lot of communication on there that you wouldn't believe . . . Some of it's music. I was four, and on this particular tape, I was singing "Sawing on the Strings." Tony was eight, and he didn't play guitar on the tape; Dad played, but Tony was singing "Battle of New Orleans." Larry could play, and he had an old guitar . . . I think he was playing "You've Got Me Under Your Spell Again."

Louise Rice:

Herb got a job at Douglas Aircraft when we first moved there. We moved to Downey, not far from Long Beach. It was a big change. Mom Rice retired and came out to visit. Pop Rice was still living, but they didn't live together. The aircraft company was just up the street, so I thought I'd go to work. That way we could have money to buy a house. I picked up an application and brought it home. When Herb came in, I told him what I did. "Oh, gosh, honey, forget that." I said, "But Mom Rice said she would be glad to keep the kids." He said, "No, my wife is NOT working."

Herb was a man who believed that the wife's place was in the home, and a woman didn't work, although his mom did. I did not go to work until years later, after the kids were grown. He wanted me to be a stay-at-home mom. It was okay with me then. I wanted to be with my kids. I made their clothes, their little pajamas and shirts; I even used to make my husband shirts. I made a lot of my clothes. I was a homemaker, and I loved to cook. Everything back then was from scratch. The boys all ate good. Tony was the slimmest one.

We lived in Downey for a while, and then we bought our first home in Artesia. All the homes in the neighborhood were brand-new. The windows went from one end to the other, and I made the drapes. It was a three-bedroom, two-bath house, and we felt like we were rich. We had a beautiful yard; it was a corner lot, and we worked very hard on weekends; we had roses and flowers and we put up a rustic fence. All the family, the boys included, would help do yard work. People would drive down the street and stop to look at our yard. I was so proud of that house.

Del McCoury (vocalist/bandleader; former Golden State Boy):

L.A. was kind of one big city even then. It was something new to me to be out there with all those freeways. Seems like everything just ran together. We lived in Downey and Norwalk, and the only two things that separated those two places was a dry creek. Wasn't no water in it. Funniest thing, never seen anything like that before.

Ronnie Rice:

Our house was at 205th Street in Artesia; there was an avocado tree in the front yard. When we moved to Elaine Avenue, it was only about three blocks away. It was like a *Leave It to Beaver* neighborhood. People took care of their yards and took pride in their homes. We were seven miles from the ocean. It wasn't very far for a bike trip. Larry and Tony would go there all the time. They always left me behind. Their bikes would go faster than mine!

Mom was like Mrs. Cleaver. Dinner would be on the table, when Dad walked in the front door . . . The house would be clean . . . She took care of us. She might have sacrificed her time for herself, to take care of the kids and her husband, I guess, but I guess they were raised old-school, and that was her job.

My father took pride in his home, in his yard, appearance . . . He was economical. He would save. People who grew up during the Depression, their thing was to save in case something like that happened again. He didn't cut any corners when it came to his kids, especially in music. He made sure they had good instruments to play. It was just the three of us, and he would take equal time with all of us.

Louise Rice:

My brother Floyd played music, and he and Herb would just get together and jam. And they had an old tape recorder and they'd tape things. I think it was mostly Flatt & Scruggs. "When the Roses Bloom" was one of them. Jim & Jesse stuff, things like that. They did gospel songs.

Ronnie Rice:

I don't think my father was a professional, but he could play everything—the bass, the guitar, the mandolin, a banjo . . . He could show somebody the basics and get 'em started. That was his talent right there. He could show me how to play the bass, and he could show Larry how to play the mandolin . . . He was very good when it come to that. Even squirrels in the yard . . . he'd have 'em eating peanuts out of his hand in two days.

Hal Poindexter, Jr.:

I enjoyed singing with Herb; he was a good tenor singer. He could go from bass to a real high tenor. He had more range than Tony or Larry. He never was much of a mandolin player. He just played simple one-string stuff, about as simple as could be. But his timing was good, and he sang real well, and he could chop rhythm on a mandolin okay.

Louise Rice:

Herb sounded like Hylo Brown, one of his favorite singers. You could listen to Herb and his dad and his two sisters. It was beautiful. With the Golden State Boys, he played mandolin, and my brother Hal played guitar. Then Leon came out and he played the bass, so there were two Poindexter brothers and a Rice there, and then with Walter, there were THREE Poindexter brothers, and Herb, and then we found a banjo player.

The Golden State Boys, circa 1961:
Leon Poindexter, Hal Poindexter, Herb Rice,
Don Parmley. (Courtesy Louise Rice)

The first time they played on the radio was around '57 or '58. They did a gospel show on the *Town Hall Party* [a KXLA radio show; *Town Hall Party* was also broadcast on KTTV, a Los Angeles TV station]. They all had matching outfits and they looked very handsome. They were sitting there at the dining room table, and they said, "We don't have a name! What are we gonna call ourselves?" Well, I went in the kitchen and I got a carton of milk out of the refrigerator, and the name on the milk was Golden State. I said, "Hey, guys . . . How about the Golden State Boys?" They looked at each other . . . "Yeah, that's good!"

Ronnie Rice:

I guess Mom owned the name, and I think Junior bought the name for $60, whenever we left California. It was Junior and Don Parmley, and whoever was in it afterwards.

Hal Poindexter, Jr.:

I'm the official owner of that name now. At one point, our manager, Bob Flowers, registered that name for me. This was at a time when we kind of had a split-up in the band with Don and Vern and Rex Gosdin. We sort of split into two bands, and Bob had the name registered in my name. That made it official.

Louise Rice:

They played for years on the Squeakin' Deacon radio show that came on every Sunday. They became well-known from that and the *Town Hall Party*. They ended up at the TV show on Channel 13 in L.A. and they played a lot of good spots. And they had to push themselves in stupid barrooms. People weren't that interested in bluegrass. There were coffeehouses, and they had music, but it wasn't all bluegrass. Not like the Golden State Boys were playing.

Del McCoury:

Hal Poindexter was a good guitar player. I think he played some runs and he was a good lead singer. He kind of reminded me of Monroe's early lead singers, maybe a cross between Lester Flatt and Jimmy Martin. He was really good, but he worked a day job.

Frank Poindexter:

They would go around and actually stop in bars and ask if they could play for the kitty.

Louise Rice:

We did good for a couple of years, and next thing I know . . . It seems like the music started it. Herb wanted to start a band, but the only places you could play back then were two-bit beer joints. That's when he started drinking—when he started playing in the beer joints.

We had, at one time, three homes in California. The one we lived in, and then we bought two homes and rented those out. But because of the drinking, Herb lost a lot of time from work, and we finally had to sell those. After that, he went through the money.

But Herb Rice was a guy who would go out and find a job where other people couldn't. It was his personality. He was an up-front guy. He was always on time for work; he didn't lose time unless he was sick. He would spend the weekend playing, and come in on Sunday night drinking, but get up Monday morning and go to work. He was very smart. If he had $2 in his pocket, in a couple of weeks, he had money in the bank.

Ronnie Rice:

The day after Thanksgiving, a Friday, in 1959, my family was in a bad car accident. I was in traction for six weeks and then I had a body cast on. I was pretty much confined to the bedroom or the living room. I had a couple of other injuries, too, but I had a pretty serious compound fracture on my leg.

Louise Rice:

Herb, Mom Rice, Tony, Larry, and Ronnie, and I had been to the grocery store, and we were on our way home—just two blocks from where we lived in Artesia. Later, we found out it was a fireman, and his wife, and another couple, out celebrating. I think they were drinking. It was right by a service station that it happened, on Pioneer Boulevard. The people that saw it said that our car kept spinning around, and when it did, bodies came out.

Tony was the only one that walked away from it. All the rest of us were really hurt. Tony took off and ran down the two blocks where we lived. He went around and knocking on doors and telling people what had happened! He was just a little tyke, and he was really scared.

I don't remember the collision or anything. They said it took ten men to lift the car to get my body out. When I was stretched out on the cement, the paramedics kept bending over me, and I would come to, and I couldn't hear what they were asking because I would black out. They put me in the ambulance, and on the way to the hospital, I was saying to myself, "Okay . . . this is my deathbed. I'm not gonna make it." I'd say, "Where are my boys?" and then I'd black out again.

They put us in two different hospitals, my husband and I in Pioneer Hospital, and Mom Rice, Ronnie, and Larry in Bellflower. When I came to, and people told me what had happened, I kept asking, "Where's Ronnie? Where's my baby?" Of course I asked about the other kids, but he was the smallest one. They didn't want to tell me what had happened to him.

I had a head injury; I had five chipped vertebrae in my back; I had a broken leg. I had to wear a steel brace for months, and crutches because of my leg. Larry had a few scratches, but he didn't get any broken bones or anything. Herb got a very bad head injury. Mom Rice had a broken leg and a broken arm, poor thing. She was in a wheelchair for a long, long time. She must have been in her late 70s, early 80s. And it was months and months before they could take Ronnie's cast off.

We hired an attorney from Sherman Oaks, and we spent so much time in his office, calling all these people, discussing what happened, and how much money we were supposed to get for it. It was settled before we went into court. I don't remember how much, because at that time, my head was a little fuzzy. And all that stuff was just left up to my husband. So I really don't know, except we got our settlement.

If you had walked in our home, you would think that we lived in a hospital because of the bandages, the crutches, the wheelchair . . . just a bunch of crippled people. Emotionally, too. It took a long, long time. When I would look at my kids, I would get so mad at the fireman for what he did to my family.

Ronnie Rice:

I guess our father was like the perfect father until after the accident. The accident was the dividing line. There was no *in between.* He was sober, and the best dad, and the kindest guy in the world, and he could go from that to just totally a different person.

Louise Rice:

Sometimes Herb and I went out to the desert to Hot Springs. This was after my injury, my back . . . I didn't think it would ever be right again. They had hot mineral water coming out of the ground. Although I didn't swim, I would get in the pool and just hold onto the sides. We had a little efficiency kitchen, and we'd go out and buy us a steak, and have a nice meal, just the two of us. Herb wouldn't drink on those occasions. We had good times.

Herb & Louise at the Village Inn in Crystal River, FL, circa 1970s. (Courtesy Louise Rice)

We didn't want for anything, as far as food and our well-being and everything. The worst part of it all was the drinking, and having to go to a neighbor's to stay the night, just to get out of the house, you know.

Ronnie Rice:

During the week, you pretty much knew everything was okay, but Friday night, you're peeking out the curtains at the driveway to see what pulled up. Not *who* pulled up, but *what* pulled up.

Frank Poindexter:

I wanted her to leave, totally, and get away from that danger. But I was not in a position for a young man to be telling his older sister what she should do. She was afraid, and you could see that. We didn't sit down and talk about it. It was just, "Hey, I'm praying that he's not gonna do anything more drastic than what he's already done." When he would get like that, she would go wherever she had to, for safety.

You know, Herb was a fairly small man. I sometimes wonder if he needed that, if he thought that drinking made him a little bigger man than what he was.

Louise Rice:

I might have been an inch taller than Herb. I was always very self-conscious about it, and I'd try to buy dress flats. He was a nice looking man, until the drinking and everything, it just it damaged him. It really ages you.

If we knew he was out picking, most likely he would come in drunk. We were prepared. I'd have a bag packed, and if he came in the front door, we ran out the back, because we knew he'd be drunk. As the boys got older, they turned on their dad a little bit, and started telling him off, how wrong it was for him to be treating us that way.

Hal Poindexter, Jr.:

Larry and Tony started a band, the Haphazards. Well, they were pretty good. They had a real good banjo player, Andy Owens, and of course, Larry was real good on the mandolin. He picked it up quick. It was just a big joke with Tony; he didn't take music seriously. He'd rather have been out riding his skateboard! But Larry, on the other hand . . . he was really into music. He spent a lot of time at our house learning to play mandolin.

Louise Rice:

I guess Larry was the first to get interested, and it wasn't long before Tony was interested. And then Larry went from guitar to mandolin. The Golden State Boys had been together for a while, and all this time, Larry and Tony were practicing. They got their little band together and they did good, the little Haphazards. I was really very proud of them.

Larry Rice (late singer/songwriter/mandolinist; Tony's oldest brother):

Our first check for playing on TV came out to $13 each, union scale. We played on the Hootenanny tour that year, at the Troubadour, the Ash Grove, the Santa Monica Civic Auditorium, on the same stage as Glen Campbell.

Ronnie Rice:

I remember the hootenannies back then. They were done in fairly good-sized auditoriums. We were on the bill, and Peter, Paul & Mary, and the Kingston Trio . . . We'd all be in the same dressing room. I remember 'em rehearsing . . . It's almost indescribable, to be in a dressing room with those people, three feet away from them, and hearing that live sound.

This one particular place was in Riverside, right along the coast. There was a park that had the big rollercoaster, the Cyclone, the one you see in a lot of old movies. We always liked to play there, because afterwards we could go over and ride the rollercoaster.

The boys in Clarence White's band were kinda quiet, except for Billy Ray, the banjo player. He was fairly talkative. Clarence was quiet. But Tony and Clarence hit it off. Tony might have been eleven or twelve. We'd play at Kernville, this place like an old Western town, and at Knott's Berry Farm, and Tony and Clarence would get together and play guitars after shows.

I remember one particular image of the two of them. There was this huge boulder at Knott's Berry Farm; probably several people could sit on top of this thing. I remember Tony and Clarence sitting on this rock and jamming together.

Louise Rice:

Johnny Horton did a song that Tony did, and my husband recorded. What was it? "In 1914, we took a mighty trip down the Mississippi . . ." ["Battle of New Orleans," based on a fiddle tune, "8th of January," which Tony recorded on his first Rounder solo project in 1978.] And he could sing it! It was a long song, and Tony knew all the words when he was little. You'd laugh, but you weren't laughing at him. He knew all the words. It was just easy for Tony.

Ronnie Rice:

Butch, the bass player for the Haphazards, had been in the band a year, maybe two. I think his mom and dad were concerned about school, and playing music was taking away from his education. I think that's the primary reason why he left. It wasn't because he wasn't a good player.

My dad said, "Okay, son. Here's the bass. Now you're gonna play it." I hated to. I didn't want to. In our family, you didn't have a choice. I don't mind playing music. I love music. But I just don't care anything about getting onstage, even today.

Dad took us in this studio in Burbank. It was a professional place, with this glass partition window between the studio part and the control room. And the engineer was in there, and he had headphones on, and we recorded a couple of tracks. "Little Maggie" might have been one of 'em. When we got through, the guy said, "Come in and give a listen." I heard the sound that came out of the speakers on the wall, and I knew right then that that's what I wanted to do for a living. I didn't care anything at all about playing the music; I wanted to be on the other side of that glass window.

Ronnie Rice during The Lawrence Welk Show *at the Hollywood Palladium, early 1960s.*
(Courtesy Louise Rice)

Don Parmley (banjoist/bandleader; former Golden State Boy):

In 1961, I was up in a little old town at a music store, trying to get a banjo. Somebody said he knew a band called the Golden State Boys looking for a banjo player. So I got in touch with 'em and went down to the house and auditioned for Hal

Poindexter, his brother Leon, and Herb. We just done some old standard bluegrass tunes. The only key Herb wanted to play in was "A"! We slowly worked him out of it.

When I first got to listen to Tony play guitar, he was just playing rhythm. About the only lead stuff he played was some of the stuff he heard Don Reno do on records. But later on, Bill Monroe come up there to a club in Hollywood [the Ash Grove], and that blind guitar player down there in North Carolina, Doc Watson, was there. Tony got to watchin' him play the guitar, and in just a little while, he was doing it too.

Louise Rice:

I don't think the Golden State Boys recorded an album, but they did record singles. There wasn't that many bluegrass bands around then. I think that's one reason they became famous in Southern California. They kept pushing the bluegrass until people just fell in love with it. Remember Barbara Mandrell? Back then she was playing drums. She was 15 when I saw her on Cal Worthington's show. The Golden State Boys played on the same stage. So the music was sort of mixed up, country and bluegrass and everything.

They did do some good shows, until the drinking stepped in, and they went their separate ways.

Don Parmley:

Hal Poindexter did the lead singing, I sang the baritone, and Herb sang the tenor. Herb was a real good tenor singer. He sold his mandolin playing better than most people that was really well-known. He just could get that mandolin and hold it up close to the microphone where he was singing and *pick it*, and people would just go crazy over it. He never was a very good player, just mediocre, you know, but he sold it real good.

Hal Poindexter, Jr.:

At first Herb and I worked together [on bandleader chores]. I led the group up till about '62, even while Herb was still with us. We had a little disagreement; I dropped out for about a month. During that time, Don Parmley took over as bandleader and remained that way after I went back. I still fronted the group, but Don was doing the heavy lifting. Vern Gosdin replaced Herb in early '62.

Don Parmley:

We had two television shows, and we also went off to different towns on weekends. We played a lot of shows for the sponsor of the TV show [Cal Worthington]. We went out and done shows for him when he'd buy a car dealership and take it over. He furnished me with a brand-new Dodge station wagon to run around in! We didn't get paid nothin'. I was sort of leader of the band at this time. We played all the time in bars. Herb didn't drink heavy when we first started out; it was probably close to four years, I'd say, before he started letting it interfere with his music.

He was a likeable person. I enjoyed picking with the whole bunch of them, till towards the end, and he got to tippin' the bottle too much. We were at a regular gig on a Sunday afternoon. He got so drunk he had to sit down on a stool. So we let him go. We picked without him.

Louise Rice:

The Golden State Boys had played at the Squeakin' Deacon show, which was every Sunday morning. We were on the way home and Herb stopped at this barroom and just left us sitting there in the car. I knew if I sent one of the boys in to tell him to come out, he would be mad. I just took it so long and then I said, "Okay, we're gonna walk home." I knew he was gonna stay in there and drink, and it wasn't fair to leave us sitting outside. I didn't want to be in the car when he was driving. So we walked home, about a mile or so.

When he came in, he was so mad. Oh, the language that came out of his mouth. It was horrible. And he just took his guitar and splintered it all over the living room. Tore it all to pieces. And that was a beautiful Martin guitar. He had a violent temper when he was drinking. He could take two or three drinks, and he would be that way.

Ronnie Rice:

A lot of times, we got drug to the bars with them. Mom would go, and the kids would be there. It didn't matter to me, because music, to me, even at an early age, was music.

There really wasn't a lot I could do. Larry and Tony were at an age where they could leave, and I was at an age that I couldn't. Dad was different with me. He would probably treat Larry and Tony the same way he would Mom. But he would never raise a finger towards me.

Louise Rice:

He would try to get a little hateful around Mom Rice when he was drinking. He'd say something bad about me, and she would always come to my rescue. One day he picked up an ashtray and he was gonna hit me. She got in between us and said, "You will not hit her! I know Louise, and she doesn't deserve this." Mom Rice picked up a dining room chair like she was gonna hit him with it! He ran out the front door, jumped in the car. You could hear the tires squealing as he went around the corner. That was his mom. She didn't say any bad words or anything, but she would really tell him off.

She lived it, too, because Pop Rice drank. But Pop Rice would just sleep it off in the haystack out beside the kitchen door. Herb had two brothers that were alcoholics. He had two sisters that were alcoholics. So he was from an alcoholic family, except he had twin sisters, Goldie and Gladys, they never drank. What was it Mom Rice said? Pop Rice's dad died with a jug of moonshine under his bed.

Ronnie Rice:

A divorced woman with kids back in that time was unheard of. It just didn't happen. It was impossible for a woman to go out and get a job and support three or four kids. She didn't have anywhere else to go. What could she have done?

I couldn't speak for my brothers, but for myself, I could say that it probably has, and probably will have, an effect on my life, for as long as I live . . . in one way or another.

Louise Rice:

Sometimes I would call the police to pick Herb up and take him to jail. He was on probation, and if he drank or anything, I would just call the probation officer, and they'd take him up in the hills to the place you had to work during the day, and he'd stay up there six weeks or two months at a time.

Herb was . . . I guess you call it *domineering*. I thought it was horrible to be mistreated like that. I didn't run around on him, never had an affair in my life. I wasn't that kind of woman. But he did me that way, and then he would come in drunk and cuss me out for no reason. He would make me get up and go in the kitchen, saying, "I want you to cook me some bacon and eggs!" And if I said anything . . .

Some people can drink and be funny; other people drink and they want to fight. And if you can't find somebody out in the world to fight with, you go home and fight with your wife. Yes, he took it out on me. When we would hear him pull into the driveway, we knew if he was out real late that he would be drunk. The boys, we kept their screen unhooked on the window, so they could just jump out, and I would try to get out the back door before he came in. We would go across the street to the neighbor's and spend the night.

Wyatt Rice (guitarist/engineer/producer; Tony's youngest brother):

Once we had to leave a place up the coast in Virginia when he came in drinking one time, and I got stuck in my room and couldn't get out. The law showed up and somehow from the outside they got my window open, so I had to go out that way. And then me and Mom left.

Louise Rice:

I have to say, Herb Rice was good to his family when he wasn't drinking. There were times when he would go almost a year without it. He provided us with a nice home and food and everything.

Young Wyatt Rice in pajamas, 1970s. (Courtesy Louise Rice)

Herb Pedersen (singer/songwriter/banjoist):

I met Tony in probably 1963, when my band came to Los Angeles and played the Icehouse in Pasadena and the Troubadour in Hollywood. We did a bluegrass festival kind of thing at the Icehouse, which included the Kentucky Colonels—Clarence & Roland [White], and Billy Ray [Latham] and Roger [Bush]—and the Golden State Boys, which was Don Parmley, Vern & Rex Gosdin, and Chris Hillman on mandolin; and our band, the Pine Valley Boys, which was Butch Waller, Rich Conley, Dale Hollis, and myself. Tony and his brothers were there as the Haphazards. Larry was maybe 14. I don't remember them being a novelty act at all. I remember them just playing straight bluegrass, but they were just real young. I guess that was the novelty in and of itself.

Chris Hillman (original member of The Byrds; childhood friend of Tony & Larry):

Tony must have been 12, and Larry was 14. Tony could barely hold his guitar. He was playing a dreadnought then. Larry and I used to play mandolin together. I'm about 4 years older than Larry. He was a real good mandolin player, but I think Tony was just starting to figure it all out. I know Clarence taught him a lot of stuff.

Ronnie Rice:

I think the Haphazards played till around '63 or '64. It wasn't a real long time, maybe a couple years. Maybe we just ran out of places to play. The early '60s was a big thing with folk music in California, and there were a lot of coffee houses and places like that. But I think it just eventually wore itself out.

Larry Rice:

We were on the verge of getting a contract with a major label as something like the Little New Christy Minstrels when my family moved back East.

Ronnie Rice:

I'm not sure why my uncles left the Golden State Boys. It could be because of the drinking, and maybe not. They left California over a short period of time. They just packed up and moved back East. I don't think making a living was an issue. I think a lot of them maybe got homesick.

Louise Rice:

Herb felt that if we continued to live in California, friends would call him and say, "Meet me at such-and-such bar." He had a lot of friends he made through the music. I had reached the point where I was saying "I just can't continue to live like this." And we decided it was best for us to move back East. So we moved to Florida.

Ronnie Rice:

It was a long road trip. It took five days to drive from California to Florida. We went to my Uncle Leon's house for a few weeks. Long enough for Dad to get settled in at his new job and make enough money to go out and get a place in Safety Harbor. In the summer of 1965, we moved to Clearwater.

I don't know why we left California. It could have been alcohol-related or not; I'm not sure. I know Dad held a pretty good job there. But whether he lost that job and had to relocate to find more work, I'm not sure. I was ten. It was just one of those things where your parents say, "Okay, son, we're moving; get in the car." You didn't really have a choice.

Louise Rice:

We had just moved in the neighborhood [in Clearwater], and Wyatt was a baby. Herb was out of work that day, the Fourth of July. He started drinking. Wyatt started crying in his crib. Herb came in and was getting real violent. I had to go next door to get a neighbor; I didn't even know his name. He came and stood in the door while I grabbed my baby and ran back. They let me and the kids stay over there. And of course, I had to call the police. It's something you don't like to do, but for the sake of your children . . . If it had just been me, I would have left. Not that I didn't love Herb; I did. But he was a different person when he was drinking. He would always say he was sorry, but then there was always the next time.

He wasn't supposed to drink to begin with. For one thing, he had emphysema, I guess from smoking real heavy night and day. He smoked in bed. He woke up two or three times a night, and he would smoke every time he'd wake up. Nights even when he wasn't drinking, he would fall asleep and drop the cigarette. I would wake up and he would be smoking and set the sheet on fire, sometimes even the mattress. I'd have to run and grab water to pour on it.

Ronnie Rice:

After we left Clearwater, we went up to Dunellen, Florida and then up to Donaldsonville, Georgia. I was in the 7th grade when we went to Rosenburg, Texas, a suburb just outside of Houston. Oh, I hated it there.

Louise Rice:

I thought I would never like to live in Texas. But once we got there, we found this very nice apartment; it was in a nice neighborhood, mostly schoolteachers and lawyers, and across from us a park with a big swimming pool, and a little pool for the kids.

We lived in Texas, we lived in Georgia . . . let's see, Virginia, North Carolina, Florida . . . seven states. A lot of that had to do with the construction business. But Herb made good money.

It was hard for the boys, especially changing schools. Growing up, my dad's limit was to live at a place for two years, and then you moved to another place. I was very shy, and I hated walking into a classroom, meeting a new teacher and kids I didn't know. I'm sure the same thing happened with the boys. I would always go with them the first day of school and meet the teacher.

Doc Hamilton (Texas banjo/fiddle player):

In 1966, I was living in a little town called Deer Park, a suburb of Houston, on the east side, and working for NASA in Mission Control Center. I think Larry Rice called a radio station looking for bluegrass pickers, and somebody at the station told him to call a guy named Robbie Shipley. I played with Robbie in a little band called the Moonshiners.

I'm not sure if they called over to my house or if they just showed up. They pulled up in an old black Plymouth, a real old fallin' apart car, and Larry was driving. They were kinda scrawny lookin'. They knocked on my door and said, "We heard you play bluegrass." I said, "Well, I play some banjo, yeah." "Well, do you wanna pick?" I said, "Yeah, come on in."

They had two old beat-up lookin' cases. Larry had a pretty nice old mandolin; it was an F model but I don't remember what year. Tony got this old guitar out and it had a hole in the front of it. They had tried to patch that thing up, took some popsicle sticks or something and wove 'em like you do a potholder, and stuck it on there, and then just gobbed a bunch of glue over that! It was the awfullest, rattiest-lookin' guitar.

Tony was a pretty good rhythm guitar player, but he wasn't anywhere near the hot licks yet. Larry was the one who blew me away. He was an awesome mandolin player, even at 17.

The only time I ever saw them was when they came over to my house. We'd pick all weekend. There was a music store down in Houston called H&H, and we would jam there on Saturdays pretty regularly. They gave us a corner of the store. There was a pretty good fiddle player named Bill Northcut, who played old-time and Texas kind of fiddle tunes. Whenever it worked out that they were off and I was off, we'd get together and play.

Larry and Tony and I, and a guy named Bill Clemmons who played the bass, threw together a little band. I think we played one gig, and we opened for George Jones at some beer joint in Pasadena, TX. We played four or five bluegrass tunes, and then George Jones actually showed up and played.

Louise Rice:

We left Texas and moved back to Florida, and Tony dropped out of school when we lived in Crystal River. That really hurt me, because I wanted him to graduate. I still think it was because of his dad's drinking. He just didn't want to be around him anymore. He would get so disgusted with his dad that he would lose interest in things. I guess school was one of them. He was probably thinking to himself, "I just want to get out of this."

Ronnie Rice:

Whenever Dad would get drunk and Mom had had enough, she would load all us kids in the car and go up to North Carolina. Tony was old enough to drive, so he would drive us up there, and the only place to stay was at Grandma's house. It was just kinda out in the middle of nowhere, not a whole lot to do.

Frank Poindexter:

They came to North Carolina when they moved back and Herb got a job—I think it was with the Schlitz Brewing Company up in Winston-Salem. Him and Louise had a problem at that time, just another instance of where he had mistreated her, and she left. That's when Tony came to live with Mom and Dad and myself.

Louise Rice:

Frank and Tony became close, playing music together, and they would go out and find places to play on weekends.

Frank Poindexter:

Tony was doing ductwork in Reidsville, sheet metal work that goes in the heating and A/C. When he and I moved up to Greensboro in late '69, into a mobile home owned by the friend of a friend, he found a job doing that same kinda work. So if he wasn't gonna be playing music, Tony seemed to have a strong interest in sheet metal work.

We got kicked out of that mobile home. The guy that ran the park there was real eccentric, and he said he didn't want us playing music. Can you imagine, just an acoustic guitar and a Dobro®? How much noise could we make?

Hal Poindexter, Jr.:

The Rice boys lived with my wife Joyce and me at times, more than they did at home. After we moved to Reidsville, Ronnie used to live with us, and then Tony. You know, this was their second home.

Tony lived with Joyce's mother [Ma Smith] and her family around 1970. Joyce's mother had lots of bedrooms in their house, and she asked Tony to come and live with them. He took all of Doc Watson's records, and started learning them one at a time. Then he started learning Clarence White's stuff, with the Doc Watson stuff in his mind. Then he went in a direction of his own.

He didn't sing any at all in those days; he just didn't consider himself a singer.

Bobby Atkins (North Carolina vocalist/bandleader/songwriter):

Joe Stone and myself were partners, working Channel 48 TV here in Greensboro, NC. We had a show called *The Stone & Atkins Show*. The first time I seen Tony and Frank [Poindexter], they came walking in one day. We got together, and they done some of the TV shows with us. I was looking for another band, so Tony and Frank joined me. We was on two nights a week, and we had a good show.

Tony in Florida in 1968 (Courtesy Louise Rice)

We started playing other places and my brother Kemp was playing bass with us. We didn't get no pay [for the TV show]. We was just doing it for free to get the publicity. We did get a lot of shows and commercials. We went around to the theatres, and played with the movie. We also played some clubs. Anything we could make a dollar at, why, we'd play it.

[The single we recorded] was "Mary's Gone" and "Farmer Man." Frank wrote both of them. The single and soundtrack were recorded here in Greensboro. We were like the staff band, because when they done commercials, we did the music and some of the singing. If you were in the studio for five minutes, you got $25. Back then, $25 was pretty good money.

Frank Poindexter:

One summer, I wanted to do something different. I said, "Tony, you wanna go to Myrtle Beach?" So we took a guitar and Dobro® and packed a little overnight bag, and said, "We'll just stay on the beach and play music." We played music till it got dark, and then it started getting chilly . . . "Hey, we don't have camping equipment." I said, "Let's find a cheap hotel room."

We went up on the main drag, right on Ocean Boulevard, and we found this place. It was the cheapest room, but it was a lot better than being cold on the beach. That's where Pam Sanders and her family were, on their last night in Myrtle Beach. That was June 1970, and we got married in November.

Tony and I were still excited about the recording we had recently done with Bobby Atkins. We had recorded "Mary's Gone," that song I wrote, and boy, I was on Cloud 9!

Bobby Atkins:

We was together around eight months. What we recorded, we recorded in that eight months, and we done that first movie *[Preacherman]* in that eight months. [Tony and Frank did not appear on the soundtrack to the sequel, *Preacherman Meets Widder Woman.*]

Tony played guitar and bass on most of the stuff we recorded. He was a great doghouse bass player. Me and Frank and Sherlie and Rita—there were some girls on that album, too, doing backup vocals with us—sang on the album, and also in the movie. Tony's doing some harmony singing with us. Tony would sing in the group, but he wouldn't sing by himself. I'd say he was a baritone.

None of us had no money, but I had a little, and Shirley had a little, and Frank had a little. We did the recordings at different times. I suspect it was five or six sessions, because we didn't have enough money to do it all at one time. There were several singles released first; one came out on Carl Story's label, and we went and done his TV show down in Charlotte. Old Homestead put it out, and they never sent us [any money] either.

Most of the movie soundtrack was originals. The first one, I had wrote a banjo tune called "Bob's Special," and that was the travelin' music in it. Then we had other little things in it, too, where we'd do maybe just like single note stuff on the banjo or guitar, or maybe the fiddle. [Fiddler] Cub McGee worked with us.

Bobby Atkins, Tony, Sherlie Tucker, Frank Poindexter. *(Courtesy Bobby Atkins)*

Frank was working for a steel place here in Greensboro. Tony, when he first come with me, wasn't working. We'd practice at night, and he'd spend the next night or two with us till Frank come back, and then we'd practice again, and he'd go back with Frank. Later, Tony got a job down in Reidsville, with Atkins & Jones Sheet Metal (we're not related) and worked there for a good while.

Tony was just a good ole country boy! As country as you would ever want to meet, and he was a great musician. He was a good singer, but at that time he wouldn't sing too much. He just loved that guitar, you know. He would put the monkey on that guitar, and the bass, but he would do very little singing, except with the group.

Him and Frank, they'd always ride around, and Tony was all the time mockin' this feller—you've seen *Hee-Haw*? The one that done the announcing for the Cornfield County thing? Tony used to mock *him* all the time. Rita, of the two girls that sang with us, Tony had a crush on her. She didn't have no crush on him at the time, but Tony had a big crush on her. She was a pretty girl.

Tommy Edwards (North Carolina guitarist):

Tony and I used to compete regularly in the fiddler's conventions and band contests and would sometimes play together informally. I have an old trophy from the Level

Cross Civitan Club Fiddler's Convention dated 1969. I believe I met Tony there or at the North Moore School convention about that time.

Our band was warming up and someone brought Tony in and we played together a few minutes. He had what I thought at first glance was a D-35 but it was probably that old guitar with the bound fretboard. I remember he was quite good, much like Michael Auman, another guitarist from the area who paired with Tony at least one contest at Oak Ridge in 1971. At that time Doc was the standard folks in these parts tried to emulate. Most of us hadn't heard of Clarence White.

At the Level Cross convention in 1969 Tony played with a group that included Ronnie Prevette (later with Jimmy Martin) on mandolin, Garland Shuping (later with the Bluegrass Alliance and Jim and Jesse) on banjo and a fiddler named Sipe.

I remember an afternoon at Camp Springs in 1970 or '71, when Tony asked if I had my guitar—the 1969 D-45. I got it out of the car. We went into the woods away from the stage and he told me he had been out to California for a while. He started playing a version of "Grandfather's Clock" with the flatpick that sounded so much like finger-picking I was mesmerized. He also played "Love Come Home" and he did some chromatic things I had never heard on guitar. He went through tune after tune, showing me what he had come up with, and it was like a major revelation. He was making me see the guitar in a whole new light.

Mike Auman (North Carolina guitarist):

I was in high school and playing guitar with a series of bluegrass bands in central North Carolina, and we regularly made the rounds of the fiddler's conventions. There was a banjo player named Garland Shuping who lived near Gold Hill, and Garland met Tony somewhere and mentioned him to me as a really hot guitar player from California. Garland also talked about Tony's connection to Clarence White, who I admired.

I met Tony probably in 1969 or 1970 at a fiddler's convention near Statesville. The format of the contest required guitar players to have just a single guitar as backup, so Tony and I were to play together. We practiced, and I was really struck by his style. He was doing some really new things. He was fast and fluid with both left and right hands, and used lots of fingerings up the neck I hadn't seen or heard before. I could see some roots in Doc Watson's and Clarence White's styles, but Tony clearly had his own style. His pickwork was a combo of cross-picking, syncopation and downstrokes, and I noticed how flexible the first joint of his thumb was—he used the movement of his thumb against his first finger to get the pick across the strings, with hardly any wrist. For rhythm, he used a little bit of thumb/finger, lots of wrist and very little elbow.

He showed me some licks I had to work on, hard, for several weeks to get right, very jazzy and syncopated. Also some very nice rhythm techniques, emphasizing different beat patterns in counterpoint to the melody, and inserting extra up-and-down strums in 16th or 32nd note timing. He used good strong bass runs, with a lot of slippery timing like Clarence used while playing rhythm. He showed me a piece he called "Slow Hornpipe" in D with the low E string dropped to D. It was very resonant and stately. Tony played quite softly at that time. I think it was later that he extended his use of dynamics, after he started with the Alliance, and certainly by the time he worked with J.D. Crowe.

I found Tony to be quite modest and self-effacing, and he truly didn't seem to know how good he was. His playing was much better than mine in every regard, but he gave me a lot of compliments. He played either "Black Mountain Rag" or "Beaumont Rag" in the contest; I know we practiced both. On stage he used a style very close to Doc Watson & Clarence White's, not too fancy. I was surprised, because that didn't come close to showing off what he was doing during practice. He was quite nervous on stage, and had trouble working the mike and being heard. I don't believe he won anything that night, which was not unusual at this type of event where local favorites often won.

I have a memory about his guitar, and I think it was the same occasion because it's the only time I ever sat down and played with Tony. He had an old D-28, pretty battered, and it had a white binding around the fingerboard like a D-35. The fingerboard was extended over the sound hole. The action was low and fast, lower than mine. I looked inside the sound hole, and there was a *pencil,* sawed off to match the depth of the body, stuck inside between the back and the top directly underneath the end of the fingerboard, as a support. There were some structural problems resulting from modifications, and the pencil was keeping the top from caving in.

Frank Poindexter:

When this Camp Springs Festival came along, we both went over there. I was on the other side of the festival, and Tony found himself jamming with these guys from the Bluegrass Alliance. When I came back over, there he was, standing there jamming. I thought, "Wow . . . *Go, Tony!*" And he was loving every minute of it. Next thing you know, he was off to Kentucky.

Louise Rice:

I think Tony left when Herb and I were living in Morrisville, NC. Herb was working with the power plant. We came down to see the festival out at Camp Springs, and that's where Tony left to go with the Alliance. I cried and felt so bad, because he was leaving home, and I knew that would be for good.

I felt good about it for Tony's sake, because I knew, in his heart, that's what he wanted to do. He wanted to be a musician; he wanted to play and get really good at it. And they wouldn't have taken him had he not been good. I did a lot of crying, but we stayed in touch, and you know the rest of the story. Herb was there with us. He knew it would happen one day, sooner or later, and he just—like me—accepted it. And he was proud.

Tony and his mom, Louise, in Florida in 1968.
(Courtesy Louise Rice)

On the Road
Part 2

Somewhere in Pennsylvania

We pause at a truck stop with a Subway in the back and Tony gets the kid behind the counter to build him the scariest sandwich ever: a meatball sub on wheat, with mayo and jalapenos, lots and lots of 'em. He eats his sub sandwich with a fork, carefully and quickly, politely holding a napkin in front of his mouth when he chews. His lovely silk shirt—today in lime, with yellow buttons—remains immaculate. He says he is presently underweight by about seven pounds, and that he stops eating when he is blue. I admire one of his rings—he wears three—and he says it's actually a woman's ring. "The one for men was just too big and gaudy," he explains. I look at his slender fingers and believe it.

New York, NY

We get to the hotel in New York. He watches CNN and Fox endlessly, and growls at the headlines. He does a spot-on imitation of James Carville. He is opinionated and stubborn, with views I do not always share or understand.

He empties his pockets onto his bedside table. There's a silver money clip and a wad of cash. His contract from his booking agent, Keith Case, shows that the gig starts at 9:00 P.M.; the venue's website says 8:00. Many phone calls ensue. Is there an opening act? Nobody seems to know. And there's no parking at the 42nd Street venue. We will have to find our own way there. He calls Marilee at Keith's office and asks her to help him find a car.

Finally he calls the front desk himself. "This is Mr. Rice," he says. Not Tony, but Mr. Rice. He arranges for a Town Car (his auto of choice, after his beloved Mustangs) and then calls Marilee to tell her they've got a car for him. He carefully tells the desk he must have a large vehicle, because some cabbies are reluctant to put his flight case into their cabs.

The next day, at the B.B. King Blues Club in Manhattan, we are led through cement corridors to the "green room"—a tiny space, absolutely without luxury. The bathroom is large, about half the size of the little dressing room, and there is a roach in the toilet—the kind of roach you smoke—and a few spent matches.

Billy Bright sits on the black leather sofa and noodles with his Gilchrist mandolin. He is still shaken by the traffic he and his wife, Bryn, encountered in the Lincoln Tunnel on their way from the airport. Tony orders a club sandwich from the abbreviated artists' menu. He chats with the Brights and eats his food. When he is finished, he takes out a tortoiseshell pick and a square of rosin and his penknife, and proceeds to trim the pick to his liking. This is so he can hold the pick without fear that he will lose his grip on it. He's been having some trouble with that lately.

Peter Rowan shows up minutes before show time. A total of 360 tickets have been sold for tonight's show, with 20 VIP seats. The floor manager is a young Israeli who tells me earnestly that B.B. King's is probably the best club in the city anymore. He says this is a great crowd for a Wednesday night.

Finally, the time comes and the band takes the stage. "Man," somebody says in awe, "Tony's so cool under those lights!" And he is—quiet and elegant and understated. He plays a little lick that is intricate and amazing, and the crowd goes nuts. He keeps his eyes down and doesn't say a thing—but the corners of his moustache twitch just a bit, so you know he's smiling.

Leaving New York

After the show, we go back to the hotel, pack quickly, and leave. We stop for dinner at an all-night Greek diner, its dining room and parking lot teeming with restless youth, pierced and profane. Tony ignores them completely.

When we are seated, Tony orders meatloaf, mashed potatoes, salad—no cucumbers. He loves meatloaf, but he hates cucumbers. As we wait for our food, we talk about the objects he carries. Things that at first blush seem mundane are actually highly symbolic. The key ring, for example. He still carries and uses the same key ring that came with the jalopy he bought from Sam Bush when they were kids in Louisville, playing for pennies with Bluegrass Alliance. The watch on his narrow left wrist is an Accutron with a tuning fork in it that chimes a perpetual F sharp. He holds it to my ear so I can hear it. He has worn this watch since he played with J.D. Crowe and the New South, for over three decades.

He talks some more about his rings. On his left hand, he wears two rings with similar settings. One is an old mine-cut diamond; the other's a sapphire. On his right hand he wears a distinctive and unusual ring with sapphires *and* diamonds, set in a geometric pattern. He says these rings are symbolic of the recording process. "The sapphires go back to the days of vinyl; they represent the cutting stylus used to create the master lacquer recording. That's done by a heated sapphire; it melts the modulations of the record grooves into the lacquer. And the diamonds represent the phonograph needles used to play the discs." He wears them to stay physically connected to that process, though he's aware that the symbolism isn't accurate anymore. Nowadays, he says, it's all laser beams and 1s and 0s. How, he asks, do you represent *that*?

At 3:01 A.M., we get on Highway 84N in Newburgh. We pass places named Fishkill Creek and Wappinger's Falls. It is raining. The odometer reads 9310 miles. He tells me he puts at least 50,000 miles on his car in an average year. "That's not a hell of a lot," he says slyly. "That's only circling the globe two times in a year." I will Google it later— "circumference of the planet Earth"—and find that he's exactly right.

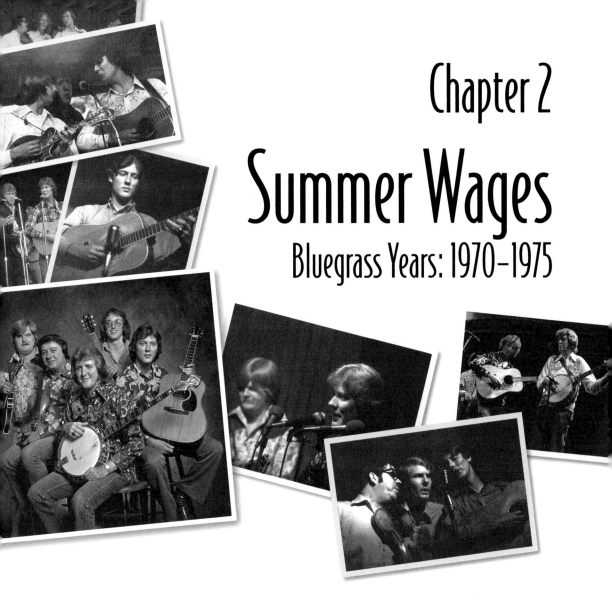

Chapter 2
Summer Wages
Bluegrass Years: 1970–1975

Tony come out and played "Sunny Side of the Mountain" with me one time. He just tore it all to pieces. He said I was his inspiration. That's the reason why he picked it; he wanted to try to play a guitar kindly like me. I've got it on tape somewhere.

I said, "Yeah, you know if it's left up [to me], what I'd do? You give me them note fingers, that left hand, I'll lay it down on a flat rock and take me a hammer and hit it!" I just said it in fun, 'cause he could outnote me. If you read between the lines, I like it!

I've never heard nobody, unless it's Tony Rice—he might come close—that plays rhythm like I do.

Jimmy Martin (1927–2005), Hall of Fame guitarist/vocalist/bandleader; bluegrass music's greatest rhythm guitarist

Chapter 2: Introduction

The period between 1970 and 1975 marked Tony's first years as a professional musician. His introduction to the world of bluegrass began over Labor Day Weekend in 1970 with a fortuitous trip to Carlton Haney's Bluegrass Festival in Camp Springs, NC. There, Tony met 18-year-old Sam Bush, who invited him to join the Bluegrass Alliance, taking flatpick legend Dan Crary's spot in the groundbreaking "newgrass" group. Within a few months, Tony had moved to Louisville, KY and was married and living the bluegrass dream, at or near poverty level.

Exactly a year later, once again at Camp Springs, Tony played his last show with the Alliance and joined his brother Larry in J.D. Crowe's New South. In *Bluegrass Country Soul,* a documentary filmed that weekend and released in 2006, Tony is seen performing with both the Alliance and with Crowe, pounding out rhythm on "Train 45." This was the beginning of Tony's education in the J.D. Crowe school of timing, tone and touch, forged over countless nights in Lexington clubs. Like the Beatles in Hamburg, Crowe and his group benefited greatly from five steady hours of playing every night. By 1975, Tony had established a reputation as an innovative bluegrass guitarist and strong, distinctive singer with two compelling solo records to his credit.

In 1974, Crowe added mandolinist, fiddler and tenor vocalist Ricky Skaggs to the New South's lineup. Skaggs joined Rice on guitar, Crowe on banjo, and stalwart Bobby Slone on bass; young resonator guitar player Jerry Douglas came aboard the following summer. Astonishingly, this configuration of the New South, which was responsible for the most influential recording in modern bluegrass history, was together only a few months.

The significance of this eponymous recording cannot be overestimated. Often called *Old Home Place* after its first track, or "0044" after its Rounder Records catalogue number, it has profoundly influenced successive generations of bluegrass musicians. In his 1975 liner notes for 0044, Jack Tottle said Tony was quite possibly the most important bluegrass guitarist alive. A decade later, 14-year-old Alison Krauss would cite the record as her biggest inspiration, and Tony as her favorite musician. Twenty years after *that,* young Sean and Sara Watkins were listening to Tony Rice *"all the time,"* according to their mother, Karen, on their way to careers that would begin with the influential young band Nickel Creek.

The sound of the New South was very powerful, but it could not compare to the new music Tony heard in the spring of 1975, when he did a recording session in Washington, D.C. with banjoist Bill Keith. The session included innovative California mandolinist David Grisman, who shared a tape of some unusual new material he'd been working on. Rice would never be the same. He would not rest until he returned to California to join Grisman's experimental group, melding jazz and bluegrass rhythms into something entirely new.

I was mildly rebuked by a reviewer in the mid-'70s for my audacity in suggesting that Tony might be the most important living guitarist currently performing bluegrass. It's nice to have history prove you right—-at least occasionally!

Jack Tottle, mandolinist/vocalist/educator/author

In His Own Words: Tony's Story

I was hanging out with my Uncle Frank Poindexter, the Dobro® player. Frank and I went to Carlton Haney's Camp Springs bluegrass festival near Reidsville, North Carolina on Labor Day weekend, 1970. I didn't go there specifically to get a job with anybody; I just went there to hang out and jam.

I met John Kaparakis there, and he was instrumental in getting Sam Bush to hear me. I was sitting on a picnic table, playing, and Sam came over and listened. We started talking, and he said, "Hey, man, how would you like to have a job, playing?" And I said, "Uh, *yeah*." I knew Sam from the previous year and by reputation; I'd heard him and Wayne Stewart and Alan Munde, and I thought, "Damn, this is *Sam Bush* I'm talking to. This is a heavyweight dude! And here he is asking me would I like to have a job in a band."

I said, "Yep." He said, "Well, you've gotta move to Louisville." I said, "Okay!"

And it was a real easy thing. My brother Larry and Doyle Lawson were playing with J.D. Crowe in Lexington, KY, so that was cool. I was in heaven, having a music job in Kentucky, and being that close to my brother, like 75 miles away. The day after I accepted Sam's offer, my father and I went to this little country bar and drank a bunch of beer. My father didn't have very much

Sam Bush and Tony. (Photo courtesy Tony Rice)

to say about it, other than "Well, if that's what you want to do in life, I know you'll be good at it." Something like that. Supportive in a real sublime sort of way.

The first time I got pleasantly stoned on reefer was right before I left Louisville one night to drive my car over to see Larry and J.D. and those guys at the Holiday Inn. I remember the 75-mile drive from Louisville to Lexington. Every one of these little hills felt like a rollercoaster. And I was just diggin' on the AM radio . . . That was my first experience getting stoned, and it was in the old Rambler I got from Sam Bush, a '62 Rambler station wagon. This thing was really ragged out, man. But it was certainly worth 75 bucks! It got me around for a while. It used about three quarts of oil on the trip to Lexington.

I was staying in this big old house where an old lady was renting out sleeping rooms for $12 a week in Louisville, right down the street from Sam. The band wasn't working so I didn't have enough money to pay my rent. The landlady found out that I had to go to the draft board one day. She came to the draft board to try to collect the back rent I owed. I didn't have the money, so she got mad enough to say, "I'm gonna have to lock your stuff in your room." I said, "Well, I've gotta have my guitar! That's the only way I've got to make some money." She said, "No, the guitar is staying."

But I remembered a way to get into the room. We got back there,

and Sam gave me a boost up to the top of the transom window over the door. I didn't care about the rest of the shit; I went in and got the guitar, and we snuck out. Later I went back and paid the money I owed her and I got my stuff back.

It was in one of the clubs Bluegrass Alliance was playing in that I met my first wife. Her name was Kate Freeman. Her father was a lawyer in Philadelphia, and he'd bought property in Woodstock, Vermont. Kate came to Louisville and was part of the University of Louisville's educational program to rehabilitate high school students that were failing in a subject for some psychological reason. I met her in one of the clubs we were playing in called the Storefront Congregation. And Kate and I were together from that moment on, for eight years, until we parted ways in 1979. She was with me through the first three major groups I was in: the Bluegrass Alliance, the

L-R: Tony, Kate Freeman, Louise & Herb Rice in Berkeley, CA, circa 1978. (Courtesy Louise Rice)

J.D. Crowe and the New South era, and the Grisman era.

We went to the local church to get married. And present at my wedding were Bobby Slone and his wife, and Larry and his wife. That was it. Kate and I had the clothes we put on that day when we got up. We didn't talk about it much. Just one day we said, "Well, this is probably a good day to go and get married. Why not do it?" As far as we were concerned, getting married by a preacher in a church was just a formality.

We lived only a short time in Louisville. It wasn't that long after we started going together that I started with Crowe.

I don't know how to describe Kate, other than she had more brains than she knew what to do with. She was a graduate of Mt. Holyoke with a major in Philosophy, and a minor in Ancient Greek. Suffice it to say there were times we didn't get along. The only thing I knew was guitar playing. Her mind didn't intimidate me, but Kate always felt better in a surrounding of intellectuals, for obvious reasons. But she never belittled anyone that had less formal education than she did. She was very mysterious. It was hard for anybody to get really close to Kate. She worked for a long time as a hostess at a real fancy restaurant. And with all her academic skills, she liked that, because it was a fancy restaurant frequented by the elite of the town where the University of Kentucky is located.

The Bluegrass Alliance played whatever gigs it could find, and there was a long period of time when it didn't work anywhere. Sam would borrow money from his parents. I would borrow money from Lonnie Peerce, and then pay him back when we started playing again. I lived with Courtney Johnson and his wife for a while, down in Southern Kentucky in a log cabin, kinda roughing it. Fireplace for heat, you know . . . I liked it a lot. I'd never really done that before. But the place I stayed longer than any other was with Sam and Kathy, Sam's first wife.

Bluegrass Alliance at Camp Springs 1971:
(L-R) Courtney Johnson, Lonnie Peerce, Sam Bush, Ebo Walker (partially hidden), and Tony.
(Photo by Akira Otsuka)

Sam and I were a couple of 19-year-old kids playing music. His musicianship was already advanced beyond mine to some astronomical degree.

Ebo, the bass player, was a big kid to me—somebody I looked up to. His real name was Harry Shelor. There was a song the Dillards did called "Ebo Walker," and as far as I know, he decided to use that as a stage name. I've never thought of him as Harry Shelor. Ebo and I had a lot of good times, a lot of laughs.

That configuration of the Bluegrass Alliance recorded a few tunes for an album. They might even be in circulation somewhere. I don't really remember the tunes, or the event—just have a vague memory of being in the studio with that band. The only conflict we had was with the fiddle player, Lonnie Peerce, who was a real traditionalist. I was with them exactly a year, and then I left to go with J.D. Crowe. I thought it was time to move on.

Before I left the Alliance, I'd talked to Eddie Adcock about joining the II Generation, a band he was forming. Eddie was a figure of notoriety, and I knew the role he'd played in creating something unique with the Country Gentlemen. We just jelled. Eddie was a journeyman—and by that point, Jimmy Gaudreau was, too, to some degree—and I was the apprentice. It was at Bean Blossom in '71 that Eddie and Jimmy and I started talking. And it really got in high gear at Renfro Valley, Kentucky, in August of '71. We decided, "Yeah, this is it. The three of us ought to be playing and singing together, no matter what." The few times we played, the vocals were extraordinary.

There was a little circle of band personnel changes that were going on simultaneously. Doyle Lawson was leaving J.D. Crowe's band to join the Country Gentlemen . . . to replace Jimmy Gaudreau, who was leaving to join the II Generation with myself and Eddie Adcock . . . and I was leaving the Bluegrass Alliance to join them. I was at Gettysburg in '71, and I had already decided to make that move. My brother Larry and I were talking. He said, "Uh,

J.D. is in the camper, and Crowe wants to talk to you whenever you got time." I knew what was gonna come down, because Doyle was leaving, and Crowe needed a guitar player and a singer. And he knew I'd wanted to work with him since 1969. Not only did Crowe have a *more* driving sound; he had *the* driving sound. There was never a time in the history of this music that four guys could drive bluegrass like that band: Crowe, Larry, Doyle, and Bobby Slone. I'm not sure it's existed since.

Plus, Crowe had the Holiday Inn scene in Lexington: a five- or a six-night thing every week, four hours a night, 9 P.M. to 1 A.M., nine months out of the year, with the other three months devoted to outdoor events. Crowe was established. And for a bluegrass musician back then, the weekly salary was *unheard of*. It was the same amount every week, it was incredibly good, and it was always there. It was a dream for other bluegrass musicians, even the ones of notoriety, because we didn't have that steady of an income.

I had to go to Eddie and Jimmy and say, "Guys, I got to go with Plan B." I was really worried about how I was going to put it to them. Bill Emerson and I talked about it up at Gettysburg. He said, "Man, just follow what you want to do. Just be upfront about it, tell Eddie and Jimmy what's in your heart and that's what you want to do." So I did.

At the same time, I had to tell Sam, Ebo, and Courtney I was leaving the Alliance. It was at Camp Springs, exactly a year after I joined. Sam and Ebo tried to get me to reconsider. They weren't shitty about it, but they said, "We're going to get rid of Lonnie and take this whole thing in a totally different direction, and we'd like to have you stay with us." Of course, then I told them I had already committed myself to Crowe. They were cool about it, and out of that came the New Grass Revival.

The one thing I didn't like about the Crowe band was the electric thing, and the drums. I didn't care for that, but I accepted it for a number of reasons. A lot of bluegrass music was headed in that direction, including the Osborne Brothers, and it wasn't long after that the New Grass Revival decided that they would go to amplified instruments and drums. I made no bones about the fact that I really didn't want to do that, but it wasn't my call. Bobby and I didn't really want it, but Larry and J.D. did. From that moment on, working with that band was like a job. We used those instruments all the way up to when Larry left in '74 and Ricky Skaggs joined.

At the Holiday Inn, six out of ten people in the audience were college students, and the other 40% were locals. We'd have a rowdy crowd occasionally, but not that often. It was more or less a sophisticated audience. Looking back, I'm sure we were probably the only band in the history of bluegrass up to that time that had anything like that—a club gig where they served lots of liquor and beer, and a listening crowd. That was almost unheard of. This was the University of Kentucky; it's a very reputable institute of higher learning. These were college students that had an *ear,* and they wanted to be involved in the spectacle

of live music of any sort that had musical validity.

That was *the* place to end up in Lexington all those years. By and large, every Friday and Saturday night, you couldn't get in the door. The only thing comparable up to that time would have been the Country Gentlemen at the Shamrock in Washington D.C. The early configuration of the Bluegrass Alliance had that kind of following at a club in Louisville, The Red Dog Saloon. But I don't think either the Gentlemen's regular gig, or the Alliance's, encompassed that many dates out of the year.

At the Holiday Inn, the innkeeper had this idea that he wanted to start a cocktail hour and have some real low-key music, from 4:00 to 5:30 or 6:00. For some supplementary money, myself and Larry and Bobby Slone would go in and sit there and play mostly instrumentals and real low-key stuff; Larry and I would sing a few duets. Do the math: it's like 24 hours of playing time, not counting the cocktail hour, which was an additional two hours a night. And sometimes it was more than that.

As a result, my musicianship was evolving, although I wasn't aware of it. I was prone to explore the guitar like some people would do. Crowe will tell you this, too: to adhere to a strict regimen of music and tunes night after night for a long time, it was quite literally going through the motions. There's no way in the world you could do anything that many hours a night, that many days a week, and keep it musically interesting. So we would mix it up. We had a repertoire of a couple of hundred

Louisville, KY, early '70s
(Courtesy of Frank and Marty Godbey)

tunes, at least. I don't remember having a set list.

I rehearsed more with the Crowe band than I did with any other band. He took a lot of pride in his work. Every once in a while he would call a rehearsal just because we would want to expand the repertoire. If it was stuff we didn't know, he wanted to make sure it was done right. But then there were other nights in the club where we knew it was gonna be an off night—we'd try almost anything because if we screwed it up, it wasn't a big deal.

I think Crowe was a very good boss. When I joined this band, there's no doubt about it, I was an inferior musician when it came to playing rhythm in time. I had not developed that yet. Boy, it would really piss him off! And he didn't hold any-

thing back when it'd come to expressing himself in that regard. In retrospect, it must have been unnerving for him. You can imagine: here's J.D. Crowe, coming out of the school of Jimmy Martin's rhythm guitar, which has never been excelled by anybody on this planet that I know of. And Doyle was an *amazing* rhythm guitar player. Red Allen was a good rhythm player, before Doyle.

It didn't take me very long to realize what was necessary to make this jell. It wasn't anything that I *practiced*. It was being aware that I was standing onstage next to a *monster*. How does this guy use his hands to make sound pour out of his instrument with the drive of a ten-diesel locomotive freight train? He was a banjo player with impeccable timing and drive, and he just wanted his guitar player to be an integrated part of that. Once I grasped that notion, it started to quickly fall into place. I learned how to be a bluegrass rhythm guitar player, and I can't conceive of it having happened had I been with somebody other than Crowe or perhaps Bill Emerson.

I think J.D. has mentioned this before in various interviews: somehow Jimmy Martin taught him what he wanted, and how he wanted his own bluegrass sound to be distinct. Martin taught Crowe how to play with that *drive.* There are very few guys that played with that precision. He was probably the most precise musician I ever stood beside.

One thing's beyond dispute: playing with Crowe shaped my guitar playing permanently. He is the guy who made me aware of the fact I have the capability of taking this guitar and having a rhythm section in my hand. That came from Crowe.

Tony and J.D. Crowe at the Great American Music Hall in San Francisco, CA. (Photo by Jon Sievert)

Sometimes well-known people would show up at the Holiday Inn. Chris Hillman from the Burrito Brothers and Steve Stills [from Crosby, Stills, Nash & Young] showed up one night. I remember I played "Freeborn Man," and Chris and Steve and a couple other guys were sitting in the front row. Steve Stills looked at me and said, "I'll give you twenty bucks if you'll play that tune again." I said, "You got it!" I remember Crowe looking at me with this look on his face like, "Are you gonna split that with the band?" I never did . . .

Maria Muldaur and I developed a relationship that became a friendship there. And John Hartford came in; that was the first time I'd actually met Hartford. Sometimes when a bluegrass band would be on the road, like the Country Gentlemen or somebody, they'd stop in, just for the camaraderie. Man! It was really cool. Of course, at the time, the New South was a very prestigious band. Other bands would stop in, and it was just *assumed* that if they weren't too tired, they would sit in. We'd *dig* it, you know? It was so cool that we, as a band, got to go out in the audience and watch somebody like Charlie and Bill Emerson and Doyle and Bill Yates get up there and play amazing music. I remember those days well.

Bluegrass musicians have sort of a built-in camaraderie. When you first meet them you feel like you've got so much in common. It's such a tight-knit music, in terms of the people that make it up. It takes a certain type of personality to have that much dedication to it. For whatever reason, people like that would take a liking to me. The list of bluegrass musicians of notoriety that I've befriended is too much to even comprehend, and there's mutual respect and admiration there.

Crowe came up with a real good sound system; the local music stores gave him anything he wanted. And in those days we had excellent microphones and sound reinforcement.

Surprisingly, most of our outdoor events were north of the Mason-Dixon line. Like myself, Crowe had no tolerance for a rude audience of any kind. And back then it was no secret: the word was out that audiences north of the Mason-Dixon line in general were ten times more respectful of artists on stage than hillbillies in the South, who had come there to fight and drink moonshine. Which later changed, of course . . .

I remember the day I found out Clarence White died. The Crowe band was playing a three-or-four month engagement at the Sheraton in Louisville. I was in my room at the hotel, and Lamar Grier, David's father, called me to tell me about it. I don't remember anything other than just sadness. It hadn't been but two months before that, Clarence and Suzie were at my house. We even jammed that night and I got a tape of it. It's Larry and I and Bobby Slone, and Clarence.

The last time I saw Clarence alive was at an outdoor event at Annapolis, MD, and he was playing in some configuration of the Flying Burrito Brothers, which had disbanded. It was only a few weeks after that, the phone rang, and he had died.

Larry Rice, J.D. Crowe, and Tony.
(Photo courtesy Tony Rice)

There was an early New South album, before Rounder 0044, that I recorded for Starday with Larry and Crowe. History has not been kind to it, let's face it, unless history gets rewritten a few decades from now. I never liked that album, to tell you the truth. We used the regular Nashville session players like Kenny Malone, Pig Robbins and Dennis Bigby. Nobody could fault Crowe for his decision to do that, because in retrospect, the idea was to reach as

many people as you could with bluegrass instrumentation. And he did a damn good job of that. Like I say, the Osbornes were doin' it . . . Jim and Jesse were doin' it . . . So I wouldn't fault him for doing that. The fact that I didn't like it certainly doesn't invalidate the concept.

It was during this time that I recorded my first solo album for the Japanese. I had a reputation as a guitar player, and a guy named Saburo Watanabe, who I'd known since '72, contacted me about doing a record. He was in a band called Bluegrass '45 on Rebel Records and had started his own label, Red Clay, in Japan. Nobody else had asked me to do an album, so I figured, "Hell, yeah, I'll do it for Sab. Fuck 'em! I'll do it for the Japanese."

Bob Trout, a real nice guy who owned King Records, got wind that I had done a record for Red Clay. Bob was real diplomatic about making the offer to release the album in the U.S., rather than have it be an import from Japan. Sab sent the master tapes back over to Bob, who put it out on King with a different cover and a different title and everything else.

There was *no* budget, no money up front or anything. I went into a cheap studio, the only studio that was practical. I put Crowe on the spot, because I said, "Hey, J.D., I gotta do this album, and you've gotta help me out. Is that okay?" He said, "Yeah." I needed a mandolin player and a bass player. Well, I already had the band there because I worked with them five nights a week!

It's amazing how many people still like listening to that album. It's torture for me to have to hear it. When I hear it again in my head, I think, "If I could do this again, I would do everything differently." To me, that invalidates what's there. Does that make sense? I'm honored it's still valid to all those people that treasure that album.

I saw an interview with James Taylor where somebody asked him about what he thought about hearing his own music. He said, "Well, to put it in perspective, I was in a restaurant the other day, and on the Muzak system, somebody decided to play an entire album of mine and I had to try to sit through that and maintain my appetite." He said it was literally torture. And the album was *Sweet Baby James*. I thought, "Damn, I'm probably one of few people who can appreciate that!"

Eric Dolphy, an *avant garde* jazz horn player—incredible musician and one of the heavyweights—said, "Once the music has been played, it'll end up in outer space, and you can never recapture it again." He wasn't talking about the recording medium. You

From Mike Auldridge's 1974 concert at the Merriweather Post Pavilion in Baltimore, MD (L-R, sitting): Tony, Mike, John Starling, Josh Graves; (standing): Akira Otsuka, Ben Eldridge, Tom Gray, Ricky Skaggs. *(Courtesy Mike Auldridge)*

can never recapture its most important components. There's no machine that will do that. Once you've played something, it's gone, and you can't recapture it.

John Starling was starting to get sick of the Seldom Scene. He wanted to get back into his medical practice, so I would fill in for him sometimes with the Scene. Around that same time, Starling got me a deal with Rebel Records. He talked to Dick Freeland and said, "Hey, this guy ought to have a record." The result was *California Autumn*.

The rhythm section on that record was pretty much the Seldom Scene minus John Duffey. Skaggs was there and Larry and Crowe were on a couple cuts. Flux (Jerry Douglas) was on a couple things. The title cut was one of my first original songs. I wrote it sometime in '73 or '74 but I never liked it. I just kind of scribbled it down one night and then did it in the studio.

"Bullet Man" was inspired by Bob Baxter, this guitar player who used to run a music store in L.A. He would play stuff that kind of sounded like that. I started fooling around with chords and different pick rolls one day, and all of a sudden there was a tune with no title. The song's title was from a real convoluted dream I had. I can't remember the dream, but there was a guy in it named "Bullet Man." Hugh Sturgill, the New South's manager at the time, said, "Well, that's what you ought to call that tune."

Larry had done a cooler version of his tune "Mr. Poverty" on his first album. I played on that, but I don't remember much about it. "Alone and Forsaken" was a really pretty tune I got from a Chet Atkins album. I had heard Ernie Watts' band do a jazz style, three-quarter-swing version of "Scarborough Fair," and I thought, "This band could pull this off," and they kind of did.

It actually turned out be a pretty elaborate production for those days, because nobody had done anything like it on Rebel other than the Scene. We did it at Track Studios, a high-dollar, 16-track facility with great mics and a good engineer, Fran Tate. George Massenburg mixed it. It was done during a couple different sessions, over a period of a few days. *California Autumn* was the first album I was fairly proud of, but that was short-lived, because I went on to better things within a couple of years.

Larry left Crowe's band in '74. Dickie Betts, formerly of the Allman Brothers Band, had just come out with his own album. My parents and Dickie Betts's parents had known each other in Florida, so there was a family tie there. And when Dickie was putting this tour together, he wanted to get back to his acoustic-oriented music roots, so he hired Vassar Clements. He was looking for a mandolin player, and somebody to sing a little harmony with, so I think he threw out the offer to Larry. Larry couldn't turn *that* down.

Sam Bush was the first substitute for Larry in Crowe's band. Sam wasn't working a lot, so he came and filled in for a short while. When he couldn't do that anymore, Ricky Skaggs was available. When Skaggs came in, it was as a temporary, but of course the sound took on a whole

new thing. I remember Ricky and I talking one night at my apartment—I was trying as hard as I could to talk him into staying on, and Ricky made it real clear that he couldn't take the drums, the electric bass, being plugged in. At that time, he was playing an F-4 or something, plugged in, and it just wasn't him.

It wasn't real hard to coerce Crowe into what was being offered to him: Ricky would stay with the band if it would go back to being a traditional bluegrass group. That ultimatum was sort of laid in Crowe's lap, and he said, "Well, yeah, we'll do that." It was that simple.

I think J.D. was ready to get back to the roots of bluegrass for himself anyway, not to mention that traveling on the road, he wouldn't have to take drums and amplifiers and whatever else. Crowe was tired of drums, and I think he figured out that his audience wanted to hear him play the five-string banjo in a traditional bluegrass setting. And by that time, electric instruments and drums had already run their course. The change that happened overnight was really incredible. All of a sudden, here was J.D. Crowe and the New South, the Holiday Inn country-bluegrass band that overnight was the force to be reckoned with, a bluegrass band playing traditional bluegrass music. Up until that time, there had certainly been no bluegrass band in history that had that much precision and drive.

Ricky had left the Country Gentlemen that Jerry Douglas was playing in. Ricky and Jerry were real close. Crowe knew of Flux by reputation. It almost went without saying: if this cat became available, we was gonna snatch him up! Well, we did. Flux wasn't stupid; he wanted to play with J.D. Crowe and Tony Rice and Ricky Skaggs. It was a real high to play with that band. But it wasn't all peaches and cream either. Just like any other band, there were days when you felt good about the gig you just did, and other days when it just didn't jell, for whatever reason.

Skaggs was really into the jazz violin thing: Joe Venuti, Stéphane Grappelli, Django Reinhardt-oriented stuff. Guys like Ricky and Jerry were really open-minded at the time; they weren't ashamed to listen to anything that sounded good to their ears. Crowe listened to things other than bluegrass, but I think his favorite music forms were real country music, and early rock 'n' roll. Elvis, Jerry Lee Lewis, early Johnny Cash—those were artists he really respected and admired.

But J.D. was amazingly receptive to any idea that anybody would throw out. His way of thinking was, "What the hell, let's try this, see what happens." J.D. was cool, always has been. He doesn't get riled up very easily about anything. We had reached a point where we really didn't have to discuss music anymore.

The *Old Home Place* album was recorded in three or four days, in Silver Spring, MD, at Track. Some of the material we had been doing live, and some of it was put together with the intention of giving that band a different flavor, like "Rock Salt and Nails." Jerry Douglas brought that in,

and I think I know why. We first heard it by Flatt & Scruggs when Josh Graves was the Dobro® player. It was an era of Flatt & Scruggs Jerry really liked.

I brought in "Home Sweet Home Revisited," "Old Home Place," "Summer Wages," and "Ten Degrees." "Cryin' Holy," of course, had been Ricky Skaggs. Crowe wanted to do "Nashville Blues"—I didn't give a shit about doing it, especially with a drummer. Crowe and Doyle and Larry had done "I'm Walkin' " as part of their regular repertoire. Crowe wanted to do "Some Old Day." "Sally Goodin" was a tune Crowe and Ricky used to do as a fiddle/banjo duet in the club. I don't know who got the idea to bring the band in. They should have left the band out—the band basically fucked the tune up. Just let Ricky and Crowe do it.

Some of that stuff came together in the studio. J.D. Crowe very rarely likes to discuss music—he's like me in that regard. Rehearsal was noodling in the wings between sets. J.D. detested going over things in detail. I'd sing a verse and chorus of the tune, we'd get on stage and he'd say, "Let's go ahead and do it. We'll learn it." I'd go out and sing "Home Sweet Home Revisited" as a solo and later on they would drift in with the harmonies after learning the words by hearing me sing it live in front of the audience.

It didn't take that long to record it. I don't think it was more than three days at the most. The original engineer was a guy named Steve Hamm. Bill Tate—the owner of the studio at the time—engineered when Steve couldn't be there. Ricky, Crowe and I went up and mixed it with Bill McElroy.

Hugh Sturgill, who co-produced the album, had a great D-35, and some of those cuts were done with that guitar. Hugh helped put up the front money and had ideas about arrangements and stuff like that, using two guitars instead of a guitar and banjo. And some of those ideas were valid. He offered general good support and was a positive force with this band.

I cut my right thumb right before we went in to do the album, and I still had stitches. Ricky Skaggs and I were sitting in the lobby of the Holiday Inn, I was whittling on a boot heel, and the knife blade closed. It was razor sharp. I remember doing this album, trying to hold a flatpick, but I had stitches in my hand exactly where the pick goes. After a few tracks like that, I got annoyed by it, so I called John Starling, who was a surgeon, and said, "Hey, come down here and take these stitches out!" Starling came down and took the stitches out in the studio.

I was pretty sick for part of the recording, too. "Rock Salt and Nails" is probably where you can notice it the most. I had a fever, but I got some medicine in me, and onward and upward . . .

Why did we have a piano and a drummer on "Crying Holy Unto the Lord"? From day one, my whole take on that album, and especially its popularity in bluegrass music, has been different from everybody else's. There has never been a moment that record's been mentioned that the first thing I think of isn't: "This record *would be better* and would have sold more

copies—it certainly wouldn't have sold any *less*—if the only people on that album was the working band." There's no doubt in my mind. I thought, and still think, "Well, we had a band. Wasn't that band good enough?" Yeah, it was. If there's anything on that album that anybody doesn't like, it damn sure ain't my fault!

The New South, circa 1975 (L-R): Ricky Skaggs, Bobby Slone, J.D. Crowe, Jerry Douglas, Tony.
(Photo by Jim McGuire)

The band's popularity went way up as a result of that album, even though the group that recorded it only played together for a few months. It's kind of like Miles Davis's best group. When you think of Miles Davis albums, you think of *Kind of Blue,* but that band wasn't together a year. The Crowe band probably didn't see any real room for improvement. I think everybody had sort of a sublime awareness of that. We knew who we were as a bluegrass band. We knew we had all the elements there: the harmonies, the drive, the tune selection. It's almost like it was so good, it was doomed to burn itself out real quick. If I hadn't left, it wouldn't have stayed together much longer anyway, I don't think. Ricky had a real staunch traditional side even back then, and he wouldn't have hung around.

But the legacy still lives on. It raised the bar for what is still going on to this day in bluegrass music.

The '75 band was really short-lived because of me. I played on Bill Keith's first Rounder album *[Something Auld, Something Newgrass, Something Borrowed, Something Bluegrass]* in March of '75, about two months after the New South recorded 0044. That was an amazing recording. Keith was able to pull more out than I thought I had in me. As far as I know, that was the first record of significance I had ever guested

on. It was probably the most significant recording of my career, in terms of setting a stage for the music that I would be most identified with, even to this day.

It was at the sessions for that record that I heard David Grisman's music with Richard Greene and John Carlini for the first time. And I thought, "This is the shit I want to do more than anything I've ever wanted to do in my life." 'Cause this music I heard Grisman play on that tape machine, it instantly started flowing through the veins. I'd never heard a sound like that. I was in heaven.

And so in September of that year, the New South broke up. I just made a commitment to Grisman to do this thing, this new band with these wild hippies who only played instrumental music.

Family, Friends & Fans

He was the right age, he had the right look; he had enough quirks about him that made him famous in the vans going down the road, the stories and stuff. Everything about him was "star." He just had this kind of aura about him.

> **Ricky Skaggs, multi-instrumentalist/vocalist;**
> **'80s country star; bluegrass legend**

John Kaparakis (D.C.-area musician and close friend of Clarence White):

I had gone down to Camp Springs with some friends of mine, and they had a trailer. We were listening to music and just picking around the campground. So I was just about ready to go to bed, and here comes a couple of guys out of the darkness. They said, "Hey, you guys doing some pickin'? We heard you across the way." I said, "Sure, let's play a few." It was Tony Rice and his uncle. And all of a sudden, Tony starts playing this beautiful lead guitar and singing . . . It was just like heaven had opened up and an angel had come down and landed at my campsite.

It was incredible. I said, "Tony, it's good to meet you. With what band do you play?" He kind of shook his head and said, "I'm not in any band; I'm a pipe fitter." I said, "You're so good, you've got to be in a band!" He said, "Well, I guess if the situation and money were right, I'd consider it."

I knew Dan Crary was leaving Bluegrass Alliance and they were looking for a replacement, which was going to be hard, to say the least. I said, "As a matter of fact, I happen to know of a band that's here this weekend that's going to be looking for a lead guitar player and a singer. Would you mind if I introduced you to Sam Bush? I think they would really like to hear you." I don't think I slept a wink that night, but the next morning I went to where Sam and the guys were, and said, "You've got to hear this guitar player and singer I met last night. Don't go anywhere, don't leave the grounds—I want to introduce you to this guy."

So, this is my recollection of how it went: me, the all-enthusiastic fan, stuttering and stammering, trying to introduce Sam Bush to Tony Rice.

Jack Lawrence (guitarist and sideman of Doc Watson):

I was at the Camp Springs festival in 1970 when Tony was hired by the Bluegrass Alliance. He and I jammed a good bit that weekend. I think he may have been playing Tommy Edwards' D-45 when Sam Bush met him.

Tommy Edwards:

I had a 1969 D-45 that Tony liked to play. He was sitting on my case playing it away from the stage at the Camp Springs festival when I introduced him to Bob Hoban of the Bluegrass Alliance. Bob rounded up Dan Crary and Buddy Spurlock who came over, listened to him play, asked me if he played with anybody and if he could sing, and shortly thereafter hired him to replace Dan, who was leaving the band. I believe a 17-year-old Sam Bush was around as well.

Sam Bush (legendary newgrass mandolinist & vocalist):

It was Sunday, the last day of the festival, and I looked across the field and saw the world's skinniest man sitting on a Martin Unipak case playing somebody's D-45. I walked up and started listening, and it sounded like Clarence White to me, only maybe a little slicker. Tony didn't have his own style so much yet—he was just the best Clarence-style player I ever heard. So I immediately—on the spot—said, "Hey, man, if you come join our band, then I can play the mandolin. They want me to play guitar, but I'm really a mandolin player. Why don't you come and jam with us?"

I basically asked him to join the band, later finding out that the youngest, newest guy in the band certainly can't ask someone to join without talking to the rest of the guys about it. We had a jam; seems like it was Lonnie, Ebo, Tony, Courtney and me. And after a few songs, after everybody heard him play, they wanted him to join the band, too.

We all ended up moving to Louisville. I had just moved there a month before that, and then Tony came up. Lonnie Peerce had helped me find a place on Southern Parkway, a street that sort of runs parallel to the Churchill Downs. We could literally hear them announcing the horses from our back porch, but never could afford to go to the track. Tony lived down the street in one of those community bathroom rooming houses.

Jack Tottle (bandleader/mandolinist/educator):

He was living in a little rooming house. It was very small and he just had his record player in there, and it seemed like all he was doing was sitting there with the record player, listening to stuff and working on music. When he and I and Sam Bush were driving around in Louisville, they were listening to Crosby, Stills, Nash & Young, and music like that. I was thinking, "Why don't you listen to some bluegrass?" Although they were playing bluegrass, they were into whatever was happening. Even by that time the Bluegrass Alliance was recording things like "One Tin Soldier."

The band wasn't rolling in money. That's the way it is for some musicians, especially when you get started. It seemed like he was in that stage of "All you do is sleep, eat and breathe the music," and that's life. And it's wonderful! Who needs anything more?

Sam Bush:

We started playing at a place called The Tam O'Shanter out in J-Town, a suburb of Louisville. We did about six nights a week there for eleven weeks, and then we were out of a gig and it was very sporadic playing. During part of the time Tony was in the band, the only job we had—we would travel down to Cave City, Kentucky from Louisville and play a Sunday afternoon jamboree at the Mammoth Cave Opry.

We were literally making six dollars a week each. My first wife worked at the telephone company, and because she had that job, we had food in the house. By around spring of '71, Tony had moved in with us; we had an extra bedroom. We were just all outta money—Courtney's dad was giving us 'taters. It was slim pickins, but looking back, we had a great time, even though we never had a dime to our names.

Doyle Lawson (mandolinist/vocalist/bandleader; bluegrass legend):

Larry Rice and I wound up living next door to each other in Lexington when we were playing in Crowe's band. His little brother would come up and stay for a while. Tony was a teenager still. I remember it being up in the day and I'd step over to Larry's; we were always in each other's house, you know. And Tony would be sitting there with his guitar at the breakfast table—he was usually a late riser, so it was usually breakfast. What was remarkable to me was how he would sit with his guitar—he'd have his legs crossed and his guitar would be there, and he'd reach over and take a bite of eggs or a sip of coffee, and then he'd go back to playing. He'd play for the longest time. And it would take him forever to eat his meal. I thought, "Boy, this kid is *eaten up* with music!" It was obvious then that he was destined to be a great musician.

Sam Bush:

I turned 19 that spring and he turned 20 that summer of 1971. What a couple of knuckleheads! We got along fine. If he only had six dollars in his pocket, we'd go in the restaurant at the corner of Third and Southern Parkway and he'd say, "Give me an order of fried shrimp and an ice-cold Coca-Cola."

We used to hang out down on Washington Street in Louisville. We'd go hear a friend of ours named Tim Krekel. Tim is one of the first guys I ever met that could do Clarence White-style licks on the electric guitar. Tony used to dig Tim's playing. A friend of mine named Kenny Smith had this real heavy-metal band called Buster Brown, a lead singer and a trio like The Who or Led Zeppelin . . . *real* heavy. A really good band, and Tony liked Kenny's playing.

Newgrass Alliance: Lonnie Peerce, Sam Bush, Tony.
(Courtesy of Frank and Marty Godbey)

We listened to the Country Gentlemen—we loved the Country Gentlemen—and we still listened to *Bluegrass Holiday* with Red Allen, J.D. and Doyle. We were listening to rock 'n' roll, but Tony was more into other things. I remember him loving Gordon Lightfoot even back then, and I remember him having the *Southbound* record by Doc Watson, and *Sweet Baby James*. Tony was the first guy I knew who had that record, and he immediately learned all those chord voicings James Taylor was doing on *Sweet Baby James*. Tony was the first guy I knew that could play those, and he showed them to me.

The Bluegrass Alliance with Dan Crary had already established a reputation for having a lead guitar player, and there weren't that many around. There was George Shuffler and Doc. And of course, Tony knew a whole lot of Doc Watson, too. When Tony first got with us, he didn't have much of his own style yet. He didn't like to play fiddle tunes, *per se,* and that was one thing he had to start doing with us. So he was probably influenced a little by the notes of Dan Crary, but certainly he never played with a right hand like Dan.

Dan Crary (flatpick guitar legend; replaced by Tony in the Alliance):

Lonnie was the putative leader of the band at that point, and he wanted to create some continuity, because he thought the fans wanted to hear things the band had done in the past, so it may be that Tony did some of that stuff. Tony did tell me that Lonnie used to get on his case all the time and want him to do what I had done. And I told him I didn't think that was necessary at all. I'd be honored to think I had influenced *anybody's* playing.

Sam Bush:

We hadn't really played for any great bluegrass audiences yet. Finally, festival season started rolling around. When we hit Bean Blossom, we were primed and ready to pop, baby, because we had been practicing so much and playing a lot, and we literally just tore it up. We weren't even scheduled on Saturday night, but there were so many requests for us to play that Bill had to put us on! So we went on and did about four or five songs, and we just *killed* the place with "One Tin Soldier." It was a big hit. It was the biggest audience response I'd ever been part of and probably at the time, Tony too. Of course, people went nuts over young Rice, you know, because he was a hoss and he was singing like a bird. All the ducks were in line.

J.D. Crowe (banjo pioneer and bandleader of the New South):

I had met Tony when he was playing with Bluegrass Alliance. I remember talking to him periodically at festivals. He always told me, "If you ever need a guitar player, call me." And sure enough, it happened. And it just so happened that he was wanting to leave the Alliance at that time.

II Generation, which was Eddie Adcock, Jimmy Gaudreau and Wendy Thatcher at the time, needed a guitar player. So they wanted Tony. It finally came down to me saying, "I did what I told you I would do. I called you when I needed a guitar player. Now you gotta make up your mind. I need to know, one way or the other, in a week." This had been going back and forth for a month. I said, "That's it." So he finally decided.

Jimmy Gaudreau (veteran mandolinist and vocalist):

Bill Emerson had taken Eddie Adcock's place on banjo with the Gentlemen and Eddie approached me about forming a new group. I wasn't all that interested until the name Tony Rice was brought up and that sounded like it might be an interesting combination. Tony had moved into Dan Crary's spot with the Bluegrass Alliance and was now making a name for himself on the bluegrass circuit and, like the rest of us, was looking for a chance to create something new and different. He made it known that he was up for hooking up with Eddie and me in this new venture.

The trouble was, when I announced my intentions to the Gents, they approached Doyle Lawson, who was playing guitar at that time in J.D.'s band. Guess who the mandolin player was? None other than Larry Rice. Naturally, if Doyle were to leave J.D., there would be an opening for a lead singer/guitar player. When Eddie and I confronted Tony with that scenario, Tony assured us that he was still coming on board with us and not to worry about the Crowe offer—and yes, he had been offered the job.

Bill Emerson warned me of what was about to come and said that I should reconsider leaving the group, but pressure from Eddie and my trusting nature convinced me that I should go ahead with the plan. Well, I left, Doyle joined the Gents and Tony went with Crowe.

Yeah, I was pissed off, big time, at Tony and also at myself for not seeing the writing on the wall. It was tough seeing Tony in his new position with the New South and we crossed paths a bunch in the years that followed, when I was working with bands like II Generation and Country Store, not exactly headliner groups. Ironically, I would join the New South in 1975 after Tony, Ricky Skaggs and Jerry Douglas left that group. By that time I had pretty much gotten over that whole fiasco. It would be years before I would run into Tony again.

Sam Bush:
Tony left Bluegrass Alliance on the Camp Springs weekend in '71. He played with J.D., Larry, and Bobby that whole weekend, and I don't know if that was the first weekend he played with 'em, but we were completing our gigs he was gonna play with us.

Lonnie jumped on him as soon as we walked offstage on Saturday night; they got in a huge argument. The way I remember it, Tony got so pissed off, he couldn't stand to play one more note with Lonnie Peerce! Well, that happened to the rest of us a few months later, so I understand what he was going through. I think we had one more set to do on Sunday. To my knowledge, the set that was recorded for *Bluegrass Country Soul* was the last set Tony played with us, and the next day Curtis Burch played guitar.

J.D. Crowe:
The Bluegrass Alliance had a different type of structure, songs, and different types of rhythm patterns. We didn't have that. We had the straight, full rhythm sound. We discussed it a lot. I knew Tony heard the difference. It would just take time to get used to it. You got to play like the band you're gonna work with. You have to play what they do.

I asked him who his favorite guitar players were. And he said Jimmy and Lester. I said, "Well, that's it." Where do you go from there? Of course, I had heard Clarence too, and I knew Tony had followed him some. I could hear that influence, but then he kind of got away from it. He started coming into his own after he was with me for a while. He started hearing stuff a little different. And Tony also listened a lot to Jerry Reed at one time.

With the Alliance, he was doing some singing, but not very many solos. There was lots of harmony. Sam was doing most of the leads. But when Tony joined me, that was his job. He *was* the lead singer. I do know that some of those things were a little high on Tony and I knew he wasn't a natural tenor singer. We did sing a lot in the clubs, and I would say, "We don't have to sing it where it's so high. Let's drop it to where it's comfortable." But the thing about Tony, he wouldn't back up. And Bobby Slone's probably heard me say, "Think we need to drop that down to another key?" Tony would say, "No, man, I can get it." He wouldn't back up, would he?

All in all, it was a lot of training for all of us. The Holiday Inn was a good place to rehearse. And it made us tighter. Oh, definitely yes. You're playing five nights a week, four sets a night. You're either gonna sit tight or you're just gonna blow up. I thoroughly enjoyed it. It was hard, though. I think we all got aggravated at times, because we were just wearing out. That's a lot of playing. I was trying to keep the job because it was a nice place to play. The owners didn't have a faint heart about canning you if you weren't effective. If you don't make that cash register ring, you won't be there long. When Tony joined, I changed the band name to the New South. With the Kentucky Mountain Boys, or any "Mountain Boys," you're labeled, let's face it. I wanted a band name where you could be playing any kind of music.

And after a while, of course, we used pickups and hired a drummer and all that, and got a lot of flack for that. And Bobby went from acoustic to electric bass. We all didn't really love it, but if you're playing in a club, you've got to play what people want to hear sometimes. I think if we hadn't done that, we wouldn't have lasted as long. I think it made us better pickers, more innovative. We could do things that we normally wouldn't do just playing acoustic.

Saburo Watanabe (Japanese bluegrass musician, producer & publisher):

I believe I first saw Tony at Bean Blossom in June 1971. I was a huge fan of the Kentucky Colonels. I thought "Wow, here's another Clarence!"

Well, when I got back to Japan, I really wondered why nobody was talking about Tony Rice? He gave me such big impact. I started Red Clay Records in the fall of 1971. I already had a plan to make an album of Tony Rice. So I started to write to Tony, "Why don't you make an album?" in early 1972.

No one in the U.S. record biz recognized him at that time, so he was very excited about my offer. All of those letters are gone but he said something like, "You're kidding. Wow! That's the first time I've ever been asked to make a guitar album." He was surprised and pleased very much.

We talked about the sessions and he sent some demo tapes with just him and Larry. I didn't know U.S. business style, so we made a kind of gentlemen's agreement which said I'll pay studio costs of $500, I'll have the rights to release it in Japan and Tony can hold the rights to release it in U.S. Anyway, Tony sold it to King Bluegrass label, then to Rebel. No emails, no phone calls . . . I think it took a year or so. Then they recorded it in late 1972 or early 1973, I believe, and our album came out in another year or so.

J.D. Crowe:

We did Tony's Japanese album over at Lemco with old Cec, Cecil Jones. Tony wanted to do a solo record. I told him, "Well, Tony, if we all play on it, it's gonna be New South. And it's gonna have your name on the front of the record." He said that was okay, and I said, "Well, we'll do it." I had fun doing it. I was helping him.

I wish the quality of the recording had been better, but you know . . . We just sat down, he turned it on and we started playing. Back then, we were playing five nights a week in an atmosphere that was so comfortable. It was like playing in your house, that little studio, with no stress, and we knew that stuff backwards and forward and had played it so much. It was just fun to go in and do it.

I could hear Tony's rhythm getting better, more solid. In other words, I was sure I didn't have to worry about him. And he didn't worry about it. When we hit it, it was there. That was it. And it's a good feeling when that happens.

Ben Eldridge (veteran banjo player and founding member of the Seldom Scene):

I think Tony was starting to get tired of six nights a week at the Holiday Inn, as anybody would. He filled in with the Seldom Scene at a bluegrass festival; it might have been in '73 or '74 at Berryville, when Starling got his car towed on Saturday night and refused to come back to play the next day! I showed up at the festival, and Duffey said, "Starling ain't coming back. We gotta get somebody." So we used Tony. He did a great job filling in for Starling; he knew all Starling's stuff.

John Starling (singer/rhythm guitarist, founding member of Seldom Scene):
I can remember hearing Tony play up in Gettysburg one fall, and thinking, "Man! I'd love to do some stuff with him sometime, before everybody else in the world finds out he's as good as he is."

So Tony helped me on *Long Time Gone*, a solo album I did over a five-or-six year period, just doing tracks here and there. Sometimes we had a little time left over in the studio. I think that's how we started *California Autumn*: we had some time left over, and we did some stuff. I cannot remember how we got together but I had George Massenberg lined up to mix this thing, and then Tony was supposed to fly in, and we were gonna go up and mix it. I went to the airport to pick up Tony, and he wasn't there! I called him—I'd gone straight from there to the studio—and he was still in Kentucky, and he said he thought it was the *next* weekend. And George was flying back to Paris in the middle of the next week.

So I said, "Well, I'll give you a choice. George and I can mix it without you, or we'll just have to find somebody else to mix it." He said, "Y'all go ahead." So we mixed it . . . but then he didn't like some of it. We had edited a lot of stuff. So we went back to Bias and remixed some of the tracks there.

I felt like if I got the right players, it would end up sounding pretty good. Tony had a pretty good idea where he was going with his music.

Ben Eldridge:
The thing I remember about *California Autumn* . . . some of the songs I had to learn were a little bit offbeat, like "Scarborough Fair." I can remember sitting down one night before we had to go in the studio, and spending about two hours trying to figure out a break to that damn thing. "Alone & Forsaken," that was one I sorta did slow, single-string. "Bugle Call Rag" and something Tony called "Dirty Tamale" when we cut it; I think he ended up calling it "Bullet Man." That's a cool tune, isn't it? I can still play that darn thing!

The sessions were real loose and laid back, and a lot of fun. Ricky was there, and Duffey, and pretty much the whole Scene. There were a lot of people in the studio. Bill Holden, the banjo player for the Country Gentlemen, was there most of the time; I don't think he did any picking . . . I think Flux was on the record . . . He was just a little kid, too. I think he was fresh out of high school.

I just remember it being a lot of fun. It didn't take us very long to do it. Seems like we might have done most of it in two or three days. And it was all done live. We did everything live back in those days.

Jerry Douglas (groundbreaking resonator guitarist; former New South member):
Tony and I met in 1974 when I was playing with the Country Gentlemen, and he with Crowe. We met at a cold outdoor November festival in Morrow, OH. Tony was about to record his *California Autumn* album at Track Studio in Silver Springs, MD. His was the third record I played on, following the Gentlemen's *Remembrances and Forecasts*,

and Skaggs's *That's It*. I only knew I was entering a cast of musicians that were more advanced in the kinds of music they were hearing than I. It was around then that I heard real jazz for the first time. I was only listening to bluegrass, country and rock at that point.

Ricky Skaggs:

When I was playing with the Country Gentlemen, I had been living up in D.C. for a little while. John Starling called me one day and said, "I need you for some session work. I'm gonna produce a guitar album on Tony Rice. He's starting to work with J.D. Crowe now and he's wanting to make a record." That was the *California Autumn* album. I don't think I played any mandolin, but I played fiddle and sang some with him. That's where I really met Tony and got to know him a whole lot more. He and I just clicked so well.

Larry Rice:

We played as the Kentucky Mountain Boys for a year and a half and as the New South for four and a half years. Dickie Betts' mom lived in Bradenton, FL, the same town as my Uncle Leon, who owned a feed store and had concerts there. Dickie came to visit his mom and invited my uncles Leon, Walter, and Frank and I to play on his record, *Highway Call*, which he put out as Richard Betts.

Then Dickie asked me to tour with him. We did a three-month tour of 26 cities in the United States, including Winterland in San Francisco and Radio City Music Hall in New York. It was Vassar, Leon, Walter, and my Uncle Frank, when he could be there. There were *five* buses on that tour!

Wyatt, Larry, and Tony Rice in 2004, Tallahassee, FL.
(Courtesy Louise Rice)

Ricky Skaggs:

J.D. called me when I was getting ready to leave the Gentlemen, because Larry was going to be leaving the Kentucky Mountain Boys [later renamed the New South], and they would need a new mandolin player. Every time I would get ready to move on, it was primarily because Keith Whitley and I had started talking after we left Ralph Stanley, "Yeah, we need to put our band together." To make a long story short, we just never did our thing. When I came with J.D., I told him, "Look, I don't know just when, but Whitley and I are still wanting to put a band together." And he said, "Well, if you want a job, you can work here until you have to leave. I really need a mandolin player and tenor singer." So I was kind of getting my fill of the D.C. area, and it was time to move on to something different.

I think Tony knew tenor singing and he had a fairly high voice, and at that time I was singing to the moon, so our voices just really seemed to have this *thing*. He was throwing his lead voice up about as high as he wanted to sing it and we'd just do silly things, like "Somehow Tonight"—instead of with a high lead we'd switch around and do it in B like Flatt and Scruggs did it, or in C, at midnight on Tuesday nights when there was eight people in there. We'd just do nutty things like that. But we would never blow it out. We were so young and had such strong chops, singing so much like that. We never even thought about it.

Ricky Skaggs and Tony.
(Photo courtesy of Frank and Marty Godbey)

Jerry Douglas:

Ricky and I had become very good friends before he left the Gentlemen to play with Crowe. We had already talked about forming a band with Keith Whitley. I think Crowe was thinking about expanding his band to put even more ground between himself and other big bluegrass acts. I was learning there was so much more out there about music that I needed to know. So the timing was just perfect for me to take the first chance in my life and move out of my comfort zone. This band pushed my limits, and I added to theirs. They were tight when I got there. They had been working in a bar six nights a week for six months. They had not only the piledriver of banjo players, but great singing and all the instrumental ability and choreography of Flatt and Scruggs to back it up.

I got there just at the end of the Holiday Inn days. I went down to visit with them and ended up filming a KET special where we all sat around and talked about our instruments. We were so little. It's kind of embarrassing to watch now. Our polyester count was very high. By the time I was really in the band, three months later, I was married and moved to Lexington into the same apartment complex Ricky and Tony lived in. They had started playing the Sheraton Inn out on the north side of town. I was only with the New South for four months, but it was the most exciting time of my life up till then. We ruled the festivals all summer, then capped it off with a trip to Japan. For a nineteen-year-old from Warren, Ohio, it was pretty awesome.

Bobby Slone (bassist/fiddler; New South member for nearly 20 years):

When we played the Holiday Inn, when Jerry joined us, all I had to do was just sit back there and watch and play bass. The people in the audience, they didn't know who to look at. There was Jerry, and Ricky and Tony and Crowe. And their eyes and heads in the audience would just move like *that* all the time, just spinning. They didn't know who to look at. And I said to myself, "Boys, something's *right*." You know? There's something's *right* somewhere.

Doc Hamilton:

I had moved to Louisville to work for the medical school, and Tony, J.D., Ricky Skaggs, and Bobby Slone all came to Louisville to play at a place called the Mason Jar, right up the street from where I was living. By that time, I'd given up the banjo; I'd got sick of it, and I started trying to play fiddle a little bit; I wasn't much good.

Well, I'd known J.D. Crowe's music from Jimmy Martin days, way back yonder. I said, "Let's go." And here's Tony Rice! I hadn't seen Tony in years, and I didn't even know if he'd remember me. I went up during the break and he said, "*Doc?* My God!" He grabbed me and hugged me like a long-lost brother. He said, "Are you still playing banjo?" I said "No, I'm trying to play the fiddle." He said, "Well, do you have it with you?" "Yeah, it's out in the trunk." He said, "Go get it and sit in with us."

Well, I was scared to death. I wasn't no bluegrass fiddler. And here's Ricky Skaggs, and Tony was on one side, and Crowe on the other . . . I got up and played a couple with 'em and got ready to take another break, and Crowe says, "Where you goin'?" I said, "Well, I'm done playing my tunes." He said, "No, you can get up and finish out the night with us here. Sounds good!"

Oh, God, when I was up there playing with them at the Mason Jar, the rhythm was *so* solid. I would just float. The notes would just come blowing out of my fiddle. I've never played that well since then. They were *tight*.

J.D. Crowe:

A guy named Hugh Sturgill was kind of helping us out doing some calling and legwork, trying to book the group. He would talk about Ricky joining the group, because I knew Ricky had quit the Gentlemen. I think at that time he was working in a factory or something up there in the D.C. area. Hugh called me, and I said, "Yeah, call Ricky and see what he says."

Hugh Sturgill (former manager of J.D. Crowe and the New South):

After Ricky came in the band, we set about trying to find a new format and different material. J.D. and I talked a long time about where bluegrass was going and where his band could be, and about changing from a hardcore Jimmy Martin hillbilly band to a more contemporary sound. When you have Skaggs and Tony Rice, you've got a much younger generation involved with exposure to different sounds.

We started working on tunes and it was a collaborative effort; we met at Bobby Slone's house over in the east end of Lexington, and had rehearsals a couple afternoons a week. They still had the gig at the Holiday Inn North that was paying the bills, and from those rehearsals came the *Old Home Place* album that was laid down January 3, 1975. That whole project took a grand total of two days. It was so well-rehearsed.

Ken Irwin (one of the founders of Rounder Records):

We approached J.D. about doing a banjo record, and a short while later, at the Gettysburg festival, Hugh Sturgill called us together and asked us if we'd be interested in recording J.D.'s band. Which sort of shocked us. I think we might have had the Del McCoury record [Del McCoury and the Dixie Pals, *High on a Mountain*, Rounder, 1973] but Del, at the time, was living in York, Pennsylvania, and was a regional artist. So we hadn't really had any major bluegrass artists . . . Certainly Del, Hazel & Alice, and a few others—Ted Lundy, Bob Paisley—went on to become national or international artists, but at the time, we didn't have anybody on the label in the bluegrass area who had made it to the next point. So we wouldn't have even considered *asking* J.D. if we could record the band! I think we were still considered by most to be young hippies at that point.

I think it was totally the band's decision. They wanted to be different, and they wanted to get attention, and I think going with a different label might have been making a statement in and of itself that *they* were different.

Hugh Sturgill:

I remember a lot of the Seldom Scene came over and had dinner with Crowe's band. It was a very interesting observation Ben Eldridge made, or maybe it was Duffey. He said, "You know, *this* is a bluegrass band! *We* play American music. *This* is a bluegrass band." Which I thought was very insightful; there was a great deal of mutual respect between the bands. We certainly loved them a lot.

I kind of functioned as a referee between the guys in the New South; I had a striped shirt and a whistle. I'd go to all the rehearsals, and kinda listen to what was goin' down, and then Crowe and I would talk, and I'd give him my opinion about it . . .

It really was a consortium. They all brought stuff to the table. I'd have to say Ricky

Jerry, Ricky, J.D., and Tony.
(Photo courtesy Tony Rice)

Skaggs was key, in arrangement, and in cleaning up vocals. Tony was a fountain of ideas for songs. He brought in the Ian Tyson piece ["Summer Wages"] and he was well into Dean Webb. Dean lived about five doors from Bobby Slone at the time, and he had written "The Old Home Place." Tony had this prolific record collection, and he said, "You know, that's a real good tune." They ran through it and they all liked it.

Tony was a night owl. His eyes didn't open till the neons came on. But I had everybody's ass outta bed and in that studio at 10 o'clock in the morning, and we finished by 5:30 or 6 in the afternoon, and went and had a good dinner.

We spent a little over six hours each day in the studio, for a double session. That whole project took about twelve hours.

J.D. Crowe:

I wanted to use steel and piano on a few cuts for a little fuller sound. For "Cryin' Holy," it gave it more of a gospel flavor, that old kind of sound I wanted.

If you'll listen to Gordon Lightfoot's version of "You Are What I Am," all that steel does is slide in behind the chord changes. And that's what I wanted. It fits so good. That's what I had in mind. Very lightly, not real abrasive. Without it, it would sound weird.

Fred Bartenstein (founder of *Muleskinner News*; musician, broadcaster, MC):

J.D. is very low-key, but he creates an environment in which people can excel. That's what happened with that band. At the time, that particular band of J.D. Crowe and Bobby Slone and Tony Rice and Ricky Skaggs and Jerry Douglas was considered to be the second coming. It was the band that people were comparing to Flatt & Scruggs with

Benny Martin and Curly Seckler. It was known at that time that this was the hottest bluegrass band to come down the road for 25 years. We thought they were gonna be the ones that would break bluegrass the way Alison Krauss and Ricky Skaggs are doing now. And *they* thought they would. People still go around talking about Rounder 0044. There aren't many records you know by their number. In fact, it's the only one that I can think of that people call by its number.

John Starling:

I think the only album they did with that particular group of guys was at the same place we did *Old Train*—Track Studios in Silver Spring, Maryland. We were doing those albums about the same time, and I heard some of *their* stuff, and I thought, "*These* guys really know how to play bluegrass. *We're* just screwing around . . ."

Ken Irwin:

0044 sold pretty well right away, and it sold consistently for years and years, and was probably our best bluegrass seller at that time. More importantly, I think that record had a tremendous impact on the way Rounder was viewed as a label. This sort of put us on peoples' minds as being legitimate. And because J.D. was so respected in the community, I think it had a little bit of cache: "Well, if J.D. trusts them, they must be okay."

(Courtesy Rounder Records)

Dr. David Haney (guitarist & historian):

The impact of this album was enormous. When I teach my graduate course on Bluegrass Traditions at Appalachian State University, I end with this album as the event that changed bluegrass.

Even though other "young" groups like New Grass Revival and Bluegrass Alliance were around, this was the first time that musicians like Crowe and Skaggs, with hard-core bluegrass credentials and a corresponding level of musicianship, brought in a different kind of beat, with jazz and swing influences that made for a whole new sound. The New Grass Revival was playing rock-style music with bluegrass instruments, while the New South was really creating a new combination.

I was playing in Buffalo, New York in 1976, and there was a very young group that played every song on Rounder 0044. The banjo player in that group was changing from a Courtney Johnson clone to a Crowe clone. I was trying to get people to listen to something OTHER than Rounder 0044 at the time, which tells you how influential this album became immediately.

Alison Krauss:

That album. *That's the one.* I don't even know how many times I've bought the J.D. Crowe album now. I don't even know how many! If I can't find it, I go and get another one. If I can't find it *within five minutes*, I go and buy another one.

All the time. I listen to it all the time! It's a little scary. Might be time to move on. But I can't seem to . . .

It's so new, even now. Even when you hear all the people who have been influenced by it, it's still so new . . . And I always think of how young Tony was—what was he, 24? That he was finding those songs at 24 . . . That somebody so young would have *that* kind of depth, and be able to deliver those tunes where I would have never known whether he had written them himself or not . . . I can believe them so much.

Mike Auldridge (original resonator guitarist with the Seldom Scene):

When Tony sat in with the Seldom Scene, it wasn't the same as Starling, but it was just as magical. Tony had a similar texture in his voice that Starling had at that point. When we sang "Old Train," or one of those classic tunes, it was just as smooth and strong as it was with John. It was wonderful.

Tom Gray (original bassist with the Seldom Scene):

Tony knew all of our songs and could sing John's part, plus he put wonderful guitar solos in everything he did. Tony was still playing with J.D. Crowe at the time. The plans were already made; we were gonna have a meeting at someone's home to talk over the plans. Starling was gonna be there, but he had announced that he was leaving the band. His replacement was to be Tony Rice. We bought him an airline ticket from Lexington to Washington for us all to get together. And much to everyone's surprise, John Starling said, "I'm sorry, guys, if it upsets any plans, but *I'm not leaving.*"

Ben Eldridge:

Starling was starting to make noise about having to stop playing, because of his medical stuff. He just had too much going on, and he didn't think he could maintain the kind of schedule we'd been doing. I think Tony got wind of that, and was really interested in taking Starling's place in '74 or '75, something like that. Starling said, "I'm gonna probably go for another six months, and then the end of the summer I'm gonna quit," and we had pretty much lined up Tony.

Then Starling changed his mind. That was at the end of the season. Seems like it was just within a few months, Tony headed on out to California. I think he got tired of that six nights a week business at the Holiday Inn, and just wanted to do something else.

On the Road
Part 3

Ancramdale, NY

It's Saturday afternoon in Ancramdale, New York, a sleepy little farming community in the foothills of the Berkshire Mountains. On sultry days like today, this little corner of God's country usually provides its own music, but today the big skies over Ancramdale are filled with bluegrass.

It seems as if the whole world has flocked to the Rothvoss Farm for the Grey Fox Bluegrass Festival. Tents and RVs cling precariously to the side of the mountain. Music lovers who have finished their suppers and afternoon jams begin moving toward the stage, hauling lawnchairs, blankets, programs and cameras through narrow dirt roads which have been whimsically named for the superstars of bluegrass music.

A sleek black car crawls up the hill. The man behind the wheel maneuvers patiently through the milling crowd, a half-smile almost hidden by his long sandy moustache.

In spite of an innate sense of direction that has served him well for decades, he makes a wrong turn in the maze of dirt passages and finds himself heading away from the stage area. Suddenly he notices something that makes him chuckle. "Hey," he says with quiet bemusement and maybe even a little pride, "there's my road!" And sure enough, there it is, running parallel to Kuykendall Crossing and perpendicular to Monroe Boulevard, the wooden sign clearly painted to give lost campers a point of reference: RICE LANE.

Eventually he gets the car pointed toward the stage. The crowds thicken, and now there are festival staff members along the way, with orange vests and bright nylon flags, to keep the roads clear. Many pedestrians turn and stare curiously at the vehicle. A 2003 Mustang Cobra with a 4.6 litre supercharged and modified 32-valve 425-horsepower V8 engine, it can get from zero to 60 mph in less than five seconds. The rising dust cannot hide the sweet purr of its engine. Crowds part as the Red Sea before Moses; folks recognize the driver and elbow each other—"Hey, that's Tony Rice!" they say. "Whoa, dude, check out that car."

One little gaggle of oblivious teenagers is slow to move, and a staff member rushes to the rescue. "Make way for Tony Rice!" he commands good-naturedly, "the best guitarist on the planet." As the road clears, the staffer steps toward the car window, rolled up against the dust clouds. "How's it goin', Mr. Rice?" he says through the glass. "Welcome back to Grey Fox. It sure is good to see you again."

The sandy moustache twitches and raises just a little. "Good to be here, man." The reply is a low rumbling growl curled around a smile. "Good to be here."

Back on the Road

"It feels like a Sunday," Tony says. "I don't give a shit what day everybody else says it is; I think it feels like a Sunday."

Somewhere in Pennsylvania, it starts to pour. Traffic slows and the cars fall back, as drivers one by one lose their nerve, let off the gas, and drop behind. They're all doing 30 mph back there because they can't see, even with their windshield wipers on hyperdrive.

But not Rice. It feels like a Sunday. He decelerates just a bit—to 60 mph—and turns up the wipers just a bit, to a fast pulse. He lights a cigarette and takes a sip of coffee, and never stops talking.

8:23 A.M. in West Virginia. Pam calls to report on her latest encounter with an unpleasant neighbor. Tony lights a cigarette as he talks to her. The lighter was a gift from his cousin, Jewell Penn. It's a fancy Calibri engraved with his initials in script, on the side—and on the top, very faintly, in quotes: "ONE TIME." "An inside joke between me and my cousin," he says shortly.

At a truck stop, he quips, "I gotta find a radiator shop . . . to take a leak." He chuckles gently, goes inside, and finally we meet at the register. He buys two atlases—one a "John & Jane Doe," as he calls it, a regular old Rand McNally—and the other, a motor carrier's map book thick with laminated pages. "Sometimes," he says, "I can't find festivals in the sticks on the trucker's map, so I need the other, but the trucker's map has the most direct routes." He also buys a bottle of Pet milk, which he says is his favorite; Tony drinks a lot of milk.

The cashier tries to scan some long, bulky item for the customer at her register, and it almost falls on Tony. She's quick to apologize: "So sorry, sir."

The moustache twitches, and there is an almost inaudible chuckle. "Lemme call my lawyer," he says. The cashier blanches, but soon realizes he is only teasing.

Winchester, Virginia, 9:15 A.M. We are talking about bluegrass festivals when he pulls into an Amoco, his fuel station of preference. He tells me that the majority of bluegrass musicians hate playing festivals anymore; they'd much rather play indoors than out, at concert halls or in theatres. For him, it really comes down to privacy. "Promoters," he says, "should make more of an effort, no matter what they have to do, to have a private entrance for the artists so they can pull up to a gig and have only their band members there." He says he wishes somebody would get all the promoters together in a room to talk about how they might improve conditions to appeal more to bluegrass musicians.

Tony hates to be disturbed before he goes onstage. He wants a private place to unwind and tune before every show he plays, and a private path to the stage, without anybody stopping him to chat or beg for an autograph. These things don't seem unreasonable, but simply things that common sense and courtesy would demand. After all these years, he still chafes when they are absent.

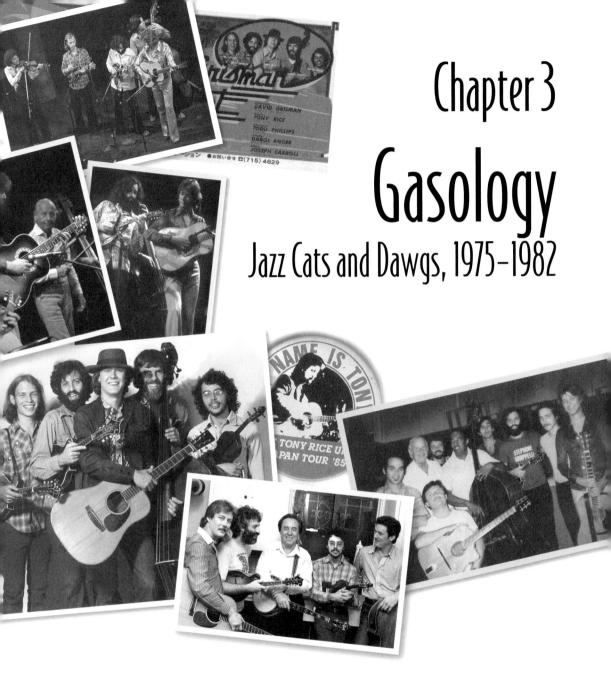

Chapter 3
Gasology
Jazz Cats and Dawgs, 1975–1982

He was good, man. He was good. He just had too much talent to be
somebody's guitar player.

David Grisman, visionary mandolinist & father of Dawg music

Chapter 3: Introduction

These were days of momentous change for Tony Rice, and for his music. One of the best bluegrass lead singers in history, he had helped make the most influential record in that genre's history, and now decided to join an all-instrumental experimental jazz group on the West Coast. Back East, in his absence the mystique surrounding Tony and his bluegrass work began to grow.

When Tony moved to San Francisco in September 1975 to join David Grisman in his quest for a new sound, he was sailing into the unknown. Leaving behind the comfort of J.D. Crowe's amazing band, and its steady six-nights-a-week gig at the Holiday Inn Lexington, Tony trekked 2400 miles on hardly a promise. Soon, the musical alchemy of the unique band of musicians he found himself living with produced extraordinary results: music that had never been heard before.

Tutored by Grisman, John Carlini and Buell Neidlinger, Rice transformed himself into a jazz guitarist, with the timing and rhythmic ferocity that had been instilled by Crowe. *The David Grisman Quintet*, the band's landmark 1977 recording for Kaleidoscope, was a stunning showcase of the new form, called "Dawg" music after Grisman's nickname. Tony's bandmates—Todd Phillips, Darol Anger, and eventually Mike Marshall—shared and reveled in his evolving eclectic lifestyle. They often stayed up until dawn, marveling at recordings of jazz cats like John Coltrane, Miles Davis, and Oscar Peterson, working constantly, listening and absorbing, practicing and rehearsing, and listening some more.

How Tony came to leave the band he once said he wanted to play with for the rest of his life is a matter of record, and also a matter of contention. After a tour with Stéphane Grappelli dissolved in arguments between Rice and Grisman, Mark O'Connor took Tony's place in the Quintet. In 1979, once again on Labor Day—a holiday that seems to bring change in Tony's life almost every time it rolls around—Tony played his last shows with the David Grisman Quintet.

He then launched the Tony Rice Unit, a vessel for his own acoustic vision, a scorching blend of Dawg and drive. In essence, it was an all-instrumental extension of the concept of 1979's landmark *Manzanita* project. The first configuration of the performing Tony Rice Unit included Tony's brother, Wyatt, on rhythm guitar; mandolinist John Reischman; Todd Phillips on bass, and violinist Fred Carpenter. The solo New Acoustic recordings Tony produced during this period—*Acoustics, Mar West, Still Inside* and *Backwaters*—proved the apex of his interest in this form of musical expression.

All the while, Tony was establishing a pattern: even as he worked with Grisman and Co. to build masterpieces within the "New Acoustic" format he helped found, he was recording some of the greatest bluegrass and related music ever committed to wax.

Tony approached jazz with a childlike honesty. He wasn't some theory jazz-brainchild. He just took the sounds his soul was drawn to and made them his own.

Brad Davis, Texas guitarist and Rice protégé

In His Own Words: Tony's Story

Around 1967, I discovered jazz. We were living in Texas, and there was a real rich girl I had a crush on who showed up at a park where I was hanging out. She had her parents' big luxury car, some kind of Cadillac convertible. Back then, if you had any kind of player device in your car, it was an eight-track. The *sound* coming out of her car ... We were sitting there, and I said, "Who is that?" She said, "Dave Brubeck. They're playing 'Take Five.' "

One of the first things I did when I moved to Lexington and started with Crowe was find a real good record store, one of those that had everything. I remember walking into this store downtown, looking for any kind of jazz that I thought sounded pleasant. They happened to be playing a record by jazz pianist Oscar Peterson, the most powerful, amazing musician on the planet. I went over and got two or three of his albums, and they just blew me away. Since then, I've probably bought 75 Oscar Peterson albums.

When I was playing at the Holiday Inn, I'd usually get home about two in the morning. We didn't have to be back on

stage until 9 P.M., so I became a late-night person, and I was ready to hear jazz or sit down with my guitar and start exploring things I thought sounded unique or jazz-like, something that could be snuck into a solo that sounds like it might have been invented by Kenny Baker. I know this sounds crazy, but it's made me the guitar player I am, for better or worse.

I heard about all these other guys I really liked in modern jazz, and they didn't discuss music. I read that Miles Davis, the king of every one of them, would play music with small acoustic ensembles, and he didn't like to discuss music, period. It was something you *did*, not something you talked about. And then I became that person. I don't like a band I gotta tell what to play. I don't like to say, "Okay, I've got this idea and it's all laid out on paper here, in this little chart."

When I met Grisman during the recording of Bill Keith's album, he had this tape of music he'd been playing with John Carlini and Richard Greene. It was called the *Great American Music Band*. I heard that stuff and I thought, "Man, I have *never* heard music this good of any kind, anywhere in my life, *ever.* I'd like to be able to play this music; it would be a dream come true." But I didn't have the technical knowledge. Grisman was really encouraging. He said, "Hey, if you can play like you do, you can play this music."

I just loved it so much. I didn't know what Grisman was gonna do with it, but I was hoping he would take an interest in continuing with it. When I heard that music, I knew that's what I wanted to do, without regard to anything else. Finances, the move from Kentucky from California—none of that was an issue. The music was the issue.

Grisman had heard the New South *[Rounder 0044]* and my other two albums while he was in California. I guess I was

his favorite bluegrass guitar player. It was a mutual instant friendship. He was scheduled to go back to San Francisco after the Bill Keith session, but I asked him to bypass his trip home and stay in Lexington for a few days. He came home to Kentucky with me, spent a week or so there and played at the Sheraton a couple of nights with the New South. He was really a hippie. And he still is! I think Grisman has been a hippie since the day he was born. And he had this new music that I had to play, so I gave six weeks notice to Crowe.

Crowe was real cool about it. He was disappointed that he was losing the band, but he was real mellow when it came to stuff like that, because he had been through it himself. I think he knew my musical soul was somewhere else. He was in no way whatsoever mad. That wouldn't have been him anyway; that's not his personality. He had sense enough to realize that if a musician is dissatisfied for whatever reason and wants to move on, that doesn't make him the bad guy.

That particular version of the New South was a real tight band. They were looking at it like, "If we've lost Tony, it'll be *real* hard to get somebody to come in and make this band sound the way we do." I don't know if I would agree with that or not; I think there were people who could have stepped in. By then Ricky and Flux might have left to form a configuration of Boone Creek whether I had stayed or not. But there were never any bad vibes about anybody leaving.

David Grisman and Tony. (Photo by Jon Sievert)

All that summer of '75, Grisman and I communicated on a regular basis, and I made a couple trips out to California. One trip was to buy my D-28, and another was just to go and hang out with Grisman. Then, when the New South was scheduled to go to Japan, I went early and hung out with Grisman again. It was no secret that I was going in that direction.

That October, Kate and I packed up everything we had—which wasn't much—in a souped-up '71 Plymouth GTX pulling a U-Haul trailer. We showed up out there and stayed with Grisman and his wife Janice a few days. By that time, I was broke. The bass player who had been playing with Grisman, Joe Carroll, was real generous and said, "Hey, here's a bunch of cash; I don't care when I get it back." He gave me enough money to get settled in a nice apartment.

The first town I lived in was San Rafael, in Marin County. I didn't live there very long, and we moved over to another apartment in Kentfield, in the center of Marin County. It's a little college community where the college of Marin is located. I lived there for a few years, until Kate and I got divorced, and then I moved to a town directly north of Mill Valley called Corte Madera. That's where I lived from '79 to '85.

I just settled in and started woodshedding with Grisman, trying to learn the music, which came to me easier than I thought it would. This was one big giant experiment.

Todd Phillips was a student of Grisman's, a bass player who all of a sudden took an interest in the mandolin, so Grisman started to show him twin mandolin parts. Todd and Darol Anger had been friends since they both lived in Santa Cruz. So Darol came to hang out, play the violin, and try to learn this new music, too. Joe Carroll, who had played in the Great American Music Band, was a jazz bass player in the true sense of the word. He had played with a lot of jazz greats.

So we ended up with this band, a bunch of reefer-smokin' hippies in Marin County. In retrospect, it was amazing how quick the sound came together. Almost overnight, it had a sound of its own, separate from anything that had ever been done. And as it turns out, it *would be* something that kind of set the acoustic music world on fire.

It was sort of a brave shot in the dark in those days for Grisman. He's a great man, and he's done amazing, considering: Here's this Jewish kid from New York that has only had a mandolin to walk out into the world with, and he's made an enormous success. He knew that sound was going to be unlike any other that had ever happened. It was way, way, *way* beyond categorization. You couldn't attach any known label to that music. It wasn't country, not classical, not jazz, not anything.

People ask me, "Can you describe that sound?" I still can't. Sometimes I'll tell people an analogy would be like asking someone if they know what a rose smells like. And they'll say, "Yeah, of course." And I'll say, "*Tell me about it.* Describe what a rose smells like. Well, it's kind of the same thing." The impact is the same. You knew what you were hearing was good, and you knew what it sounded like, but you couldn't break it down, just couldn't describe it.

I don't think Grisman wanted to present it in public as something that would be interpreted as experimental. He wanted to present it as an entity all its own, with its separate musical identity. It was a long time from the time I first went out and we got together—September of '75—until we started playing, early in January of '76.

There was a lot of rehearsal, but I liked it because it was a combination of playing and practicing. It wasn't a bummer. It was something I really enjoyed, because as it was coming down on the fly, you could instantly hear results. And this was sound that had never been created before. In the early days, most of the material was tunes that were more elementary than others Grisman had written. He would throw us whatever he thought we could play and sound good on. I didn't care what it was. I was in heaven because I was playing this stuff.

I was listening to mostly modern jazz at the time. Walking into Grisman's music library was like walking into a radio station! He was real encouraging, all the time putting on music that sounded real, real foreign to me. He'd say, "Take this home and just listen to it." It'd be a Miles Davis record, or a Coltrane record. It was amazing. The more I listened, the more I started to hear . . . and vice versa.

I took a very valuable ear training class in 1975 from Wynn Westover at Family Light, a music school I taught at in Sausalito. It was a real elegant school. They had

a staff of at least 20 teachers. Ronnie Bloomfield taught there; Grisman and Richard Greene had taught there. Grisman got me a gig there teaching bluegrass guitar, so I had free access to Wynn's class. It wasn't about playing an instrument, but about training the ear to hear and appreciate intervals that are outside the norm. After I started taking those classes, I began hearing Miles Davis records in a way I had never heard 'em before. I started to hear the value of the stuff those guys were doing—Bill Evans, Cannonball Adderley and the rest.

Improvisation was the hardest part at first, because I hadn't had the training. It's one thing to play an improvised bluegrass guitar solo on *Old Home Place,* but another thing altogether to play an improvised guitar solo over a tune that's got 20 different chords. It was a learning process, trial and error. John Carlini and I hung out all the time; he actually lived with me when I was married to Kate. Without him, I wouldn't

Tony, Bill Amatneek, and John Carlini.
(Photo by Jon Sievert)

be the guitar player that I am. Carlini had a way of showing me what kind of scales would work against certain chords; how you could simplify them and it wasn't really as complicated as you thought. We played a lot, and he was really patient. Guitar—or the role of the guitar—was just a constant thing with us.

Grisman and Carlini showed me how chord construction works. They showed me the individual notes that make up the chord, what they represented, and how they all worked together. A lot of the material was already on paper, charted out. Grisman had been playing with a little mandolin chamber ensemble, and was involved with doing sight-reading with them, so he carried that over into his music. Darol Anger also was good at sight-reading, so the music was very well-logged; it was just a matter of getting thc band to execute it the right way.

At some point, Grisman implied that in the music he envisioned, the role I would eventually end up filling would be that of the keyboard player. He explained how the guitar was the only instrument that could lend a chord voice to the music in the same way that an acoustic piano is the chord voice of a modern jazz ensemble. To this day, even as I grow as a guitar player, that's what I'm after. I get cues from keyboard players of how they back up solos. That's the way I use the guitar. That growth process, for me, will never stop.

Of course, this was an all-instrumental group. I didn't miss singing at all. Not since I could play with a band like *that.* Every-

body involved was so dedicated to that music, we just knew it was gonna fly, and it did. And it's still flying. I believe with all my heart that if it had not been for that band, other genres of music that acoustic string musicians play wouldn't even *exist.*

I remember telling David, "You know, this is *your music;* this is your own innovation, your own idea. You ought to put your own stamp on it." We were talking about band names, and I said, "Well, why don't you call it what it is? It's a quintet. Why don't you just call it the David Grisman Quintet?" He thought about it for a couple of days, and the next time the band got together for rehearsals, he said, "Hey, man, I've decided on a name for this band. It's the David Grisman Quintet." He will tell you to this day that I named his band.

Before we had any gigs, we did what we could to survive. I had some royalties coming in, not very much. Kate worked as a dental assistant. Somehow, we scraped by. On rare occasions, Grisman and I and a banjo player would get together and do some sort of bluegrass gig, just for the hell of it. Grisman, Bill Keith, Richard Greene and the remaining members of the Quintet and I even did a tour of Europe in '76.

Also around this time, we did Grisman's bluegrass project for Rounder, which was called *The David Grisman Rounder Album.* Everybody was there: Bill Keith, Vassar, Flux, Skaggs, Buck White. Tony Trischka was in town, and he said, "Hey, let's record." So we went in and did his record [*Banjoland,* Rounder, 1977] at the same time. I had a horrible head cold; I can hear my blocked-up nasal congestion on both those records. It was the first time I had fulfilled the dream of recording with Vassar Clements. I didn't give a shit what else was going on around me. All I could think was, "Hey, this is my man here. I'm recording with my No. 1 hero!"

I remember the first Quintet gig it like it was yesterday. It was in early '76, in western Marin County, at a community center in Bolinas. At that time, the whole San Francisco Bay area, and especially Marin County, was just a hotbed for all kinds of musicians from every field. All the rock stars—the Grateful Dead, the Jefferson Airplane—lived out there. But you could almost smell acoustic music in the air.

When we did that first gig, there wasn't any advertising in newspapers or on the radio or anything. It was totally word of mouth. But through the process of rehearsal, different people would come and go from Grisman's house: Taj Mahal, Billy Wolf, people who worked in the crew with both Garcia and the Grateful Dead; the list goes on and on. They would come and hear us playing this music.

By the time we got to that gig at the community center, it was so packed you couldn't breathe. We didn't use any microphones, just stood onstage and picked. Grisman wanted to do that. It was a good-sounding room. And the reaction to it was equally as intense. This crowd went absolutely *nuts.*

We knew then that there was an excitement about this music, and a potential market for it. I had known it anyway, be-

cause of the sound. I got enough faith in human beings. Contrary to popular belief, there are enough of them out there that are open-minded enough to simply enjoy what they like, without regard to categories or what their peers might think.

Having said that, I don't think it could have happened anywhere else besides California at that time. It might have happened back East, but it would have taken much longer to latch on. Besides, where would we have gigged? We would have been stoned to death at most bluegrass festivals!

David Grisman Quintet, August 1977, Great American Music Hall in San Francisco, CA.
(Photo by Jon Sievert)

Recording the first Quintet record was real hard. We knew we could be loose in performance, because we had a fan base that really didn't give a shit if they heard this growth process going on with this constantly evolving band. But Grisman knew that in the studio, it was time to tighten it up. You didn't get to miss chords; you didn't get to experiment like you could onstage. That made it kinda hard, and it meant doing a lot of takes of the tunes. We might do a day or two at a time and then listen, throw something away, go back in and do it later.

There was an outtake from one session that was real good, a version of "Minor Swing," which we recorded later with Grappelli on *Hot Dawg*. We didn't use it on the first Quintet album, so it stayed in the vault. I actually liked it better than the one we did with Stéphane. [This track is included in the CD version of *The David Grisman Quintet*, released in 1993.]

"E.M.D." was a tune Grisman had written for a movie called *Eat My Dust*. It was an "A" movie that was almost a "B" movie, but not quite. Ron Howard was in it, and some other people I can't remember. Most of the tunes on the record were Grisman's, except for "Swing 51." I wrote that shortly before the album. It was named after the year of my birth. Django Reinhardt and Stéphane Grappelli both had a couple of tunes that had been called "Swing" something; "Swing 42" was one of them.

Through Grisman and Richard Greene, I had befriended a guy who is a true musical genius, a bass player named Buell Neidlinger. Buell was one of these cantankerous curmudgeon sorts that had done it all. He'd played with Frank Sinatra and the Boston Symphony Orchestra; had played so much incredible music in his life. I started putting a little melody and these chords together, and I took the chart for this tune down to Buell's house in Hollywood. It's like I wanted his approval. I sat down with the chart and said, "The idea for this tune was to create a melody, and a chord se-

quence, and to have an E note in every chord." He's looking at the chart, and he'd never even heard the piece of music, and he said, "Yeah, I know." He picked it up right away, just looking at the chords written out on a piece of paper! I know I wouldn't have been able to write that tune if not for the stuff Buell, Carlini and Grisman showed me—chord inversions and things like that.

I wrote three tunes fairly close together: "Devlin," "Swing 51," and "Old Grey Coat," a tune that Grisman recorded but we never released [The tune later appeared on Tony's *Acoustics*]. Later on, I started writing more things like "Neon Tetra." Then I just quit; I went through a period where I wasn't writing at all. The next time I would start writing instrumentals was for the *Acoustics* album I did in '79. I really started writing heavily around *Mar West*. I wanted as much original material as I could get, because I was looking for a different sound.

Some of the tunes on the Quintet record were easier for me than others, like "Opus 57"—Clarence had actually played that with *Muleskinner*. In fact, the bridge I play is very similar to what Clarence played.

Other songs were hard for me, like "Fish Scale." It wasn't until after we recorded the album that I figured out the right way to play that, a totally different fingering. Carlini showed me how to do it way up in almost 3rd position. On the record I did it in 1st position. It was easier up in 3rd position, where you could almost play the whole head without moving your thumb. It sounded better up there because you had access to all the notes, so there was more continuity from one to the next. The phrasing was more deliberate-sounding, as opposed to playing it like the recording. When I hear the recording of "Fish Scale" off the Grisman album today, it sounds kind of convoluted—I can hear an open note in the middle of nowhere. Even though it's the right note, it kind of sticks out like a sore thumb.

"Dawg's Rag" was one of the first tunes of Grisman's I heard, from when Richard Greene and Carlini played with him in the Great American Music Band. I still remember hearing this shit go by and thinking, "There is no music on this planet any better than this that I've heard in my life, by anybody at any time." To me, that tune is still the epitome of Grisman's music.

I wasn't supposed to be on "Ricochet." The tune was supposed to feature only mandolins. While they were practicing on mic, before I got up out of my chair to go somewhere, I started noodling around, playing these major scale-oriented arpeggios. Grisman said, "Hey, man, wait a minute before you go. Keep doing that." And he just decided we would leave it on there.

At some point during that recording, I started calling David and I "The Gasoline Brothers." We were in the studio listening to a playback of something really fast; it might have been "Opus 57." We were smoking our usual amount of adult herbs, and Grisman kept saying, "Man, that's *hot shit!* That is really hot shit!" I said, "We *are* kind of putting it down, ain't we?" He said, "Yeah, we ought to call ourselves some-

thing separate from this." I said, "Why not call us the Gasoline Brothers? We're just about ready to explode."

The real genius on that album was Billy Wolf. What he did, the assembling and editing and construction of that album, was just unbelievable. It also raised the bar in acoustic music for consciousness of real good audio that had not been there before. Other than maybe the Seldom Scene, most bluegrass bands were like, "Hey, go in the studio, walk in the door, start playing the music, and who gives a shit? Let the engineers deal with it."

The first time I remember Billy working on anything was at Arch Street. He was engineering Jerry Garcia's stuff and he was Garcia's main man on the road at that time. He came over and listened to the band and then he would come over to the house and hang out at Grisman's. Billy and I were friends right off the bat. He just knew what he was doing. His approach was very common-sense, in that you put a pair of microphones in front of an instrument and the idea is to be able to reproduce that sound as accurately as you can, with no

Billy Wolf, Tony, David Grisman and cast during the Manzanita *sessions. (Photo by Jon Sievert)*

frills, so that the listener is hearing what they would hear sitting in their room. And Billy pretty much nailed it. I had never heard playback that concise, with that much clarity, in a control room.

We recorded on one-inch 8-track tape back then. I recorded so many things on that same console and on that same machine at Arch Street. It was the old 3M machine, an M23. The console was a good-sounding old MCI with custom API modules in it. The cue system and control room playback were real good. You had to stack tracks. The bass used one mic and the violin used one, while Grisman, Todd, and I were miked stereo.

Believe it or not, the reverb used on that record was a combination Orban, basically a spring reverb. You could only push it so far before you heard the actual spring. So Billy added some supplementary echo with an old Ampex machine, where you used the delay between the record and the playback head a little bit, just enough so that you didn't have to push the Orban to its limits. He had to run that at 15 IPS on a ten-inch reel while the mixing was coming down and it was only good for a few minutes. But it worked. I mean, that recording was quiet, boy.

It ain't been that long ago that I put on the first approved test pressing of that record at my house. Somehow I ended up with it. And it sounded as refreshing a month ago as it did 30 years ago. In fact, it even sounded better, because it had been so long since I had heard it and I had forgotten how good it really was—not just the individual components, but even if there's a solo at any given moment in time, there's still a sublime sound going on overall. Through all those things, a real connoisseur will hear that as not just individual components, but as this overall effort by everybody. It's a sound, and that sound never changed.

I think that album was even popular with a lot of people who thought, "Well, the unmitigated gall of these guys, to take these axes and not do Bill Monroe tunes, and not have vocals on there!" We had what was essentially a bluegrass band minus the five-string banjo, playing this weird music that sounded like a cross between classical chamber music, bluegrass, and jazz.

In 1976, we played a very successful tour in Japan. I had been there with Crowe in '75, and it wasn't a lot different—there was just more of it. Seemed like we crammed a lot into a week and a half. By that time, Japanese fanatics—as well as the promoter Hiroshi Asata—had somehow got hold of live tapes of the Grisman band playing somewhere. These cats were just absolutely crazy! We were rock stars over there. It was nuts. We stayed in the finest hotels, and made good money.

What was really weird was that the younger bluegrass musicians, even the die-hard Southern traditionalists, heard that music and went *ape* over it. Most people really liked that sound. But I didn't see that until we went on a tour back East in '79. I sort of figured the bluegrass community back East would be curious as to what this new sound was all about, but I had no idea it would be as exciting as it was. Every place we played was sold out.

For the four years I worked with Grisman, I think people perceived that band as playing all the time. But we didn't. Grisman didn't like traveling or playing live all that much, so the band didn't play near as much as bands do nowadays. And he would do other things, like a couple of movie scores. *The King of the Gypsies* was one of 'em. It worked out okay, because I ended up doing my first two Rounder albums during that period.

On the first one, [*Tony Rice,* 1977] I wanted to get back to bluegrass roots, or at least keep my foothold. I hadn't done an album like that since *California Autumn.* So I started calling people that would be available for it: Richard Greene, Crowe, Grisman, Jerry Douglas; my brother Larry's on some cuts, and Todd and Darol. Unfortunately, Billy Wolf wasn't available to do that album, so Bob Shoemaker engineered and mixed it.

I didn't know what I was doing when I went in to do that record. It was just time

to do a Tony Rice album. A lot of people tell me they like "Hills of Roane County," but if I could go back and do it again, I wouldn't have used as many ornaments with the vocal. I overdid it, but in the moment, you don't know that. "Way Downtown" was pretty much Doc Watson's version, while "Farewell Blues" was one of Clarence's signature tunes that I sort of knew, and really wanted to hear J.D. Crowe play.

David Nichtern wrote "Plastic Banana." Nichtern produced Maria Muldaur's first album, the one with "Midnight at the Oasis." He and Grisman had played together in New York. He said, "Hey, I got a bluegrass tune," and played it for me. I don't play it exactly like Nichtern, but the gist of it is there. Larry and I used to play "Stoney Creek" when we were kids. I wouldn't play lead guitar on it, but I always liked the tune. I just hoped I was playing it melodically enough that it could be identified as "Stoney Creek," because it's certainly not Jesse McReynolds's version of it.

We had been playing "Eighth of January" in the Grisman Quintet. When the Quintet started, we had a lot of compli-

An ad from the Quintet's 1977 tour of Japan in 1976. (Courtesy Jon Sievert)

cated material—"Fishscale," "Dawg's Rag," and stuff like that—but Grisman wanted to play some tunes that were really back to the roots, so he would just pull something out of the hat, "Big Mon" or something like that. We recorded that stuff because Grisman and I had played it together and we knew it.

I don't like that album. Something is missing; I can't explain what it is. As soon as I was done with it, I went back to playing with Grisman. The only two albums of my own I can't stand are the one I did for Sab Watanabe and the first one I did for Rounder. If I never hear them again, it would be too soon.

I was always involved with recording with someone, or doing something musically. Grisman and Darol Anger and I and a couple of other guys in the Bay Area would get together and go do some bluegrass shit at a nightclub somewhere. At some point, Grisman said, "Hey, we gotta do a Shasta commercial and you gotta sing it." I said, "Okay." [This appears on the 1996 Quintet retrospective *DGQ20* as "Shasta Bull."]

Later, Todd, Darol, Mike Marshall, and I played as the "'Ook 'n 'M" band around San Francisco and Santa Cruz. That was something that Buell Neidlinger's kid kept saying: "'Ook 'n 'M! 'Ook 'n 'M!" Buell could never figure out what it meant. He told us about his kid, and somebody had to do something with that phonetic bunch of letters thrown together.

We played real free-form stuff, because all of us at that time were into free-form jazz players like Ornette Coleman, Albert

TONY RICE
guitar

DAROL ANGER
violin

MIKE MARSHALL
mandolin

TODD PHILLIPS
string bass

PLAYING ORIGINAL MATERIAL FROM DAROL'S NEW ALBUM "FIDDLISTICS" *AND* TONY'S "ACOUSTICS" - *BOTH SOON TO BE RELEASED ON* KALEIDOSCOPE

kuumbwa june SAT 16
info: 427-2227

(Courtesy Jon Sievert)

Ayler and Cecil Taylor. We had a ball playing these juke joints. But it never was a functioning band, *per se*. Some of that stuff ended up being recorded in bits and pieces here and there, like on Darol Anger's album [*Fiddlistics*, 1981].

One of the best solos I've ever played in my life was "Round Midnight" on Mike Marshall's record *Gator Strut*. Mike just kind of showed up at my door one day. He was a kid I had met when the New South was together. J.D., Ricky, Flux, and I had played in Georgia and Florida on a run of gigs and here was this little kid playing the mandolin. Well, back then, there wasn't that many young kids playing mandolin that were good, maybe three on the planet, so I remembered him real well when he called. I said, "Hell, yeah, man, come on over." He just kind of showed up, and then he stayed!

As dedicated as Mike was to the music, it was logical for him to become the second mandolin player in the Quintet, and then Todd switched over to bass. In retrospect, Joe Carroll and Bill Amatneek, who also played bass with us, were grounded in metronomic rhythm: a steady, rock-solid, metronomic beat. They were from the school where you do not deviate from that, no matter what. And all of a sudden they were involved in this music form that required timing to breathe, to constantly adjust, slow down a little, speed up, slow down, speed up. Todd Phillips was a natural for that; he still is.

Todd shared his "hobo in the boxcar" analogy for timing. Imagine a hobo in a boxcar on a train riding down the rail. The speed of the train represents the speed of the tune, but the hobo represents the beat. The hobo is free to move from one end of the boxcar to the other while the train is going down the track. That's what music is all about. It's gotta breathe. And that's a real, real sophisticated thing to do, very tedious and hard to cultivate—that ability to allow your musicianship the flexibility to let time breathe, rather than creating a metronomic pulse; to go with the other band members' feelings and do whatever you have to in that moment to make good music.

It's unfortunate that configuration of the Quintet never did an album. It would have been amazing, and there are good live performances that exist. But by that time, the concept of the Quintet was changing. One of the things I learned from Grisman is to not consider yourself a boss or a bandleader and have guys at *your* mercy for their living. You don't do that because you don't *have* to. Grisman's attitude about every gig ever played—and he made no bones about this—was "I reserve the *right* to call up anybody I want to that can play the music I want to play for a particular gig or album." That really eliminates *every* problem, right there.

On the second Quintet album [*Hot Dawg*], I'm the only guy, other than Grisman, that's on every tune. There were a lot of different players on that record: Stéphane Grappelli, Todd Phillips, Joe Carroll, Buell Neidlinger, Eddie Gomez. Darol was on the cuts that Grappelli wasn't on. That should tell people where the Quintet had evolved to in just three years, because the *Hot Dawg* album was recorded in '78. By then, Grisman didn't want his band restricted to a certain number of players all the time. But he did go back to that in later years, after I left. He would go for long periods without a single personnel change.

It wasn't long after we did *Hot Dawg* that I started to get that notion myself: to assemble my own strictly instrumental group and go play some gigs. Prior to 1980, it was only a concept. The *Manzanita* album was billed as The Tony Rice Unit; so was an album I did in 1979 called *Acoustics*. Inspiration for the name came from an *avant-garde* jazz piano player named Cecil Taylor. No matter what Cecil did, his accompanying instrumentation was in a constant state of flux. One band didn't have a drummer; the next one wouldn't have a bass; the next band would have ten horns. But as a concept, he called whatever configuration he happened to have "The Cecil Taylor Unit," which implied that it could be anything at any given time, as opposed to a definitive band with expectations from a listening public.

The name implies it can be anything. I'm not deliberately trying to throw anybody a curve, so that if they buy a ticket to come and see the Unit they won't know what to expect, but through all the years, it's been the Tony Rice Unit. The spirit of it is there no matter what configuration.

The idea behind *Acoustics* was centered around Richard Greene. We both had done a tour of Europe with Bill Keith, and I knew what Richard was capable of doing. If you could present him with the right music in the right circumstances, you could capture the best of him. I had some original tunes I wanted to do again, like "Swing 51" and "Old Gray Coat," which the Grisman band used to do live all the time. I wanted to do a different take on those things with Richard and Sam Bush, who had never played together. Richard was Sam's hero on the fiddle.

That also ended up being the first session Mike Marshall did that you could call something of notoriety. I deliberately wanted to put this guy on this album on a few tunes to expose him.

When Mike was staying at my place, we started noodling around with what became "New Waltz," and he wrote a bridge

for it. "Fast Floyd" was a tune without a title. No matter where you drove in Berkeley, you saw it, because some kids had spray-painted "Fast Floyd" everywhere—on busses, buildings, you name it. I never knew what it was about. To me, this tune is all of that, arrangement-wise. It almost kicks off so fast you can't get to the next part. "Four on Six" came from Wes Montgomery, the jazz guitarist. Carlini and I used to play that. "So Much" was one of mine, as was "Gasology," a tune whose head is all in the third and fourth positions, pretty far up there. It was just a melody I put together. In those days, I would take a tape recorder and put down the melody before I forgot it. And then I would put chords to it, or I would find a sequence of chords that I liked and would commit them to tape before I forgot 'em. And then I would put the melody around it.

Acoustics was the first all-instrumental thing I did, playing what I thought was an extension of Grisman's music. I don't know if it was, but it was different: structured more around improvisation than fixed arrangements. By that time, through Grisman, I'd learned about all these jazz people who became my idols: Oscar Peterson, Bill Evans, Coltrane, Miles Davis. They were doing what I wanted to do: rather than have tight-knit, defined arrangements, I wanted a simple melody of some kind or another, and to allow the other musicians—myself included—more improvisational freedom.

The cover and interior shots were done at the Great American Music Hall in San Francisco. I played there a lot, and the acoustics were amazing. There was something magic about that room. It was like an ideal jazz listening club. I'd never played at any showcase club of that quality. There's very few of 'em that fit that bill.

I didn't get the vibe from Rounder that they wanted *Acoustics.* Kaleidoscope, the record company that had put out the first Grisman album, loved the idea of a Dawg music album that featured me, and they put it out. Then I re-signed a contract with Rounder for three instrumental albums, so I did those—*Mar West, Still Inside,* and *Backwaters.* To tell you the truth, at the time I knew that contract meant a source of income, a sizeable cash advance. The only thing I knew to do was write the music, so I did.

I left the Quintet after Grisman booked a tour with Stéphane Grappelli that I didn't want to do. The collaboration with Stéphane had become a separate entity from the music. Grisman wanted to play with Grappelli as a hero. And I didn't like the tune selection. At a rehearsal, I told Grisman, point-blank in front of the whole band, "You know how long it's been since we did 'Dawg's Rag,' or 'Dawgology,' or 'Fishscale'? It's almost like these tunes have been forgotten. If I'm going to go out with this band, that's what I want to play. If we ain't gonna do that, count me out." Grisman said something and I got real pissed and said, "David, if you want a guitar player to go play 'Tiger Rag' with Stéphane, you got the wrong guy."

And I didn't go, and that was the end of it. When I refused to go on the tour, I got replaced. Mark O'Connor was around by

then, so he came and took the guitar chair. I think I played two more dates, one in New Mexico and one in Arizona over Labor Day weekend of '79.

I have no regrets to this day. I know Stéphane never held it against me. I was a special musician to Grappelli, because he had never heard anything like my music and he loved it when we played together. But I was kind of concerned: would Stéphane hold it against me if the reason why I refused this tour got back to him? If he did, it was never mentioned to me.

From the time I joined Grisman until the time I left, my allegiance to him and his music and the friendship was real strong.

Tony and legendary jazz violinist Stéphane Grappelli in 1978. (Photo by Jon Sievert)

He and I have had disagreements and ups and downs, but our friendship is unconditional, no doubt about it. Grisman will be the first guy on the scene to bail you out if you are in trouble or in need. And when it comes to integrity and honesty, he's absolutely flawless. When it comes to all the qualities that make up a good man, Grisman is not lacking in any of them. He has compassion. He's a good teacher. I'd have to say I owe as much to Grisman as to J.D. Crowe, in terms of somebody who had the patience to work with *me.* If I had to name a single person I've learned from, in terms of listening, playing, improvisation, freedom to experiment, being unafraid of the process of trial and error—all that stuff came from Grisman.

At the same time, Grisman probably learned some things from playing with me. I think he would tell you that he had never played with a guitar player, rhythm-wise, who had that sense of *drive.* Del McCoury had it, when Grisman played some with Del, and also with Red Allen. But it wasn't just with my right hand that I drove Grisman. I think it would be safe to say I drove him to pursue his music more aggressively than he otherwise would have. I loved his music so much, and he knew that. Having me as a rhythm player was only gonna bring out the best in him, and make him enjoy playing more.

Once I tried giving him a wristwatch, because he was always asking what time it was. I gave it to him as a gift at rehearsal one night. He said, "Uh, no thanks, man, you can give it to somebody else. I'm not into time." He was serious. That was Grisman.

As I mentioned, Grisman would go off and do other things with other people. And he would encourage us to do that, too. He would get us together and say, "Hey guys, I wanna go do this other thing for a while. You guys should go out and play with whoever you can." The concept of freedom to explore had kind of kicked in by the time *Mar West* was recorded in late '79 or early '80. I wanted it to be a more polished version of *Acoustics.* Other than that, *Mar West* is kind of unremarkable.

A radical change happened with the next album, *Still Inside,* because it was made by a working band, the first Tony Rice Unit: myself, Todd Phillips, Fred Carpenter, and John Reischman. The band eventually flopped, but a couple of classic things came out of it. By the time we recorded *Backwaters,* the Unit did have an identity of its own, separate from Grisman.

Fred Carpenter came out of the fiddle contest circuit. That's just what he was—a Texas swing fiddler *à la* Benny Thomasson. Mark O'Connor was his hero. I knew Fred had the ability to play some of this stuff. Some of the fiddle solos he played on it are unbelievable. That tune "Within Specs" flies by at the speed of light, and Fred plays a beautiful fiddle on there. And coming out of that solo on "Moses Sole," back into the last head, is just phenomenally beautiful, the way he threw those notes out like that. I deliberately put Richard Greene on *Backwaters* because I wanted to include some stuff I didn't think Fred could do. There's no way Fred Carpenter could have played "Green Dolphin Street" and pulled it off

The original Tony Rice Unit in the early '80s: Fred Carpenter, Tony, Todd Phillips, John Reischman. (Courtesy Louise Rice)

like Richard at that time. And on "A Child Is Born," Richard makes the fiddle sound like he's got a bow three yards long.

Finding John Reischman was a stroke of luck. I walked into Paul's Saloon in San Francisco one night, and here was this mandolin player onstage with Kathy Kallick and the Good Ole Persons, who played a regular gig there. I asked Todd Phillips if he knew the guy. I said, "Do you know how good this guy can play? We've got to try to get him." And we did. For the *Backwaters* album, where in the hell would you go from there? The mandolin playing was exquisite, the tone absolutely beautiful. He didn't overplay, he didn't underplay; he just nailed it. Reischman was a Grisman aficionado, but at the same time, his concentration was on Jethro Burns. It was obvious—you could hear it in his arpeggios.

The first gig the Unit played was in Cotati, a place near Santa Rosa, at a real good folk/acoustic music club called The

Inn of the Beginning. Everybody played there, including Grisman. The reaction was great. If Grisman wasn't working somewhere else on that night, whoever would have otherwise gone to see Grisman's Quintet would have come and seen the Unit.

The first Tony Rice Unit was together for a long time, but there just wasn't that much work. Most of our shows were on the West Coast, but there was sort of an underground market back East. The Unit did an Eastern tour in 1981. We played in New England, the South and places in between, like Colorado and Utah. Kari Estrin was sort of managing me at the time, and she wanted to do it more than I did. Like Grisman, I didn't want to travel that much.

When we did the tour back East, I was kinda pissed off that there would be so many people in the crowd yelling for me to sing. There were a few dates where we were accepted for what we were, and in some places the response was overwhelming and shows were sold-out. But in other places, like in the South, I think there were a few gigs where people left because I didn't sing. Now that I look back on it, I kind of understand, because people thought, "Tony Rice hasn't been back East in so long, and here he is! We wanna hear 'Blue Railroad Train' and 'Old Home Place.'"

There are some things on *Still Inside* that are kind of sophisticated, like "Maker's Mark." I'd really like to see somebody resurrect some of those tunes. I can't do it, but I'd like to see *somebody* do it. "Moses Sole" is one of the best pieces of music I ever wrote in my life. Nobody's done it since I recorded it. We're in a different world now, though. There's no specific reason anybody would want to resurrect those tunes because it's a generation later, and this generation has music that's even more sophisticated.

Backwaters was done in '81 and came out in '82. Though I knew it would be something special, it was kind of an extension of *Still Inside. Backwaters* was going to be far superior to any of the previous three records. I thought the original and non-original tunes I put together with those musicians were just a good combination. The unfortunate thing was that Billy Wolf wasn't available to either record or mix it. But by then, Bob Shoemaker was flexible enough to do it; Billy had become a hero of Bob's. So Bob recorded it very well at Arch Street. And Danny Kopelson, now very famous in the jazz world, was a second engineer at Fantasy, and I talked him into mixing it. He did an amazing job. *Backwaters* has got a lot of punch, a lot of power. It's the most powerful album I've ever recorded, and still my favorite of all my records for that reason. The guitar is in your face.

I know I was playing a guitar real hard back then. Maybe sometimes I pushed it too hard, but I felt like I had an unlimited amount of power. Back then, I could have played a D-28 as loud as a banjo. I wouldn't do that now. For one thing, I *can't,* but I wouldn't, even if I could.

I haven't recorded with all that many jazz musicians, but I *have* recorded with a handful of the greats: Eddie Gomez, the great bass player who played with Bill Evans for all those years . . . Buell Neidlinger . . . of course, Stéphane Grappelli, and Ray Brown. When Grisman did the music score for *King of the Gypsies,* he assembled Ray Brown and Stéphane and myself, and a couple of other people, to record tunes he'd written for the score as pieces of music, separate from the score. To my knowledge, they haven't been released.

Branford Marsalis is a fan of mine. He likes my music. I haven't met him, but we both played on Béla's album *[Tales from the Acoustic Planet, Vol. 1, 1995].* I'd love to do some recording with Marsalis, or another jazz musician. Probably its only value would be purely musical. It wouldn't have any salability if I did what I wanted to do, which is go into a studio with a jazz trio rhythm section of good players and let it fly. The bluegrass world would go, "What the hell is this?" And the jazz world would go, "What the hell is this?"

Family, Friends & Fans

When I heard David was forming this instrumental band that Tony was
gonna be part of, I knew something historic was about to happen.
Mike Marshall, Florida mandolinist & Rice protégé

David Grisman (mandolinist & father of Dawg Music; Tony's former boss):

I first heard Tony play the day I met him . . . it must have been when we made that
album with Bill Keith in '75 *[Something Auld, Something Newgrass, Something Borrowed,
Something Bluegrass].* I kinda said to myself, "Clarence is back!"

Tony had a certain thing Clarence had—the way he phrased things, the whole
approach—that I hadn't heard anybody latch onto. It wasn't that he was copying
Clarence note for note. Tony got the big picture. His playing had a vibe I didn't believe
I would ever hear again. Very subtle syncopation, but so finely tuned, so accurate.
They both messed with the beat, but you knew exactly where it was. And Clarence was
actually a delicate player. Tony projected more, seemed more powerful.

Bill Keith (melodic banjo pioneer & former Blue Grass Boy):

When we made that record, we were
staying at a friend's house out in Virginia.
Tony ended up there when we were
rehearsing and hanging out during the
day and evening and during studio time;
it was pretty much a 24-hour deal. The
chemistry that was involved was just the
beginning of what took place in David's
band.

David Grisman:

We were in a living room full of
people having breakfast and talking, and
Tony asked me what I was doing. I played
this tape of the Great American Music

*David Grisman, Tony, and Bill Keith at England's
Cambridge Folk Festival, summer of 1977.*
(Photo by Barry Lane)

Band. It was the prototype of my Dawg music. He was really into it. I'll never forget it:
he said, "I'd give my left nut to play that music!" No one else was paying any attention
to it, but it was something he'd been waiting to hear.

Ken Irwin:

I sensed it during that session. Have you ever been to a party where a couple looks at
each other, and they start talking, and you just say, "This is gonna happen"? Musically,

it was like that. There was a magnetism there. You hear stories of a couple being in a room and not being able to see anybody else. That's the sense that I got.

David Grisman:

Tony insisted that I come back home with him to Lexington for a couple of days, so he could start learning these tunes. He and Ricky both lived in the same apartment complex. I went down several nights and sat in with the New South at the Sheraton. I was blown away at how few people were there. It was just depressing. And by the third set, they would be playing the wrong chords, just goofing off. To me, it was real sad: the best bluegrass band in the world, playing to eight people.

We rehearsed a lot of tunes. I remember writing some chord charts . . . Tony was heavy into jazz. He was playing bluegrass, but he was listening to jazz. He had all these records, and he was listening a lot to one in particular: an Oscar Peterson record with Niels-Henning Ørsted Pedersen and Joe Pass. Tony was very into Niels's playing—that's where his head was at. He was ready to try and play that stuff.

I think he was looking for the next thing, and obviously he had a great affinity for something beyond bluegrass and jazz, a kind of freedom, I guess.

After he went back to Kentucky, Tony would call me up and say, "When's the gig?" And I was like, "*What* gig, man?" Richard Greene got an offer from Loggins & Messina and he left the Great American Music Band. Carlini got a gig with the Ice Capades. I was left with a bunch of tunes and a bass player. Joe Carroll liked the music; he just wanted to keep coming over and playing it. And I had met Todd Phillips, who was building mandolins. He took a class I was teaching for a while at a music school, and he was trading me mandolin business for lessons.

I got this idea. When I was in Old and In the Way, whenever I stopped playing rhythm, the beat would sag. So, like Django Reinhardt, I figured I'd get another guy to play mandolin rhythm while I soloed. I started training Todd to do that. I liked the sound, and I also liked the ability of two mandolins to play harmonies and lots of other things. One day Todd brought over Darol Anger, who had had tapes of the Great American Music Band, and who had learned all Richard Greene's solos note for note. All of a sudden, there it was. Tony was the missing piece.

Todd Phillips (second mandolinist & bassist with David Grisman Quintet):

Once I met David, all I did was hang out in his living room every day. *Everybody* came through there. The entire New South, on their way to Japan, stopped by, and I met everybody in J.D.'s band all at once. At the time, David's band was just me, David, Darol Anger, and Joe Carroll, and we thought, "Well, we'll just have no guitar; this is it."

And then David returned from a Bill Keith session back East and said, "Man . . . *I just met the guy.* I just met our guitar player."

David Grisman:

One night I got a phone call at about 3 A.M. from Tony in Japan. He told me he had just given J.D. his notice, and he was going to come out to California to join my band.

I never asked him to do that, and it wasn't like I was really trying to start a band. But these guys literally showed up on my back porch wanting to play! When Tony did that, I said, "Well, okay, I'll make a go of it."

I mean, Tony was a big talent. Not just guitar playing, but he was a great singer. I just figured, "Okay, we'll have a band, and you can sing . . ." He said, "No, we're gonna play your music." And *he* named the band. He wanted to play Dawg music, and he recognized it was my music, and he felt it should be called that: the David Grisman Quintet. I just said, "Well, shit! If a guy this *good* is gonna leave this great band to do this, I better get my act together." But I never asked him to quit his gig with J.D.

He went back to Kentucky, got everything he owned, and brought it out here, and moved into my basement with his wife, Kate. They got a place of their own after a while. We rehearsed for about three months, pretty much every day, before we played a gig.

Sam Bush:

When Tony moved to California, it was a big step, to go play with David Grisman. It was a big step to stop playing with Larry and leave that area and go all the way back to the West Coast. But he was always talking about wanting to live there again. He missed California. He loved it. That must have been a hell of a culture shock, when he moved to North Carolina. He was always into "California-style."

Once that Grisman record came out, it was just incredible. I thought Tony got even a new step of progression better since he started with David and opened up his voicings. He had gotten to be such a bluegrass kick-you-on-the-head kind of guy, but with David, he could lighten up a little bit and play with more finesse. He couldn't do that when he was railing in B-flat on "I'll Just Stay Around." It was different music. And he was playing appropriately for both.

Todd Phillips:

The first recording we did was *The David Grisman Rounder Album,* over Thanksgiving of '75. It was just hilarious. Tony would do takes with a towel draped over his head, like some kind of sheik or something, making us laugh. And then he'd lay a towel over his left hand and the neck of the guitar, and say he didn't want nobody stealing his licks! Just as a joke . . . He'd go into these characters. Jerry was there, Vassar was there . . . it was amazing for me to see those guys working together.

David Grisman:

I realized this was a new music nobody had done before. I had a jazz bass player who had really never played bluegrass, two young guys with a lot of enthusiasm but not a lot of experience, and the world's greatest bluegrass guitar player. To bring that all together, and make it sound like what I was hearing, took a lot of time. I wanted a lot of extended solos, and that ran against Tony's grain, even though he was listening to jazz records all day long. He didn't quite know how to do it. He didn't have experience going out on a limb. He was conditioned that you play an eight-bar solo and then you start singing again. To me, it was mostly rehearsing how to play the music, rather than the parts.

I was just trying to have the kind of *freedom* in this music that jazz musicians have. They seem to be able to play these extended solos and take 'em from one place to another. The question was, how to do that with bluegrass energy?

Billy Wolf (engineer on many of Tony's records; one of his closest friends):
I had worked with David since about 1968. He was aware that I was a pretty big fan of Doc Watson and Clarence White, and played a little myself, but I didn't know the young people. When it came time for him to make the first DGQ record, I remember very well Grisman looking at me with that twinkle in his eye, and saying, "I've got this guy coming out and I think you're really gonna like him."

Well, when I met Tony, of course I was blown away. Grisman had that twinkle in his eye because he knew, with my interest in the guitar, what I would think of him. Tony was a surprise, a tremendous surprise.

John Carlini (jazz guitarist, arranger, producer):
David had collected these incredible young players—Darol, Tony, Todd Phillips—virtuosic players who had basically come out of the bluegrass tradition. But David, with what he was doing with Dawg music, required them to be able to do other things: play and solo on jazz changes; play Samba rhythms, Latin rhythms, swing rhythms, Django, etc. So he hired me to coach these guys. I write charts and I orchestrate and play, and I've studied jazz all my life. I was in a good position to help those guys learn those idioms, and they knew that I had a deep love and respect for bluegrass music, so there was no conflict.

The original David Grisman Quintet.
(Photo by Jon Sievert)

I showed Tony the concept of the mode, particularly Dorian, Lydian, and Mixolydian. Those were the three modes that lent themselves to what David was doing, so we concentrated on them. "Fish Scale" keeps floating around with different key centers, but it's really a Dorian tune. I worked with all the guys on that context, on hearing those modes from their roots, as opposed to hearing them related to the major scales from which they come—on hearing them as coming from their *own* tonal centers.

I would show Tony things, jazz chords and voicings and stuff, and then *he* would go home and work like the *devil*. He would come back to rehearsal already comfortable integrating those things. His technique was in a state of development, but I wouldn't say it changed into what you would call a *jazz* technique. He retained his original flatpicking technique, and applied this other harmonic and modal knowledge to it.

Darol Anger (original violinist with the David Grisman Quintet):

Tony was always coming up with stuff. At first it was tough, because there was a lot of jazz in there, and Tony knew his Chet Atkins chords . . . You could tell he was ready, though, to just *explode* into that stuff. When John Carlini came out to spend a day at rehearsal, Tony was a little shy . . . *and John was completely knocked out by Tony.* He was just bowled over. "That's the most amazing stuff I've ever heard. Let's go to your house, and I'll show you how to play these jazz chords." They went home, spent four or five hours together, and Tony came back the next day with "Swing 51." *He had figured it out.*

Todd Phillips:

I was talking to Stéphane about Tony, and he said, "Oh! Tony swings like *mad*." In Stéphane terms, "swings" would be the way to put it. He would just pin you to the wall with his rhythm. Same with the articulation of the solos: when I occasionally hear that first record now, each note is as definite as a marimba player or something. The pick is almost like a *mallet.*

Bill Amatneek (second bassist with the David Grisman Quintet):

His right hand was doing something jazz guitarist Howard Roberts called the "spin-drive" method. Tee [Tony] held the pick between the upper side of his curled-in index finger and his thumb, like most folks. But most folks flatpick just from the wrist and forearm. Tee moved his thumb, flatpick and index finger as a unit. Squiggling this unit around furiously, like writing with pen on paper, Tee got all over the guitar, popping the strings with his tortoise shell pick.

Tee attacks the note. He jumps on it. He lashes out at it. He rips it. He whips it. No one attacks the notes like Tee. His furious attack makes the guitar sing out, pushes the instrument to its vibrational limits. In this I believe Tony brings sounds out of the flat-top Martin that have never been made before. [From *Acoustic Stories,* Vineyards Press, 2003, pp. 64–65.]

David Grisman:

Tony had his own kind of chord shapes. It was all there; it just hadn't been applied to anything but bluegrass. And I was trying to take it further.

A lot of these tunes had nothing to do with bluegrass, other than the fact they were being played by a guy like Tony Rice, one of the great bluegrass innovators. He was steeped in bluegrass and had developed that style probably to its limit, but *this* music was designed to let it out of the confines of those kinds of songs. *This* music had a lot of the same sensibilities, but it was much more open and harmonically different, with different chords.

If I wrote a Latin-type tune, I probably would have preferred a real Latin rhythm, or a swing, but Tony was so good, he played his own way and you couldn't change it. I was always trying to get him to do other things, and that was probably good for him. I had him playing mandolin a bit. We did this tune "Pneumonia" and I wanted to have three mandolins. When one guy was playing the solo, Tony played mandolin. On *DGQ 20,* the second cut is the theme I wrote for the film *Capone,* and he's playing mandocello on that. He was an apprentice. He was very open to doing different things. I don't think he'd do that now.

It was a labor of love. I was trying to push it to a level I'd heard with jazz groups. And it's not like I was a big expert on this music. It was like the blind leading the blind. It's always been easier for me to write tunes than to play 'em. Improvising was new to me, too. We were all in new territory.

Arthur Stern (archivist of the David Grisman Quintet):

I think the biggest part of the Quintet's learning process were the tunes David wrote. They can't be overlooked as a vital part of the evolution of Tony Rice. With complex heads and tails, more harmonically challenging than bluegrass, but also with chord progressions designed for improvising, these tunes provided a vehicle to stretch out and improvise. It's like the guys signed up to go to the graduate school of Dawg music. They all learned, including Grisman. It was a great era of growth and excitement.

Darol Anger:

It was a group thing. But Tony never really followed anything. David was really anxious for Tony to create his own part. That was what he wanted to happen. David tried to sort of keep control over which way a tune was going, and usually couldn't. It became kind of a joke . . . "Hey, man, I've got an idea! Do what you just did! Keep that!"

Todd Phillips:

Tony changed the band! We all just had to adapt our roles a little bit and learn from him. He brought the J.D. Crowe school to it. The music was a lot looser back then. It was slower and a little sloppier, to tell you the truth. It was easier going; it was a little bouncier, and he brought that drive into it. Not that David didn't have drive, but I always feel like I reaped the rewards of Tony's years with J.D., because he just *laid it on* us. I got a secondhand schooling from J.D. that way!

Tony approached David's music the same way. And he found chord voicings. It was real slow at first; none of us knew what to name a chord. Calling out the name of some

Darol Anger, Todd Phillips, Bill Amatneek, David Grisman, and Tony onstage in 1976.
(Courtesy Darol Anger)

fancy chord wouldn't have helped Tony anyway, so we did it all by ear. Eventually we started figuring out what to call the accidentals and the chords.

It was like a workshop, every day. We did a lot of interesting things. We taped our rehearsals. Me and Tony would pick a tune and play it as a pair. Then Darol and Tony. Then Darol and me, or Bill Amatneek and Darol. We'd work on each pair of elements and tighten them up, and maybe do the tune as a three-piece, and then a four-piece, to get really self-reliant, and to know our roles and how they interacted. It was kinda firing-squad style, but it's a really great technique. I gained sensitivity to the rhythmic interaction of all the elements of a band, and that is so valuable to me, even to this day.

Mike Marshall (Florida mandolinist & Rice protégé):

Some of the magic of that first band was that they took a lot of care with Tony. They were very patient with him and let him work through these complicated tunes and helped him understand harmony at whatever level he needed to understand it. David and Todd and Darol really walked him through all that stuff. That's when his music really took on this expanded harmonic sense.

Of course, what *he* brought to the party was this idea of tone and timing he got from J.D., the idea that *that* stuff had to be there. No matter what you were doing harmonically, tone production and accuracy of timing had to be at this insane level. There was a nice exchange going on at that time.

The groove they had going was primarily Tony's, but in many ways, the combination of Tony and David created this floating feeling in the music.

John Carlini:

You couldn't believe what was going on with that Quintet. We would rehearse, rehearse, rehearse, and they worked really hard to get that first release out. When they weren't rehearsing, they were listening. Tony and I would go to jazz clubs and hear McCoy Tyner, Bill Evans, Dexter Gordon . . .

If you saw Tony's CD collection, you'd be amazed. He's a guy who appreciates somebody who can play his instrument well, period, regardless of the genre in which he's playing. That could be anybody from Earl Scruggs to Isaac Stern, and everybody in between. Some might say, "What's Tony Rice doing listening to all that Coltrane?" Well, in Coltrane, Tony heard a guy who had mastered his instrument and who also had beauty of tone. Tony learned and applied what he heard to what he did. He has that ability.

Todd Phillips:

We listened to music endlessly. And that was a real education. Tony taught me how to listen to music, how to get wayyyy into it. We listened to a lot of small ensemble stuff, usually classical string quartets, or jazz quartets. We listened to a *lot* of John Coltrane and Oscar Peterson. We would listen, and we would also talk to each other at the same time, and point stuff out to each other—check *that* out, check *this* out! We'd laugh at great drumming, at the inventive, unique expressions that come out of jazz drummers. Tony incorporates all of that. He doesn't study it; he just listens, and sure enough, sooner or later, some of that phrasing, and the shapes of those patterns, will come out in his playing.

Coming home from Grisman's house one night, probably a little buzzed, we were listening to a cassette of John Coltrane, and when we would hear something we liked, a phrase or the way he tagged a solo, we'd hit rewind. Tony was so busy listening, and he went past my house! I said, "Hey, man, back up." And he pushed rewind on the machine, because he thought I was talking about the music. To this day, he'll look at me and say, "Hey! Back up!"

Darol Anger:

I remember driving around a lot with Tony in his car, listening to Oscar Peterson . . . Oscar was a great model for Tony in a lot of ways, because Oscar's got a limited but incredible repertoire of licks that he plays great. Those guys are very much related in a lot of ways. Oscar delivers the goods, every time, and it's *right,* goddamn it!

Barbara Higbie (violinist & pianist; former wife of Darol Anger):

Tony and Kate lived in this pretty nice apartment right on a really busy road, and he had it really nice; he had THE top-notch stereo, and a padded chair, and he'd look out the window . . . he kind of had his own command post! Everybody would come over and he'd say, "Okay, listen to *this.*" It was this intense musical thing. We were at their house all the time. I was so lucky to be a part of it.

The camaraderie between the guys was so great. They all wanted Tony's approval. Amatneek and Darol and Todd really revered him, put him up on a pedestal. I know Darol just sweated bullets that Tony would disapprove of something he did musically. Darol was born in '53, but Tony seemed much older; I don't know why.

They were all really into jazz, listening to mostly John Coltrane, or Miles Davis with Coltrane and the band . . . some Dexter Gordon . . . "Dexter" was Darol's nickname. And they were really into Django Reinhardt and Stéphane Grappelli.

Bill Keith:

When we did the European tour, we were at the Gurten festival and there was a bona-fide Gypsy band there. I mean, I'm talking there was at least one man in the band named Reinhardt, which I understand is a common name among Gypsies, but even so . . . And David, of course, was blown away, and so was Tony. These guys were first-class Gypsy jazz players; they lived the life, they walked the walk.

I had made some inquiries in Paris about getting some tortoiseshell picks. I got an address, and we went and there was this old guy in there. I was speaking French with him and asked him if he had any tortoiseshell picks. He said, "Oh, I don't think we've got very many." And he pulled out this wooden drawer; it was over a foot long and probably six inches wide and four inches deep. You could see the bottom of the drawer here and there, but there were still a few hundred tortoiseshell picks in there! Tony and David flipped out. They started pawing through them, and David picked 'em up one by one and flexed them and dropped them back in the box. He filtered out a few nice thicker ones and Tony did the same. They had fifteen or twenty tortoiseshell picks out, and David said, "Well, how much?" And the guy said, "Oh, you know, I was in Paris when the Americans came and liberated it. So you can have 'em!" And immediately, of course, they wanted to get back in that drawer!

Bill Amatneek:

Tee and Dawg picked up this name, the Gazole Brothers, as we were touring France with Bill Keith. *Gazole* (pronounced gaz-WAHL, I believe) means diesel fuel. We saw the sign on a gas station as we were driving around in Keith's orange Mercedes mini-van.

Not knowing the true translation of the word, and seeing it on a gas station sign, the word *gasoline* was used as a translation. But the correct translation was soon revealed, and they came to call themselves by both names: Diesel Brothers and Gasoline Brothers. In any event, the two made some hot music together.

Mike Marshall:

The first Quintet record was a life-changing experience for me. It leapfrogged over so many developmental stages that were clearly coming, but that band, and the sound of that record with Tony and David, and the effort they put into those arrangements, and the sonic quality of those recordings Billy Wolf did, all of that was so profound . . .

All these developmental things were hurtling in this direction, but David and those guys gave it tremendous focus. I think it really blew the heads off an entire generation of people. And those of us who were focused on being instrumentalists and not singers—it gave us all a direction.

Arthur Stern:

There was an offshoot band called 'Ook 'n 'M (spelled differently for about every gig). It was Tony, Todd, Mike & Darol, basically the DGQ without Dawggie. When there wasn't Quintet gigs, they would play their own brand of New Acoustic music. They were writing their own tunes, a bit less structured on the arrangements, and often DGQ tunes at different tempos. They really messed with the rhythm. They all knew exactly where the beat was but some played in front, others behind it. They called that push & pull "'Ook 'n 'M." When someone played really outside, they called that "zeit buba." All these guys were big into bebop jazz at the time.

'Ook 'n 'M in the late '70s (L-R): Mike Marshall, Todd Phillips, Tony, Darol Anger. *(Courtesy Louise Rice)*

David Grisman:

Tony had released these records with him singing, and he continued to make 'em, even while he was playing with my band. He didn't want to, though. When he was making his first solo record with J.D. Crowe, I said, "Gee, you can sing some with the Quintet." But he just didn't. I didn't see it as strictly my music, the way *he* did. He always had his slant on what I was doing.

Todd Phillips:

Seems like every six or eight months, Tony would make a bluegrass record. We called the first one *Rattlesnake* because of the song of the same name. That's what Tony was gonna call it, and then he never put it on the cover. I think he was kind of missing J.D. and everybody, and he got a record deal to get those guys out to play with him. Those records were done quick. It was like a three-day weekend for those guys.

Richard Greene (trailblazing New Acoustic violinist; former Blue Grass Boy):

He wrote some amazingly good compositions, and just played the hell out of them. I did three or four albums with him, and I remember noticing that he was doing then what *I* did many years later . . . *he would come into the studio with his parts totally prepared.* Every take was the same music—on the solos, on the rendition of the composition . . . His solos weren't improvised, because they were the same every time. And he would have *us* do all the improvising, which was very clever, because he was able to deliver his part of the recordings consistently, while seeking out the strangest, most exotic stuff from us.

Every time he flew me up, I knew I was going to make good money, and play whatever the hell I wanted. An unbeatable combination. Usually when you make good money, you're told what to play. You never get both. Usually it's one or the other.

Jon Sievert (Bay Area photographer who often shot the David Grisman Quintet):

Meanwhile, David had begun recording *Hot Dawg,* during which he developed a severe case of tendonitis and/or carpal tunnel syndrome. That slowed everything down and eliminated the possibility of live gigs. It all came to a head in the summer of 1979, when Darol and his then-wife Barbara Higbie decided to take an extended trip to Africa. David's solution to losing his violinist was to do a Quintet tour with Stéphane. That's when David told me that Tony had quit because he did not want to tour with Grappelli.

David Grisman:

It got to the point where Tony was a powerful force in the band, and sometimes he would take it his way. And then he turned down the tour with Stéphane Grappelli.

I got an offer to do this three-week tour with Stéphane, where he would play with my band. I came to rehearsal and said, "Hey, guess what? We got this tour with Stéphane Grappelli!" I thought everybody would go "Wow, man, that's fantastic!" But Tony said, "I'm not doin' that." I said, "What do you mean?!?" He said, "I came here to play 'Dawg's Rag,' not 'Sweet Georgia Brown.'"

I love Tony. I loved having him in my band. But I felt Tony had made certain decisions about what that music needed and where it was going. He just had his own direction. He used to complain about everybody in the band.

I guess he had *his* version of my music in his mind. And maybe sometimes he'd try to play that. It was like Benny Goodman and Gene Krupa. Tony was strong enough to drive the bus himself. Sometimes he would, and it just wasn't where I wanted it to go. We never had a real conflict over it, but I remember one night, one of the last gigs before he left, we played in a place called Rosie's in New Orleans. There was a problem collecting the money, and we waited in that place for hours after the show. Tony and I got into a discussion—or an argument—about the music.

Darol Anger:

That was the first—and one of the LAST—gigs that we didn't get paid for. That was a really unhappy experience. For David to get stiffed for a gig, that's major, major, major—that just does NOT happen with David. He and Tony got really drunk that night, and they were shouting at each other in the hotel room for *hours*. Like they were fighting, but they were on the same side? It was a trip.

David Grisman:

I like to be able to run things in my band. For better or worse, I know what I'm looking for. Once somebody's in there who thinks he knows more about it than me—well, he might know for *him,* but not for *me*. I could see there was this conflict Tony wouldn't quite admit to, and it went down on other levels. At this stage, if he wanted something to go faster, he'd just take it there. You could not control him.

Todd Phillips:

We had done some soundtrack recording for *King of the Gypsies,* and David was getting involved with Stéphane on some projects; the Quintet was just *changing*. It had been a good five years, and I was burned out on it; I don't know if Tony was burned out, but he didn't like the direction things were going. We didn't really want to play "Sweet Georgia Brown" and "Lady Be Good" and back up David and Stéphane, so I took a break for about six months, and then the Tony Rice Unit started.

Musical cast of the "King of the Gypsies" soundtrack: L-R, Andy Statman, Stéphane Grappelli, Diz Disley, John Carlini, Ray Brown, Frederico DeLaurentiis, David Grisman, Bill Wolf, Tony.
(Courtesy John Carlini)

Darol Anger:

It was bad enough being compared with Clarence White all his life, and now he was being compared with Django Reinhardt. Who needs it? I think he was a little uncomfortable around Stéphane, anyway.

David Grisman:

It got to a kind of shaky state for me. I was in a dilemma and I didn't really want to lose control of my thing, especially because Tony didn't really have a game plan except "This guy's not good enough, and that guy's not good enough . . ." I think he probably wanted me to convince him to do the Grappelli tour. I just let it go and started looking for another guitar player *and* another bass player. Several guys called, wanting this gig, including Mark O'Connor. He had sat in on my band on guitar when he was 15, and we had helped him make a guitar record. But I never heard him play any of my tunes.

He came out, and in one day he learned about 20 of the tunes, and got the gig. Then he asked me, "Hey, can I stay, after this tour?" And I said okay. I guess I just took Tony's declining the tour as his resignation. I think he expected the tour would be over, he'd come back, and he was upset at me when he didn't.

Mark O'Connor (celebrated multi-instrumentalist and composer; replaced Tony in the David Grisman Quintet):

After the first phase of the Grappelli tour concluded, the big moment came concerning the future of the guitar position in the band. Was I going to be asked to leave and make way for Tony to come back in, or was it going to be a permanent replacement? It was a tough time for me because Tony was also my musical hero. It was almost too much stress for anyone to take, let alone a teenager who did not have all his emotions in order. I wished it all could have happened differently, but in the end, I had to replace my hero on guitar in order to work with my violin hero Grappelli and mandolin hero Grisman. I would not wish that on anybody with a sensitive heart like mine, that's for sure.

As a guitarist who not only looked to Tony Rice as a personal model for my own playing, but who replaced him in one of the great acoustic instrumental bands of all time, the David Grisman Quintet of the 1970s, I certainly devoted much time to figuring out how he was able to play like he did. Some of the material the DGQ played with me had such a Rice stylistic stamp on it that I knew I needed to incorporate as much of his sound as possible into the re-interpretations. I suppose I had such a strong musical personality to start with that it did not really matter how much I tried to incorporate Tony's style—it just was not going to sound like him anyway. In a way, it gave me room to try to play like him without having people saying, "Aha, you're a copycat!"

David Grisman:

He was still living a mile and a half away from me, so we'd see each other, and it was never spoken about. I think he was mad at me, but he wasn't *actively* mad. Then he started his own Tony Rice Unit. He had been making records all along, and I believe he made that *Acoustics* record when he was still in my band. In fact, Buck White and Ricky Skaggs were in town, and Buck White called me up one day from Arch Street, where Tony was working on his record, and said, "There's a robbery goin' on down here!" I said, "What do you mean?" He said, "They're stealing your music!"

They say imitation is the sincerest form of flattery, so it didn't bother me. I recognized Tony needed to do his own version of the music. He couldn't do that in my band, because I wouldn't let him. It's like he got into this new thing, and figured, after four years, that he had mastered it, figured out how to do it *better*.

I looked at the albums he did later, like *Mar West* and *Still Inside,* as *his* music. I mean, I was *glad* he was taking that idea and doing something with it. I didn't look at it as competition so much. When you're in the music business, you're competing with everything, in a sense, but I felt good enough about my own thing that I didn't feel threatened. I was doing *my* material, and even though it had similar instrumentation, it wasn't the same. I thought Tony's music was good, but I also always thought, "Gee, why isn't this guy *singing?* He's so good at that." But I guess he just grew increasingly uncomfortable with it. I don't know. I think he wanted to be more like a jazz musician or something. I think he looked at instrumental music as more sophisticated, especially when he latched onto the idea of more harmonic complexity.

Todd Phillips:

Tony was always alternating. We'd do a Quintet or Unit project, and then he'd bring someone from out East to do one of his vocal records. This is just a theory, but you know how an athlete needs to keep in shape to not hurt his body? I wonder if doing that kind of singing only occasionally might have been hard on his voice— just singing it all out, like he was doing it six or seven nights a week in Lexington, for a four-day session, and then not singing again for ten months.

Jeff Troxel (2003 National Flatpick Champion and Rice jazz protégé):

I first heard Tony Rice on his recording *Acoustics*. I was a student at Berklee College of Music in the early 1980s and that album appealed to me in some very fundamental way. I was interested in jazz music but, having grown up in Wyoming, there was something foreign about the urban sounds of straight-ahead jazz. Tony's music immediately filled the gap between music that had rural roots and music with enough harmonic complexity to interest a budding jazz musician.

Jeff Autry (Georgia guitarist with John Cowan Band; Tony protégé):

Well, Tony's music, to me, isn't mainstream, straight-ahead jazz, *per se*. Straight-ahead jazz is kinda swing, with a lot of chords linking it all together, the Charlie Parker stuff. But Tony's stuff . . . well, I don't know how to describe it. It's not necessarily an offshoot of Dawg music; it's similar, yet more aggressive and kinda high-speed. Like on the *Acoustics* project, "Gasology" and those things. Phew! I listen to that stuff now, and it still just freaks me out, you know?

Fred Carpenter (first violinist with the first Tony Rice Unit):

I tell you one thing about Tony that really was incredible for me. Tony was not a fiddle player, so he wouldn't tell me what to play, but he had a way of acknowledging whether what you were doing was working or not. While not knowing a thing about fiddle, he really helped me a lot about learning how to play the fiddle, especially for that kind of music. And he turned me on to Miles Davis, just outrageous CDs. I was so

Caucasian square, WAY bad! He needed to get me loosened up a little bit, so I'd have a cup of tea every morning and put on some *avant garde* jazz stuff.

John Reischman (first mandolinist with the first Tony Rice Unit):

I think he had musical ideas he wanted to explore that were not being met in the David Grisman Quintet. I think he was tired of things being heavily arranged, and wanted to have more of a jazz approach to his music.

Fred Carpenter:

He basically humbled me to a point that I hadn't ever been humbled before.

In the summer of '80, Tony had left the David Grisman Quintet and started doing the Tony Rice Unit with Todd Phillips and John Reischman. They were looking for a fiddle person. I saw Mark O'Connor and Darol Anger at a fiddle contest, and they mentioned it, and I asked 'em if they'd call Tony for me. So instead of going home to Maine, I changed my flight to San Francisco.

I didn't know any of Tony's material. Darol showed me "Old Grey Coat," and Mark showed me "Gasology" or "Mar West." Tony picked me up and we went back to his house and played a bit, and I stayed overnight with him and Leela [Tony's first wife]. That was in June, and he felt I was good enough where I could learn the material and go back out in the Fall and do a few gigs. They'd booked the Great American Music Hall and a few other venues; I think we had three or four gigs in October.

I spent a lot of time that summer working, but I also spent a lot of time just bumming around and having fun. In the fall, I went back out to California for the gigs, and I did pretty darn good; I was well-received. People clapped after solos. I was ready to go home and take how proud I was of myself to a whole new level.

I was sitting in Tony's living room; he was about to take me to the airport. He was talking about going in the studio the first of the year to do *Still Inside*. And *he just got in my face!* He said, "Fred, you know what? I'm not gonna tell you that you can't cut it. But you're *not cutting it now."* He knew what he was doing, man. If he hadn't done that, I wouldn't have come back with a kind of vengeance: *I want to show him I can!*

It was the best thing that's ever happened to me, musically. I will be forever grateful he did that to me. Instead of going home and partying with my friends and bragging, I went home and *woodshedded.* And it made a complete difference. Tony knew exactly what he was doing. He wanted me to be the best I could be, and I had three or four months before we were going in the studio. As it turns out, *Still Inside* has a really good chemistry that came through.

Kari Estrin (producer, manager, publicist):

I met with the folks from Kaleidoscope Records and I told them I loved Tony's music and I'd like to produce a new concert. I had this concert series over at Harvard University and wanted to do a show with him. They passed my name on to Leela, who was his manager. She called me and said, "We hear you really like Tony's music." I said, "Oh, yes, absolutely!" And they said, "Would you be our agent?" And I was like, *Wow. They want me to be his* agent?!

   I said, "Well, let's talk about this." Tony had just left David Grisman. He had toured with Crowe and with Grisman, but never with the Tony Rice Unit. It was a really pivotal point in his career, actually, taking the Unit out on the road for the first time. It was a huge obstacle when he switched genres, and something we dealt with the whole time we worked together.

Fred Carpenter:
   I think there were opportunities we didn't really grab, because it was riding the coattails of the Grisman thing. He didn't want to do it that way, and I can understand that. There was something he wanted to distance himself from.
   I remember Leela, his wife, would book gigs, and then he'd say, "No way! We're not doing *that.*" She'd have to call up and cancel. It was tough, you know.

Recording the NPR Car Talk *theme ("Dawggy Mountain Breakdown") at Arch Street Studios in Berkeley, 1983 (L-R): Tony, producer David Grisman, Earl Scruggs, Darol Anger, Rob Wasserman. Not shown: Mike Marshall.*
(Photo by Dix Bruce)

On the Road
Part 4

Charlotte, North Carolina

July 2005: Tony again picks me up at the airport, this time in an enormous Ford truck. It's a sort of electric blue that isn't surprising, given his penchant for colorful ties. The immaculate truck bed is covered and locked and has a plain board across the end to prevent his guitar case and other luggage from sliding around.

He looks exactly the same as he did two years ago—lean and narrow in straight Levis and a simple long-sleeved shirt, in spite of the 100% humidity.

As he gets on the highway, he pops in a CD of Shirley Q. Liquor, a white guy who makes comedy recordings as a black female. It is raunchy and hilarious and very politically incorrect. Tony says Jerry Douglas gave him a CD at MerleFest, and he shared it with Billy Wolf, who ordered him a boxed set for his birthday. As it plays, I realize that many of Tony's pet expressions these days, the ones he's used a lot on the phone in the past few weeks, were borrowed directly from Shirley Q. Liquor.

He drops me off at my hotel a few miles from his house and leaves. The following morning he calls and says things have gotten a little complicated. We're supposed to be leaving shortly for a festival in Kentucky and a recording session in Nashville. The schedule for the next few days looks like this:

> **Saturday, July 2:** *Terrapin Hill Farm, Harrodsburg, KY*
> Hippiefest 2005, says Tony, who adds that we'll be rolling up three minutes before the gig, and leaving three minutes after, just to avoid those hippies. His set is at 10:30 P.M., right after Crowe's.
>
> **Tuesday, Wednesday, Thursday, July 5–6–7:** *Hilltop Studio, Nashville, TN*
> Recording session for new Rounder project by singer/songwriter Donna Hughes; Sam Bush, Tim Stafford, Scott Vestal, Ron Stewart, Wayne Benson, Rob Ickes, and Mike Bub will all be there.

Tony is a little pissed about this session. Donna Hughes has just self-published a couple of her own tunes, but Rounder Records (her new label) had requested the right to publish them itself, and there is some tension. Tony says he may walk off the project, after having produced only about seven tracks. "Donna wouldn't blame me," he says, adding that Keith Case, his agent, would ordinarily negotiate these somewhat murky waters, but Keith is in Colorado with his sister, who is very ill.

Finally Tony works things out with Donna and Rounder, and we get on the road.

Terrapin Hill Farm, Kentucky

Saturday, July 2: It's a glorious Kentucky evening and the fireflies are everywhere. We take a country road through rolling green pastures and arrive, after a few wrong turns past crude and misleading signage, at Terrapin Hill Farm.

As we make our way backstage, the New South is just launching into its encore. "Boy, listen to that," Tony says, as he listens to J.D. Crowe's banjo kickoff on "Old Home Place." "Ain't but one guy in the whole world can make a banjo sound like that." When lead vocalist Ricky Wasson begins to sing, it's a little bittersweet. Ricky's a fine singer, but this is a tune that Rice all but made his own when he recorded it 30 years ago with Crowe, and it's odd to hear anybody else's voice after that distinctive kickoff.

Half an hour before Tony's set is scheduled to begin, he unloads the heavy flight case containing his Santa Cruz, carefully unhooking the bungee cords that anchor it to the truck bed. The hillside beyond the rough fence near the stage is covered sparsely with hippies and hillbillies and everything in between. The performer's area is a white yurt-like tent with open doors on four sides. There's a table covered with picked-over finger foods, an old Persian rug, a loveseat, and an ancient floor fan which moves the heat from one side of the tent to the other. It's quite dark, but there's no lamp and no festival staff to hunt one down.

When the New South comes offstage, Tony and J.D. greet each other warmly with a hug and a couple hearty claps on the back; they haven't seen each other for a while. There's Ronnie Stewart and Dwight McCall from Crowe's band, and—from the Tony Rice Unit—Wyatt Rice, Bryn Bright, and Rickie Simpkins; Wyatt's wife, Diane, and Rickie's wife, Annie, are also here. Suddenly, there is a tremendous explosion outside. Fireworks!

It is a long and generous show; the crowd roars its approval. Sparks fall on the yurt. I hear a guitar being tuned, little riffs quiet and distinct under the explosions, and I know it is Tony. As the last twinkling sparks are absorbed by the night, he emerges from the artists' restroom—a large porta-john. "You're ON!" someone warns him. "They've already introduced you." Bryn and Rickie scurry to the stage.

J.D. is by himself in the yurt, and we talk for a few moments, our conversation turning to the perils of the road. He tells me he found it very hard to drive long distances in short periods of time, back in the day. Like the rest of the world, J.D. seems amazed that Tony still drives to all his gigs, usually by himself. "Boy, that's hard. I used to see critters that weren't there, out on the road," he says, shaking his head with the memory, "and trap doors that would open up in the pavement." He says he only plays 50 dates a year, and he's cutting it to 40 and asking for a little more money. He wants to golf and go to car shows, and not have to play music on weekends.

A half-naked hippie stumbles into the yurt. He's young and elfin, almost blind drunk, barefoot and smelly and clutching a beer. Around his neck is an instrument strap; it's been autographed in Sharpie marker in a half-dozen places. He asks me to take a photo of him and J.D. with his disposable flash camera. The flash doesn't go off, and it's the last exposure on the camera. He rambles boozily. J.D. is gracious and sweet.

Finally, the boy stumbles away, but not before hugging on J.D.'s neck a little. J.D. sends him off with a few kind words and a good-natured shrug. We talk for a few more minutes and he leaves to drive home, banjo case in hand.

Onstage, Tony is coolly elegant, somehow removed from the rest of the world. And this configuration of the Unit is so good. They play "Red-Haired Boy" and "My Favorite Things," weaving in and out of each other's melodic and rhythmic paths with effortless grace.

Tony introduces the next song, "The Storms Are on the Ocean." It's a lovely instrumental version of the old Carter Family tune, but when the chorus comes around, the drunks in front begin to bellow along at the top of their lungs, off-key and unwelcome. Tony actually stops playing for a moment and glares them into a more respectful volume.

He and Bryn play "Summertime," and it's melancholy and wistful, with an outrageous bass solo. Their entire show is really extraordinary, the sort of set that should only be played for a quiet, appreciative crowd. Perhaps, I think, the Unit should not have been booked as the evening's last band.

Tony finishes his set and the bands exits stage left. "Let's get the fuck out of here," he growls, as he finds his way back to the yurt. The yahoos in the front roar for more, but there is no more; they've blown it. Bryn makes a chopping motion with her hand in the direction of the sound techs—that's all, folks. She retrieves her bass from an empty stage in front of a legion of drunk and disappointed young men. But she does it gracefully, with a sweet smile on her face. The drunks boo half-heartedly, but they don't make an issue of it.

The band moves to the yurt. Tony eyes the picked-over trays on the hospitality table and I realize that he hasn't eaten today; we drove fast with very few pitstops to get here in

Tony onstage at Terrapin Hill Farm, July 2005. (Photo by Caroline Wright)

time for his set. In the soft light of the old table lamp, he looks very tired. Slowly but steadily—first one, then two, then a dozen—the fans come to pay their respects. Finally, Tony sees somebody who looks like a festival official. "Can my band just have five minutes of privacy in here?" he asks. "Certainly, certainly, of course!" the official says hastily, and the fans obligingly move outside. After a moment, Wyatt and Diane take their leave, then Rickie and Ann.

Tony is standing near the hospitality table when the half-naked hippie boy comes barging back inside through one of the yurt's unguarded doors. He stumbles over and drapes himself around Tony's tall, thin figure. It's a tense moment, but Tony does fine for himself. He says just a few words, polite but so strong, so final that even through his haze, the boy realizes he needs to leave, and finally he is gone.

Wearily, Tony joins Bryn on the sofa. He puts his head back. Something is wrong with his neck and shoulder and he is in considerable pain. He finally turns to me and says, "It's a damn shame, because I really felt like playing tonight."

We all share a few more words, and then it's time to leave. He finds a bottle of water and drinks it down. Fans throng around one door of the yurt; we escape quietly through another. We load up the truck, trying to ignore the disappointed little crowd, and then we are moving on again, through the soft Kentucky night.

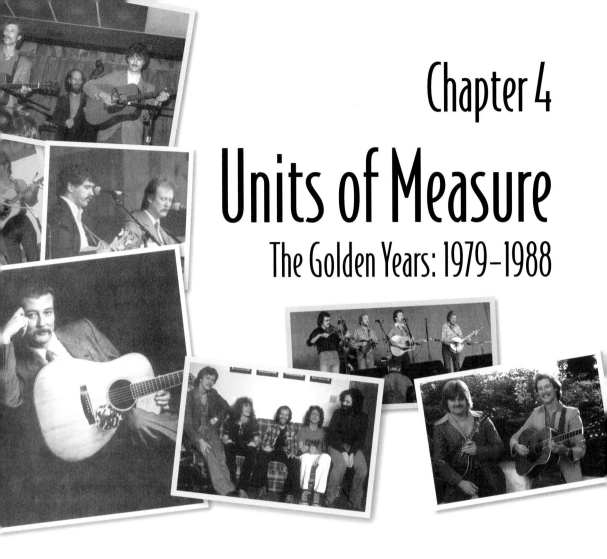

Chapter 4
Units of Measure
The Golden Years: 1979–1988

His exquisite tone, the swing and drive of his rhythm playing, the phrasing and emotional depth of his singing, and his inclusiveness as a musician are all lodged deep in my musical bones. I worked for it, but he also gave it freely, and his legacy is expressed to some degree in every musical endeavor that I pursue. For that I will be forever grateful to him.

Mark Schatz, Tony Rice Unit bassist (1985–1990)

Tony is the ultimate guitar picker. He arches that wrist out there, puts his pick on the strings and out comes a sound and power no one else comes close to. Many imitate him but none capture the tone and excitement in his playing. He won't take credit for inventing his incredible style, but he should; it belongs to him alone. He has stretched the envelope beyond all expectation and taken bluegrass guitar to places it's never been before. There will never be another like him.

Bill Emerson, banjo legend

Chapter 4: Introduction

The years between 1979 and 1988 would prove to be the most prolific period in Tony's career. Mike Marshall, who lived with Tony for a time in California, recalls the exhilaration of those days: "Here we were, busting out this intense 'experimental jazz,' and he recorded that duet record with Ricky Skaggs at the same time," Mike says. "The next week, here would come the Bluegrass Album Band, and they'd cut one of *those* records. And the week after that, it was *Manzanita*! You talk about a fertile time . . ."

As Tony focused on his own projects, he followed his muse on a merry path between bluegrass, jazz, folk, country, and even pop, with little regard for the traditional boundaries of any genre. He played on records with David Grisman and members of the Quintet as they began to branch out with their own solo adventures. He contributed to albums by artists as diverse as Don Reno and Kate Wolf.

And to satisfy a yearning to return to his roots, Tony recorded the Bluegrass Albums. "I want to show those people my love—and our love—for this music," he told Doyle Lawson, when he called to invite Doyle to play on the first recording (which began as a simple Tony Rice bluegrass project and grew into a veritable movement). "I want it to be nothing but hardcore traditional bluegrass."

Like many others in the Southeast, North Carolina musician Jason Burleson saw the Bluegrass Album Band on its first tour in the mid-1980s. This was the first time Tony had appeared at Eastern festivals since his days with J.D. Crowe, and the excitement was very high. A whole generation of fans had grown up listening to Tony's music but had never actually seen him perform. Jason, who saw the band at Doyle Lawson's festival in Denton, NC, remembers watching Tony take the stage and step up to the microphone. "Da-ding! Da-ding! *Strummm* . . ." Jason says. "The crowd went *wild*. He got a standing ovation for a *mic check*."

The quality and number of musical masterpieces Tony created during these years is especially astonishing when we consider the turbulence in his personal life. He battled crippling anxiety and depression and consumed "adult beverages," as he calls them, as much for self-medication as for recreation. He divorced his first wife, watched helplessly as his heart was shattered by his second, and began a relationship with the woman who would become his third. Also during this time, his father lost his life in a tragic apartment fire. Over twenty-five years after his death, Herb Rice's influence on Tony remains strong.

As it has turned out, all of Tony's recordings from this "golden era" have proven deeply significant for generations of musicians who have followed him. Of course, as Tony made these records it was impossible to predict their impact. "I guess when you're as involved in the music as we are," Doyle reflects, "your attention is focused on what you're having to do, and you don't think about the effect it will have, or the ripples it will cause."

I saw him live in Belfast, VA in 1982. It was the most awesome sound I had ever heard. It made me want to learn how to play music.

Shawn Lane, Blue Highway multi-instrumentalist and vocalist

At that time, now, nobody had seen Tony. He was like Santa Claus. He was somebody you hear about, but he didn't make many appearances!

**James Alan Shelton, guitarist with Ralph Stanley &
the Clinch Mt. Boys**

The first thing I heard was this incredible lead voice that I thought may have been the finest bluegrass lead vocal I'd ever heard. I still believe that. Then I heard his first break on guitar and just couldn't believe that someone could sing that well and also eat up a guitar like that. All this with such drive just tore my nerves up.

Alan Bibey, mandolinist with Grasstowne

I first saw Tony Rice on November 25th, 1982 at 8:00 P.M. at the Greensboro War Memorial Auditorium, in the Bluegrass Album Band with Bobby Hicks and Jerry Douglas. Changed my life.

Clay Jones, North Carolina guitarist and Rice protégé

In His Own Words: Tony's Story

Manzanita was recorded in January and February of 1978, two different sessions. Crowe was slated to be the banjo player, then he got sick. Since he couldn't do it, I said, "I'm doing this record without a banjo." I was used to playing with no banjo anyway. It ended up having a sound of its own. But it certainly wasn't planned. I mean, look at the material: "Hold What You Got," "Blue Railroad Train," "Nine Pound Hammer . . ." Those are tunes that would have featured J.D. Crowe! The core

band was supposed to have been Crowe, Sam, Ricky, and Flux. It would have been like the New South, with Todd Phillips on bass and Sam Bush on fiddle.

Crowe couldn't make it. And then Ricky got pneumonia, so we did it in two different blocks, a month or six weeks apart. On a couple cuts, Sam is playing fiddle and mandolin. We started in January '78 and the whole record was done by February. We had a ball doing it. The spirit was there when we were all together. It was almost like the magic of the first Grisman session. It was a bluegrass sound like had never happened before. And everybody was digging it. To tell the truth, *Manzanita* was just one big giant drunken stoned-out bash, a big party.

I had actually started the album, eight or nine tunes at least, in September of '77 or so, with Grisman, Bill Amatneek, and Darol Anger as the primary band. We did "Little Sadie," "Blue Railroad Train," and the classic tunes, but it just wasn't there. I was so displeased with what was coming down that I canned it and threw it away.

The name of the title track came from when my father was in jail in Los Angeles. I was a kid. He brought home this lamp he'd made of manzanita. I always thought it was such a pretty lamp. When I'd written the tune, I don't know why, but the memory of him came to mind. Plus, I was surrounded by manzanita—in Marin County, it was everywhere.

The song "Manzanita" was based on a tune called "Afro Blue," written by a Cuban percussionist named Mongo Santamaria, one of his most requested songs. If you listen to "Afro Blue," you'll hear similarities in the structure of "Manzanita." It kind of came out wrong, because the idea was to have a very well-defined stop to dead silence, and then have the next soloist come in whenever he wanted to without regard to pulse.

It became the title tune even though it's really very much separated, conceptually, from the remainder of the album. You've got "Manzanita," this one Dawg tune, on

there, and then the rest of the album is "Little Sadie," and "Nine Pound Hammer," things like that. But that was deliberate.

I think everybody knew, once "Old Train" was kicked off, there was something magic there that had not happened before. There were two takes. I chose the first, and it was the first time we'd ever played it. Kick it off? *I had no idea who was gonna kick it off!* There was no arrangements on anything. I said, "I wanna do this tune Herb Pedersen wrote; the Seldom Scene did it . . . Who wants to kick it off?" I was looking at either Sam or Ricky. Flux or somebody said, "Well, *you* ought to kick it off."

I noodled around for a few minutes, and then said, "Yeah, I think I can get us into this." I counted off and kicked it, and the version that's there is what came down. I remember thinking, "This thing ought to be done with some balls." Skaggs played the fiddle solo and it was breathtaking. I mean, he *nailed* that fucker.

What inspired "Little Sadie" was Clarence Ashley doing that on one of the Vanguard *Live at Newport* things. I heard that old-time version and I wanted to sing it that way, with the instrumentation I had. Grisman suggested "I Hope You Have Learned." He came down for a couple tracks. I didn't want to overdo it, because Grisman had tendonitis and wasn't supposed to be playing. He was in the middle of the movie score for *King of the Gypsies*. He had quit playing for all practical purposes, but I remember calling him from the studio one night and asking him if he felt up to it.

Due to Ricky's absence, and me having gotten sick, there were vocal overdubs.

I didn't want to overdub *anything* on that album, and there's very little, but some was done out of necessity. "Little Sadie" is one of them: Sam is playing mandolin and fiddle, where Ricky was slated to be on the tune. Grisman's on "Nine-Pound Hammer," "Stony Point," and "Blackberry Blossom."

There was one conscious underlying theme. I wanted it to sound Grismanesque, to have a real well-defined Dawg music flavor in the rhythm section. And it does. Grisman coined the term "spacegrass" in the studio during *Manzanita*. We were in

Manzanita *sessions, January 1979 (L-R): Tony, Sam Bush, Todd Phillips, Mike Marshall, David Grisman.* (Photo by Jon Sievert)

the control room, and somebody said, "God, this is really some different sounding stuff. What do we call it?" Grisman said, "Hey, man . . . how about *Spacegrass?*" I said, "Yeah, that'll work." I've never used that term much, but others have.

Kate was my wife when I was recording *Manzanita*, and during some pretty creative years of my life. I mean, think about

all that happened when I was with her. The J.D. Crowe stuff, the Grisman stuff, the *Manzanita* album, all the way up to *Acoustics*. She was there for all of that.

Coincidentally, Kate and I were breaking up at the same time I was leaving Grisman. I had found a new love, and it hadn't worked for Kate and I for a long time.

I was performing with Grisman on the Quintet's East Coast tour we did in '79 when I met Leela Satyendra at the Bottom Line in New York.

She was beautiful. She was born in Chicago, but she grew up in Los Angeles. She was Korean and Indian. Her father was a physicist from India, and I think he met her mother at Northwestern University.

Her major in college, at UCLA, was ballet and modern dance. I think she was just trying to be around the modern dance scene in New York. By night, she was working as a cocktail waitress, and she'd had it with that. She was gonna move back to L.A., and when we got together, she moved to Marin County.

I didn't have any interest in anybody else. She was very intelligent, very beautiful, but with a chip on her shoulder. Once in a while, she would talk about it and say it was real hard because she grew up in a world of 99% white affluent kids. But she carried the chip on her shoulder well into adulthood. I never could figure that out.

Leela and I both got into photography at the same time. She booked dates for the Unit; she helped coordinate recording projects, like *Mar West* and *Still Inside,* and at least three of the volumes of the *Bluegrass Album.*

Skaggs and Rice. (Courtesy Tony Rice)

In 1979, Ricky Skaggs was playing with Emmylou Harris, and he was in San Francisco with about three days off. He came over and we started catching up on the last few years. He had his mandolin, so we started playing. Somehow the subject of our fathers came up. We would play a tune, and then Ricky would say, "My father used to like that a lot," and then I'd throw out a tune, and say, "Yeah, my dad used to sing this tune with Mom's brother."

I don't remember who had the idea, but we decided, "This needs to be captured on tape, this format of just guitar and mandolin, two voices singing." It was spur-of-the-moment.

The first session for that album, we called up Arch Street, and yeah, we could get in the studio. They said, "The only problem is, we don't have any tape." The last session had drained the studio of tape! They called

Billy Wolf, who had a couple of reels that were new. We did about six tunes.

Billy Wolf recorded it, and if Billy records something, unless somebody tells him otherwise, he assumes he is doing the whole project: mixing and mastering to what was then vinyl disk. Billy always did the complete project. Billy recorded it—pristinely, I might add—and somewhere along the line, Ricky got the masters and took 'em to the Enactron Truck. Brian Ahern owned the Enactron Truck, an elaborate mobile recording facility. It was in a semi truck, with a console, tape machines, a fully functioning studio.

The main engineer was Donivan Cowart. That's the reason Billy's name is not on the album. Billy's always said no disrespect to Donivan but he thought it was his project . . . The world assumes that Donivan Cowart engineered, mixed and mastered the album, which is not the case. Billy Wolf was the tracking engineer.

J.D. Crowe said the *Skaggs & Rice* album is the greatest learning tool for a baritone singer in the world. He went on to say, "It's because of the way you and Ricky did it in a traditional way, where it's not always exactly a third interval above the lead that Ricky's doing." In good three-part harmony singing, of course, sometimes you have to switch parts. But it would be an amazing learning tool for somebody to learn how to fit a third part into that and make it work.

In 1979 and the early part of '80, I did two albums with Emmylou and then played some gigs with her, with her band. She was pregnant with one of her kids; she was married to Brian Ahern. One session was done at Emmy's house over a few days. I had never used cocaine in my life . . . but while the session was going on, and after it was over . . . with the exception of myself and Emmy and Ricky and Albert Lee, everybody else had their nose in a mirror what seemed like every few minutes.

After all this was over, I played a gig with Emmy at the Palomino in Hollywood. And I decided to find out: what *is* this Hollywood drug that everybody's so involved in?

I had a couple of days of that, and something told me that it was real *evil.* That was the end of it. I have not thought about it since then. It's not anything that I want. I've seen too many people lose everything with it. I'm just glad I never . . . I mean, I just didn't *want* it.

It wasn't big in the bluegrass community. Well, people were experimenting with it, some of the more progressive, younger people. From that moment on, I started to see that it wasn't as innocent as Hollywood had cracked it up to be, and these people were in for a rude awakening at some point.

The *Roses in the Snow* album is considered a classic, but there were *two* takes that ended up on the following album, *Evangeline,* and those were the takes I was glad got

released: "Millworker," and "How High the Moon." Ricky just had a natural instinct for constructing vocal harmonies with Emmy and I. I got a standard fee . . . it might have been double union scale or something. I was paid well, and treated very well, by Emmy, Brian, and everybody.

Working with Emmy was something I wanted to do, but my head wasn't there musically. And I don't think her head was there musically full-time. She wanted to do other things. I don't think anybody was disappointed with *Roses in the Snow.* But being on the road with Emmy and that band, it wasn't me. That wasn't where my heart was as a musician. I didn't do it that long, because I couldn't take it. She had a loud band, and it just didn't work. She had me working with her more as a singer than as a guitar player, anyway.

Church Street Blues was what I considered, at the time, as my own attempt at getting back to early Lightfoot. I liked that first Lightfoot record so much. "Well," I thought, "if nobody is going to do this, then *I'm* gonna do it. It doesn't mean I have to perform it, but if I can get it on tape . . ." I called Ken Irwin at Rounder and said, "I want to do this solo album just for me and it's gonna be hard." And Ken's reaction was, "We don't think that's the direction you ought to be going."

I wasn't under contract at the moment. So I called Barry Poss at Sugar Hill Records and said, "I want to do this album." And he said, "Do it [for Sugar Hill]." And Rounder was really pissed, because they didn't even know I had recorded it until it came out.

They got over it because they knew it was well-documented that I wanted to do this album and I laid the idea on Ken Irwin and he rejected it.

Church Street Blues is not anything that I could have ever walked out on stage and done live. Let me put it this way: I didn't like doing the album but I was proud of the results. It was a struggle to do it, real hard. By the time I had done it I had been playing 25 years already. All of a sudden it was as naked as anything. Worse than sitting in a room by myself. All of a sudden you don't have that bass in there, that banjo roll, those Dobro® fills; you don't have the fiddle playing backup. It's like you've got to be a different musician as soon as that tape is rolling.

Wyatt was staying with me and Leela at the time, playing rhythm good enough for me to let him do it on a couple of tunes. I didn't want to overdub anything; I wanted it to be real. The concept of that album was Tony Rice's guitar and voice in the raw.

I was doing *Church Street Blues* when anxiety was really a problem, and I was doing *Backwaters* right before I sought treatment. I didn't start heavy drinking until probably '85 or '86. And it would come and go. There was no real pattern to it.

Anxiety has been a problem since sometime in the late 1970s, one I sought professional help for in 1981 or '82. It manifested in different phobias, like agoraphobia. That was when I was really losing it. I was trying to drink it away, and that didn't work. I ended up seeing a clinical psychologist in San Francisco. I did bio-

feedback, and was enlightened greatly. I got it under control.

I think more people have anxiety than we're willing to admit. They have their own ways of fighting it. I knew something was weird when I was afraid to go away from home very far by myself, or to be by myself in huge crowds. It would bring on severe anxiety. It was hard to fight that while being a musician and having to perform.

I'm glad I learned how to keep it controlled. Occasionally, it still exists. It made me less fearful of everything else. You gotta learn how to get through it. And you learn there's a rhyme and a reason for everything.

The first Bluegrass Album Band album was originally slated to be a Tony Rice bluegrass album. After I started hearing playbacks of everything, I thought, "This sounds like some sort of a *band.*"

I didn't invent the name "The Bluegrass Album Band." I've always detested it. Milton Harkey is the inventor of that name. By the time the band had decided to go on tour, it had to call itself *something.* By then, there were two or three volumes out. Nobody knew what to call it. The bluegrass world had been buying three volumes of this stuff, and they were calling it "The Bluegrass Album." So, Milton's logic: "Well, this is the Bluegrass Album Band. This is not just the album, this is going to be the *band.*"

On the early Bluegrass Albums—the first three volumes—there were no overdubs. The idea was that when you edit, you've still got the entire ensemble playing together, rather than piecing it together

Bluegrass Album Band in Denton, NC, mid-'80s (L-R): Terry Baucom (filling in for Bobby Hicks), Todd Phillips (hidden), Doyle Lawson, Tony, J.D. Crowe.
(Courtesy Louise Rice)

one guy at a time, or making tracks and going back to overdub vocals. And no matter how much you edit, you've still got the band playing live.

The Album Band did the first three albums with no headphones. You could hear everybody so good we didn't need them. There were two rooms at Arch Street, in this mansion of a house: a big, elegant room with a control room, and an isolated, conventional studio downstairs that adjoined the control room. The first two volumes of the Album Band was done in the upstairs room, and you could hear a pin drop. When you get guys gathered around, you could just hear every little nuance. We were individually miked, and Billy hung a Neumann quadraphonic mic over the top of the entire ensemble to capture the room sound.

Live was always preferable and still is. I will accept mistakes to be able to have it live if it's got the spirit. Listen to those Album Band records—they're loaded with mistakes: off-pitch harmony vocals and weird tuning discrepancies here and there; missed fiddle notes. But who gives a shit? It's almost like the discrepancies have a value of their own.

By Volume 3 we had Flux. We didn't do overdubs, but we recorded it in the smaller room. There's imperfections in all those tapes, but they're live all the way through most of Volume 4, and that's still my favorite of the series. We did a few cuts at Track, but we did most of it at Arch Street.

My choices for musicians were very well-thought-out. Doyle and Hicks could do it better than anybody I could think of.

I knew I was going to be doing a bunch of Monroe and Flatt & Scruggs stuff—that was conceptually what I wanted: a bluegrass album that was just as pure as it gets. I needed a mandolin player and tenor singer that could cover both of those sectors of bluegrass and do it well. Doyle was the only guy that could have done it. No other musician could have played mandolin like that. A Monroe tune, he could give it a Monroe flavor, and he could give it a Monroe tenor. On a Flatt and Scruggs tune, he could give it that Everett Lilly or Curly Seckler flavor, tenor too.

Back then, Bobby Hicks was really riding the wave of a bluegrass fiddle renaissance. There was the smoothness of Kenny Baker and the unusualness of Vassar Clements, but there was a fiddle player in Hicks that was almost like every damn bluegrass fiddle player from Howdy Forrester, Chubby Wise, all the way down through the ranks, rolled up in one. Not only that, but he could play it so hard and deliberate. And when it came time to back up something, he knew *exactly* what to do. That's the reason his backup on those mixes is real loud. His backup is in your face as much as the solos are—it was too pretty not to have it out there.

It was kind of a collaborative thing. I came up with a list of 20 tunes before we went into the studio. And Doyle would bring out a couple things, and a lot of times we'd do just whatever came to mind.

I remember thinking back then that bluegrass music was really in the toilet, maybe its lowest point in its history. It was a rarity to see a good bluegrass band that used an acoustic bass. Bands were spread out all over the stage, individual microphones ten feet apart, and it was a different world. The Bluegrass Album was kind of a deliberate attempt to get back to that traditional approach. It hit the bluegrass music world with ten times the impact I thought it would. Even the more contemporary players liked it. The traditionalists *really* liked it. All of a sudden here was this *sound* again, and it hadn't been done since Flatt & Scruggs and Monroe & Martin and Jim & Jesse and Sonny & Bob at their best.

Everybody was playing so good back then. They were just playing their asses off. I think Doyle talked me into any guitar solo I played on the first couple volumes. I didn't want to do any. But Doyle kept prodding, "Well, I don't want to play a mandolin solo there. People are going to expect you to play a little bit."

I wanted to use Vassar on Volume 5, because we'd already done four of 'em with basically the same configuration. I don't remember Bobby expressing any resentment. But by then I'd also been working on a regular basis with Mark Schatz, and I used Mark instead of Todd. Vassar just had a radically different approach, a nontraditional bluegrass fiddle approach. You know how Vassar is: he knows how to play traditional bluegrass fiddle, but if left to his own devices, he *won't*. He's like me with a guitar.

By Volume 6, that band had said everything it had to say. I had no voice by then, and wanted to do an instrumental album anyway. After Volume 5, that band would have only started to repeat itself. Over those five volumes, we had covered so much of what I thought was the best of the best of traditional bluegrass material.

In November of '83, the Bluegrass Album Band was getting ready to go on a tour. I got a phone call from Larry and Mom. And they were both just hysterical.

I don't know. I wasn't really surprised. My father kinda lived on the edge. There was something in that house that started a fire, and nobody knows what it was. My father was one to not care about smoking in bed, so it could have been that, or something else. He would get in his own little world, drinking beer and being loud. He'd run everybody off. So my mother was staying with Ronnie, who lived around the corner, when that happened.

The Rice family, circa 1980 (L-R, seated): Larry, Louise, Herb; (L-R, standing): Tony, Ronnie, Wyatt. (Courtesy Louise Rice)

I went back to help my mother make arrangements for the funeral, and then I had to leave immediately and go on to the tour. I wasn't able to go to my dad's funeral. You can imagine the commitments the Bluegrass Album Band had, because the only place that band had ever played live, prior to that, was one time at the Great American Music Hall in San Francisco. By the time we did the tour, I think Volume 3 had just been released. Without exaggeration, the whole damn bluegrass world back East, that's what *they* wanted to see. It just would not have been good for me to cancel any part of it. I don't think my father would have wanted me to have done that anyway.

He spent about a week with me in California not long before he died. We had a good time hanging out, catching up. It was real good. I didn't spend a lot of time with my parents after my professional career started; I only saw them once a year, once every three years, something like that.

I don't think the cause of the fire was ever determined. It started in his room. The story I initially heard from the fire department was that it was electrical in nature. Possibly by the dog kicking a wire or something like that. That little dog died in the fire too, and it was so sad—everybody loved that little dog. That whole damn thing was sad.

He was 54, and he was already aged way beyond his years anyway. His work meant more to him than anything in the world, and he was good at it, so he just did that until the end. He was the most respected welder in the United States. If anything heavyweight had to be done, he'd be the guy they would call in, like for NASA jobs, and when something had to be fixed and the only way to fix it was with a very small heliarc welder. He could weld stuff backwards, looking in a mirror, reaching behind his back. There wasn't anything in the world he couldn't weld.

My father would not have liked the world we live in now. He couldn't have tolerated it, to see what has happened to our liberty, and our freedom. He wouldn't have wanted to live in this society as we know it.

He had the bad side, which was alcohol abuse, but he had a good side, his personal integrity and his honesty. He was liked by everybody. Other than that, there's not a lot to say about my father. He left this world when he was supposed to.

The last conversation I had with my father, he was on the telephone on his end with a bunch of beer, and I was on the telephone on *my* end with a bunch of beer, and we just had a real good time. I loved him very much.

Cold on the Shoulder and Volume 4 of the *Bluegrass Album* were done right about the same time. *Cold on the Shoulder* was done in two studios in Berkeley. You can almost hear the work that went into it. I mean, *I* can hear it. But I can also hear musicians collaborating in a way that created enjoyment.

(Courtesy Rounder Records)

The best thing about *Cold on the Shoulder* was that it was the first time I had recorded with Vassar and had him as a guest on my own album. Leela shot the cover photo in Chicago in 1983; we were having Christmas with her family in Evanston. It was real cold that year. A lot of people died, it was so cold.

I did want a banjo on it, but I didn't want traditional bluegrass banjo. If you think about it, J.D. Crowe or Bill Emerson or Bill Keith—as good as they all are, they wouldn't have been flexible enough to play a lot of the stuff on *Cold on the Shoulder* that Béla played on there. He was the only guy that could have done it.

The first time I remember meeting Kate Wolf, the Grisman band had played an outdoor festival up on the Russian River in Northern California. Kate got a record deal with Kaleidoscope, so we met, and I really liked her voice and thought it might be great to use her on some harmony vocals. She's on two or three cuts, I think. An amazing writer and singer . . .

It was kinda shocking she died when she did. Only a very few months before, I was at home and Kate came by for a little bit, and she was telling me about not feeling good. She thought it was something serious. I told her, "Well, you can't ignore this, whatever it is; you need to get this checked out." By the time she got to a doctor, it was too late.

My father died in November of '83, and Leela had had a lover; I found out about him in January of '84. It was only a few months.

The last thing I heard from Leela was that I had never done a damn thing wrong, that I was a good person, a good husband, a good man. But she couldn't hang on to the identity of being Tony Rice's wife. I have always felt that I was on the wrong end of a five-year bluff. I think she knew all along she was gonna hit the road one day. It kinda came crashing down, and it crashed pretty hard.

But I managed to pick myself up. Some people go, "Well, I'm just throwing myself into my work." I always wondered, "Okay, how can you *do* that?!" I'm not one that can throw himself into *anything* at a time like that. That marriage unfolded—I mean, *crashed*—in '84. I wasn't very active that year. *The Bluegrass Album Volume 4* was recorded during the breakup of my marriage. The only other thing I did, outside of playing various sessions with other people, was the first instructional video for Homespun. Other than that, I made trips back and forth from San Francisco to Florida, to be with family, and get over all of it.

The first time I went to an AA meeting was in San Francisco in 1984. It's been 21 years since I've had that instilled in me. I quit for good in May 2001. I'm still very much aware of the foundation of the

Unit front line: Jimmy Gaudreau, Tony, Wyatt. (Courtesy Tony Rice)

Twelve Steps of sobriety. Anybody can quit drinking, but if you quit drinking, are you *living?* I started to become more and more aware of that, as a way of life. You try to practice those principles, although nobody does it with perfection. As it says in AA, "We are seeking progress, not spiritual perfection."

I went through all the depression that goes along with the breakup of what you think is a good marriage, and you don't even see the end coming. Then BAM, one day it's gone. It was sometime in '85 when I had found my *own* identity, separate from Leela. And when that happened, I became very productive, very happy.

When I came back East, I was ready to start expressing myself again poetically. I put together a band. Actually the first band I had was me and Wyatt and Gaudreau. We played a gig in Canada without a bass. It was a co-bill in a real nice auditorium in Toronto with the Country Gentlemen, who Gaudreau was playing with. And Gaudreau and I had been talking about forming a vocal-oriented Tony Rice Unit. He was really excited about it. So we formed the Unit, and the next date we did was at Sanders Theater at Cambridge. By then I had a full band. Todd flew out and Stuart Duncan. We played a remarkable gig.

Kari Estrin had already coordinated a tour for the instrumental Unit back in '83. She was real good to work with, and I needed management for the new Unit. For a while she served in the capacity of manager and agent. She had an office in the Rounder warehouse. In those days, Cam-

bridge was a great town. At one time, I seriously considered getting some kind of a little space up there.

Gary Oelze had taken me under his wing to work a lot at the Birchmere. He served as my business manager for a while, too. I owe a lot to Gary and Linda Oelze, for moral support. Their friendship was a healing for what I had been going through with my breakup with Leela. Things started to happen. I really felt good about being alive.

I stayed at my mom's in Florida on and off for about a year. But I wasn't at Mom's for the entire year; I'd go home to California, and there were gigs occasionally. I was into photography then. And I was drinking a lot. You get just the right amount of alcohol in ya, and you can hold the camera a lot stiller.

I had a lady friend from Colorado, very pretty and a load of fun. I'd call her and say, "What are you doing next week? Do you want to come to Florida?" We took a boat out on the river to this little cove. I saw this nice brick house with a sign that said HOUSE FOR RENT, INQUIRE AT RESTAURANT. I walked over to the restaurant. I happened to have a pocket full of cash. I said, "I'm Louise Rice's son." The owner said, "Well, boy, yes, I know Louise, and I knew Herb . . . you're the musician they talk about all the time." I said, "Yep. What's the deal on that house?" She told me how much it was per month. I reached in my pocket and laid it down, with a one-month deposit. I lived there for eight years.

Gary had been encouraging me to forget California. It wasn't gonna work for me to live out there. It was impractical. So Gary threw a bunch of money at Billy Wolf and Wyatt, and told them to go get all my shit and my car, and pull it back East to Florida. And they did. They showed up with my stuff, dumped it in my living room, and backed my car off the trailer.

Billy was fighting his own demons in San Francisco. I said, "Hey, I got this place on the Gulf of Mexico, and I'm fixing to move in there. Why don't you come hang?" So he did. We both started drinking a lot. In a good-spirited way, not habitual-type. Coors! Coors Light, at that. And we used to party with John Duffey up in D.C. Billy finally talked Duffey into giving him his recipe for whiskey sours. There was a time that Billy and I were drinking a lot of whiskey sours in Crystal River.

Crystal River, FL, mid-1980s. (Courtesy Louise Rice)

When I get old and look back on the eight years I had in Florida . . . it was good. It was musically productive. I was single, without any long-term commitments of any kind, until Pam and I got together in October of '87. Yeah, I was having a ball out there in the world.

It wasn't long after I got down there that I saw this speedboat that I wanted . . . It was just a runabout, a ski boat. It had been used to pull professional water-skiers. When we didn't have anything to do, we'd load that boat up with beer at around 11:00 at night, and some good reefer, and go out and hit the river!

One of the things that made consumption of alcohol so easy was there were a lot of bars on the river. There were at least three or four places where you could just pull your boat up, get out and walk into the bar. You didn't have to worry about a DWI back then.

By the end of 1987, Billy was spending more time in D.C. than he was in Florida. Gary Oelze had discovered Billy as a soundman, so Billy started as house soundman for the Birchmere. And then Bias Recording Studio had discovered his engineering talents, so he was a staff engineer there.

The Seldom Scene had become so busy that Gary couldn't handle the load. It was just too much on him to try to manage and book the Seldom Scene, and manage and book the Tony Rice Unit. Gary got me in contact with Keith Case. Since then, Keith has been my agent.

Me and Gaudreau and Schatz and Wyatt played the Birchmere one night.

Flux was on the bill with us. Afterwards, we were all feeling good, man, we wanted to party and we wanted to play. I said, "Well, let's go party at Track. We'll get Billy Wolf over there." Billy said, "Hell, yeah. I'll go over there." So we go in with a couple cases of beer and all this reefer and cut some of the best shit I've ever cut, if not *the* best stuff I've ever cut. "Greenlight on the Southern," "Walls," "Song for a Winter's Night." That stuff came out of that all-nighter. It was a good time to do it. Yeah, they were raring to go! Especially Schatz. He was like a ball of energy. He could record 24 hours a day.

Fran Tate had recorded *California Autumn* at Track. I liked that studio so much, I wanted to finish *Me and My Guitar* there. Some of it had already been done in Nashville, with Sam and Vassar. "Me and My Guitar," "Port Tobacco," "Hard Love," "Four Strong Winds," had been cut at Studio 19 in Nashville. The album ended up being done in four different studios.

Port Tobacco is in Maryland. It was a place where John Wilkes Booth hid out. As part of his escape route, one of the stops he made was Port Tobacco, where he found Southern sympathizers.

Gary Oelze introduced me to a book called *Twenty Days* that, as it turns out, was kind of sensationalized, and filled with inaccuracy. The more I read, the more fascinated I became. I ended up buying more books, and wanting to photograph places like Ford's Theatre, the tombstones of the co-conspirators, things like that. I really took an interest in it.

What made it fascinating was that John Wilkes Booth, who we're all taught was nothing but a deranged madman, was just the opposite. Not only was he *not* crazy, but he was the greatest and most popular actor of his day. So, anyway . . . that's how "Port Tobacco" got its name. I wrote that for John Wilkes Booth, hoping maybe somewhere he'd hear it.

That was a first take. And if you listen close, you can hear spots where Vassar doesn't know what's coming next. This is his real genius. The only thing he knows is that he can't rely on one road to get him into the next section. He's going to have to totally change modes. He's gotta play something that will linger over into the change, the transition. "Tipper" was the same way—same situation. He didn't have to rehearse it. Sam did, Jerry did, everybody else did; they made chord charts. I don't think Vassar knew how to read a chord chart.

"Early Morning Rain" was done in California while we were doing Volume 4 [of the *Bluegrass Album* series]. The original track, which ended up on *Me and My Guitar,* was myself and Flux, Todd and Doyle. The four of us did "Early Morning Rain" for Volume 4 and the version on *Me and My Guitar* is with Doyle's track cut.

I didn't really relate "Hard Love" to my family directly. My manager before Gary, Kari Estrin, probably had almost every folk music album in existence. I heard the song on one of her Claudia Schmidt albums. There was something about it that just hit me. The more I listened to it, the more I wanted to try to figure out a way to do it. I wanted a soprano sax or an English

Tony, Todd Phillips, and Wyatt at the Birchmere in Alexandria, VA, mid-1980s.
(Courtesy Louise Rice)

horn on "Hard Love" and a tune of Larry's called "About Love." Schatz had worked some kind of jazz session with Cole Burgess. I trusted Schatz, and he called the guy, and he came over and started playing his horn. And I thought, "Wow! You're the guy I need." There was another tune Cole played on, "Sweetheart Like You," the Dylan tune.

When I did "Fine As Fine Can Be," I was kinda singing that with Leela in mind. It was at the point where it was iffy, whether we were gonna break up or stay together, but I did it with her in mind. And there's a retraction of that dedication on the back of the album. It was obvious to anybody reading it that I retracted its original dedication in favor of dedicating to whoever will faithfully receive it.

At some point, Leela would have seen a copy of that album, and she would had

to have read it. I was *pissed*. Here was a way for me to take a swing and let the whole damn world know.

Three tracks were part of the *Me and My Guitar* sessions that were never released on it. "About Love," the song Larry wrote; a Lightfoot tune, "Whispers of the North," that ended up on the Lightfoot compilation . . . and then there was "Never Meant to Be" [released on *Night Flyer*, Tony's 2008 Rounder vocal compilation]. Alison Krauss occasionally does the tune live. I wrote it in '85 at Mom's house in about ten minutes.

I had no reason to believe that the album would fail because it would alienate some of the diehards of the bluegrass community. By then, the number of those had started to become insignificant anyway. There just wasn't enough of them anymore.

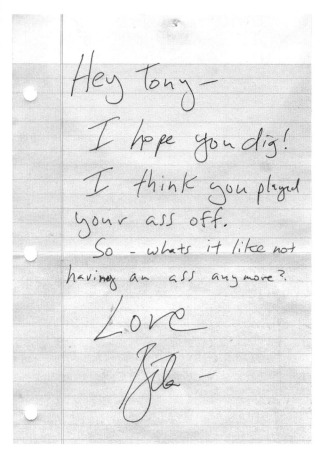

Note from Béla Fleck. (Courtesy of Pam Rice)

What I think of as some of my best work is hidden. Serious guitar aficionados are probably aware of it . . . For example, Todd Phillip's album *Released.* There's a tune on there by Coltrane called "Miles' Mode," and it's some of my best work. On Mike Marshall's album, *Gator Strut,* the guitar solo on "Round Midnight" is some of my better work, and some of the stuff off of Darol Anger's album called *Fiddlistics.*

Béla Fleck's *Drive* was a real in-depth album. One of the best sessions I ever did

in my life; one of the most musically trying. Very difficult for me. I was the only guy that wasn't rehearsed. Everybody else was, so I had to come in cold and hit it off paper. I wasn't available until the day before the time to go to the studio. There was time enough to get to the hotel the night before, get up the next day, go in, and have this music laid out for me. I spent a lot of time listening to *Drive* thinking, "Damn, I wish I could have played guitar that good on some of my *own* albums!"

One of my prize works is Emerson's album called *Home of the Red Fox.* There were some magic moments on that record. It was heavy. When Emerson had the concept, I said, "There's a damn good rhythm section in town, Mark Schatz and Gaudreau and myself . . ." I think Jerry Douglas was with us then, if memory serves me right. Béla and I, and Gaudreau and Schatz, had just done a recording with bluegrass fiddler extraordinaire Jimmy Buchanan, who played with Jim & Jesse all those years, and then with the Quintet for a while. I played a hunch to see if I could talk Jimmy into coming to Maryland to the studio. He said, "Hell, yeah! How do I get there?" It was one of the magic bluegrass albums.

In 1985, Rounder had this big celebration to commemorate 15 years of Rounder Records. I had just played a gig at Harvard, and Norman Blake had played there. I had met Blake back in the early '70s, when I was with Crowe. We would talk casually about hooking up someday. And we were both at the Rounder after-party, and we started talking guitars, and we took 'em out, over

Tony and Norman Blake. (Photo by Jon Sievert)

in a little corner, and started playing. We instinctively knew we were on to something that should be recorded.

It wasn't long after that that we did the first *Blake & Rice* album. We talked on the phone: "Do you like this tune? Do you like that tune?" Very easy-going, easy to collaborate. The success of it hit the acoustic music world with enough of an impact that Rounder requested that we do another one right away. So we did Volume 2. I did a co-bill with Doc at the Birchmere, when he was in town. And all the pieces were there: Doc was there, Norman & Nancy were there in the area, and the Unit was there. So Doc and Mark Schatz are on a couple of cuts, and Nancy Blake. That's what happened with Volume 2.

Pam and I got together in October of '87. I'd known her since we were kids. I'd come up occasionally and stay with my grandmother, and I would see her when she visited.

I played an outdoor event in North Carolina, and I saw her there. Then, on September 30, 1987, I went to visit my grandmother and Pam was there. My grandmother said, "Sparks started to fly!" That's when Pam and I started talking on the phone. I invited her down to Florida and she came. She stayed for a long time . . . for good!

She was drop-dead gorgeous and witty. I was ready, by then, for a steady relationship. The last time Leela and I had lived together as husband and wife was in January of '84. That's almost four years where I was a single guy. I'd had enough.

We got married August the 8th of '89, at a town called Chatham, the county seat of Pittsylvania County in Virginia. It just kinda *happened.* She woke me up that day and said her friend Fuller Dibrell pulled some strings and we could get married without having to do blood tests. Getting married in North Carolina is a big ordeal. I said, "Yeah, okay."

Native American might have been recorded over a span of two years. There was a long lapse in sessions because I did a bunch of stuff for it, and then I didn't know what to do.

John Jennings and I were palling around with Mary Chapin right before Chapin became famous. We did a lot of hanging out at the Birchmere and would go to clubs in the District and play at these hootenanny-type things. Anyway, Jennings offered to produce some tracks for *Native American.* He ended up with Chapin's band—Jon Carroll on piano, Robbie Magruder on drums, Rico Petrucelli on bass, and John Jennings on electric and acoustic guitar—and he produced "Nothing Like a Hundred Miles," the remake of

"Summer Wages," and two other tunes. That might have been the first time I ever thought, "Okay, I don't know what to do to finish this album. I don't know how to give this concept continuity . . ." I kind of just dumped it in Jennings's lap.

I met Chapin through Gary Oelze. It was very common after a show at the Birchmere, you'd sit around with Gary and Linda and friends, and drink beer till four or five in the morning. Chapin was there and we were hanging out. She overheard Gary and me talking about John Wilkes Booth. I told Chapin, "You know what? If anybody could write a good song that would present John Wilkes Booth in the light of reality, it would be *you*."

I bet it wasn't two days later her and Jennings came in the club after everybody left and put on a cassette over the sound system. I said, "Damn, how in the world did you do this so fast?" And Chapin said, "I went to the library."

The chords I ended up playing the tune are the same chords Jennings played when I first heard 'em. If I was driving down the road in a car by myself and had three hours, I would remember the lyrics . . . *[he proceeds to recite them all]*.

Everything on that record was recorded at Bias and engineered and mixed by Billy. The stuff with Sam and Flux and the other guys was live. The Jennings stuff was constructed tracks with overdubbed vocals and guitar solos.

"St. James Hospital" came off Doc's first album. With *that* band I could pull it off. It had to be in that swing time. "Night Flyer" was from this guy me and Sam used

to listen to, John Mayall. You keep tunes in your head all these years, thinking, "One of these days I'm gonna find a way to record this." I didn't really like arranging anything, but what gave that tune impact is the same arrangement on the kickoff and the interludes Mayall did with just a bass player and guitar player. They all played that unison line, so I stuck with that.

"Urge for Going," written by Joni Mitchell, came from Tom Rush—it was on one of his albums, just him and guitar, very simple. "Summer Wages . . ." At the time I thought it was worthy of being done in a way that couldn't be associated with the bluegrass world. It was done by the New South and I wanted to try to dress it up. I like the *Native American* version better than the New South version, but 99.9% of the listening public likes the original.

Alison Krauss played quite a few dates with us all over the United States, and she was real gracious about it. I didn't know a thing about Alison's singing, but I liked the way she played that fiddle. Every time I had a Unit date I thought was good, I'd call her and say, "Hey, I've got this date and I want a good fiddle player. Will you come and play?" And she was always there.

She might have had two albums by then on Rounder, but when I heard her sing, she sounded almost childlike. At some point, we were backstage somewhere and Schatz said, "Play 'Cry, Cry Darling.' I want you to hear Alison sing this." She went onstage and sang it into the fiddle mic, and that was the only song she sung.

As good a voice as she had, I didn't care

about her singing. I wanted her fiddle playing. I love her fiddle playing—there's something unique about it. And she fit right in. There was no rehearsal or anything. No matter what the Unit threw at her on that stage, she fell right into it.

This was a whole era in which I was doing stuff where I was proud of the results, as opposed to previous albums where I just went in and did an album because it was expected. With most of those albums, you can hear it: the desire to create the music.

But starting with *Hot Dawg*, everything was changing for me. It was like musical heaven; I could do no wrong. No matter what I went in to do, I was going to come out of there with something that was damn good. That spirit and enthusiasm probably started to diminish somewhat, right after *Native American.*

(Photo by Tim Talley)

Family, Friends & Fans

I thought *Cold on the Shoulder* was the greatest thing I'd ever heard. I'll just never get over that record. I would listen to it eleven hours a day. Every waking moment, that record was on.

Alison Krauss, bandleader of Union Station

The collection of songs on *Church Street Blues* is very moving to me. This is how I think people make decisions about music: it depends on where it finds you in your life. I found that record when I was living hand-to-mouth, struggling so hard. The only thing that made me happy was to be able to listen to songs I loved. The songs on that record were very moving to me in that regard, and I loved to sing along to every one.

Mary Chapin Carpenter, country artist

Buy *Manzanita* and get your butt kicked.

Tim Austin, rhythm guitarist & Lonesome River Band founder

Manzanita . . . Because it's goddamn good, that's why.

Audey Ratliff, mandolinist & luthier

Barbara Higbie:

I was there when he started writing the *Manzanita* material, and that was exciting. It was like, first he thought he wasn't capable of that, and then he just dove into it . . . and then he was capable of it *all*.

Darol Anger:

Manzanita . . . Tony's going, "I'm out here in the middle of nowhere . . . do I still have a career? Who am I? *I better make a record.*" Well, Tony likes making records. And being home all the time, we didn't play that much. That was one nice thing: instead of going to the Holiday Inn every night, he would stay home and work on ideas. That was actually kind of a catalyst.

Sam Bush:

When he'd been in California a year, he called and asked me to come out . . . He was gonna make a bluegrass record, but we weren't gonna have a banjo. I'm thinking, "Okaaaay. . . ."

That was the first time I ever got to play with Flux and Ricky. I think that's when Ricky found out I'm not just a hippie, if you know what I mean. I can play bluegrass. The singing, with Tony and Ricky and I, was really fine. There's no editing on that record, and Tony's guitar and vocals were recorded on the spot. He didn't overdub a lick.

Jerry Douglas:

Manzanita wasn't really an attempt to leave out a banjo. It was Tony's adjustment and mixture of the two worlds of music he was playing at the time. Anything we recorded for that record could be played with a banjo, but he chose not to. It was smoother in an ethereal way.

Jeff Autry:

This is the truth: I had three of those LPs in my life. The first two I had within five years—I wore 'em out! I never put 'em back in their jacket . . . they never came off the turntable. It's been a long time. Unfortunately, the more complex life gets, the less you can get lost in something like that.

(Courtesy Rounder Records)

Ricky Skaggs:

It's such a great record, very influential. It was a great banjo player's record because there wasn't a banjo on it, but boy, you could sit and play banjo to it.

Sammy Shelor (banjoist with the Lonesome River Band):

I spent three years playing to that record. That's what taught me timing, and how to *create*. There was no banjo to try to emulate, so you listened to the mandolin and you might pick up a lick. You listened to the resonator guitar and the fiddle and you might pick up a lick. You ended up designing your own breaks to play to that record. It was the best timing lesson ever.

Billy Wolf:

You have to have done a lot of records to have a feel for this, but there's no *room* in a five-string banjo roll. It's constantly going. When the banjo goes to chops during breaks, it's being a mandolin. While it's doing the five-string roll, it's constant notes. I remember David in particular talking about that: there was more space without the banjo.

Mark O'Connor:

Tony took me under his wing a bit during the *Markology* and *On the Rampage* sessions in 1978 and '79. He introduced me to Coltrane, Davis and Monk and told me I had to absorb this music. He wanted to be my mentor and take care of me as part of his legacy, but the music business that is sometimes thrust upon musicians in a harsh manner can get in the way.

When we found out through David Grisman that Tony would love to play rhythm on *Markology,* I was just blown away. I was 16. He also played some lead on one of my compositions called "Fluid Drive," along with flatpick guitar great Dan Crary. What a dream this was.

Mike Marshall:

I moved in with Tony and Kate in October or November of '78. It was a tumultuous time. I think Tony wanted me to move in with him just to create some semblance of sanity around the house. Here I was, getting to hang out with my hero, but meanwhile, he was in the middle of a breakup. He did his best to weather it. After a couple months, I ended up moving out.

I remember Kate as being pretty well-educated . . . but it was a very short time that we hung out. A couple months. Mostly it was Tony grabbing me and saying, "Let's go to Berkeley, Gator Bait!" We'd jump in the Trans-Am, drive 90 mph across the Bay Bridge and go buy a jazz record.

Barbara Higbie:

Kate was a wonderful person, very kind-hearted. She was working some straight job. She really loved Tony, but I think it was not a healthy relationship for her. There was a lot of high drama. It was very hard to be ANY kind of feminist in that scene. They weren't mean-spirited guys, but women were supposed to be in support roles. It was the era when everybody was working that stuff out. It was wonderful, very high-level, but the values in the music were male values.

Billy Wolf:

Kate loved him dearly, and I think she was devastated when it didn't work out. I remember going to their house after they'd split, and her listening to Tony's recordings over and over again . . .

Mike Marshall:

We were at the Bottom Line in New York [in 1979]. I remember Pierre Bensusan opening the show. That was an amazing tour, very intense. Tony wouldn't fly . . . I think he flew *after* that, but for that tour, he refused to fly. I agreed to take a train with him to the first gig—in Denver—from San Francisco. That was fricking misery. A train? Are you kidding me? Instead of flying for two hours, we take a train for, like, *twenty*. Tony on the smoker car . . . Yeah, that's a *great idea.*

Are you looking for logic? Come on! We all kinda took care of him.

Billy Wolf:

Leela was an educated girl, the daughter of educated people. Tony doesn't have a tremendous education, but he's incredibly intelligent. This is a guy who can fix Accutron watches. He does the Rubik's Cube in a minute. I don't want to say she threw the big words at him, but I think Leela took advantage of her extensive education to get under his skin. Not a warm person.

Ricky Skaggs:

I brought Tony out on *Roses in the Snow* [1980]. I really wanted him in on that. Brian [Ahern] gave me freedom to bring people in I wanted to play with, because he knew that would be better than him trying to pick bluegrass guys. That was a genre he loved, but didn't know anything about. Hearing Tony and Albert Lee playing on the same track was pretty cool.

Emmylou Harris (legendary country & bluegrass singer):

I did some recording on John Starling's first solo record (*Long Time Gone,* 1977) that he took so long to make . . . but it was great, because we had Tony Rice—I was singing with *Tony Rice!*—me and Tony and John. It was just *fantastic.*

Tony was really an important part of *Roses in the Snow.* And he was still singing then. "Jordan" with Johnny Cash . . . That's me, and Ricky, and Tony, and we had Johnny do the bass part. We did that whole album sort of live off the floor, at a studio off Coldwater Canyon. Everything was pretty much live off the floor, but we came to Nashville to overdub John.

Ricky Skaggs:

Then we wanted to do a duet record, old Stanley Brothers, Blue Sky Boys, Monroe Brother-sounding stuff. I got a list of songs together and he got a list together. I was with Emmylou, and I was going to have two or three days off. Seems like I flew from L.A. to Berkeley. I didn't even have a mandolin with me. I borrowed David's '25 or '27, a really good-sounding mandolin.

Barbara Higbie:

There was one night at Grisman's house that was just *amazing.* It was Ricky Skaggs and Tony when they were getting ready to record that duets album. They were singing ALL the songs. My hair was standing up on the back of my neck.

Ricky & Tony at MerleFest in 2001.
(Photo by Caroline Wright)

Ricky Skaggs:

I can't remember which songs I brought and which ones he brought, it's been so long. The singing and playing was all live. I think that's one of the reasons it's got such a great sound. My vocal is in my mandolin mic, and his lead vocal is in his guitar mic. It was a real magic thing, so simple and easy. We thought, "Man, ain't nobody gonna buy this! It'll be something for our moms and dads." And we dedicated it to our parents . . . We had no idea it would be so well-received. We practiced enough where we knew the phrasing. Sometimes we'd blow a line. It's not a perfect record, but it feels good.

Billy Wolf:

There were six tracks. Two vocal mics, and four instrument mics. There would have been a vocal mic, and the instruments would have been in stereo. They were organic takes.

I pulled my name from the recording. I won't record anything I don't mix. Actually, that's probably the only thing in my life that I recorded that I *didn't* mix. And I wouldn't have done it if I had known. I was not happy.

Mike Marshall:

Tony was recording all this amazing vocal music, and we would go play these shows and he would not sing! That was his big thing: *I'm in California, playing jazz . . . it's not about singing.* He tried to draw a very hard line in the sand with that one. It was frustrating for some audience members. They'd yell . . . "Sing one, Tony!" And he'd just grumble.

He'd play all this instrumental music for six months, and never open his mouth . . . and then he would book a session with the Bluegrass Album Band or Ricky Skaggs and for a week, he would do nothing but sing in the most intense way. This was before ProTools and tuning vocals. You had to sing perfectly. The amount of focus and intensity it took . . . He gave himself no warm-up time; he'd just make a list of tunes, and BAM! start recording.

Béla Fleck (ground-breaking banjoist):

I was making my second album [*Natural Bridge,* 1982], in the period after Tony and Grisman split . . . I thought, "Maybe they'll record together for me!" I was egotistical enough, or foolish enough, to think it might happen.

Tony agreed to do it; I think Mark O'Connor was gonna play fiddle, and Grisman was gonna play mandolin. As it got closer, Tony was realizing he wasn't ready to play with Grisman yet. He was very uncomfortable. He said, "Isn't there somebody else?" I really wanted to play Dawg music with a banjo in it. That was my vision for these five or six cuts.

The night before I'm gonna fly out, I get this last-minute call from Marian [Leighton] at Rounder: "Tony's not gonna do the session." *Ack!* We had to cancel the whole deal. We decided to get Mark to play guitar and have Darol play fiddle. Mark had been playing guitar in the Grisman band for quite a while, and he was really looking forward to playing fiddle. But we had a magic session. Mark played some of the best guitar I've ever heard; he was so influenced by Tony at that time. The delicacy and dancing quality were there.

Gary Oelze (proprietor of the Birchmere in Alexandria, VA):

First time I met Tony was in about '82. I did a concert at the Lisner Auditorium in D.C. We put together the original Country Gentlemen, the original Seldom Scene, and the original New South. We recorded it, and the New South, with Tony, won a Grammy for that show in 1983. [Best Instrumental Country Performance for "Fireball"]

John Cowan (bassist/singer with New Grass Revival):

When Courtney [Johnson] and Curtis [Burch] left the New Grass Revival, Sam and I had this idea of approaching Tony and Jerry Douglas and inviting them to join. Tony's name came up a couple times. I remember our conversation was, "Well, that'd be a long shot." We knew Tony as a jazz guy approaching bluegrass through that genre, and we clearly were rock guys. I think Tony's a bit more John Coltrane and Miles Davis than Duane Allman and Carlos Santana. My remembrance is that Sam went ahead and called him, and Tony very respectfully declined.

Wyatt Rice:

I used to call him and bug him about coming out to California. One time I got to stay, and when I got back home, I called and said, "Man, I gotta come back out." I bet he was thinking, "Yeah, for what?" I'd bug him all the time, at least once or twice a week I'd call. I'd say, "Man, I need to get a ticket." And the next thing I know, he said, "All right, here you go."

I was 17 when I did *Backwaters*. And Tony called me out to play on *Church Street Blues*. It was around the same time. I was tickled to do that, even though it was only two or three songs that I just played rhythm on. I was out there for a couple weeks for that one. The *Backwaters* thing took a little longer, because I didn't know any of those songs or those chords or anything.

Tony & Wyatt at Terrapin Hill Farm, Harrodsburg, KY, July 2005.
(Photo by Caroline Wright)

J.D. Crowe:

Tony owed Rounder a bluegrass album. He called me and wanted to know if I would help. I said, "Yeah!" He was talking about who to get for tenor. There was Gaudreau, there was Ricky, there was Doyle. For the mandolin playing, timing, tenor pull, the phrasing, Doyle was the one to have.

After we got about halfway through, we were listening to the playbacks. You know how Tony gets all hyped up. He said, "Man, that sounds so good, we ought to do a whole series." I said, "Isn't this supposed to be your bluegrass album?" He said, "I'll do my bluegrass album later." I said, "Well, that suits me."

Doyle Lawson:

That was a joy, just getting to be there and not have to do anything except play mandolin and sing tenor. I was in seventh heaven.

Most of the time, J.D. and I would meet in Atlanta and fly to California. We'd write down a list of songs. We'd have ten, twelve, a whole slew. And when we got out there, Tony would have *his* list. We might run through them one time to figure out what we were going to do. When we did "Back to the Cross," Tony wasn't familiar with it. I sang a verse and chorus, and we cut it. They went down surprisingly easy. We never did put in a lot of time on rehearsing.

Tony didn't want to do any breaks. He was almost adamant. We said, "You've *got* to." We were *all* like that. There were some songs that didn't have a mandolin break on the original record [by the original artist] and I didn't want to do it. They said, "No, you've got to. It needs a break there." We were really concerned about paying the highest respect we could to the first generation.

Todd Phillips:

Downstairs at 1750 Arch Street, there was a "dead" kinda studio. I think we did all the Bluegrass Album stuff down there. As far as I remember, the lead vocal line was live, and tenor and baritone parts were stuck on after. But everything else was live. The room is weird; it's narrow and long. I was at one end. Basically we were all in one room, and the baffles were only little half-walls, three or four feet tall. You could see right over the top of 'em.

Doyle Lawson:

California Connection, Volume 3, was actually cut in the hallway of Arch Street Studios. The guy who owned Arch Street was a classical violinist. His hearing started to go, so he had an acoustics engineer design the room so he could hear his violin. It was a *great* room for acoustics. Oh, I *loved* it! Hardwood floors, natural reverberation. We couldn't get the room upstairs so they said, "Let's do it in the hallway." Billy pulled everything out there. We only had four 8-tracks. J.D. and I shared a mic. We had to do edits because of the bleed; that's the only way we could get it to match up. I thought, "Man, this is going to be a *zoo.*" But it worked good.

Ken Irwin:

I don't know when the term "supergroup" developed in the rest of music, but I think the Bluegrass Album Band was probably considered the first one in the bluegrass world. There had been records with lots of guests, but that first record came out, and then they decided to actually tour, which was never a part of the original plan. As it was successful, they decided to do a second record, and a third, and kept going as long as Tony's voice was there . . . and even one record after.

Doyle Lawson:

During that early period, we really came close to saying, "Well, let's make this a permanent thing." Then we let that idea go and went back to our own groups. I don't have any regrets about that. What I regret is the fact that we didn't get to keep doing what we were doing, with Tony's voice being the lead anchor and me getting to sing tenor with him.

We did the sixth volume all-instrumental, and we had pretty much covered everything with the way we heard our music, the people we were influenced by. I think we all felt, "Well, this is a good place to wrap it up." I've never said we won't ever do another one. I wouldn't want to do one just for the sake of doing it, and I know the rest of the guys would feel the same way.

Steve Dilling (banjoist with IIIrd Tyme Out):

The first time I ever saw Tony was in 1982. Milton Harkey, the promoter of the Bluegrass Album tour, had the Album Band play in Denton. This was their first East Coast gig. When Tony got out of the car at the festival, Milt had to get security to keep people back! He had to be whisked in backstage. Tony didn't deal with it well at all. He just wasn't used to it.

In November 1983, I'd have been 18. I already had been playing for five or six years. Milton Harkey is a family friend. He knew that being around those guys would be a career builder for me.

At the time the tour was organized, Tony was almost a mystery around here. He was in Camp Springs with Crowe in the early 70s, and then he went out West, and when he came here with the Album Band, everybody here was Tony Rice *crazy.*

My parents went to my school and arranged it where I could miss a few days of school to go on this tour. I was on the bus with J.D. Crowe, Tony Rice, Doyle Lawson, Jerry Douglas, Bobby Hicks—he was on the first four shows and then Terry Baucom played fiddle the rest of the time. It was unreal.

Steve Dilling and Tony on the Bluegrass Album Band tour, 1983. (Courtesy Steve Dilling)

Kari Estrin:

Five days before the tour, Tony's father died. Tony was such a trouper that he went on the tour. He was very introverted, and there were a lot of little power struggles, and he wanted nothing to do with them. He decided not to do any of the emcee work. He went the whole tour without saying one word—until the last night. He broke a guitar string, and he said, "Shit." And the entire crowd almost gave him a standing ovation.

Ronnie Rice:

My dad had been drinking and it got to the point where nobody could stand to be around him. Mom left first; she was staying at Larry's. Wyatt and Michelle were staying with Vicki and I. They hung in there a couple days after Mom had left.

Wyatt Rice:

I was the one who found him. I came home and the doors were locked and there was smoke on the windows. One of his buddies was out on his front porch, and I said, "Man, there's something wrong. He's got the doors locked and something smells like smoke in there." He busted the door in. He went in and I was right behind him, and here's the strangest thing: right there where my father was, where the cigarette caught the bed on fire, there wasn't no bed except the springs. I walked in and all around and then back out . . . I walked right over him and never seen him.

I had a feeling that one day that it was going to happen. I was still shocked about the whole thing, but I wasn't that surprised about it.

Louise Rice:
Tony was in California, and he and Leela came out. He and the boys were with me, making arrangements. We had to take him to the airport; he had to go to Myrtle Beach to play music. He said, "Mom, I don't want to do this! But I'm obligated." That's his living, and he had to do it.

And he cried just about all the way to the airport. Leela sat there like a stone. She didn't put her arms around him. She did not show any emotion. I never felt so sorry for anyone in my life as Tony.

Steve Dilling:
He flew to Florida and was a day or two late getting back for rehearsals. My first assignment, so to speak, was to go to the airport. In one day, I picked up J.D. Crowe and Todd Phillips and Tony and his wife Leela. They rehearsed Tuesday and Wednesday night at Milton's in Asheville, and then we left Thursday morning to go to Myrtle Beach.

I didn't ever ask about it. I was just a kid. When he came back Tuesday, he got his axe out, and man, they went to it. It was just like nothing was wrong . . . on the surface.

Doyle Lawson:
We just tried to overcome it, never said anything about his father, because we felt if he wanted to share something with us, he would. But he handled it quite well.

Steve Dilling:
Leela was the only wife on the tour. She was super-nice to me. I think she picked up how much I idolized Tony.

It was over in, like, ten days. The guys in the band got more comfortable with each other as the tour progressed. They played pretty much the same setlist at every show. Doyle kinda organized all that. He was the one that got the pen and paper out.

Cold on the Shoulder was getting ready to come out, and Tony played a demo of it. I got to go home and tell all my buddies I'd heard an advance copy of Tony Rice's upcoming record. They did some tunes off it—"John Hardy" and "Wayfaring Stranger" and a couple things, to preview his next record. But I'd say 80% of the setlist was Album Band tunes off those first three records. "Freeborn Man . . ." and "Train 45" were probably the biggest crowd-pleasers. Anything Tony took a guitar break on, he blew the roof off the places.

Doyle Lawson:
You talk about excitement in the air . . . It was amazing. You could feel the anticipation from the wings of the stage. One fan bought tickets for every date we had. I said, "Aren't you tired of this show? We're doing the same one every place we go." She

Bluegrass Album Band, early 1980s (L-R): Bobby Hicks, Doyle Lawson, Tony, J.D. Crowe, Jerry Douglas. (Photo by Steve Dilling)

said, "Oh, no, it's just as fresh as the first one."

They would introduce us one at a time, and we always kept Tony until last. Audiences saw *us* pretty much any time they wanted to, but they *didn't* see Tony. And it was *electric*. I witnessed it.

Happy Traum (founder of Homespun Tapes):

I had met Tony sometime in the late '70s when he was playing with the David Grisman Quintet. I called him about making some instructional tapes for Homespun. Back then it was all audio cassettes, so I brought my tape recorder to his place in Marin County. We spent several days together and made a set of six one-hour lessons on traditional and "new acoustic" guitar.

I was completely into his singing and, of course, had never heard anyone play guitar like he did, so I was pretty blown away. For some reason I was expecting him to be prickly and difficult to work with, but when I got there I found the opposite to be true. He was extremely gracious and willing to put in the time we needed to get it right. At that time he was doing a lot of photography, particularly of birds, and we talked about that. We spent about three days doing the recordings.

Once Homespun started getting into video, he was among the first we worked with. In '84 we got him to come to Woodstock to shoot, and we booked Todd Rundgren's Utopia Studio, which had a fairly primitive video set-up by today's standards. The studio's heating system wasn't working, it was bitterly cold, and the equipment kept breaking down. I remember finishing after midnight, cold and tired. In spite of this, Tony sang and played beautifully, and never complained.

Béla Fleck:

After *Manzanita* became my favorite record, I was thinking, "It would be so cool to be able to play banjo in music like *this*." There was a whole movement going on about banjo not being in the music. And frankly, Crowe couldn't really go to some of the places Tony wanted to go.

Getting the call to be on *Cold on the Shoulder* was the most exciting thing that had ever happened to me. From the second we all sat down, every note was perfect. It was one of those things I've only gotten to experience a few times. Every note was locked, everything was *right*. And Tony and Sam together . . . that is a banjo player's home turf, man.

Wyatt Rice:

I was in California when Tony went to pick up the master for *Cold on the Shoulder* at Fantasy Studios in Berkeley, where that record was recorded. He was really into that—picking up the lacquer masters. He'd say, "You know, these are only good for about ten plays." But he'd get them home and play them, then he'd say, "God. Let's play it one more time."

Alison Krauss:

I think *Cold on the Shoulder* was the latest record when I saw him play live for the first time. There are pictures of me sitting there watching him, and my mouth is hanging open! I was so star-struck, seeing him that day. I had never seen people react to anybody like they reacted to Tony. I remember thinking, "Wow—*cool*. These other people feel the same way I do!"

There was a house in Savoy, Illinois we would drive by whenever we were driving to Nashville, on a road you take to get to the highway. I would sit and daydream about *Cold on the Shoulder* and "Song for Life" would come up. In my mind, that house is the one he would pull up to, the house the woman he was seeing lived in. I thought about that all the time.

Gary Oelze:

When *Cold on the Shoulder* was out, a lot of people said they'd like Tony, just solo, to come in and promote that album. He told me he absolutely would not go onstage by himself.

Kari Estrin:

When Tony toured Japan, he hadn't been back there for nine years. And he was like a god: this tall, commanding presence walking about. All he had to do was move and legions of people would be snapping pictures. They idolized bluegrass.

After the tour, he stopped playing for a while. I was just his agent at that time. I never talked to Tony on the phone; it was always Leela. If Leela called me, then I could explain his actions [to promoters]. But if not, there was nothing to do.

And one day Leela confided in me about her marriage. She wasn't working it out with him, and it was a hard road. There's no judgment on my part. I adored Leela, and I really believed in her. They had things they needed to work out, but she told *me* about them instead of *them* working it out.

(Courtesy Masahiko Abe)

And when they split up, Tony started calling me. Then Leela would call. Tony's career was going nowhere because Leela was his manager. I desperately wanted them back together. But fate is as it is, and that didn't happen. I was in the middle of their divorce, and it was very painful.

Billy Wolf:

Musicians live different lives than regular people. Leela was working at a bank, nine to five, and Tony was eating dinner at 11:00 at night. They weren't connecting.

Gary Oelze:

When he and Leela split up, I heard that Tony was having this huge *pity party;* he just sort of disappeared from the face of the earth. I called him and said, "What in the hell are you doin'? You need to get outta California!"

Louise Rice:

When Tony and Leela broke up, he came and stayed with us in Florida. It just about killed him. He stayed for months. I made sure he had the right kind of food to eat, and that his clothes were clean. If he wanted to talk I was there to listen. Sometimes he would talk to Leela on the phone. Sometimes he would want ME to talk to Leela, and I would . . . but there's only so much a mother-in-law can do.

Mark Johnson (Florida clawhammer banjoist and Rice family friend):

He was just devastated. I told him, "You call me any time you need to talk." And I'd get these calls at two in the morning. I would drive down and pick him up and we would head north through Citrus County, up into Levy County, Florida, just driving, and we would talk and talk. That's where our friendship got forged, right there.

Todd Phillips:

I took him on the road. I had just had my first record come out. He tried to back out of it, wanted to sit home and do nothing. I got him out of the house and on the road. Man, he was in really bad shape. He would just sit in a corner and stare at the floor. He still played well. In fact, maybe he kinda let out some of the emotional stuff.

Kari Estrin:

Rounder called me into their office down the hall and said, "We're flying Tony here to talk to us, and he needs a place to stay." I lived in a group house—there were six of us—and I said, "He can sleep on the couch." I should have said, "Get him a hotel." But I think they planted a seed in me that he needed a manager. They saw his career stalling.

So Tony came. I talked to him about being his manager, and he loved the idea. I said "Look, I have this concert with David Bromberg in February. Why don't you open for him?" He didn't want to, really. He said, "Well, I need to put together a Unit." We sat in my little office in Cambridge and thought up who was going to be the new Unit. We booked gigs at the Birchmere and Sanders Theater at Harvard.

Jimmy Gaudreau:

Tony sent me a bunch of LPs and a list of songs to learn for the first show at Sanders Theatre. Besides all the harmony choruses, he wanted me to learn "Midnight on the Stormy Deep" *à la* Skaggs! I was supposed to learn all this stuff AND be ready to take a break when I got the proverbial Tony Rice "nod."

I was picked up at the airport and driven to the theatre where I met Todd and Wyatt for the first time. After Tony came strolling in, we rehearsed in a room behind stage. Tony didn't appear to be nervous about the fact that the theatre was packed with rabid fans who showed up to hear him sing. The show went over like gangbusters.

Wyatt Rice:
One of our first shows with the Unit was in Canada, just Tony, me and Gaudreau, and there wasn't a bass player. I can't recall one rehearsal. The Country Gentlemen were there and Jimmy was doing a gig with them. That's when Tony got Gaudreau. The three of us just went onstage and started playing.

Jimmy Gaudreau:
Rehearsals, what rehearsals? After those initial shows, Tony said he wanted to book more gigs, but it wouldn't be cost-effective to fly Todd from California—Todd always buys a seat for his bass when he flies—so we needed to look for another bass player. I suggested Mark Schatz, and Tony told me to give him a call. Same story. Mark agreed, he was sent some LPs and showed up with barely enough time to head for the stage at the Birchmere. Again, full house. Again, we managed to pull it off with no major train wrecks.

Wyatt Rice:
Tony stayed at my house in Crystal River while all his shit was still in California. That was a pretty rough time. Even though the Unit was already doing some shows, I kept seeing him drinking, worried all the time and not eating right.

Something kept telling me we needed to get his stuff. I said, "Tony, somebody's gonna get in all your records and your damn hi-fi gear. Let's get this out of the way." He finally said yes.

I went out and packed every bit of it up. I got a big Ryder truck with a thing on the back to pull his car, Spacegrass. During the move, I called him and he said, "I want you to pick up Billy Wolf. He's gonna move down here with me." I had to go to Billy's and load all his stuff on the same truck.

I think Tony will tell you to this day how relieved he was to see me pull up in that truck. He had already located a house. And after that he started getting his shit together.

Billy Wolf:
I liked Florida. It was restful. Tony had the big stereo in the living room, and we'd listen a lot. There was a TV we'd sit up and watch. I remember a lot of laughter, a lot of good times. Going out in the boat, fishing . . . It's a great place to fly to gigs from. He was still flying then, and we'd do the tours and come back and have a week or two without anything. It was a blast.

We had some scares with the airline, flying out of Tampa, losing his Herringbone . . . This one time, it turns out the tag for Dulles and Newark are the same color? Continental sent the guitar to Newark instead of Dulles. I had a couple sleepless nights, but I figured out what had happened. I reached somebody at the Newark airport and bribed them over the phone to put it aside. They got it to Dulles, and I picked it up the following day.

Gary Oelze:

He just started getting *busy*. He started doing things he wanted to do . . . I had to control his money, and he had it all sent to me, because he knew he'd spend it . . . He called me one time and said, "Hey, Raj, I found this boat and I wanna buy it!" He called me *Rajneesh*. He had the money. I talked him into talking the guy down a bit, and paying him half now and half later.

Wyatt Rice:

Seems like it started happening overnight. The Unit started getting all these gigs after *Cold on the Shoulder*. He dedicated that album to Leela, and then, in the liner notes to *Me and My Guitar* he said, ". . . Otherwise known as the low point in one's life . . ." or something like that. By the time he did that record, he had gotten his shit together pretty good.

Jimmy Gaudreau:

Other than an occasional solo tune, we'd perform tunes from a set list and infiltrate an occasional piece from his jazz bag. The rhythm groove had so much drive; it was easy to fall into that and express yourself by simply letting loose and not playing conservatively.

Mark Schatz (bassist with the Tony Rice Unit, 1985–90):

We might have rehearsed once, spent a few days drinking beer, and maybe working up some new stuff. Maybe it was for a new record. But generally, the tunes get worked up in the studio. We would just gather round . . . he'd say, "Here's the tune." And we'd work it out.

Jimmy Gaudreau:

There were certain things he demanded of you if you were to play in his band. First, you get to the gig the best way you could. Drive, fly, hitch-hike, walk, whatever. Next, you had to be in tune when you hit the stage. We had an unwritten rule that we wouldn't use electronic tuners, because anything other than a tuning fork would make you look like a wimp. We were wearing jeans and sport shirts, but you didn't want to show up looking like you had slept in them. Above all else, don't be daydreaming on stage and wander out of the groove. And when you got the "nod," you'd better play your ass off.

Mark Schatz:

He'd hit the "A" fork, tune his guitar perfectly, because his pitch is impeccable . . . and all of us would just tune to him. Of course, at the time, tuners were not prevalent, but that's how we always tuned. We'd get backstage, and he'd get the fork out of his case, and have his guitar tuned up in about 30 seconds. He's got an uncanny ear.

Tony Rice Unit at the Berkshire Mountains Bluegrass Festival in the mid-'80s (L-R): Jimmy Gaudreau, Mark Schatz, Tony, Wyatt.
(Courtesy Tony Rice)

Jimmy Gaudreau:

More often than not, we'd show up at the gig in separate vehicles and convene backstage. Sometimes we had played the night before and other times we hadn't played together in a month. Didn't matter. Just like riding a bicycle, you simply jump on and go. Tony would get his guitar out and tune it up to a fork and the rest of us would tune to him. He would pace back and forth like a caged tiger and he and Wyatt would fill the room with smoke. Warm-ups were usually brief. We never used a setlist and had to be ready for anything Tony wanted to do. No whining. You got used to living on the edge.

Wyatt Rice:

A lot of times I didn't know the song, so I'd pass it on. He'd nod, and I'd pass it on over to Gaudreau. You can bet your ass the next time he nodded at me on that song, I was ready for it.

Jimmy Gaudreau:

We were booked to play at a fair in Haines, Alaska and we got in a day early, so a local guy drove us around to see the sights. We stopped by our guide's house to pick up some fresh salmon and some local brew, and we headed out toward the mountains. It was a clear day in August. We got to this meadow next to a clear stream and a breathtaking view of the mountains and Tony breaks out his camera and starts snapping pictures. There were some climbing rocks nearby so we proceeded to act goofy, like young kids. When we finally broke out the picnic I can vividly remember Tony's comment: after a bite of smoked salmon, and a swig of his beer, he said, "Boys, this might be one of the best days of my life."

Keith Case (Tony's booking agent since the 1980s):

The summer of '86 or '87, he had played Telluride and a bunch of other big shows and just *stunned* people.

That New Year's I remember him playing at Jekyll Island at this kinda old people show. Half the crowd left after the act that preceded Tony. When he hit the stage, they were heading for their campers. He was playing to an audience at 30–40% capacity!

Jimmy Gaudreau:

If Tony didn't feel like taking an encore, he'd stand backstage and ignore the wild applause, screaming and foot stomping until they'd finally give up and begin to exit . . . often booing. To this day I cannot understand why he would choose to do that, and it remains one of my most unpleasant experiences while working in the Unit, if the truth be known.

Wyatt Rice:

Sometimes we'd finish off and the audience would be clapping and wanting more, there'd even be standing ovations, and the first thing he'd say was, "Tell 'em to turn the house lights up." To this day I don't know why he done that. I never have questioned him.

Kari Estrin:

He wanted to do *Me and My Guitar* and to use Billy Wolf on piano and he wanted some horns. I said, "I think you should consider putting drums on a couple tracks. I'm suggesting this from a musical standpoint." You could tell he was stricken. Two days later, we had this interview in Japan, and he goes, "Yeah, we're gonna put drums on the album."

Rounder was very resistant at first. Tony and I had a meeting with Ken, Bill [Nowlin] and Marian. I said, "You've got to let him do this." It was a departure for him, putting piano and horns and drums on a couple of tracks. But Tony was so convinced musically about it. And it was a great-selling album and it made a difference in his touring.

Billy Wolf:

I can almost think fondly about *Me and My Guitar,* because there were a couple tunes that were almost groundbreaking. Listen to the mandolin on some of it. You've NEVER heard a mandolin sound like that before. It's like you're sitting in front of Sam, and he's leaning over and playing the mandolin to your *face!* That's how Tony describes it.

Kathy Chiavola (Nashville-based singer who sang on several cuts on *Me and My Guitar*):

I used to live in a duplex with Mark Schatz, in the early-mid '80s. He had one side, and I had the other. Tony and Wyatt used to come over, and we had jam sessions. We had Sam Bush, we had Jerry Douglas . . . we had *everybody* over.

Mark was playing with Tony, and he kept recommending me. Tony asked me to sing harmony on a session, four songs. Seems like it was two or three hours. It was some original songs of his, a Gordon Lightfoot song ["Whispers in the Wind"], and "Hard Love."

(Courtesy Rounder Records)

I hung out for a couple of days. I just wanted to soak it up, and get to know Tony as well as I could. He was in a very serious mood. I had a lot of respect for him. He was in a sober period, and he seemed to be taking life pretty seriously.

Billy Wolf:

I don't think there was EVER a situation where a day of recording with Tony did not result in at least two tracks. There was never a session that was a waste, because of alcohol or anything else. In terms of L.A. standards, that's acceptable. Remember, I've worked with rock bands. You talk about *excess . . .*

But in the context of bluegrass, where the potential rewards are lower, there's an expectation of going in there, breaking your back, and getting eight songs in a day. That, I think, IS impossible in a relaxed atmosphere.

Kari Estrin:

I did want Tony to have mainstream success, which is part of the reason I wanted to add drums. I thought we could work a couple of those songs to radio. And Tony could have the most incredible mainstream career. I think it was outside of his comfort zone. I think he had external personal pressures in his life that had nothing to do with his music career or me, but at the end, it got transferred to me.

Mark Schatz:

I can't remember how many days we worked. We were busy enough that I was suddenly not scrabbling after my rent payment. Kari was doing the management, and I think she was instrumental in helping get him back on his feet. They ended up parting ways on not the best of terms, though they've since worked things out.

Bill Wolf was road-managing and doing sound, and eventually he got a job at the Birchmere and stopped coming out on the road. And there was a vacuum, which I filled: I became the road manager.

Tony is incredibly loyal. Once you play with him, unless you quit, you're *in* there. Of course, it's a two-way street. I had involved myself very deeply with him. I road-managed him; we figured out how to do the soundchecks without him. I was booking everybody's travel, and interfacing with Keith Case . . . In '90, when I went to play with Tim O'Brien, it was very jarring for Tony.

I thought he had the potential to be like James Taylor, especially with the material we were cutting on *Me and My Guitar*. I said, "Let's do some promotion. When we get to a town, let's find out what radio stations are into this stuff and do some interviews." We'd set these things up, and Tony wouldn't show. I was acting in this quasi-managerial kind of role . . . dabbling in an area where I did not have expertise. The first thing a manager would do is sit down with the artist, and say "Is this something you're interested in?" You don't push somebody to do it. Either Tony didn't care, or there was something going on where he sabotaged these things for himself.

Mike Auldridge:

Sometimes Tony would take John Starling's place when John had something medical to do. He did it eight or ten times over the course of a couple of years, mostly at the Birchmere. I always liked it because he took such great guitar breaks on *my* instrumentals!

That's what probably started us talking to him about taking the job. It's hard to *imagine* what it would be like to not have Tony have his own thing going, to have him be part of the Seldom Scene. I remember Duffey and I talking: "Damn, if Tony takes the job, we can really . . ." well, I don't know if we could have *doubled* our asking price, but it would have been a huge thing to have Tony in the band, because he was already successful. It would have changed everything.

As it was, John hung on for another year or so, and in the meantime, Tony sat in a lot. We did all the classic stuff . . . "Wait a Minute" and "Old Train" . . . the stuff that had been on *Act II* and *III*.

Billy Wolf:

When Tony would sit in with the Seldom Scene, it was like they would *stand up straight,* suddenly. Duffey was a showman, but a lot of time we forget the skill he had as a mandolin player. Duffey took a lot of liberties, and when Tony was in the band, he would play his *butt* off. They *never* sounded like that! Tony's one of those musicians that when he sits in with someone, it's greater than the sum of the parts.

I worked Seldom Scene gigs once a week for I don't know how many years, and I've done all their recent records. But it was a treat with Tony. That would have been a special band, and he really did consider it.

Jimmy Gaudreau:

In 1988, Tony decided he wanted to add a fiddle to the Unit. We did shows with Ray Legere, an outstanding fiddle (and mandolin) player from Canada, and later a young Alison Krauss, whose dream was to play fiddle in the Unit. Not for an extended time, mind you, as she was already making plans to make her own mark on the music.

Mark Schatz:

I think I introduced Alison to Tony. We were at a festival. I had heard her play, and I knew she was a phenomenon. So I asked Tony if he felt like getting her to sit in. I don't think he'd heard her before. She got up there, and he said, *"Whoa!"*

Alison Krauss:

I played the show and he gave me $50. I said, "I can't take that money!" And he said, "You're taking it, you played." And I saved the $50. I still have it in a little frame.

I ended up doing a series of dates with him after that, ten or fifteen shows maybe, and I think, "What an amazing thing for him to have asked me to do." When I was just sucking all over his show and he was so nice!

Mark Schatz:

He asked Alison if she wanted to join the band. She loved it. I mean, who wouldn't? But even then, she had a strong sense of her own band. She said, "This is an honor . . . but I've got my own thing going." And there were no hard feelings.

Alison Krauss:

We played a gig in Maryland and he wanted me to drive his car because he had a little too much to drink. I don't think I had my license yet. I said, "I got a *permit!*" He said, "You'll be all right." So I'm driving his Lincoln, right? Me and Tony in the car, and I'm thinking, "I'm driving *Tony Rice* in his *car*, and I have a *permit*." We were listening to Benny Goodman and Leon Redbone. He was talking about music while I'm driving him with my *permit* back from the gig!

Pam Rice (*née* Hodges; Tony's third wife):

Alison was about 17 and we had been in Virginia for a few days. She was going to play with the Unit that last evening, and she had been shopping. She and I were in her room all afternoon laughing and trying on outfits, trying to come up with the perfect stage outfit for her. I noticed her skirt was wrinkled in the back so I got my makeup case and pulled out an iron I brought from home. I pressed her skirt quickly and I had just enough time to let it cool so it wouldn't melt my makeup case. Then Tony was knocking on the door for us to head out to rehearsal with him.

We were so high-spirited I didn't think anything could dampen our mood. Just as we were driving off the ramp about to get onto 395, Tony slammed on the brakes and brought the car to an abrupt halt. "What is that?" he yelled. "What is that smell? What's on fire?" I had to tell the truth and say, "Oh, it's just the iron in my makeup case; it's barely warm. It's not going to set the trunk on fire."

He got out of the car and nearly slammed it off the hinges. In no time he was going through our girl stuff in the trunk of the car, digging like Fire Marshall Bill. Alison got so nervous she tried to get out, but Tony's abrupt exit had activated the automatic safety locks. "Let me out!" she pleaded. "For what, pray tell? I can't let you out on 395; it's too dangerous!" I said. "No, let me out, he is mad." "Oh, crap, Alison. That man has the fastest temper in the world. He will be really sweet in two to five minutes, believe me. He angers quickly but then his rage passes in a few minutes, tops."

Poor little thing was scared to death, thinking we had nearly set the Town Car on fire, and Tony was furious with us both. He got right back in the car . . . and of course had to slam the door as a statement. But two minutes later, he was saying so sweetly, "Look, sugar! Look, Alison. See that building over there? Do you know what it is?"

I just turned to the back seat and silently mouthed "Toldja," to a very shocked and relieved Alison. He was an absolute charmer for the rest of the night, and the show was one of the best I have ever seen or heard them do.

Tom Gray:

When we did the Seldom Scene's 15th Anniversary show at the Kennedy Center, we wanted Tony Rice to be part of it. Starling planned that whole program and suggested tunes each person would participate in. That 3,000-seat concert hall was packed; there were people in the aisles.

We spread the word that there would be a lot of special guests. We couldn't really advertise Ricky Skaggs and Linda Ronstadt, but we put out the word that folks we'd performed with over the years were gonna make an appearance. People were expecting something big. We leased the concert hall for the night, and there was a party afterwards. Oh, man. It was a big party, and a wonderful night.

Mary Chapin Carpenter (Washington, D.C. singer/songwriter and Tony protégé):

I was falling in love with bluegrass music. I lived in the Washington, D.C. area at the time. I started going to the Birchmere. In whatever incarnation Tony would play, I'd try to catch it. Gary Oelze would let me sit behind the soundboard by Billy because I didn't have money to sit in a chair.

After the shows, people would sit around and play, and that's when I got to know Tony. I was pretty shy, so it's not like I ever had deep conversations with the man, but I loved him so much, and he was always so kind.

I don't remember the exact chain of events, but Tony asked me if I knew anything about John Wilkes Booth. I said, "No, other than what we read in our history books." Evidently, Tony had become fascinated with that era; he'd spent time around Port Tobacco and Ford Theatre. He said, "Well, maybe you should write a song about him."

The next day found me at the library, pulling out books to familiarize myself with the infamous event Booth was involved in. At that point, I was pretty immersed in Tony's style, but I also felt like I was well-versed in terms of the kinds of non-bluegrass songs he was drawn to. When I started writing, I think I tried to hear those songs in my head.

I wrote the song, and demoed it up with my buddy John Jennings. I handed it over to Tony, and never expected to hear another word. And then he told me he really liked it. Needless to say, the fact that it ended up on the next Tony record was the greatest compliment to me.

Gary Oelze:

Chapin was very shy. She was always around the Birchmere. She called me from Bias Studio and said, "Could Tony come over and play something?" I took Tony over there and he did this piece on her record. Her manager gave me a check, and he said, "I don't want this! I did it for her." But they insisted, because of legal stuff—"No, Tony, you have to take it."

John Jennings: (D.C.-area guitarist)

Chapin and I took him down to an open mic at this little club in Washington. It was pretty funny. A third of the people there really knew who he was, and they were sort of gobsmacked. And the other people got educated. "Do you have records out?" "Yeah, kinda . . ."

I worked on a record with him, *Native American*. That was fun. He had a few songs he wanted to lean in a sort of pop direction, and asked if I would come hang out and throw some ideas around. "Let's not be afraid of electric keyboards and stuff like that. Let's put a drum kit behind us and see what happens." All that works, just as long as you don't get in the way of the song. I think it was a good stretch for him.

Jerry Douglas:

Cold on the Shoulder, Me and My Guitar, and *Native American* all remind me of when Tony was so sad. He was going through some very hard times. There were times we wouldn't record at all; we would fly out to find Tony in a depression and unable to work. What would start off as a wonderful journey—the chance to play with my favorite musicians—would end in a blur of mental strife I didn't understand until I actually found myself in the same place.

Of all those records, my favorite remains *Native American.* It seems that was when he found his way out of the maze. Maybe I had gotten out, too. It all just seemed so much fun to listen to. The songs were great, his voice was strong, and his collaboration with Billy was at its peak.

Pam Rice:

Tony and I got together on September 30, 1987. I still have the ticket from that Labor Day show he played, as well as my airline ticket he purchased to fly me down two weeks later (to visit his mom, he claimed). We talked by phone—yeah, he called me all night long, every night . . . he would hang up long enough to walk the dog and call me again. I was so sleep-deprived I agreed to come to visit, thinking if I was there I might finally be able to take a nap! It is true I never left after that. We got engaged after three days and lived together for two years before I was convinced he was safe enough to marry.

Béla Fleck:

When we did *Drive,* there hadn't been an instrumental version of the sound we had when we played *Cold on the Shoulder.* The sound of that band—Sam and Tony and Jerry and me, you know? My dream was just to feel that rhythm again, the way that group played together, which was the most magic thing.

People who knew Tony would say, "He can be kind of self-destructive. He can get into a drinking thing . . ." He was always a bit difficult about rehearsing, which I found curious, because everybody I knew, with a difficult session coming up, would want to be prepared. Somehow, I got Tony to agree to let me show him some tunes in his hotel room. He got them so fast, it was almost unnecessary.

When the actual session came, we're all there—but no Tony. Sam went to the hotel and got him. When he walked into the room, it was time to play. Maybe you'd wait for him, but when he sat down in front of the mic, you were *going* for it.

The first thing we did was "Whitewater." We did a bunch of takes, and everybody liked the first one. Though people didn't really know the song, there was a groove you couldn't believe. Then we wondered, "Okay, NOW what are we gonna do?" It was two-inch tape, and it wasn't quite good enough yet.

I got Tony to go back in. He did one solo, put the guitar in the case, stood up and walked back in the control room. I was nervous, because this was gonna set the stage for the whole session. I said, "There's some really good stuff there, but would you mind giving me one or two more?" He was like, "Okay, but *why*?" He had *played* it. I imagine Miles Davis was the same way, and Charlie Parker, all these great jazz players. There was something very classy about it, but it was also frustrating. You're trying to make a great recording, and maybe the thing on the track is better than anything he's gonna overdub, but if it isn't . . . you're *stuck* with it.

Mark O'Connor:

There is one thing Tony backed me on during Béla Fleck's *Drive* recording. We just got done recording "Sanctuary." My solo at the end was done live on the keeper take. Béla wanted to make sure the solo was good enough for the album. After we listened, Béla said, "Let's start at the beginning and do the violin solo again." I said "WHAT? Are you joking!?" Tony stepped in and said, "I don't think you want to go over that, man, that's the *shit*." And we didn't. Thanks, Tony.

Mark Schatz:

Tony was not driven to keep fresh stuff in his repertoire. We would do the same thing, month after month. And then we'd have a new record come out, and we wouldn't do the stuff off the new record. It was weird. Was it artistic laziness? Or he felt like, "I can't do this stuff, with this band that's not gonna do justice to it"? I never understood.

Billy Wolf:

Native American was the last of a certain type he recorded, his last what I would call *fully creative recording* that included voice. I have a couple of tapes from a Worcester gig in '87 where you hear how great the voice was, and the following year, you can hear a bit of strain. I don't think it was diagnosed, but it was starting to show. In '87, it's starting to get a little bit of that rasp. But the '86 one is clear as a bell.

J.D. Crowe:

I noticed when we did Volume 4 of the *Bluegrass Album* [released 1985], it sounded like Tony was straining a little bit. And when we did Volume 5 [released 1989], I could definitely tell something was happening to his voice. I didn't say anything, but I could tell it. I think when he went to California, that had a big impact on him, hurting his voice. I wonder if he really even wants to sing. Tony was a picker first, and singing was secondary to him.

Doyle Lawson:

During some of the Bluegrass Album recordings we started noticing his voice would tire more easily and quicker than before. It got progressively worse. By the time we got to Volume 5, it was really getting tough.

I was devastated. I loved singing tenor to Tony's lead. I thought we had a really good blend. Our voices suit each other. And I loved it. It hurt me when he started struggling with it. I still grieve over the fact that we had to quit.

On the Road
Part 5

Hilltop Studios, Nashville

July 6, 2005: It's the second day of the Donna Hughes sessions. We turn onto a suburban road and see the sign that says HILLTOP; Tony hasn't been here before. We go up the hill to the building; a sign points to STUDIO A and another to STUDIO B, and a yellow sign at the crosswalk shows a pedestrian with an electric guitar.

Tony notices a red truck in the driveway. "Wonder who owns that F-150," he says. Scott Vestal, as it turns out. Most of the vehicles in the lot are American-made pickups.

We enter the studio and are greeted by Mike Bub, Tim Stafford, Rob Ickes, Wayne Benson, Ronnie Stewart, and Carl Jackson. Donna, a sunny, colorfully dressed blonde with an easy smile, appears after a moment and invites us to listen to the tracks she recorded earlier. As the rough tracks of her new CD play over the studio's speakers, it is clear that she is a tremendously talented songwriter. Others have noticed, too. Last year, "My Poor Old Heart," a tune on her first CD, caught the ear of Alison Krauss, who recorded it on *Lonely Runs Both Ways*. [The CD will end up winning the Grammy for Best Country Album in 2006.]

We all go into the control room, except Tony, who is still in the soundbooth with engineer Steve Chandler. Donna plays a tune on Tim's guitar. Nobody has heard it yet, but they learn it almost instantly. It's called "Where Are You Darlin'?" and it's simultaneously upbeat and wistful, a fine bluegrass tune. Shortly they decide: Scott and Wayne will do a split break after the first chorus; Ronnie and Tim will do a split break after the second.

All around the perimeter of the room there are church pews covered with power cords and equipment, and a few guests. The vocal booth is close to the control room at the end of the hall and has a tiny window through which the engineer can maintain eye contact with the vocalist. There are three closed booths—one for Ronnie on fiddle, one for Bub on bass, one for Rob and his resonator guitar. Scott Vestal is behind a plexiglass partition; Sam Bush will be, too, when he gets here.

Donna plays her song again. Tim makes a suggestion for an alternate chord at the end of the chorus. After she plays it a few times, considering it carefully, she politely says she feels it would change the tune too much. She tells a story about a friend who once helped her work out the weak spots in a song she'd been struggling with.

Ken Irwin from Rounder Records is there. "Donna?" he says. Donna interrupts her story, the smile still in her voice. "Yes, Ken?" she says cheerfully. "FOCUS!" he scolds, in a voice that raises eyebrows all over the room.

At some point, we return to the control room to listen to everybody's favorite track, "Talking to the Wind," a haunting tune about a Native American recorded during earlier sessions for this project. As the last notes fade, all of the musicians return to their posts in the studio. Donna goes to her vocal booth. Steve, the engineer, settles into one huge executive leather chair, and the other is left empty for Tony.

Donna sings the day's first track again. She gives it punch, but the punch is deteriorating. There's a break, and Tony's not in the control room yet. When he comes in, he goes straight to the boards and begins working with Steve, checking levels and getting the musicians settled.

Finally, Donna enters, quietly but visibly upset. Tony's back is turned and he does not see her. She grabs a soda from a little cooler she's brought from home. "What's wrong?" asks a friend who has accompanied her to the session. Donna is too upset to reply. She scurries out and her friend follows a moment later.

Tony fiddles with some levels and gets things settled. "Where's Donna?" he asks. Ken leaps up and goes to find her. When he returns, he says she's using the restroom and will be out shortly. Within a few minutes, she emerges and goes to her booth and begins working on the next track, but it is immediately apparent that her warm and powerful voice has been affected by her emotions. The take is flat and spiritless.

Tony listens and watches the monitors. "Hey, Donna," he says, pressing the TALK button so she'll hear him in the booth. "I don't know what's going on, but you're dropping out on the low notes here."

"I'm sorry, I'll try to do better," she says, her voice small and sad. "I've just been crying."

"Huh," he says. "Crying?"

"Yes . . ." she sniffs. "I've just been having some trouble here."

"Baby," he says, with comforting warmth in his voice, "we got all the time in the world. You just relax."

They try to get through it a couple of times, but Donna misses her cue and doesn't come in when she should, or she sings a verse when she should sing a chorus. She tries it in A and it's too high; she tries it in A flat and the instruments all sound odd to Tony's ear. Finally, he tells her to take a break. Ken has quietly left the soundbooth. Donna comes in and tearfully apologizes to Tony.

"I'm sorry," she says. "I'm not used to this pressure. Everybody's really great, but Ken keeps telling me to *focus,* and it's making me nervous. I don't know how to work like this!" She shrugs helplessly. "I've got to be able to cut up and have a little fun. I don't know how to be all serious."

"Listen, darlin', I'm here and you can just be easy," Tony says. "I'll never forget one night in the studio . . . We were working on *Native American.* Somebody showed up with a case of beer in a cooler and a bunch of reefer and we put our best tracks down at about 2 A.M. that night! So don't you worry."

Donna is goggle-eyed. "Are you gonna let her write about that in the book?" she asks, pointing at me.

"You bet, honey. Every word," he says emphatically.

With that, she goes back into the booth, ready to sing.

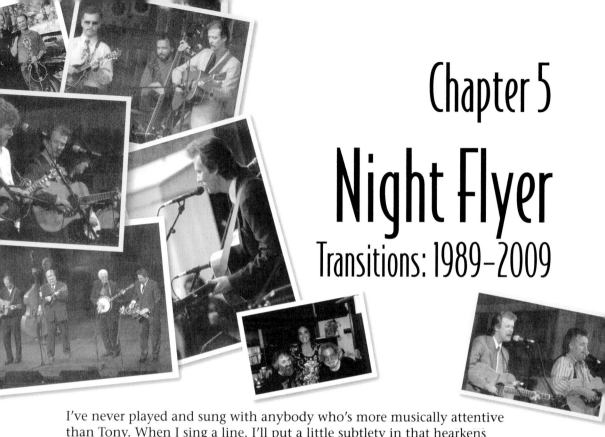

I've never played and sung with anybody who's more musically attentive than Tony. When I sing a line, I'll put a little subtlety in that hearkens back to everything we know about our bluegrass tradition, and Tony will always go, "Yeah!" He'll always, always respond to it. And that is really rare. That's what makes being onstage fun. He doesn't mail in his part!

> **Peter Rowan**, founding member of Old & In the Way;
> Rice collaborator

Tony's timing . . . that's what he really got from Clarence [White]. Somehow, he absorbed that. Tony feels it. His rhythm playing astounds me. I love his solos, but his rhythm stuff, these little subtle things he does . . . he'll play a little run in there that's just outta nowhere . . . he *swings*. That's the best thing I can say about him. He just makes the whole thing swing.

> **Chris Hillman**, original member of the Byrds; Rice collaborator

With Tony, there's so much contact and communication on the stage. The way he communicates his point to you in the middle of a song . . . it's really telepathic. He gives you that look, and you know he wants you to tear it up, or he wants you to hold back . . . or he wants you to sing . . . None of it's spoken. It's completely communicated through the feel, and the looks . . . Tony can just take over, by just being Tony. We all look to him. And he'll lead us, without a word spoken. Pretty amazing.

> **Larry Keel**, flatpick guitarist, vocalist & bandleader

Chapter 5: Introduction

Tony's deft flatpicking and ability to select and arrange diverse, interesting material helped define a trifecta of recordings he made at the end of his "Golden Era." But fans could now hear hard evidence of his diminishing vocal range on these albums. Careful listeners had perceived changes in his voice even on *Native American,* released in 1988. Tony's peers and friends who played on the same stages in clubs and on the festival circuit were all talking about it.

First came *The Bluegrass Album, Vol. 5: Sweet Sunny South,* released in 1989, which featured Tony's beloved Vassar playing twin fiddles with Bobby Hicks. *The Rice Brothers,* Tony's homey 1989 release with Larry, Ronnie, and Wyatt, included "Grapes on the Vine" by songwriter Steve Gillette, the No. 1 song in the very first *Bluegrass Unlimited* survey in 1990. On both recordings, Tony's voice, even for its flaws, was still warm and appealing.

That year also saw the release of *Blake & Rice 2,* a follow-up to the 1988 collection of duets from Tony and flatpicking/songwriting legend Norman Blake. "Georgie," with its haunting old-English melody, included a few challenging top notes that obviously took everything Tony had to deliver them. Most of the material on the Grammy-nominated *Tony Rice Plays & Sings Bluegrass* was recorded at least three years prior to its 1993 release; Tony blames allergies and sinus issues for any vocal deficiencies on that album. By the time he sang John Starling's heartbreaking ballad, "All the Way to Texas," for Rickie Simpkins' *Dancing on the Fingerboard* (released in 1997, a few years after he recorded it), Tony's voice was almost gone. Subdued and hoarse, his rendition of the tune was still extraordinarily beautiful.

That was the last vocal he recorded until he went into the studio with Chris Hillman, Herb Pedersen, and his brother Larry to record their final project (*Running Wild,* released 2001) as a quartet. Tony wasn't at all happy with the band's sound; years later he would say it was a Flying Burrito Brothers vision that did not need resurrection. He got quite drunk on the last night of the sessions, much to the dismay of Hillman and Pedersen. Late that evening, when everything for the album had been nailed, Tony approached Jon Carroll, the piano player who'd been hired for the session, and said there was one more track he'd like to record. He didn't know the lyrics by heart, but he had the CD sleeve for reference and his reading glasses. He put them on, and unsteadily at first, but with increasing confidence and obvious pleasure, he began to sing in a voice that evoked a million miles of hard road . . .

> I've seen it all, boys
> I've been all over
> Been everywhere in the
> Whole wide world
> **PONY**
> **Written by Tom Waits**

With its references to a Manzanita cross, a lost watch and chain, and an old dog curled up around the feet of a weary traveler, Tony's cover of Tom Waits' tune "Pony" would find a home as the last track on *Night Flyer,* his vocal compilation released a full decade later. It seemed a fitting epitaph for the end of his career as one of bluegrass music's most acclaimed lead singers.

He insists he does not miss his own voice. To those of us who fell asleep or in love or apart as we listened to him sing those songs, it is hard not to be incredulous at his indifference. Tony says he disliked singing onstage almost as much as he disliked *talking* onstage, and the combination of those two things was something he absolutely detested. He says he makes more money as a guitar player than he ever did as a vocalist. That does not stop him from keeping a mental list of songs he would record if he ever *did* start singing again.

The last time he sang onstage at a bluegrass festival was in Gettysburg in 1994. After that performance, Tony found it was harder and harder to get bookings for a vocal Unit led by a Tony Rice who no longer sang. He finally disbanded the group and tried to figure out how to continue making a living. Essentially, he had to repackage himself as an instrumentalist who simply did not sing. That was something he'd done when he'd taken a job with David Grisman's non-vocal group in 1975, but now Tony was a free agent. It was *his* voice and guitar playing that defined the sound of the Tony Rice Unit, and now half of that sound was gone.

Since '94, Tony has appeared as an instrumentalist on dozens and dozens of recordings. He recorded *River Suite for Two Guitars* with John Carlini, his old mentor from the Dawg years. He's made a half-dozen well-received instructional videos for Happy Traum's Homespun Tapes. He's toured extensively with his buddy Peter Rowan, playing "that Mexican bluegrass," as he calls it, and made two recordings with Rowan, the second even better than the first. He's done some interesting tours, including a few dates of a *Manzanita*-themed show, playing material from his timeless classic with the guys who had originally helped him record it.

In 2007 he did a very special tour with Alison Krauss and Union Station. As images from high points in his life and career projected on big screens in the background, the members of Union Station, every one of them a self-professed Rice fanatic, joined Tony in playing his music in the ultimate retrospective tribute. He continues to work with bands like Mountain Heart and Larry Keel & Natural Bridge. His own Tony Rice Unit, which he resurrected as an instrumental ensemble in 2003, only seems to get better with each new configuration. As of 2010, Josh Williams sits in a lot, and since Josh is a superb vocalist as well as an award-winning guitarist, it only makes sense to let him sing a few of those great old tunes.

But the swift river of time only flows in one direction. As Tony ages, and as his hands and joints and back and bones begin to weaken under the tremendous strain of the tasks he has demanded of them since he started playing guitar, he once again finds it necessary to reinvent himself. Instead of a powerhouse, lightning-fast guitarist, he becomes a master of nuance. Instead of the pioneer of a new sound, he becomes the lion in winter, watching with bemusement as the kids gather at his feet to learn his tricks as building blocks for the techniques they will eventually develop on their own.

He is also trying to adjust to the recording industry, as it, too, scrambles to reinvent itself. Music sales continue to follow a trend that shows no sign of changing: digital sales are up, physical unit sales are down, and overall revenue continues to plummet.

These are unsettling days for recording artists, but high-quality live acoustic music is still a hot commodity. Tony Rice continues to make his living as a touring musician, driving himself to all of his own gigs, working with Rowan, Keel, Mountain Heart, and his own always-spectacular Unit, making music that sounds good and brings in a paycheck. The road takes its toll, but he's figured out how to make it work for him; he's made an uneasy peace with his hands and has found ways to hide any shortcomings, and he knows how to get through a show.

In spite of what he has lost, he still has much to offer. There is a lot of damn good music left in those hands.

"Nobody," he says, "has complained so far."

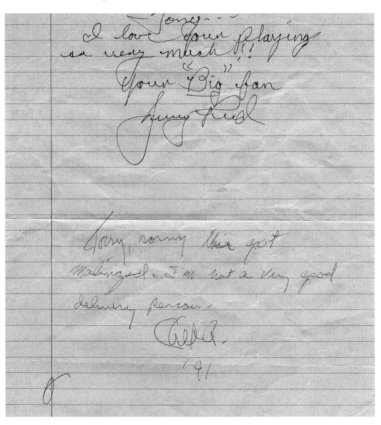

1991 note from Jerry Reed via Chet Atkins. *(Courtesy of Pam Rice)*

*"Tony - - -
I love your playing so very much!!
Your 'Big' fan
Jerry Reed"*

*"Tony, sorry this got malingered. I'm
not a very good delivery person.
Chet A.
'91."*

I was as impressed by his singing as his playing. The words were so clear. The tone was so nice. Kinda like a bluegrass Sinatra. It was a real loss (for bluegrass) when he lost his voice. Almost like someone died.

Phil Leadbetter, resonator guitarist and former member of the New South

I was at some of the first Unit shows when he wasn't singing anymore and it was tough. I often thought what courage it took to do that. Most football players leave the field when something like this happens, never to return.

Kenny Smith, Virginia guitarist and Rice protégé

In His Own Words: Tony's Story

In the fall of '89 I had surgery. I'd had a deviated septum since childhood, from jumping out of a crib. I had only one open nostril. John Starling is a fanatic about wanting to fix faces that are not lined up the right way . . . He kept poking at me for years, saying, "When are you gonna let me fix that?" Finally, I said, "Let's do it."

It happened at the local clinic [in Fredericksburg, VA where Starling had his surgical practice], but I stayed at his house for two or three days and did everything I was supposed to do, and then I had the surgery. The next few days were spent being driven around town with John Starling, barhopping, with my eyes all black!

My nose was certainly better. It used to be very conspicuous. I used to turn my head to the left when I was photographed. It's still crooked now, but it's not near as bad as it was.

The voice deterioration started before the nasal surgery, in maybe 1988. It was al-ready in the works. And I know why. By nature, I'm not a tenor singer, but that's what I ended up doing. No matter what it took to get that high lonesome sound, I was singing *way* out of my natural range.

Do that long enough, and the dam is gonna break. All through my career, I found a way to tighten up the right muscles and squeeze down on those vocal cords enough to achieve the desired result. With the aging process, it reached the point where the muscles started to protest. It wasn't painful. It was uncomfortable at times. On rare occasions, I'd open my mouth and sing, and it came out naturally.

I was in Dayton in 1990 and I got pulled over and arrested for DUI one night and Red Allen came and got me out of jail. I bailed myself out; I had money, but I needed a character reference from somebody and Red knew the local law enforcement people down there, and a good lawyer . . .

Tony and Red Allen at Doyle Lawson's festival in 1989. (Photo by Pam Rice)

Before we went in to see the judge, I was really worried, wondering if I was gonna have to go stay in jail for 30 days. Red looked at me and said, "How long has it been since you shaved?" I said, "Red, it's probably been two or three days." He said, [*imitating Red's slow twangy drawl*] "Well, get in there and shave. You look like a fuckin' bum."

Six weeks later the lawyer called and said the officer had written the ticket wrong. I was charged, but I was never convicted.

I think the Rice Brothers albums turned out tenfold better than I had initially thought they would. They were kind of hard to do, but in the long run, I'm glad we did 'em. There's some good moments on *both* those albums. But there's just some level of musical incompatibility there. The four of us grew in different directions.

Steve Gillette wrote "Grapes on the Vine." I heard him do it when I was doing the first Homespun video for Happy

Traum in the mid-'80s. Steve and his lady friend were staying with Happy and Jane in Woodstock, NY. We'd play tunes at night after dinner, sitting around. Steve knew Larry from L.A. when he played with Aunt Dinah's Quilting Party. He started playing all these tunes, and I said, "Steve, I'm always looking for good material. Send me some stuff in the mail." He did. And it was laying around for years. I drug out this cassette and played it, looking for material, and lo and behold, there was "Grapes on the Vine."

Lightfoot sent "Let It Ride" to me in the mail, and "East of Midnight," a then-unrecorded great tune which I've always wanted to do. Lightfoot played that to me in a hotel room one night. He was playing me tunes he wanted me to do, that he had either written a long time ago or that he just didn't do for whatever reason.

My brother Larry and I had a good time doing *Hurricanes & Daydreams* [1986]. That was a real good-spirited thing. I liked his tune "Mr. Poverty" well enough to do it on *my* album [*California Autumn*, 1975]. And I've recorded some other things Larry wrote: "If You Only Knew," a tune called "About Love . . ." A lot of his music is personal to him on a real deep level a lot of people wouldn't understand. He wrote some tunes that *I* don't understand. We kinda grew up with separate ideals and goals as musicians. It carried over into the Rice, Rice, Hillman & Pedersen albums.

Some people are not meant to lead the life of a professional musician. Larry was one of them. He didn't have the wherewithal it takes to do that. But he still had the music in his soul, so once in a while, he got an urge to do a recording.

We didn't see each other much. Maybe once or twice a year, Larry would come up, or I was in Florida and I'd meet up with him. But that's not to say we weren't close. All of us were close. It's just sometimes with siblings, that closeness is unspoken.

Plays and Sings Bluegrass came out two or three years after it was recorded. I thought, "I want this album to be vocal-oriented, but I want that sound we captured on *Home of the Red Fox.*"

What's remarkable about that album is Bill Emerson. Man, banjo players ought to listen to that real close. That was the first time Duffey and Emerson had been in the studio together since the 1950s. Duffey and I were hanging out on a regular basis and talking about resurrecting a couple old Country Gentlemen things, and "Galveston Flood" ended up being one of them. "Girl from the North Country" was an old Gentlemen tune, although the version I ended up doing was more influenced by Dylan.

Hylo Brown was on Capitol, and my father had a 45-rpm single with "I've Waited as Long as I Can" on one side and "Thunderclouds of Love" on the other side. That's where they came from. I wanted to do "On and On" because this was a bluegrass album and

that tune is just about as bluegrass as you can get. "Ain't Nobody Gonna Miss Me," that's right off of Martin's second album.

Sam wanted to do "Will You Be Loving Another Man." He started imitating Lester Flatt singing. I said, "Roll that tape!" We were almost laughing our way through it.

It was just whatever tune and whoever was available. I wasn't worried about how long it would take or who I was going to have on it. I concentrated a long time on the first six cuts we did with Emerson. I thought that was some of the best bluegrass I'd done in ages.

I was already having problems with my voice, in a different kind of way. It was more allergy and sinus-related problems. In some of the songs on *Plays and Sings Bluegrass* you can hear a different tone in

Sam Bush, Tony, Béla Fleck at MerleFest.
(Photo courtesy Tony Rice)

the voice. It wasn't anything to do with the vocal chords or anything.

When Leela and I broke up in 1984, I tried to stay in my house in San Francisco by myself and fight out the memories and all that shit. I could only do that so long, and then I had to get on a plane and go back to Florida and be with my family. My father hadn't been deceased that long. I went back and forth between both places, and in the summer of '85 I lucked out on a real nice place on the river in Florida. And I lived there until the flood in 1993.

I don't think the storm had a name, because it wasn't a hurricane. Usually you associate floodwaters like that with a hurricane in Florida, but it wasn't. It was just an intense tropical storm that happened to coincide with an extreme lunar tide.

In the middle of the night I woke up and heard water sloshing. It wasn't in the house yet. I said, "What the hell is this?" I went to open the door and it was about an inch away from coming in the house. Because it was only a tropical storm, I thought the tide would go back out any second. I called the Coast Guard. They said, "As a matter of fact, it's gonna get real bad. Where you live, at the very mouth of the river where the springs are, we're predicting it's gonna be anywhere from three to five feet." It turned out to be right at five feet.

Mom went with the Coast Guard. I put quite a few things of value up a few feet, thinking, "Oh, well, they'll be okay." Photographs and records and stuff like that . . . and the Antique (Tony's nickname for his 1935 D-28 Herringbone). I was trying to

get the boat somewhere where it would be okay. My dog Pokey and I left in the boat. I thought the water wasn't gonna get that high.

Well, I missed the call.

I'd had the Florida place before Pam and I got together, so it was our primary home. We had a place up here in North Carolina as an alternate. Very few people are fortunate enough that when they have one place instantly wiped out, they have another one to go to.

The only good reel-to-reel machine I had got lost in the flood. Stuff got totally submerged—masters, multi-tracks to the *Manzanita* album, all that. The first thing I tried to clean up worked: outtakes from *Me and My Guitar* that didn't make it on the album. One tune, "Whispers of the North," already came out on the Lightfoot compilation. "Never Meant to Be" was an outtake from *Me and My Guitar* and its only version was on a real good rough that was in the flood, as was the tune Larry wrote called "About Love." [Both were released in 2008 on *Night Flyer*.] Billy Wolf made the audio on them sound amazing.

I'm sure there's a lot of stuff in my archives that got in the flood and could be restored. It's a nightmare. All the labeling got washed away. You open boxes and the only thing you see is white mold. And you don't know what's there. And if you don't clean it, you can destroy a machine by just threading it up and playing it.

In 1993, in the middle of a Unit set, I told Jimmy he was gonna have to finish singing the remainder of the set. We played

Jimmy Gaudreau, Ronnie Simpkins, Tony onstage at MerleFest.
(Courtesy Tony Rice)

some instrumentals and completed the set. That's when I knew my days as a singer were probably over. The last time I sang onstage at a bluegrass event was at Gettysburg in 1994. I'd had voice deterioration happening for two or three years. In the middle of a set, it got so bad I couldn't go on. I had no control over pitch *or anything*. And that was it. There were a few isolated things after that where I sang and I could barely get through. Occasionally Jimmy did the vocal stuff. We did a lot of instrumentals. We just didn't do as many gigs. I don't remember a lot of that period.

A few times since then, back in the late '90s, 2000, and 2001, I was brave enough to sing baritone with Peter Rowan and Bryn Davies on "White Dove" at some hippie fest . . . It was always good, too. I only did that at select events. I was always afraid of getting a rumor started . . . "Tony's getting

his voice back! Listen to that three-part harmony." I didn't want that.

But I've since recorded "Pony." I mean, if you can call that singing. Even Bob Dylan would listen to that and say, "Man, that guy sings *rough.*" I heard the tune on a record of Tom Waits, *Mule Variations.* I thought, "I don't give a shit if I ain't got a voice or not; I'm gonna do this tune." And it was recorded when Larry, Chris, Herb, and I were doing the last album, *Runnin' Wild.* It was at the end of that session, and I threw the tune out; everybody knew I was gonna do it while they took a break. I said, "I'm gonna do this tune as a novelty . . . I ain't got a voice, but I think I can growl it out. And after it's all over with, if you want to put it on the album, you can. If you don't, hey, I understand. Maybe it'll get released a few years down the line." Which it did [in *Night Flyer,* 2008]. The combination of those lyrics, and the way Jon Carroll played it on the piano . . . it's almost like whoever had sung it wouldn't have mattered, whether it had been Enrico Caruso or Bill Monroe.

I never liked to sing anyway, man. I always saw it as a distraction from what I wanted to do best, which was play the guitar. With me, one always interfered with the other, *real* bad. There were two things I hated to do onstage. One was sing; the other was to talk to my audience.

People were like, "Oh, what's happened to his voice?" It's not really that mysterious. If you use it incorrectly, it will wear out. The best I remember is it took a while before I went to a doctor about it, maybe even a year. Because it didn't bother me that I couldn't sing, not one iota. If I could sing now, would I? *Yeah, I would.* Would I structure a Unit album and/or live shows around vocals? *No, I would not.* I wouldn't want to do that.

It was unremarkable, the transition from being primarily a vocalist to being a guitar player. I don't remember any moment where I was *one,* and then the *other.* But I've been more active, and I've been paid more money, as a guitar player than when I was singing.

Oscar Peterson had the most amazing voice of any jazz singer in the idiom, but he never felt comfortable singing. George Benson, my favorite guitar player, is also an amazing singer. George Benson does not like to sing, so now he's a jazz guitar player.

You know what's really weird? You listen to early Bill Monroe, and how amazing he was, when Bill and Charlie sung together in the early years of bluegrass. Even when Martin was with him, Monroe really nailed it. But sometime in the '50s, Monroe just wore out as a singer. The records prove it: *the voice wore out, and it never recovered.* It wasn't that long into his professional career, maybe two or three decades, that some of his recordings started sounding *atrociously* bad. And there were times, after the '50s, when he sang on occasion, but the last few decades of his life, he was vocally a mere shadow of what he was once capable of doing.

My vocal history is very well-documented, in terms of ultra high-quality audio recordings available to anybody at any time. I did an awful lot of singing in the period spanning a little over 20 years. Most musicians only dream of being able to sing such a diverse repertoire.

Once in a while, I wish I had a voice so I could express myself poetically . . . but it's not enough for me to pursue voice restoration. My two speech therapists in Florida have no doubt that my voice could be restored, but it would mean a regimen of moving there and talking to nobody but them for months.

Maybe I'll get back to it at some point. If I want to do it bad enough, I'll pursue it. I can make it come back if I think about it. It's just real hard. The muscles have atrophied, and they have to be retrained.

I don't know what the future holds. I have no idea.

Tone Poems [released in 1994] was really work. I can't just switch instruments.

It's very rare I pick up somebody else's instrument and get anything out of it, and all of a sudden I was faced with all these different guitars. There was only one instrument that I was familiar with, and all the rest of 'em were foreign.

The bulk of it was done in one sitting. A few months later, I flew to California and we completed it. Grisman bought out all the equipment from the old Arch Street Studio in Berkeley, where so much of the classic stuff was done—*Manzanita,* the first three Bluegrass Album volumes; *Skaggs & Rice,* all that stuff. He bought the equipment—the console, tape machines, outboard gear, the whole nine yards—and reconstructed the studio in his giant house. It was almost like recording there again.

The stuff we did on *Tone Poems* was done direct to two-track. Some of those axes came from a vintage instrument retailer in Carmel named Dexter Johnson. Grisman and Dexter were friends and they decided to collaborate and find the instruments. Other than my own axe, the instrument I had the most fun with was the *cheapest* vintage instrument. It was a black painted guitar called a Diamond, with dice inlaid in the fingerboard.

We only had to do one tune for *Tone Poems* at the last session. At some point, somebody suggested that the only thing missing was what we currently were using as *new* instruments. Grisman said, "Hey, to make it complete, can you bring your Santa Cruz?"

My Santa Cruz was very new at the time. It sounded *amazing.* The idea was to show the music world that a good axe doesn't have to be a half-million-dollar vintage instrument of some kind to make you sound good!

The idea was also to present the sound of the instruments in state-of-the art *analog,* just for the purity of it: direct to analog tape, with minimal outboard equipment used in the process to keep it pure.

It turned out good, I think. It certainly was an interesting concept. It worked, because it's still selling, and it was Grisman's best-selling album on his own label, although by now, it's probably been exceeded by *The Pizza Tapes.*

We got together with Garcia the second time I went out to finish *Tone Poems. The Pizza Tapes* were pretty much just a jam session. We got together and just recorded it all as a party. The mics were set up, we could hear each other really good in the room, and it was just conducive to being able to play together, with headphones and echo and all that stuff. We started playing and it was so fun we didn't want to stop. We recorded everything. Garcia was having a ball.

It had been a few years since Grisman and Garcia had started hanging out. I think Garcia had been sober for a number of years. I had met him before, but that was the first and only time we played music together. He had a reputation for not liking a whole lot of guitar players. He had a handful of favorites, and I just happened to be one of them.

Pam was there. She took the picture that ended up being on the inside of the tray card of the CD. There wasn't hardly anybody else there: David, and Dexter Johnson, and Garcia's wife. It was just kind of a *party.* You can actually hear that on the CD, that it wasn't slated to be a proper, defined album, constructed from the start.

Garcia had to have a memory like a calculator to have known all those tunes. I have no reason to believe he would have been in any kind of environment to have sung them for years and years. But Garcia's like a lot of other rock musicians that came out of bluegrass. They were bluegrass musicians before they were anything else.

There was a lot of mystique in his voice. It was really genuine. He was born and raised in California, and he was like a library of ancient mountain tunes. And he sang with an authenticity that was unbelievable.

David Grisman, Tony, and Jerry Garcia in Berkeley, CA, February 1993, during the sessions for The Pizza Tapes.
(Photo by Pam Rice)

Garcia said, "Hey, I want this stuff; make me a copy." I think Grisman made him a DAT, a digital audio tape. The story I heard was that Garcia left it at his house on the counter. The pizza delivery guy saw it, snatched it, and it was gone! And all of a

sudden, it spread like the plague, and there were third and fourth generation cassette copies floating around everywhere. Grisman finally said, "As long as it's already out there, I might as well give 'em the real thing in high fidelity."

I'm pretty sure that session with Garcia was recorded in January or February of '93. It was in the can for years. [*The Pizza Tapes* was released in April 2000.] The main thing I remember was that we were just having a good time. Garcia still had two vices: reefer and cigarettes . . . I had my Coors Golden, and the reefer . . . and Grisman probably smokes more reefer than anybody I've ever known, on a daily basis.

River Suite for Two Guitars . . . We talked about it ever since Carlini and I met, as just a raw, naked album. We recorded a lot of stuff in Florida in '92 and we liked the way most of it turned out. So we got together here in North Carolina and re-did a lot of the stuff. We recorded *River Suite for Two Guitars* in my listening room with a single Audiotechnica AT825 microphone plugged directly into the mic inputs of a Sony DAT machine. More often than not, Carlini and I had played together in somebody's house, or a hotel room. We thought since there was only the two of us, why not do this as simply as we could? Why not go back to the roots of stereo recording: just hang a mic between us and play? That's the way the album was made.

Carlini and I played at the Turning Point in New York. And these rich people hired us to come up to this little town in extreme southwestern North Carolina. It

Tony and John Carlini recording River Suite.
(Courtesy John Carlini)

was this giant house with a giant living room, a private thing, and they just invited all their friends. They set up mics and a little sound system. We might have played a couple other gigs. Carlini likes doing that more than I do, because he pushes real hard. He's the kind of guy who would say, "Well, c'mon man, we did this 20 years ago. I know you remember this." Some jazz tune with five million chords that look like this *[his fingers bend into a painful contortion].* Man, I can't remember that stuff.

To this day, if I do a session with somebody, I request that they write out the chords instead of numbers, because I don't relate to a number. That throws me for a loop, when I see a number coming at me. I just haven't done it enough.

The first Rice, Rice, Hillman & Pedersen record happened because of Larry and Chris. From childhood, they had played together, and Herb Pedersen was on the scene. Those guys were right out of high school, but they were just bluegrass fanatics.

Those three voices are almost like

magic in terms of the harmonies. Herb and Larry and Chris singing together could do no wrong. What I wanted was to assemble that band—Larry, Chris, Herb, I, a bass player and Flux—and roll that tape—not "produce" anything, just do it live and let those voices sing.

The conflict was Larry and Chris and Herb. The vision they had for that album, and the second one, too, was from the Flying Burrito Brother days. That's where they were coming from, musically. The results were something that had already been done.

I'm convinced to this day if we had just done an all-acoustic, simplified thing, those albums would have ten times the impact. By the time *Running Wild* came out, I felt like a fly on the wall, just sitting there playing a few guitar fills and a solo here and there. I didn't want to do it. If they were willing to just approach it a different way and simplify it, it would have been much better.

The Unit played its last date at the Birchmere on January 1, 1996. At that point, that band had been together close to eleven years, with one personnel change: Mark Schatz left after five years and then Ronnie Simpkins joined in '88 or '89. Rickie Simpkins had played on and off with the Unit, and the band he was in folded, so he jumped onboard full-time.

I'm very proud of *Unit of Measure*. But it happened to come along at a time when there wasn't really a place for it. I wanted to do it because that band had never gone in as a band and done an album. Maybe it was a day late and a dollar short, in spite of how good it is.

It was done in two different sessions in '96 and '97, not counting the live tune, which was done in '92. Why did it take so long to release? I don't know. I've done that before with records, ever since *Manzanita*: record something and then deliberately stay away from it for a while. Long enough so when I approach it again, it sounds fresh to me.

There's a couple of tunes where the arrangement was done on the fly, like "Jerusalem Ridge" and "House of the Rising Sun." Those arrangements were not written out or anything. I think that proved you don't have to have long discussions, write out chord charts or anything like that.

I don't mean any disrespect for bands that need to do that, because with some music forms it's a necessity. I'm just not one that ever wanted to do it. I think I inherited that from Crowe. He said, "You only ever talk about any of that if there's a need to. Otherwise, here's a piece of music. Play it!"

There's a line in an amazing tune by Cheryl Wheeler about an old couple . . . "They speak across the garden, and not a soul can tell . . ." I'm sure that old couple was having a conversation as intimately as you and I are right now, but they weren't speaking. Musicians have that. It's an intuitive thing.

I worked on "Shenandoah" for a couple of years before I recorded it. I wanted to bring a beauty to it that had never been

MerleFest (L-R): Tony, Peter Rowan, Tim O'Brien, Jerry Douglas.
(Courtesy Tony Rice)

there before. Then I heard a big choir sing it . . . it was absolutely breathtaking to hear all those voices with that much precision and vocal pitch in the parts. The chords formed by all those voices would bring tears to a rhinestone.

And I like that version of *Manzanita* ten to one better than I do the original cut.

There is something that's kept me playing with Peter Rowan since 1998. It's a freedom. When it's good, it's real good. The tunes are good, the music has spontaneity—it's never boring, never repetitious.

I'm really proud of *Quartet*. It's got some amazing stuff on it. I like it a hundredfold better than the first one [*You Were There for Me*]. There's nobody on it but the Quartet, no guest artists. All the tracks are live. We went back to Bias with Billy Wolf again. Peter was singing better than he ever has. Good original material and a couple of Monroe things.

Peter and I started working together in late '97 or early '98. And that's kinda what I've been doing ever since. I hear the comments people make: "Oh, I'd rather hear Tony in another format." I've enjoyed it enough to hang in there and keep doing it. It's an easy gig. More often than not, that band sounds real good.

Almost invariably, we start a show with "Panama Red." Every time I start playing that solo, it's different. Yeah, it's absolutely fine with me that we do that, and then move on to "Midnight Moonlight" or something. Peter's constantly coming up with new stuff. There's never a dull moment.

I missed Bryn when she toured with Patty Griffin in 2007, because we were just a pair when it comes to the rhythm section. Over the years, we evolved into a rhythm section that was really special and intuitive. Nobody can blame Bryn for wanting to move on. I'm sure there were times when she missed that sound we created. She liked the moments when the rhythm section was cooking.

Of late, Mike Bub usually plays bass with the Quartet, although Bryn did play one date with us recently. We got in a situation where we didn't have a bass player and she was available. Mark Schatz has also done a couple of dates with us.

I started doing isolated dates with an instrumental version of the Unit about two years after the vocal Unit's last show at the Birchmere. Usually it was me and Wyatt and Ronnie and Rickie Simpkins. I missed playing instrumental music with that particular rhythm section. Bryn is now working with us again. The only other bass player the Unit has had in the last two or three years has been Tim Surrett.

Josh Williams is also working with the Unit—that's Wyatt, myself, and Bryn, and either Rickie or Josh or both, and sometimes Rob Ickes. I think it's the best Unit I've ever had. It's a vocal Unit; Josh is a great singer. We're doing a bunch of stuff from *Manzanita* and *Cold on the Shoulder* and *Me and My Guitar*. When Josh and Bryn and Rickie sing harmony, man, that's really good. It's good for me, because I get to stand there and play guitar and listen to it . . . hell, I don't even have to play rhythm if I don't want to; Wyatt can do that. I can just noodle around.

In 1997, I was almost home, a quarter mile from my house near a golf course, and I had swerved to miss a deer, or what I thought was a deer, and the road was wet . . . I ended up with the car upside down in the creek. It banged me up pretty bad, a few broken bones, and blood coming outta my nose and my mouth and one of my ears . . . Shoulder bone fractured, and broken ribs and collarbone broke all to hell . . . I was hospitalized for only a few days. That was the same year Pam had quadruple bypass heart surgery.

I quit drinking on May 29, 2001. I don't think it had negative influence on my playing until about the last year and a half. I would keep myself in check and then it reached that point where I was so bored with music that I didn't want to play with anybody on a stage unless I could get half shit-faced. If I wasn't drinking, I had no use to be around a bunch of people. I just didn't feel comfortable.

And then it reached the point where I said, "I don't want to be drunk anymore." So I just quit drinking.

I was never the guy that stayed drunk every day for 15 years. I never had DTs, was never hospitalized for alcohol treatment or anything like that. The *last* time I quit drinking, I'd drunk enough that I got scared. I think it was the realization of how many bottles of beer I had consumed in a 24-hour period. There's people out there that can drink a case of beer a day, but for me, it just wasn't working anymore. It was that simple.

So I went to the hospital and my doctor said, "Yeah, you've had too much to drink.

I want to keep you here and observe you for a few hours." And he did, and he sent me home, and said, "Go home; don't drink."

I started to be aware of heavy drinking when Leela and I were separated. It was getting to be something I was doing to excess. But I was conscious enough of it to keep it separate from my career. I guess it got in high gear for a while when I moved to Florida. But it wasn't drinking away depression or anything; it was just drinking to feel good.

It got consistently bad around '97 or '98. It was short-lived, that chapter. But I had to go through that to get to the point where I didn't want to do it anymore. I was starting to show up drunk at gigs I didn't give a shit about. If there was a damn good gig, and I thought it was important, and the pay scale was fair, then I would show up dead on the money, be serious and deliberate, and put in a good performance. The gigs I felt otherwise, it would have been a hit or a miss whether I played good or not. Some of 'em, I played bad.

But the last time around, I started to really enjoy the sobriety and how that had changed my outlook on life in general. It changed it enough that I decided to latch onto it. And I've been latched onto it ever since. I know one thing: there isn't a damn thing going on in my life right now that a drunk wouldn't make *worse*.

What's amazing to see . . . I've witnessed this firsthand: Some of my peers look at me, and various other people who, for one reason or another, have decided to quit alcohol or drug use or whatever, and they're taking a different view of themselves as a result. See what I'm saying? It rubs off on somebody else automatically. I'm not talking about things that are benign, like reefer, or people that are able to drink beer and control it. I'm talking about people that have a serious problem with either alcohol or drugs.

John Cowan said it best. He said, "It's only a problem if it's a *problem.*" And that's *it.* That would be the best way for anybody to assess if they're consuming too much alcohol, or using too many drugs, or whatever they're doing. It's only a problem if it's a *problem.*

For the past ten years, Alison Krauss has been my favorite artist. Within the range of my own genre, whenever I really want to hear precision music, I'll listen to her.

The tour with Alison was something she wanted to do for a while. I think the forces behind it were Jerry Douglas and Ron Block. The way it was first put to me was that it would take the form of a couple of isolated dates. It started to grow real fast. I think somebody realized the potential after the first couple of dates *sold out,* almost overnight, by word of mouth!

On the tour, I used an in-ear monitor

L-R: Gospel artist Buddy Greene; Jay Orr of the Country Music Hall of Fame; Earl Scruggs; Alison Krauss; Jerry Douglas; Tony Rice. (Photo by Donn Jones)

fitted by Cliff Miller at SE Systems—that's Alison's sound crew in Greensboro. All the members of Union Station use them, rather than monitors on the floor, and they talked me into it. The last time I had used one was in Colorado in maybe 2000 . . . me and Béla and Sam and Flux and Stuart Duncan did a gig in an amphitheater, and they were trying monitors where you have one little headphone in one ear. I got through a couple tunes, but it was just too confusing. I said, "Enough! I'm taking this thing *out.*"

But it's a whole different world now. They make a mold of your outer and middle ears, all the way up to the eardrum. They send that mold off to a company that makes a real high-quality transducer mounted in this rubbery stuff that's in exact conformity to your own ear. They're, like, seven hundred bucks.

There was a bunch of stuff Alison was dying to do, where she'd take the lead vocal. She sent me a list of those ideas, and then another list of stuff Dan Tyminski would be singing. The first list had "Urge for Going," "Night Flyer," "Four Strong Winds," "Early Morning Rain," "Church Street Blues," "Shadows," "I Think It's Gonna Rain Today," "Any Old Time," "Song for a Winter's Night," "Sixteen Miles," "The Last Thing on My Mind," "Pride of Man." And for Dan to sing, she had "Cold on the Shoulder," "Likes of Me," "Orphan Annie," "Ten Degrees," "You Don't Know My Mind," "Age," "Muleskinner Blues," "Freeborn Man," "On My Way Back to the Old Home," "Greenlight on the Southern," and "Ginseng Sullivan." She had Cliff load a bunch of stuff

into an iPod, hundreds of tunes, just ideas. What we wanted, by the end of the rehearsals in mid-April 2007, was a list of about 25 tunes everybody felt confident doing. That was more than enough to do a fairly entertaining show.

That musical format was a more tightly run ship than any I've probably ever worked in. Even with Grisman . . . it was arranged, but there was still that improvisational freedom, as much as you wanted, for the most part. With Krauss, tunes were arranged in terms of orders of solos, and who backs up *this* verse, and who backs up *that* verse . . . You know *my* technique on that shit . . . just give a nod to whoever you want

Old Home Place *reunion at IBMA 2003 (L-R): Tony, Bobby Slone, Ricky Skaggs, J.D. Crowe, Jerry Douglas. (Courtesy Pam Rice)*

to come in next. If somebody's singing a verse and there's a hole, then somebody jump in and fill it up. Whoever gets there first gets to have it for at least eight bars.

This was like harkening back to the days of the New South. That band was a well-oiled machine. There was a formula for almost everything, and it really wasn't a bummer to adhere to it. You had a repertoire of tunes with a particular arrangement, and you played the solos like you did on the original recording. That's Krauss' thing. She's a commercial artist, and a commercial artist basically has to go out and keep the material pretty consistent. Their audiences are conditioned to think they don't want spontaneity. They think they want to hear an exact replica of what they hear on the radio, note for note. Her audience is 180 degrees opposite of a John Coltrane-type audience. A Coltrane audience—or a Tony Rice Unit audience—can't *wait* to see what's gonna happen next. They want it to be a surprise.

The older I get, the more and more I drift toward improvisational freedom and music that's not structured. It's almost like you're playing it, and listening to it played back at you, at the same time. You don't know what's coming next, not even out of yourself.

There was a period of about a year where Alison worked a *lot* of dates with the Unit, so she knew the gist of my musical convictions, and that I'm a musician that has to work *in the moment*. I can only go so far, in terms of being able to adhere to a real strict format of *any* kind before I start feeling trapped.

Whenever I thought it was starting to get complicated, I told everybody, "Look, show me my microphone, turn it on, and I'll do the rest! I'm gonna be doing what I've been doing for 35 years. The curtain is gonna go up, somebody's gonna call my name, and I'm gonna walk out there with

my guitar and try to create music. The other stuff? To me, that shit is *details.*

The biggest challenge was having to go back through my memory bank and try to remember some of the tunes I hadn't done for 15 or 20 years. There were a couple things I had *never* done outside of the studio.

It was all great. It was one of the best musical collaborations I've had in many, many years with anybody, playing with that band, and having some of those old tunes resurrected. It sure sounded better hearing HER singing 'em than it did hearing ME singing 'em! I don't think I'd do anything differently. All those shows were so good. They were amazing.

Night Flyer, my new vocal compilation, has been out for a while now. I don't know how it's doing. When a statement comes to me from the record label, I can't figure it out; more than half of it is not retail CDs. More than half is downloads of XM and Sirius radio and whatever they play on satellite TV, and stuff like that. It's usually a couple hundred pages. But I only look at the first one, the total amount due to the artist, with the check attached to it.

The last song I wrote was "Never Meant to Be," in 1985. That appears on *Night Flyer.* I've written one instrumental since then. Carlini transcribed it right after I wrote it; the Unit played it live a few times. It's called "Wacahoota Station," after an old train depot in Florida. An instrumental, up-tempo bluegrass kind of thing. I don't even know how to play it anymore. But other than that, I haven't done anything but freelance and play Mexican-style bluegrass [with Peter Rowan].

I have played on a couple of Béla's records since *Drive.* He hires me because he wants me to come in and do whatever I want to do. There have been some other good sessions. The Donna Hughes stuff turned out good. I produced two albums for the Isaacs and played on them, and that's some good playing. I produced some stuff for Karen Peck. It's been real spontaneous over the last few years.

I've worked with Larry Keel some. . . . I like working with Larry. Those wild moonshine reefer hippies . . . man, it's really loose! That's the way I like it nowadays. And playing with Mountain Heart is like playing with a locomotive. We've done quite a few shows, and it's really been successful. Anytime they want, I'll do it. And their mandolin player is so good, he's *off the scales.* He's a young guy, about 21 or 22; his name's Aaron Ramsey. He's doing an album soon, and I've gotta go do some stuff on it.

Other than that, I'm going to devote as much time as I can to putting everything in motion for the documentary. A guy named Tim Cowling is filming a documentary on me and my old D-28. It's going well; the contract is fixing to be closed. . . . John Carter Cash is involved, and I believe Robert Duvall is doing part of the narration.

I've been involved in so many different projects and recordings. There've been countless numbers of career highs. It happens at gigs where everything is gelling just right. As a professional musician, I live for

those moments when you're sharing the stage with good musicians and something is so good that it raises the hair up all over your body. And you can feel it from the audience, and you know it's raising the hair up all over *their* bodies too. You can feel something during those moments. Whatever mental or physical afflictions you may have, in those moments where you're that *elated,* somehow you can feel a wash of something running through your body in a process of healing.

It's all changing so fast I can't keep up with it anymore. I've still got bluegrass in the veins . . . I love to play it, but it's got to be right on. It's got to have that *feel.* The confidence factor is something that comes and goes. But there's other times I know what my musicianship is worth. I know what it's worth when it's on, and I know what it's worth when it *ain't* on. A lot of musicians don't know the value of their musicianship. I do. And as an ensemble player, whether it's going to be good or not is contingent on the situation I happen to be in.

It was certainly not intentional that I would become a model for musicians on the guitar. Isn't it weird how for so many years, I was notorious for being a lightning-fast, powerhouse D-28 player? And the last few years, what really gets people off is to hear a solo version of "Shenandoah." That's sending me a message. I've got physical disabilities that may or may not ever correct themselves. Some of them will not. So, in order for me to sustain my craft, I've got to change it, to alter it in a way I approve of, and with the hopes that my audience will also approve. So far, the most radical alteration is concentrating on different elements of musicianship than just being that powerhouse lightning-fast player.

Right now, there's probably at least ten guitar players out there that can play circles around me at my own shit, with much better precision and articulation. So I've gotta throw 'em a curveball. And I'm gonna do it, if I live long enough. I will really throw their asses a curve. Just play a little slower and laid-back, things that are real melodic and pretty, where any idiot can hear every nuance coming out of that old antique instrument.

It's already there, especially on the most recent recordings I've done with Peter. I'm not really hot-dogging anything, and I don't want to. People probably wonder, "Why has Tony Rice been content to play with Peter Rowan?" Well, *Peter's music offers room for nuance*, and needs that. And it works.

I've been playing this damn guitar for over 50 years. I've got a right to be worn out. And I am. *I'm tired.* The voice is a good example. I loved that high lonesome sound so much, but I didn't have the natural ability. I did it anyway. It's like a sprint runner that would injure himself for life in an attempt to run the four-minute mile. Maybe he does it, but in the process, he overtaxes his heart. And I did that with the voice.

My hands feel like shit. The arthritis is getting worse. On a good night, nobody'd know it except me. And on a bad night . . . STILL nobody would know it except me! If the music is good enough, I'm not aware of the arthritis. And nobody complains so far. I don't think I've gotten any feedback on my website or anywhere, "Tony's arthritic and he didn't play worth a shit last night." I've got tricks and ways I can hide it. Oscar Peterson had osteoarthritis in both of his hands for most of his adult career. It doesn't necessarily mean the end of the world. You have good days and bad days with it, and on a bad day, it's just a bummer.

The way I play requires that my hands be in perfect synch. If something is wrong with one hand, the other hand is also gonna be fucked up. I have osteoarthritis in my left hand, and I've wore my right hand out. To fix it, I'd have to change the way I play. I have heard promising stuff from Scandinavian countries that are doing a surgical procedure to correct this problem very successfully. They're taking smaller joints of the body and doing microsurgery and replacing them with Teflon. If you go under the knife with the right guy, the use of the hand could be as good as it ever was. But if the surgeon has had a bad hair day, things could go drastically wrong.

I think I'll be viewed more in a historic context at a younger age than most musicians, more than somebody you could look at and say, "Well, God, imagine what the future holds for *this* guy." I don't think that's gonna happen with me.

With the music business as unstable as it is, I'm not really as motivated as I otherwise would be. Most of my career has been making and producing good records. And now there's not even any use to make a fucking record! If things pick up again . . .

God only knows what kind of changes are coming in the music world. But everybody's going through this. Professional musicians are scratching their heads and going, "How can we keep making records? And WHY do we keep making them, if people are going to steal music for free?" I don't have $20,000 or $30,000 to go into a recording studio and make a record somebody's going to listen to for nothing.

I can't retire. I've got to somehow be involved in some aspect of the music, enough to share it with other people and make money at it. There are a couple things I could certainly enjoy doing: seminars, teaching serious students some of the philosophical aspects of musicianship that would be helpful to them, clearing up a lot of myths and legends they hear about the so-called "correct ways" of doing things.

No doubt about it, I'm aging very fast. But I've accepted it. It's just part of living. Considering the abuse I've done to myself, I think I'm doing pretty good.

I'm just going with the flow right now, trying not to worry about where I'll be in ten years, or what I'll be doing, and if what I have to offer will be accepted by enough people to support me. I'm pretty sure it will be.

And I'm still grateful for every day I wake up breathing.

(Photo by Nancy Gatling)

Family, Friends & Fans

I think Tony is doing exactly what Tony should be doing, and all of us, even though we miss hearing him sing, should respect and honor his own personal choices in life.

> **Brad Davis, guitarist and Rice protégé**

Many, many people consider him one of the all-time great bluegrass singers. I feel the loss of his voice is one of the biggest tragedies of bluegrass. The truth is, it hasn't hurt his drawing power with the public, because his powerful guitar playing is just as widely loved and respected, if not more so, than his singing. I think his career will go on as long as he cares for it to go on.

> **Mike Auldridge, resonator guitarist & original**
> **Seldom Scene member**

I think Tony had one of the greatest voices in bluegrass but when he lost it, it certainly did not hold him back. He just sings through his fingers now!

> **Rickie Simpkins, mandolinist/fiddler with the Tony Rice Unit**

John Starling (original Seldom Scene lead singer; U.S. Army surgeon):
The operation was probably back in the late '80s [actually, in October 1989]. Tony had a deviated septum, and his nose was a little crooked on the outside. We did the whole thing and straightened out the septum and the nose a bit. It was an outpatient procedure at Mary Washington Hospital here in Fredericksburg. He stayed with me for a week while he was healing up.

Tom Gray:
John did say that his work on Tony's nose should have improved his singing. Tony had had that broken nose all through his young life, and early pictures of him show a nose that's leaning over to one side.

Mike Auldridge:
In 1990 I did an album called *Treasures Untold*. He sang two songs. I remember thinking, "There's something wrong with Tony's voice. There's something a little *different*. It's not like that smooth, silken voice that he had." He was getting a little ragged.

Ronnie Rice:

Kari Estrin and I made a trip down to the Rounder building. She took me through and introduced me to Ken and Bill and Marian. Kari mentioned about there being a Rice Brothers project. That might have been the point that got us started.

A friend knew this guy who would go to major cities and run an ad in the paper that he would buy old instruments. He would take 'em home and alter them and try to sell them. He had a bass, but it was not very playable. I wound up buying it for a couple thousand dollars. I took it to Tony's, and him and Billy are blasted, and they put on Blues Brothers sunglasses and they're sitting there playing this bass, looking really cool . . . They said, "Do you think you can learn to play?" I hadn't played acoustic bass since I was ten years old.

"Whisper My Name" was the first song we recorded together as the Rice Brothers. I think we started in March of '87 at Bias Studios in Springfield, Virginia. We didn't practice . . . We were running it down and we made it about a quarter of the way through, and it just come together. Tony said, "Stop right there! Let's roll the tape, Billy. I think we've got a groove going." That set the pace for the whole project. I'd never played that song before in my life. We had no idea what we were gonna do till we got into the studio. We didn't start till 5 or 6:00 in the evening and we went till 4 or 5:00 in the morning.

The Rice Brothers at the Larry Rice Benefit in Tallahassee, FL, 2004: Larry, Tony, Ronnie, and Wyatt.
(*Courtesy of Lee Kotick*)

Billy Wolf:

I loved Larry; he and I got on pretty good. Ronnie didn't do music professionally so it was hardest on him, although he did great. There wasn't a lot of belaboring. It might have had something to do with the fact that the budgets weren't really high. There weren't any serious hang-ups. Larry wasn't drinking at all at that time . . .

There wasn't always agreement about choice of material. I think Larry had a sweet side in his song taste that Tony didn't share . . . Tony would privately say to me, "Oh, I wish he wouldn't make us do that tune!" Back then, he didn't appreciate the sweet songs so much. There's always an edge, even with Tony's pretty things.

Ronnie Rice:

Wyatt and I would sit back and watch Larry and Tony be jealous of one another . . . Tony never did agree with most of the songs Larry had written. "Keep the Lamp On, Sadie." Tony hated that! I don't know why. The short time we played shows, that was the most requested song.

I think the total budget was around $22,000, including what people were paid up front. In order for Rounder to recoup their money, they had to sell at least 17,000 copies. I think they've gone way beyond that on sales.

Rickie Simpkins (fiddler/mandolinist):

I first met Tony at a festival near his home in Florida. I was performing with the Virginia Squires and we invited Tony and Larry on stage. Shortly thereafter I was asked to fill in with the Unit on a few occasions. That eventually turned into my spot. I primarily played fiddle but occasionally banjo. When the Unit became all-instrumental, I became the mandolin player.

Tony is one of the fairest bandleaders I have worked for. He has always treated everyone with respect and kindness. It meant the world to me to have the privilege to play with the Unit. I believed it would allow me to push my skill to its maximum, and it did.

Billy Wolf:

I was on the road with him when he was drinking a case of Coors Light every day. My biggest concern was driving. But I never said a word. Having been to some AA meetings myself, it's something you have to decide for yourself.

I never saw a mean Tony Rice, drunk or otherwise. He could be a little harder-edged sometimes, when he'd been drinking . . . but never mean.

Mark Schatz:

His drinking certainly had an effect on the workings of the band. To his credit, there were not many times he went onstage where he had drunk enough to be impaired so he wasn't playing well. Generally, the excessive drinking would happen after the show.

He was a real happy drunk, a bunch of fun. That's maybe why he did it. When he's *not* drinking, he's a little bit covered up, kinda shy, almost awkward. He seems sometimes almost uncomfortable in his own skin.

There were some mornings where we had to get up and get to the next gig, and I couldn't get him out of bed. Sometimes, I got scared that he'd killed himself. I'd knock on the door and he wouldn't answer. I'd get in there and pull him out of bed and his eyes were rolling back in his head, and he'd say, "Okay, I'm up . . ."

Billy Wolf:

That one year he had the terrible accident, maybe '97, it was the same tax year in which Pam had her heart surgery. Usually we don't deduct the medical expenses, but that year, he had enough. I figured he was an auto fatality waiting to happen, unless he quit drinking. So it was prayers answered when he did.

Now, I don't know the specifics of alcohol consumption. But the way Tony used to consume, a hangover would be enough to impair your judgment. The accidents happened when he was in North Carolina . . . I think there were two accidents in a short period of time, but one of them had hospitalization for days. *Days.* I remember how he felt when I hugged him afterwards . . . Everything looked *broken*.

The whole top part of his bone structure got pretty mangled. He's never stood quite as square-shouldered as he did before the accident. He always dresses well and looks good, but one of his shoulders slumps a little now. He tells me it's arthritis, but arthritis can be aggravated or triggered by bone damage.

Mark Schatz:

Tony continued singing, but he was starting to lose his range, and if he'd go a couple nights, he'd start having trouble. The material not being fresh was frustrating. Some of these things I tried to do with him, in terms of promoting the record, had been kinda frustrated.

It would have to take a pretty powerful draw to lure me away from him, even when things were difficult. The thing with Tim O'Brien came along, and well . . . I think he's an incredible artist. And this thing with Tony had gotten frustrating and contentious and difficult. There was a lot of enabling going on around him, and I was part of that. And I didn't really realize what I was doing.

So I came to him, and not real ceremoniously, said, "Hey, I've decided to work with Tim, and it's not gonna start for another two or three months. I'd really like to keep playing until that happens." Well, he was devastated. I should have approached that with a lot more sensitivity. I mean, it's like a divorce. Within a couple weeks, Ronnie was on the gig.

Bill Emerson (banjo veteran and former member of the Country Gentlemen):

Being a part of Tony's *Plays and Sings Bluegrass* project was a great experience. The material he chose allowed me to do what I do best, but the best part was what I learned from watching him in the studio. Jimmy Gaudreau told me, "He really knows how to get it out of you." Tony does it without saying a word. Just his presence is plenty.

Ken Irwin:

We held up a whole long time—at least a couple years—before putting out *Plays and Sings Bluegrass*. I kept thinking Tony's voice would improve. I wrote a letter which pleaded

(Courtesy Rounder Records)

with him to take better care of it, saying something like, "I think there are many people who care more about you than you do yourself." I never got a reply.

Mark Johnson:

I guess it was 1992, Christmas time. We'd had a friendship for years. I went to the Rices and said, "You guys are all going to be home for Christmas. It would be fun to make some cassettes for the Rice family and the Johnson family. I got this studio up in Gainesville. Would you like to join me?" And Tony said, "When and where?"

All four of those guys came up, and we recorded *Clawgrass*. It started out as kind of a goof, and then Tony said, "You know, you're doing something very different here." He even brought me out with the Tony Rice Unit, for four or five gigs. I had never had any stage experience or worked on a microphone. We'd start playing duets, and Tony would see me tensing up, and the crowd's just going nuts, and he would lean over and joke in my ear, trying to get me to relax. He was teaching me how to be on a stage, how to work with a crowd, how not to tense up. He taught me all that.

David Grisman:

Tone Poems was just an idea I had, to do a project where two guys would play a lot of different instruments. I thought of Tony for that, and asked him if he'd do it, and he did. *The Pizza Tapes* was during that *Tone Poems* thing. I invited Jerry over to meet Tony, and we ended up jamming. I didn't really intend to release that as an album. I thought there were some cuts I could use at some point, but it got bootlegged. It's the only tape that ever escaped from my studio. It got played on the radio in New York City, like, ninety minutes of it. I got real upset. For the next couple years, people would come up to me with these tapes and CDs, and say they loved this stuff. I'd just get pissed.

I hired a guy named Rob Bleetstein to be my publicist. He kept saying, "You really should put out those tapes, man. They're great!" They were all over the place for several years. Finally Rob brought over a CD one day, and said, "*This* is what people are listening to." It just sounded so bad, the fidelity of it.

I said, "Okay . . . I'll try to put this together." And I did. I think the pizza delivery guy got a cassette that was 90 minutes long, and there were different takes . . . the complete session, or most of it. I said, "Well, gee, what am I gonna do? Put it *all* out? *Two* CDs?" I decided I was just gonna make one good CD. I found some stuff that *wasn't* on those tapes, and several tunes were made off the multi-track. Several of 'em ran off, but there were backup DATs, so I was able to reconstruct a few tunes. I put it out and it was a huge success.

Pam Rice:

We had backwaters very near in Florida. Every day, Tony and I would put our dogs in the boat and go out. We'd spend a lot of time out in the sawgrass, looking at the gators and photographing them. Tony'd do a lot of fishing, but he always threw the fish back.

Mark Johnson:

We'd put the boat in at the Dunnellon boat ramp and head out into an area of the lake called "The Backwaters." Remember the CD he did called *Backwaters*? The photo on the cover of that CD was taken about 500 yards in front of my home in Dunnellon.

I truly believe that Tony's all time favorite pastime was fishing for large-mouth bass down here in Florida. I believe that he liked it for the solitude it provided and the simple pleasures that fishing held, and it reminded him of when he was a kid. He and I spent a lot of time together, fishing on the Backwaters.

Pam Rice:

You think you can imagine a flood, but you do not even come close to imagining it. I was not there. Tony was, and his mother was in the house with him. The fire department came in the evacuation, and they took her. Tony said, "Can I leave by my boat?" They said yes. What they didn't know was that he wasn't gonna go with them because he had the little puppy . . . If you're rescued, you have to leave your animals behind. And that's not gonna happen with us.

He called me that morning and said, "The water is coming in . . . Is there anything you want to save?" When he got it moved as much as he could, it was 100 mph wind gusts, 30

Summer of 1985 on Lake Rousseau, Dunnellon, FL. *(Photo by Mark Johnson)*

degrees, and snowing. He zipped Pokey up in his jacket and got in our boat. He said, "Pam, it was so scary, trying to steer against the wind . . . I was driving over peoples' docks. I didn't know where I was." When he finally found a place to get out and tie up, he was in the middle of a motel parking lot.

He got out of the boat by this restaurant called Charlie's, with a ramp up the side. The water was up to his chest, and he was trying to keep Pokey up. He got to the ledge, and there was a payphone, and it worked. He called me and he was just terrified. I said, "Hold on, I'm gonna get the police to come after you. Just go to Cumberland Farms." He said, "You don't understand. There IS no Cumberland Farms."

So I called the police, and the officer said, "Lady, I wish *everybody* was on the ledge at Charlie's! At least they'd be safe." And he hung up on me.

Larry and our friend Mark Johnson had to launch their boat five miles inland. They got to our house and saw our stuff floating out to sea. They went in and got the gold albums and the Grammy, and put them in the boat. Our coffee table was originally the hatch of an old ship, and it floated.

What people don't understand about a flood is, you'd think that the water's gonna come in, and go down, and then everything's gonna be exactly the way it was, only wet. It's not that way at all. It's like an agitation. And you would never believe how much paper is in your house. All this paper starts floating around. It's very nasty. Anything that's in the ocean, any trash on the ground, is gonna be in your house.

And of course, the D-28 was in the house.

Ronnie Rice:

He couldn't move back into the house. It wasn't livable. He had to get everything out and move it to North Carolina in a short period of time. I think he might have planned on going back. Maybe he figured out he was just as happy in North Carolina as he'd been in Florida.

Pam Rice:

We rented this house in North Carolina for my son Roman to go to police school up here. He was my son that died. When we lost our home in the flood, if it had not been for this house, we would have been homeless.

I believe things happen for a reason. It's not the house either Tony or I would have chosen. It's a tri-level, four bedrooms . . . I did the best I could. I took a piece of mud from the high mesas of New Mexico and I had my other son, Chris, take it to Lowe's and get the paint matched exactly, and that's what I put on the house. I tried to make it look like the French Quarter in New Orleans. Mostly I try to keep a lot of things growing up in front of it, so nobody can see it.

Jimmy Gaudreau:

I was in the audience at Gettysburg—the year was 1994—watching Tony perform with a reunion of the New South. I vividly recall him getting progressively worse as the performance went on. Every time he'd go for a note, his voice would break, or nothing would come out except a squeak. It was not pleasant, especially for him. He finally exited the stage and said to both Rickie Simpkins and me those exact words, "That's it. I can't sing anymore." He didn't stick around for the reaction. Basically he just wanted to put his guitar back in the case and get the hell out of there.

Rickie and I looked at one another and he said "Well, what do we do now?" Good question.

Keith Case:

If he'd kept his voice, God knows what would be happening with him now in the current environment. With what's going on in the music now, he'd be a *huge* act.

Wyatt Rice:

His voice thing happened over a period of time. I don't know—he's never really talked to me about it. I talk to him sometimes even now and he sounds like he used to sound 20 or 30 years ago. And I'm thinking, "My God, you're getting your voice back!" I'll catch him in it every once in a while, and then he'll go back to that "ruhr, ruhr" . . . *[imitates Tony's low growl].*

John Cowan:

I lost my voice a couple years ago for about four months. I didn't know if it was coming back; nobody did. That was the scariest, most harrowing thing I ever experienced. If you identify who you are with what you do for a living, that's not such a great thing. For myself, the possibility that I was never gonna sing again, well, it just broke my heart.

Having said that, I can't bring myself to talk to him about it.

Gary Oelze:

I read a piece on George Jones, where he talked like a duck for a whole year. He did not sing. He could not. And the way the author was describing what George Jones was doing, I said, "Well, shit! I've watched TONY do that."

Billy Wolf:

One time, I remember, he demonstrated to me . . . it was *spine-chilling* . . . if he concentrates and works very hard, *he can make his voice sound like it used to* for a line or two. I just about fell out of my chair! He only did it for me once. He said, "The problem is that I have to think about every word to do that, and it's very difficult." I guess part of what happened to his vocal chords has to do with controlling them.

John Starling:

At one time, there was a rumor going around that my surgery caused his voice to go south. But I read somewhere on the Internet where Tony was talking about his vocal problems, and I think he had a pretty good read on what was going on.

There's a term, *dysphonia plica ventricularis,* and it basically means you're phonating with your false vocal chords. It's caused by memory loss of the small muscles. You have two sets of vocal chords: false vocal chords, which close when you swallow to keep things from going down the wrong way, and true vocal chords, whose function is phonation. They're very thin, below the false vocal chords, and when you breathe out, the small muscles bring them together so you can talk, sing, whatever.

I think he got into the habit, when he'd talk to somebody out on the road *[growling like Tony]:* "Hey, man, how you doin'?" After a while, your muscles forget, and the muscles that control your true vocal chords are pushed to the background. It's not a pathology as such, other than the fact that you can't sing and you talk funny. It is correctable, but with a lot of work, by taking your vocal cords to the gym—to a *voice* therapist. They make a video of your vocal cords in action, actually put a little scope at the back of your tongue to look. The voice therapist gives you exercises. With a lot of work, you can teach those muscles to remember. But the longer you wait, the longer it takes to restore the memory.

I got an appointment with Tony with Bob Ossoff, the chairman of the ENT Department at Vanderbilt, who was one of the world's experts on this. That was eight, nine years ago. But I don't think Tony kept the appointment.

At some point I talked to him about it, and he said, "You know what? I'm just enjoying playing the guitar so much. I don't miss singing."

Peter Rowan:

Shit, man. If Tony was on his deathbed, I'd bring him his favorite cigarette, and say, "Man, you want one more?" Because *what the fuck* . . . I'm not gonna begrudge Tony. It's only hurting him. And he must be aware of it.

I mean, it's a pain in the ass, man. "Please don't fucking *smoke* in the dressing room! It bothers my throat. How inconsiderate." But you love somebody because of just *who they are,* not how you would like them to be.

Béla Fleck:

He was a big part of both *Tales from the Acoustic Planet,* Volume I and II. On Volume I, he did a solo on the first tune; it was great, but I wanted another, and he wouldn't do it. He said, "Well, that's about as good as I can play . . ." He looked back on it as some of his greatest playing, and it *is* some of the best I ever heard. I just wanted to see what else he would do.

[For Volume II, *The Bluegrass Sessions*] I actually went to his house. Trapped him in his lair—I wanted him to play a guitar melody on some things. He had time to get into the songs. That's what happened. You get that first-take intensity when you're first playing a song, and then maybe by about the fourth take, it peaks, and then it'll start to go down. But if you keep going for another half-hour or hour, it will start coming back up, and get this locked-in thing.

Tony and Béla Fleck. (Courtesy Tony Rice)

Jerry Douglas:

I've always admired Béla's interest in keeping Tony involved [on *Acoustic Planets*] when maybe he could have gone some other direction. Tony is the wildcard that made it all work.

Béla Fleck:

He didn't do any of [the shows on *The Bluegrass Sessions* tour]. He was originally booked for them, and then he cancelled. Something about being out of control . . . being on a bus with a bunch of guys . . . not being able to come and go at his own will . . . I think it made him uncomfortable. And we were gonna be hitting it *hard,* six nights a week. He was also starting to have some hand problems. All I know is that he cancelled, and we got Bryan [Sutton], and Bryan did a great job.

I was happy with every cut for what it was, and how everybody played. And it's done better than *Drive;* it's sold 130,000 or 140,000 by now, and it keeps selling. I intentionally put the word *bluegrass* into the title for Volume II, because if people were listening to all my new stuff, they would go get *this* record, and then they would hear all *these* guys.

Richard Bennett (flatpick guitarist, former member of the New South):

Tony was working in Knoxville with the Unit, and I was in Asheville. I called him the night before and asked if he was coming back home that direction. He said yeah. I asked if he would mind helping me do some tunes [for *Walking Down the Line,* 1997]. He said, "Sure, where?" That was all the preplanning there was. It was straight out of the case to the microphones, and very few retakes. We did six songs in four or five hours, maybe.

Sammy Shelor:

When I did my record [*Leading Roll,* 1997], it was like, "I'm going to get my heroes together and we're going to play. Whatever it costs, I don't care." Luckily I found a studio that was, like, 29 miles from Tony's house. I hadn't done any formal gigs with him at that point. But I had picked with him on Larry's records and felt comfortable enough to call him and say, "Hey, would you play rhythm on my record?"

It was so cool. We were starting to work up stuff, and I'd say, "Well, do you want a break on this?" He would say, "No, that's not my thing." So he would do the rhythm. We

Tony and Sammy Shelor in 2005.
(Photo by Mike Kelly)

would work on another song—"Do you want a solo on this?" "Yeah, I think I would." I just let him do his own thing, and we worked on his schedule. It was so relaxed and fun. There were no overdubs. Some of the stuff speeds up, but it felt good when it did.

Herb Pedersen:

I had seen Tony and Larry up in Grass Valley, when I had my band, the Laurel Canyon Ramblers. Tony said, "It's so cool to see all the California guys again; it'd be great to do a record together." I said, "Sure!" To celebrate the fact that we've known each other for almost 40 years . . . just put something together, tunes we liked to do, and some original stuff.

About a year later, Larry called, and he had talked to Ken Irwin at Rounder, and Ken thought it was a good idea, so . . . That was that.

Chris Hillman:

We recorded [1997's *Out of the Woodwork,* the first Rice, Rice, Hillman & Pedersen album] in Nashville, and Jerry Douglas was on that one from the get-go. The second one [*Rice, Rice, Hillman & Pedersen,* 1999], I was real sick. They did all the tracks back in Virginia, and they brought 'em out, and I did the vocals on 'em.

Herb Pedersen:

Sitting across from Tony for five days was very reminiscent of sitting across from Clarence. He had that sense of tone and timing. I would kinda chuckle to myself: "Wow, here it is. It's still happening!"

Rickie Simpkins:

We would never spend time rehearsing, as was the case in recording *Unit of Measure*. It was a great experience to be part of that recording. The performance would just evolve. Playing with people who know when to play and when *not* to play makes a world of difference. Tony allowed for the music just to happen. We followed his cue.

Jimmy Gaudreau:

Tony had other dates contracted that year and we managed to get through them with Rickie and me splitting the duties as lead singer and me doing the tenor in a duet situation, which was about as far as we could go with it. It also put me in the uncomfortable position of acting as emcee and trying my best to explain why we were having to perform in this manner—without apologizing, of course, since Tony didn't particularly want to compromise his asking price.

Finally, I'd had my fill. I eased my way out of the Unit as dates trickled off. No formal resignation; I found myself performing more dates with Chesapeake and Tony would use Mark Newton (or Dan Tyminski if he was available) to cover any Unit dates that conflicted. It simply became a matter of Tony not calling, and me moving on.

Wyatt Rice:

It was always good on stage, even when we were hung over. At least it was better to get onstage with a hangover and the shakes than to be fucked up from the night before. He and Larry was involved in kind of the same thing. Larry would go for ten years without a drink. Then he broke into his thing, and it was worse every time. Tony's was gradual. He'd party with the Unit, and then he'd quit for a year and not have anything. Then he'd get involved with AA, and the next thing you know, out of the blue, a year later, he's back on the roll again.

Peter Rowan:

Around 1998, I had been working with Charles Sawtelle on my recording, *Bluegrass Boy,* and Charles had passed away after a long battle with cancer. I finished doing this series of bluegrass records for Sugar Hill. I didn't know what I was gonna do. We'd lost John Hartford, Bill Monroe, Roy Huskey, and Charles, all within a couple years. I felt very unattached and a little at sea.

So I was at the end of that period, and at MerleFest sort of floating free, and lo and behold, they put Tony and me on a stage together . . . He had sort of retired. I hadn't seen him for three or four years; I think he'd trailed off on the Unit thing. This was right around the time he wrecked his car and broke his collarbone. He showed up, and he was half in the bag.

I'm thinking . . . All I've ever heard is that this guy has to have everything all worked out beforehand. I said, "Uh . . . hey, man, what do we do?" And he says, "Man . . . whatever you wanna do!" He was loose; he was a little high, you know? He said, "Fuck. Just play."

Soon after that, we started taking dates, just the two of us, with Mark Schatz on bass. In 1999 we toured the West Coast. Occasionally Kester Smith, Taj Mahal's drummer, played snare drum and congas with us.

Later I pulled in Bryn [Davies] Bright and mandolinist Billy Bright [Bryn's husband at the time] from Texas, and we had a quartet. Bryn is pretty advanced. She was brilliant. A lot of bass players get caught between trying to find a nice medium place where it seems comfortable for the vocals. But Tony plays ahead of the beat a little bit, on the front edge of the rhythmic pulse. When somebody can find the right place to lay the rhythm in there, it works fine.

Bryn Davies (California bassist):

The first time we played together was about six months after I'd started playing with Peter; the spring of '99 was our first tour as a quartet. Billy and Peter and I showed up at the club and I met Tony for the first time. He was sweet as could be. We went over a couple things and played the show, and it was like meeting my long-lost musical soulmate.

Peter Rowan:

His accident happened when drinking was playing a bigger part in his day-to-day life. But even while he was drinking, we did shows. If we had a date in Texas, Tony would drive all the way from North Carolina, and often have somebody with him as co-driver. We'd pull off a good show, but he would drink in the second half of the day . . . I remember one night in Texas. He kept saying, "It's so colllllld, man!" and playing not really *there*. The crowd did nothing but scream its approval. I've heard tapes . . . it's all out of whack, but it has a strange beauty. Maybe the sign of true genius is you play to what the moment *really* is. And if it's all fucked up, you play all fucked up.

When we were working with Billy and Bryn, and we were out there hitting every Midwest theatre . . . I've never been so tired in my *life*. Tony was driving the whole thing, and he'd be calling from a hundred miles away an hour before show time.

Bryn Davies:

Billy [Bright, former mandolinist with the Rowan & Rice Quartet] wanted to do an all-instrumental record [*Billy & Bryn Bright,* 2002]. Well, Tony was still drinking. So there was the whole issue of getting him to the studio. We would all show up around noon, and Tony would usually show up around four. We would have his case of beer for him, and he would lay down the tracks. Some stuff he got really crazy on, and it was great, but when it would get to overdubbing twin fiddles on some stuff, Tony would be sitting there on the couch: *[in a slurred approximation of Tony's voice that night]* "Damn it, man! It's not gonna work. The only person that can play twin fiddles to Vassar Clements is Bobby Hicks!"

Chris Hillman:

We did the third Rice, Rice, Hillman & Pedersen album [*Running Wild,* 2001], back in Virginia with Bill Wolf. In hindsight, I should have been more opinionated . . . I should have convinced Larry not to use drums and steel. The magic was obviously in the acoustic thing. Larry wanted to make a country rock record, and what's the point?

Jon Carroll (former pianist in Mary Chapin Carpenter's band):

I knew the *only* reason I was at that session was Tony. It was obvious the other guys there did not have use for a piano and didn't understand how anyone else could, either.

I was playing on the last cut. They'd been there for two weeks, and it was very clear that no one really cared if this song got on the album or not. It was just, "Okay, we're SO done. We were done three days ago . . ." This wasn't from Tony, but from everybody else.

Tony came in and said, "I really wanted to do this Tom Waits song ['Pony'] with you." He didn't know the lyrics, but he had the CD sleeve, and he put on his glasses. I don't think we actually got through the whole thing once, but we did about five different takes. He said, "Oh, I haven't sung in four years." That's why I really wanted it to be good.

Keith Case:

The 2001 Wilkesboro festival [MerleFest], before Tony quit drinking in May, he was in no shape to play. He had a show with Rice, Rice, Hillman & Pedersen, a show with Pete, and this jam setup with Sam and Jerry. The week following Wilkesboro, I got feedback from these guys, and they were all saying, "We love Tony dearly, but we're not playing with him anymore." Nobody was talking to Tony. Over the next couple weeks I talked to him about it. I said, "You need to know what's going on. Your old friends aren't willing to go onstage with you anymore."

Sam Bush:

It was a terrible situation. Keith Case said people called and told him, "We just won't work with Tony anymore." Keith had to call Tony and say, "Man, *they're* not gonna tell you, but *I'll* tell you this . . ."

Keith Case:

I guess that got his attention. He started talking to a psychiatrist in his hometown, and got into a very serious outpatient program. He took it very seriously, and he hasn't had a drink since. Not even a beer.

John Cowan:

The last year before he got sober, it was Darol Anger and Mike Marshall and Todd Phillips at the MerleFest Midnight Jam. Tony was just drunk, drunk, drunk. There were some moments of brilliance, because it was those four guys playing, but more often than not, it was a mess.

I thought he was gonna die, I really did. He wasn't eating; all he was doing was drinking. I confronted him during the festival, and then shortly thereafter. We talked a whole lot during that period. I think he felt some real healthy shame about showing up places and being too inebriated to play.

It was within the next few weeks that he went and cleaned himself up.

Keith Case:

It's made an amazing difference. I never saw him happier in his own skin than he is these days.

Ronnie Rice:

At Grey Fox 2001, Larry pitched a pretty good drunk and said some embarrassing things onstage, and I guess Chris Hillman took offense. I imagine there's been a time or two Tony's been onstage and said something stupid. I was at the Birchmere and Vassar showed up so drunk he couldn't play. He *hummed* his part into the microphone! I'm sure Chris did some crazy things when he was with the Byrds . . . I don't think none of 'em have the right to point their finger at one another.

Chris Hillman:

It wasn't always pleasant, to be honest, but Tony's a monster, and he's got the Jimmy Martin rhythm. Clarence had that, too. It *swings*. It makes you play better. And in defense of Tony, he was really nice to work with.

The few shows we did were disastrous, the last one being Grey Fox. I'd go to take a solo, and Larry would start playing rhythm out of time . . . it was a nightmare. I wish we could have left a better last performance together. That was a tough one, that night. I was harsh with Tony. I said, "I have worked with so many guys that have died from drugs and alcohol . . . Gram Parsons and others. Why am I being put through this again?"

Sam Bush:

When Tony and Peter Rowan were on this JamGrass tour in 2002, we were on at least 20 gigs together. He was playing great, and looked great; he was sober, and driving himself. He'd pull up in time to pick, and when he was done, he'd hop in the Mustang. He likes driving himself, and he likes being the Lone Wolf out on the road. That's maybe why he's doing it that way. Maybe he doesn't give himself time to hang out and be tempted. Whatever it is, it's working.

Dave Talbot (Canadian banjoist):

When we did Aubrey's record [Aubrey Haney's *The Bluegrass Fiddle Album,* 2003], we hadn't rehearsed, we hadn't even played together—and the first song we cut was "First Day in Town," an old Kenny Baker song. We hadn't even run through it. We tuned up and rolled the two-inch tape, and Take One was the one we kept. I don't think we even tried a Take Two.

The experience over the three days of making that record with Tony was an absolute emotional rush for me. I had a real hard time for quite a while afterwards, because I had just finished playing with unbelievable, moving, emotional, rhythmic . . . It's hard to put into words. It was really, really difficult for me to come off that. I had a hard time in terms of having to go somewhere else. At one point, I thought it had ruined me.

Bryn Davies:

Billy Bright and I split up in March 2004. When MerleFest came around, we were still on the road together, but separated, and it was emotional turmoil all over the place.

Tony and I were talking on the phone a lot, trying to be a friend to each other, and he asked me to play the Midnight Jam with him. We did this version of "Summertime," just the two of us. And he said, after we were done, "The Unit hasn't been able to work as much as I want, because Ronnie Simpkins is working so much with the Seldom Scene . . . would you be willing to do Unit stuff?" And I said, "Oh, *hell,* yeah!"

The first gig was May 2004. I asked Tony a week ahead if there was anything weird I should listen to. He was like, "It's mostly fiddle tunes. Instrumentals, bluegrass. We'll throw in some jazzier stuff like 'Devlin' and 'My Favorite Things.' " We went over a couple things but it was basically get onstage and *go*. It was such a natural thing to walk into that group of players. It felt like I'd been playing with them for years.

Peter Rowan:

We made that very sweet first album *[You Were There for Me]*. It was me, paying the bills to go in the studio and just get *something* on tape, and we put it out on Rounder.

Bryn Davies:

We spent four years recording *You Were There for Me.* Whenever we had time on the road, we would go into a studio . . . a studio in Maine for a couple days; in Texas; in North Carolina. That record was very fragmented, with different studios, different engineers all over the place. Every time we got into a studio, we would re-record stuff because Peter would change it completely—the chord changes and the time and the feel. Tony and I got really frustrated during that process.

Peter Rowan:

When Sharon Gilchrist joined the band, she said, "I'm not gonna play with Uncle Earl; I'm gonna play with you guys. What's the game plan?" And Tony and I were like, "Uh-oh . . . What do you mean, *what's the game plan? What's the game?*"

So we had a big meeting in Nashville with the agency, and they're like, "Gosh, with a steady band, and a new record, we can probably get you up into that magic figure where you can get better gigs and—" Well, it didn't happen.

Sharon Gilchrist (New Mexico mandolinist):

The first gig I did with Tony was for the Jam Cruise to the Bahamas in 2005. It was maybe three weeks before that Peter asked me to play with them. He told me to call the booking agent and ask them to send his CDs to me.

The next thing I know, we're on the boat, getting settled in; we had a show that first night, and I got up onstage, we shook hands and jumped into the first set.

It went pretty well. And Peter is so spontaneous, he was having me jump in on harmonies on the first night. Peter and Bryn had their harmonies worked out, and it was pretty easy to add a third part.

Bryn Davies:

You wouldn't have thought to put Tony and Peter together at all, but in the end, it's just the most beautiful thing. Tony adds a beauty to Peter's music that nobody else could.

Bryan Sutton (North Carolina flatpick guitarist):

He does so many intricate subdivision things with his pick rhythmically. Playing with him, I try to do things he might not have heard from any other guitar player. Hopefully I can inspire him as much as he has inspired me. I'd like to think I captured some of that on my record [*Not Too Far from the Tree,* 2007].

"Lonesome Fiddle Blues," we talked about that around the time Vassar was in pretty bad health; everybody knew he was on the downhill turn. I wanted certain kinds of songs with certain kinds of guys. I wanted to get the hard-driving bluegrass, but Tony's been such an influence with the jazzier approach. I thought "Lonesome Fiddle Blues" got a lot of what I wanted out of a duet from a producer's standpoint.

Sometime after that, Tony said he told Vassar we had cut the tune and it made Vassar really happy, so I knew that was the right thing to do.

John Cowan:

I talked to Tony every day, almost, the last six weeks Vassar was alive. Vassar didn't really want to talk to anybody else. Sam liked to visit him, but Tony was his day-to-day guy. It wasn't that he didn't love the rest of us, but I think Tony became a paternal figure in his life. A confidant, maybe a protector of some sort.

I think Tony felt very honored. It was hard because he loved Vassar so much and Vassar was dying, but I don't think he would have traded places with anybody in the world on that walk.

Sharon Gilchrist:

Tony went through several deaths within a year. Every time I was around him, I thought there was a grieving process. I know he made the effort to be there with Vassar, and stay up on everything. It was fairly consuming for him.

Pam Rice:

My brother Dale was taken care of by Tony and me until his death. We got him on hospice, and Tony came off his tour to be with him in his last weeks. Dale passed away in our arms . . . we held him for hours and hours to make him feel comforted and safe until he took his last breath. Less than a month later, Tony would be doing the same with his own brother.

Frank Poindexter:

(From e-mail dated March 24, 2006) Larry's health is a constant day-to-day monitoring situation. He's taking some physical therapy trying to stretch him back from the way he has to favor that right side. His right lung barely moves now so basically he's working off the left, good lung. We all know there isn't a cure for this disease, except the fact that God himself can heal him if it's in His plans.

John Cowan:

This stuff with Larry happened really fast. Once I got wind of it, and started trying to communicate, Tony went into shutoff mode. I sent him a text message, told him sorry and I knew how he felt . . . My brother died of cancer. But he did not respond. I just thought, "Well . . . I'm not puttin' my two cents in there."

Pam Rice:

After Larry died, Tony left the hospital, drove to the motel, got a waterfront room and just sat on his porch there, staring out into the Gulf. That was where he and Larry had spent so much time together. That was the only way he could connect to comforting memories, the only place he could feel close to Larry. Most of the time he was on his cell phone with me, and the only thing he talked about was Larry—how he felt so helpless. He was crying most of the time. If I had been able to get a babysitter for the dogs, I would have jumped a plane and gone to him.

Tony and Larry in 2004 during the photo shoot for Clouds Over Carolina, *Larry's last recording.*
(Courtesy Larry Rice)

After Tony sat staring at the Gulf for three days, he got really homesick. He had to jump in his truck and drive home. I was going to return to Crystal River to attend the funeral, but Tony was in such bad shape over Larry's passing that I was not able to leave him. So neither of us was at the funeral. I know that looks really bad to the rest of the world, but I was not going to leave him in that crushed, incapacitated state. He was certainly not in any shape to make the drive to Florida by himself, even if he had the ability to deal with funerals.

Peter Rowan:

We did all the promo behind *You Were There for Me,* and on the second record [*Quartet,* 2007], there was *no* promo. We were doing interviews in Nashville, we were on radio, doing all kinds of things for *You Were There for Me* . . . and come the next record, there was absolutely *zero,* very much a lack of interest on the part of the record company.

I think both records have sold 12,000 or 13,000 each. In this age of the shipwreck of the music industry, you've gotta be selling 20,000 to 30,000 to have it in the pocket.

When we got Rounder involved, Ken Irwin wanted more input from Tony. Tony said, "Let's just do the best of what we do live. 'Cold Rain and Snow . . .' 'The Walls of Time . . .' These are the tunes people love." Tony's call to redo "Midnight Moonlight" was brilliant. That song on the record is *on fire.* It's the best of the original songwriting. It's also the best of Tony's contribution of his genius. That made it all worth it. And he pushed us to do "Dust Bowl Children" which we had performed only rarely before that.

Tony and Peter Rowan
(Courtesy Tony Rice)

Sharon Gilchrist:

Tony told me one time he didn't understand bands that HAVE to play different songs every single night. He didn't understand needing to be fresh, when instead you could play the same song every night and find something new, go deeper and deeper . . .

By the time we did *Quartet,* it was a year into the four of us playing together. I felt like the band was in a groove. The first three months of that year were a lot of work. I definitely felt a little more in my stride after the album. It resulted in Tony and Bryn and I having a rhythmic texture not common to a bluegrass band. Instead of a straight-ahead, *boom-chuck, boom-chuck* bluegrass beat, there was all this interplay going on. It felt like bubbling water.

Bryn Davies:

We had rehearsal for three days. Then we went into the studio and banged it out for a week, and came back about a month later and finished the overdubs and vocals.

I had the flu that whole week, and I was concentrating on making it perfect so I didn't have to keep doing it. There are *no bass overdubs* on that whole record. All the bass is live, even the solos. I credit that to having just Tony's guitar and me in my headphones. That's all I needed.

Billy Wolf:

When Tony and Peter were recording, he was having a problem. He had to make a new pick, and that's really an event, when a pick he's been using a lot finally gives up. I think it was a little bright, a little too hard-edged, until the tortoiseshell got broken in. Keep in mind, we've got the microscope turned up pretty high. Would the average listener know? I couldn't bet on it. But this is the kind of thing that makes it fun to work with Tony.

Sharon Gilchrist:

I've always been frustrated with the lack of momentum that surrounded *Quartet.* Maybe that's exactly how Peter and Tony wanted it. We did eight dates on the West Coast before it was released in January, three dates in February, another eight in March, and two or three in April and May. That's just *nothing.* I don't know who dropped the ball.

Bryn left that January . . . I think there were eight dates, and she left to join Patty Griffin. It all happened really quick, Patty deciding to bring her on. The last night, Bryn was backstage sobbing . . . "I'm gonna miss youuuuu . . ." I'm like, "Wait a second. This is the end of an era, of Bryn's playing with Tony and Peter . . ." Nobody said anything negative . . . but it almost wasn't even *acknowledged!* It was extremely weird.

John Cowan:

[January 2007] I talked to Tony the other day and he told me they'd made a really good record with Peter. He said he wanted to honor his commitment by promoting it, but that he wanted to focus on the Unit this year.

I can't wait to hear Tony on tour with Alison Krauss. To hear her sing those songs will be fabulous. This whole thing is gonna give him a golden opportunity. I would tell him to have a band up and running, and oodles of merchandise to sell. She has a much larger audience than he's ever been exposed to.

I don't know what happened on that *Bluegrass Sessions* thing. Well, he didn't do the tour. Béla was very pissed about it. I just hope that Tony can accommodate Alison, and they can accommodate him, and it'll work out really good.

Jerry Douglas:

Dan, Tony and I were on our way to the stage to play a Union Station show at the Opry one Saturday night. Tony was in town to do the CMT Video Awards with us, "Sawing on the Strings" and all that. I asked Tony if he would like to do some dates where we were essentially his conduit to the songs [we recorded with him], do "Manzanita" and reinvent the albums we had made. He was very receptive to the idea, and at RockyGrass the next summer, we did a show with Sam, Dan, Barry, Gabe Witcher, myself and Tony, and it went very well. We did another at Michael Smardak's festival in Salem, Virginia later.

When I heard about the possibility of Tony doing a tour with Union Station, I was happy, but remembered the *Bluegrass Sessions* tour he had cancelled himself out of right before we started rehearsals. I still think he may have felt self-doubt over getting his arthritic hands through two hours of intense pounding every night. The material for that tour was very intricate. For a week, there was a chance he wouldn't make the tour because of a fall. But after he made it to rehearsals, it was clear he was in for the duration.

We refined the setlist with breaks so he could rest his hand.

Powerhouse: Tony, Jerry Douglas. (Courtesy of Donn Jones)

We never used them. He stayed on stage with us every night through "Let Me Touch You for Awhile," putting himself into the guitar role of that usually Dan-dominated part, slightly altering it to fit his style. It was refreshing. He played extended intros to "Manzanita" and our duet of "Summertime." Every night his stage banter would get a little more dramatic, as in his introduction of Alison for "Streets of London," and especially "Manzanita," when he would step up to the microphone and exhale *"Manzanitaaa!!!"* Which I clued Sam Bush into, before our Telluride show. That particular show, I looked to my right during this display, to see Sam and his entourage on their knees in the monitor booth, bent over in tears. If only Tony had been wearing a Zorro hat.

In my view of this tour, Tony pulled out the stops, stepped up to the plate and hit the Grand Slam. I was so proud to stand beside him every night and watch him pull it off with ease, the statesman among his people. I was there with him through all the terrible ups and downs of making those records, but felt as though I was seeing and hearing it all for the first time.

Sharon Gilchrist:

The first time I saw Tony with Alison Krauss & Union Station was at MerleFest on their 2007 tour. He stood up and did this five-minute solo. It was Saturday night; 80,000 people were there. It was just so cool to see. You can imagine the expectation . . . Seeing him deliver that level of mastery was one of the most impressive things I've seen musically.

Every time he has a chance to have his music presented at that higher level, with the best players he could work with, he really rises to the occasion.

Jorma Kaukonen (original guitarist/vocalist with Jefferson Airplane):

Tony came to the Fur Peace Station last year with the Tony Rice Unit. My son (he was nine at the time) was visiting that weekend and I took him with me to see the show. Now, Zach is not really consumed with music yet . . . he listens to what his peers listen to, which is something else entirely. After the first set, I expected him to want to go home . . . but he said, "Dad, these guys are great. I want to see the second set!"

Happy Traum:

We've just issued a wonderful DVD with Tony and Peter Rowan. Peter does the singing and basic guitar parts and Tony shows his accompaniment and lead soloing improvisations.

We started experimenting with the split screen idea after the first couple videos we produced. It was a little crude when we did *An Intimate Lesson,* but I think it worked. We've gotten a lot better, but the idea is still the same: give folks as close a view as possible of everything that's going on.

Peter Rowan:

We have a great relationship with Happy Traum and Homespun Tapes. The way you work with him, you kinda get together and have dinner and talk, and one of the different things I'd been talking about with him was Tony's unique approach to backing up my songs. Happy said, "That would make a *great* video!"

Happy Traum:

I was very struck by the way Tony and Peter, two very different players and personalities, work together so seamlessly. I thought their two Rounder CDs were exceptional and wanted to capture how they created their guitar parts, and how Tony backs up Peter's singing.

Billy Wolf:

I recently finished Tony's compilation for Rounder [*Night Flyer,* 2008]. "Never Meant to Be" was recorded during the time of *Me and My Guitar.* "Urge for Going," "St. James Hospital," "John Wilkes Booth," "Night Flyer . . ."

And it also has "Pony," the Tom Waits song, at the end. Tony was up for releasing it, and Ken [Irwin] spent money on the session, so he was pushing to put it out. And *I* was the stick in the mud. I just didn't want to put Tony out there like that. I was being protective. But he played around with it and came up with the parts he thought were good. There were four or five takes. We had to get the lyrics right, because Tony didn't sing it correctly each time.

I ended up really liking it. It's *sad,* in a way. And he had had a snootful. That's not who Tony is now, with his drinking behind him. But the net effect of the piano and voice together is very moving. It's one of those juxtapositions: the hard, scratchy voice, and the beautiful, gospel-style piano.

Sharon Gilchrist:

He wasn't really one to talk about it, but we all knew it was happening. Every now and then, you'd see him backstage, shaking out his hands a little. You could tell some nights were harder than others.

Bryn Davies:

He's had some problems holding his pick. In the last year or two, he's had to put violin rosin on it so it will stick to his fingers. But it seems like his playing has gotten stronger. There was a time, when he first quit drinking, he was playing great, and then, for about two years, he didn't really seem into it. I think he was going through some personal stuff. In the last year or two, he has just been on fire. Every show, he's been a madman.

Sharon Gilchrist:

There was one gig where he tore out of the festival in a big, loud diesel truck as we started our encore. He wasn't happy with the music that night. The band was in a weak spot. Our routing was almost physically impossible. I don't know how Tony did it, driving by himself. I think we were sleeping three or four hours a night and driving nine hours a day, getting up and playing, driving another four hours at night. It was really hard toward the end of the summer.

Peter Rowan:

I think his frustration now is *it's either all or nothing.* You're either gonna hard-drive it to the wall, or you're gonna play with the nuances. You have to realize, Tony's *always in pain.* For his hands, playing with the nuances is better. But playing hard is what he's famous for. So we're stuck sometimes. If we play "Wild Mustang" or "Muleskinner Blues" or one of those real hard-driving tunes where he has to tear it up, it's gonna ruin Tony's hands, but it's gonna hit the show hard. And he's always up for it, that's the thing.

Keith Case:

He likes to have the financial *comfortableness* from success, but I think hot sessions with hot players, regardless of crowd size, is what gets *him* off. When they have one of those magic nights, that's what gets him off.

Mary Chapin Carpenter:

Tony always struck me as someone who is fairly comfortable pursuing his muse where he found it. If his ambitions were to be James Taylor, I never sensed that in him. He was always king of the Birchmere. King of any festival. If there was any gathering of musicians, Tony Rice, that's the shit.

Ken Irwin:

Tony's best-selling records, according to SoundScan, are his bluegrass guitar compilation, *Unit of Measure,* and *Manzanita.*

The guitar compilation *[58957]* is approaching 30,000 copies, which is nice money for Tony. We've had this vocal compilation mastered for about two years, and we have liner notes, but we still can't find a photo from the mid-'80s for the cover. And it might not do as well as the guitar record. It might do *better.*

Billy Wolf:

Physically, it is becoming more difficult for him to play. Developing his assets is something I'm concerned about—these live tapes. I've purposely waited. When something becomes an antique, it becomes a lot more valuable. This stuff is now rare.

He really doesn't want to work that much. It's hard for him. Playing music is a wonderful thing, but for Tony, it hurts to play. So the thing you love has gotten to be like work.

Larry Keel (guitarist and jam grass bandleader):

We had a really good bunch of dates in late 2007. Tony was taking extended solos on some of the Miles Davis stuff we were playing. I've been to many of his shows, and I've never seen him do anything like that. We did "All Blues" for about 25 minutes and a couple guitar duets, like "The Last Thing on My Mind." The sound was good, and everything was working right. I believe he was having a wonderful time.

We got three or four shows in; I think we had five more. Before the one at Mountain Stage, we got a call . . . Tony's dogs were out, and a neighbor's dog came through the fence and bit his hand. I hope things work out where we can do more with him. It's always a blessing to work with him.

Peter Rowan:

If Tony and I aren't working a lot, I assume he's doing what he wants to do. When we get together, we have a pretty good time.

He seems to be on a higher professional plane right now. I think Keith Case can call any of those promoters that have worked with Alison, and they'll put together five or six dates for the Unit, and know they'll do okay.

Right now, there's magic. We've had better response and bigger crowds than ever. My writing is moving in different directions and I haven't forced it to be tunes for our next album, but we'll see. It's not that Tony and I can go no further; it's just that you have to plateau at a certain point. And for us, it's better to leave room for some spontaneity.

Richard Bennett:

In Pigeon Forge last summer, I said, "You still holding cool, man?" That was our code for staying sober. He said, "Oh, yeah! Six years." He said, "You?" I said, "Yeah, man . . ." He said, "Good deal. I think we got it by the balls now."

Bryn Davies:

The Tony Rice of 1982 is definitely gone, but nowadays I think he's willing to experiment more in his lead playing and not so worried about playing perfect bluegrass. It makes playing with him so much more inspiring to me.

Ron Block (songwriter & banjo player with Union Station):

I love hearing Tony play "Danny Boy" or "Shenandoah"; I've told him he needs to make a whole record of just his guitar playing.

Peter Rowan:

Tony's a very romantic player, when he's left to play ballads and things like that. I've always wanted to get him into the studio with a rhythm section and have him do a jazz album.

John Cowan:

He expressed his jazz bone through his guitar so often. I'm really surprised he never did any Joe Williams or Jon Hendricks material . . . Even Sinatra! If Tony's voice was still operating, I'd love to hear him sing "In the Wee Small Hours of the Morning" or something like that.

Wyatt Rice:

I've asked Tony several times, "Man, look, if you ain't gonna sing, get together another Unit and let's go play some fuckin' *jazz* shows. You've got a ton of songs we've never even *played*." I only played them a few times onstage with him, stuff like "Gasology," "Within Specs . . ." All these incredible songs he *wrote,* man. I think he thinks we might have to rehearse or something.

Mark Schatz:

I think Tony's very demanding of himself, to play perfectly. He creates a little bit of a tension. It's always just a little bit . . . on edge. It has to do with him being a little bit . . . wound. And the environment of the band is gonna reflect the guy in charge.

One time, we were playing at the Station Inn, and he kept talking on the mic. He said, "You know, I had a dream last night that I was back playing with Grisman, and I made a mistake, and he turned around and shot me!" It was like this window opening up. I saw Grisman as his superego, an aspect of himself. That's how demanding he is of himself. It's part of what drives him to be as good a player as he is.

John Cowan:

The thing about it is, even if he never makes another record, the body of work he's given to this universe is *enough.* Anybody that's able to create brilliant work like that, under these conditions . . . it's *enough.* With the exception of Alison Krauss, there's no mansionaires in this ballpark. This music is a true art form, and people do it because they love it. It dawns on them at some point that they're not gonna be rock stars, and there's not gonna be any limos, or retirement accounts . . . That's *enough,* to ask somebody to live like that.

Peter Rowan:

I'd like to tell one last story. Tony and I were hired to play with Rick Danko from The Band one April at the Old Settler's Music Festival up around Round Rock in Texas.

Being Texas in April, it started to rain, then snow, then sleet. It was one of my first times with Tony onstage. I was thinking, *Man!* Here's Tony, this amazing, pristine, precise guitar wizard, and the weather is just *dumping* on us.

I looked over at him, in this driving hailstorm. He just smiled and said, "Hey, man, it's a gig!"

(Photo by Steve Johnson)

On the Road
Part 6

A Waffle House, Somewhere in Transit

July 2005: It's 2:45 A.M. on a dark highway somewhere between Tennessee and North Carolina, and Tony Rice is behind the wheel. These days he seems to spend more time on the road than anywhere else.

Since 9/11 and the advent of heightened airport security, Tony won't fly. His decision to stay earthbound was a long time coming. This is a man who detests anything that cramps his considerable style or stifles his beloved freedom. Back in the '70s, he'd fly to California for a booking or to record, decide to stay a weekend—or a month—with Grisman or somebody, without paying an arm and a leg to extend his stay. Disgusted by the airlines' inflexibility, he drives himself to all of his gigs now. He estimates that he put 75,000 miles on his car last year.

Rice allows himself few real luxuries. He keeps good books and music on tap, and he drinks good coffee when he's home. Over the years he has collected a couple of birds, a half-dozen dogs, and a complex stereo system. And then there are his vehicles. This truck, a 2005 Ford SVT F-150 Lightning pickup with a heavily modified 331-cubic-inch Triton V-8 engine, is a recent purchase. His 2003 Ford Mustang Cobra is at home, in need of four new tires; he says he can get about 20,000 miles out of 'em before he has to replace them, at a cost of about $1,800 a set.

(Photo by Laurie Hillis)

Today, we spent about six hours at Hilltop Studio for session work on the Donna Hughes project, which Tony is producing. It's almost three o'clock in the morning. Neither of us has eaten since about noon the day before, and Tony says he might be a little hungry. He pulls into a Waffle House, parks the truck with customary care, far from any other vehicle, and strides into the diner.

He orders two scrambled eggs with a side of bacon, raisin toast (which he eats with a fork) and a glass of plain white milk. His stamina for the road that seems to define his life is astonishing. When he finishes his meal, he plays a couple of rounds of poker on his cell phone. He seems relaxed and alert.

After Tony's omnipresent travel mug is filled to the rim with strong coffee, he pays the bill and we rise to leave. Then Tony spots something on the wall. "Hey, looky here," he says quietly, as he reaches for it. "A lightning bug. How 'bout that!" Cupping it gently in his hands, he slowly moves toward the exit, a door opening into a small vestibule with an outside door just beyond it.

His empathy for animals is legendary among those who know him well. Over the years, Pam's e-mails are filled with stories of Tony and his dogs, and how he fusses and frets over them and treats them like his beloved children. Tony himself will confide that the deaths of his pets have been some of the most heartbreaking moments of his life. And he obviously has great compassion for animals in the wild, even insects and reptiles. As Pam recounts later, "We were driving through Florida and he tried to save a baby rattlesnake he saw on the road, only to watch it get hit by a car. I hate to tell you what he yelled after the car."

He carries the insect so naturally, as if this were something that happened every day. I open the first door for him, and then the next. The moment he is through the second exit, he raises his hand to let the creature fly away. But it doesn't seem to want to leave him. We both watch it meander over his palm and wrist and sleeve. Then it is airborne—and heading back into the vestibule through the still-open door.

Tony, holding the door open, cannot reach the tiny wanderer. I reach up to intercept the firefly as gently as I can. I hold it aloft, my palm outstretched into the warm evening. It explores my hand for a moment or two. Finally it lifts off, once and for all, and soon it disappears into the darkness.

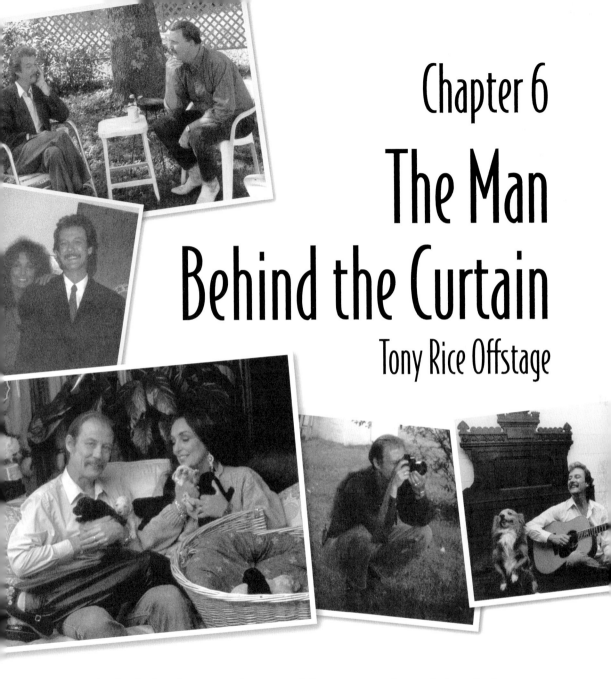

Chapter 6
The Man Behind the Curtain
Tony Rice Offstage

People think they know you because of the way you play and sing. And I am so guilty of that with Tony. I think I know who he is because of his records. I think I know what kind of person he is . . .

Don't you go, *[whispering]* "Who IS that???" When I was watching that video of him singing "Georgia on My Mind," I'm like, "Who is that man? Who *is* that?"

Don't you want to know so *bad?*

Alison Krauss

Chapter 6: Introduction

Onstage, Tony Rice is immaculate and graceful, a model of elegance and fine tailoring on a frame whose painful thinness belies its power and endurance. It is easy to imagine Rice in grand surroundings that echo his onstage persona.

The reality is somewhat different. Tony lives in a modest brick split-level house in a very pretty community at the foothills of the Blue Ridge Mountains in Rockingham County, NC, not too far from the Virginia border.

He shares this house with his wife, Pamela Hodges Rice. Once described in an article by a co-author of this book as a "half-wild Southern tombelle," Pam Rice is exotically beautiful, creative, imaginative, funny, and smart. She and Tony keep odd hours and devote themselves to their own pursuits and hobbies. Pam works at the historic old Chinqua Penn Plantation, where she is manager of the wine division, and she enjoys being surrounded by graceful antiques and chatting with curious, friendly strangers and wine lovers.

The Rices' much-loved housemates in this occasionally chaotic Ark include six standard poodles, a thundering herd of good-natured, playful dogs whose average weight is about 60 lbs., as well as several cockatiels and a small Jack Russell terrier.

Tony, when he's not on the road, spends most of his time in his "listening room," the big basement room in his house. In most other homes in the community, these half-underground spaces have been turned into family rooms and dens. In Tony's house, it is his center of operations, his control room. It's where everything happens. His wife calls this room "the dungeon."

If you stood in the crowded center of Tony Rice's listening room and slowly turned around in a circle, here are some of the things you'd see:

An old crank telephone. A rocking horse. Bibles, old and new. A special gold record award from the now-defunct Disk Jockey Records for the *Bluegrass Albums*, Volumes 1–4, their best-selling bluegrass records of all time. Uncashed IRS refund checks from several years for $1.57 and similar amounts. A 1972 photo of Tony, Stéphane Grappelli, and David Grisman. A framed triptych photo of Branford Marsalis and an envelope with the NBC peacock. A photograph of Herb Rice, Tony's dad. The Grammy for "Fireball." A stereo microscope for watch repair. A 1995 letter from Congressman Richard Burr regarding an NPR program about gay and lesbian books for children. A photograph of Bill Monroe. Vintage Coke bottles, dozens of them.

An oscilloscope. A photo of the Antique. An engraving of a violin. Scores of IBMA and SPBGMA awards. A guitar award he received in Turin, Italy in the early 1990s. License plates. The platinum record for Alison Krauss' "Now That I've Found You." Pam's oil portrait of John Wilkes Booth. A letter from the office of Governor Wilder, designating June 10, 1990 as Tony Rice Day in the great state of Virginia. Books on a variety of disparate topics . . . and a stack of Accutron service manuals. The gold record for Emmylou Harris' *Roses in the Snow*. A small burlwood-and-seashell lamp Mark O'Connor gave him for Christmas in 1979; Tony says it is one of his prized possessions.

Keep turning, and you'd see a snakeskin. An enormous Navajo medicine shield. NARAS Grammy nomination certificates. A globe. Accutron watches in a thousand stages of rejuvenation. An award from the Virginia Folk Music Association that begins with the greeting "To A Native Son Who Has Reflected Honor Upon Virginia." A photo of Tony at the grave of John Wilkes Booth. A fireman's helmet. Tens of thousands of dollars' worth of stereo components from Marantz, Bryston, Ortofon, and other names only an audiophile would recognize, with a sign over the stereo that says DANGER, DO NOT PUT ANYTHING ON TOP OF THIS. EVER. With a skull and crossbones at the bottom for added emphasis.

And there is music everywhere, *everywhere* in this room: thousands of CDs, vinyl recordings, cassettes; obscure Japanese pressings of his material and everybody else's; lacquer masters; autographed rarities from jazz and bluegrass legends . . . A survey of his collection reveals a profound truth about Tony Rice: his musical curiosity has no boundaries. There are discs by songbird Eva Cassidy, '80s rocker Huey Lewis, violinist Regina Carter, Hawaiian slide guitarist Sol Ho'opi'i, a Mahler symphony, a trio of R&B vocalists—Vanessa Williams, Anita Baker, and Angela Bofill; a pair of jazz guitarists—Lee Ritenour and Pat Metheny; jazz violinist Jean-Luc Ponty; Tony's beloved Oscar Peterson; Bob Dylan's *The Times They Are A-Changin';* Paganoni's 24 caprices by violinist Midori Goto, just 17 when she recorded them . . .

This is where Tony spends most of his waking hours when he is not on the road. He has been known to sit for hours and hours in front of his microscope, working on his beloved Accutron watches. "I'm not restoring them so much for myself," he says. "I'm restoring them so that somebody, 500 years from now, will be able to put one of them on their wrist and tell time with it, because it will still be running."

Sometimes he wishes he were better organized, but he says he's mostly content with things the way they are. "I don't really aspire to live any differently or have anything more than I have now. I might even be happy if I had less, I don't know." He pauses, looking around the cozy room at his treasures, as if taking stock. Finally, with satisfaction in his voice, he concludes the thought. "I enjoy getting these old timepieces going again, and spending time with my animals, and being home whenever I can. As much time as I can spend here, that's where I want to be."

Anything he takes an interest in, he takes it to the fullest. Whatever it may be, he wants to know everything there is to know about it.

Doyle Lawson, mandolinist & bandleader

Tony could solve a Rubik's Cube far faster than anyone I had ever witnessed.

Jon Sievert, concert photographer

I just think his whole persona is the coolest. He's the cat daddy all the way around.

Alan Bibey, mandolinist; member of Grasstowne

In His Own Words: Tony's Story

On making a living

As a recording artist, I make records for a living. It's not only that I want to express myself musically, but also I want to be able to make a house payment. That's a reality for a lot of artists. Most of 'em.

On photography

When I go on the road I feel empty without a couple camera bodies and a few lenses. If it's not that, it's usually something good to read, or some little audio device, like a digital audio machine. I like to read anything concerning the art of photography, anything to better myself at that particular hobby, at which I consider myself to be a serious amateur.

I like older Canons, manual focus F1s. I've got eleven of them, believe it or not. At last count I had 33 or 34 lenses, different lenses in Canon's FD mount system.

I'm now on the borderline of being able to have a book out of my color wildlife and landscape photography. At some point, I will do that.

On taking students

I took students years ago. They all told me I was the worst teacher they ever had. I don't have the patience. Sitting down with a guitar and showing people how to do something is really hard.

On his favorite venues

I really like small, restored opera houses. One of my favorite venues, Sheldon Hall in St. Louis, is coming up at the end of the month. Everybody loves it; it's notorious for the way it sounds. Chicago School of Music is another one of my favorites. There's some clubs that sound pretty good, too.

My *least* favorite is outdoor gigs. The sound of the guitar, my own comfort . . .

that's the reason. Outdoor gigs do a lot of damage to instruments. They have to mine. Back in the days of chamber music, Stradivarius violins and cellos, chamber music and orchestral music were seasonal. They shut the damn season down around May, and didn't continue it until around October, depending on the climate, because the instruments just could not take the heat and humidity. How often do you think you're gonna play an outdoor gig where the temperature is about 72 degrees onstage? It just ain't gonna happen.

My heart and soul is in acoustic music. And when I say *acoustic,* I mean unamplified instruments. That's real hard, once you reach a certain level, playing in bigger venues to larger crowds. It's almost impractical to try to pull it off.

The ideal is a gig in an intimate setting, where the crowd is fairly up close, the sound is real good, and you can hear every nuance, and you start playing for a crowd and you *feel* something coming off of them. It's nothing you can see, or hear, or touch, or taste, but you can feel it coming off a crowd: that they are enjoying being entertained. It starts kind of a feedback loop: the more I feel it coming off of the audience, the more I want to give it back to them. Those gigs happen once in a while. But sometimes they don't. Sometimes you pull up there, you take your axe out, you go play, and you get the hell out of there.

On his appearance

I don't know who said, "Clothes make the man," but he was right. That's kind of a primitive part of me that adheres to that.

Clothes make the man. That's not to say that I haven't shown up somewhere in life looking like a slob, but if I ever did, it's usually at the tail end of a three-day drunk.

It's a weird world, when people accept that the musicians on the stage are dressed just as badly as the people in the audience.

American society as a whole . . . all you gotta do is take a look on a holiday weekend, and you're looking at a bunch of fucking slobs. I'm not kidding. Maybe the reason I dress like I do goes back to the day where, if you went out on the street, unless you had some sort of ditch-digging job to do, you made an effort to not look like a slob.

On his hair

The last haircut I had was right before the flood in '93. India [Pam's daughter, who Tony loves as his own] was visiting me in Florida with a friend; they went to Disneyworld. I told India, "While you're here, what the hell, I'll pay you to cut my hair." So she did. After that . . . I don't know. I don't have an explanation for why I just kept letting it

(Photo courtesy Nancy Gatling)

grow. I think I was working on the car one day, and I wanted to get it out of my way, so I pulled it behind me and grabbed a rubber band to tie it back. I thought, "Hey, I could start a movement with this." Which I never did, obviously. Hey, look—at my age, and with my stature in this music business kind of sagging, anything charismatic is a plus!

Doesn't that look a little bit weird, for somebody to walk onstage in a tailored suit and a tie, but have hair all the way down to his waist? Doesn't that look a little weird? *I want it to look weird.* Those two things don't go together.

On his clothes

Back in the heyday of Miles Davis' most famous bands, you wouldn't have seen Miles without a tailored suit on. *My musical heroes wear suits.* You won't see Wynton Marsalis without a tailored suit, or Branford . . . If they don't have on suits, they will have dressed in such a manner as to leave no doubt that they are conscious of their appearance.

If I can find 'em, I get Yves St. Laurent suits, because I can't buy a suit off the rack and just put it on and wear it. I've got to take it to the tailor, for the waist in the pants, and the length. And then the coat's

taken in. I like a European or Italian fit, in a suit—without regard to whether it's in style or not. I don't give a shit if it's in style.

If I didn't wear a silk tie, I'd feel like I was wearing something fake. All my jewelry is real . . . I've got so many pairs of boots, I don't even know where to start talking about them.

(Photo by Nancy Gatling)

Clothes are like a lot of other things you buy. You usually get what you pay for. I've got tailored suits at home that I've wore onstage for at least ten years, and they still look good and are quite nice.

I don't iron anything; I do my own clothes at home, and suits go to the dry-cleaner; I pack 'em a certain way so that by the time I get to the hotel, they're not mangled. I once read in the liner notes of a Robert Johnson album that he had a way of folding his suits; he knew how to do it just right—a combination of folding and rolling up, and he carried them in a bag. All he had to do was pull his suits out of the bag, shake 'em down, and they looked like they had just been pressed. Somehow he'd figured out a way to do it. I never figured *that* one out . . . I'm able to pull it off with

(Courtesy Tony Rice)

a garment bag, and that's good enough for me.

On food

I'd have to say my favorite food, as an entrée, would be coldwater lobster tail, and any of the trimmings that go with it. As long as I have plenty of lemon and sourdough French bread.

I was in Maine two or three months ago. I went up by myself with some camera equipment, and came across a little mom-and-pop seafood place up on the coast. I couldn't remember the name of it to save my life. But I have never had lobster as good.

When I lived in San Francisco for ten years, I got spoiled there. There were gobs of good restaurants of all kinds. I used to love Thai food. And one of my favorite places of all time was Alioto's #8. It's a renowned restaurant in the most densely packed area of Fisherman's Wharf.

It's not beyond me to feel real satisfied going into a Taco Bell. I'm not a connoisseur. I don't think I'm a connoisseur of anything, to tell you the truth.

On his late nights

I like to listen to music late at night, sometimes into the wee hours of the morning. That's when it's quiet.

I quit adhering to any kind of schedule years ago. I like to take it a day at a time. If it's the right time of the year, and I want to be outdoors fishing or taking photos, I'll get on an early-morning schedule so I can make the best of that. And I get into night moods, where I like the night more than I do the day.

On his coffee habit

I like good coffee . . . although I'm not the guy that's gonna go to Starbucks and pay $75 a pound for coffee that came from Antarctica or somewhere. Two pots a day is my norm. I drink a pot of coffee over a few short hours after I get up. Then, come mid-evening, 9 or 10:00, I'll start on another pot, and will generally finish it by 1 or 2:00 in the morning.

But a good grade of coffee doesn't give me near as much nervousness and anxiety as regular old domestic freeze-dried, jarred coffees. Good coffee will not produce the nervous side effects of some of the more commercial coffees.

On his weight

I have always been very fine-boned.

I was kind of a whopper during some of the years I was with Crowe. I got quite big. Not fat, but I was certainly what you would call a big person. I was maybe 15 or 20 lbs. overweight, technically, maybe for two or three years.

My father was always very slender. My father appeared to have two things: bones, and on top of his bones was nothing but this stuff that looked like *power*. And *it was*. He was extremely strong. You could take a look at his arms and see brute power, and he wasn't doing anything.

On flying

I don't fly anymore. I used to do that on a regular basis—in fact, I used to fly everywhere—but it's something I don't do anymore. The airline industry has gotten out of control. I'm not the one who knows who to point the finger at, but the bottom line as to why the airline industry is in such trouble would probably be corporate greed.

The appealing part of traveling, back when I was flying, was having the option to go somewhere and maybe stay for an extra couple of days and record if necessary. When the government deregulated airlines, things really started to go downhill. Airlines started to herd people around like cattle. Having to buy a ticket two weeks in advance, having to stay over a Saturday night . . . All of a sudden, there came these rules where you had to adhere to your original flight plan, destination, time of return and all that, and no deviation without serious penalties. Stupid little rules that really don't make any sense. When that happened, it became an inconvenience for me.

I can guarantee you: any musicians who have to fly to execute their craft, nine out of ten of them are absolutely disgusted at what they have to go through, taking their musical instruments on and off planes . . . it became a nightmare, where years ago it used to be so easy.

On sentimental possessions

I still have the key ring from the car I bought for $75 from Sam Bush when I was 18 years old. Every car I've ever had since that one, I've put all my keys on that same key ring. There hasn't been any reason to change it.

When I go on the road, I wear the same Accutron watch I've been wearing for 35 years. I bought it brand-new in 1973. I think I paid about $135 for it, which in those days was real unusual. I walked into

the Holiday Inn with it one night, and J.D. Crowe looked at me and said, "Tony, what in the *world* are you thinking? Have you lost your *mind?* A hundred and thirty five dollars for a watch?" Well, here it is, 35 years later and I'm still wearing it . . . I guess I got my money's worth.

On Accutrons

Max Hetzel was a Swiss engineer who invented the Accutron in 1953, under the auspices of Omar Bradley, a five-star general who graduated with Eisenhower from West Point. Omar Bradley was Eisenhower's secretary of defense, and he also owned the Bulova Corporation. The Accutron was designed as a gentleman's wristwatch, but NASA was getting into high gear in the mid-1950s, and they had heard about a watch that ran off a tuning fork and would be unaffected by the lack of gravity. They figured, "Hmmm, we might be onto something here . . ."

The very same Accutron movement that a person would wear on his wrist was used in timers on 46 outer-space missions. They were used in the cockpits of X-15 fighter pilots. The Accutron still doesn't have any competition in terms of timekeeping ability if you rebuild it right.

I traveled with my Accutron for a while. I'd take a few tools and a few watches to be refurbished, and my stereo microscope, and if I had two or three days in a hotel room, I had something to do. I work on them all the time. I don't do it for money. I can't even count the number I've built for special friends and given away as gifts. I'm now one of the global techs that people contact to troubleshoot their Accutrons and find out how to fix them.

On his politics

Politically, if the truth be known, I am probably more in the center than any other human being that's ever been born. I see the best and the worst of both sides. But the sad part is I see a nation politically divided in a way I never saw before. There was a time when Democrats and Republicans could sit down and talk politics and enlighten each other. You don't get that anymore. If they talk at all, they're trying to ram their own political convictions down the throat of anybody that's politically opposed to them.

I carry a copy of the Constitution and the Declaration of Independence in my back pocket. It's always with me. I don't go onstage without it. I keep it with me as a reminder of what our Founding Fathers went through to escape the terror and the torture in England, to come here and set up a land of liberty. And how intelligent they were for writing that document! It's damn fine the way it is.

On the right to bear arms

I am a firm believer in our second amendment. I am pro-gun, and pro-ammunition. I think it's also important to make sure the guy who's sold one is not a lunatic, and to make sure that people who want a permit to carry a concealed weapon all have to go through the same thing I did: take a firearms class, and be tested on it.

Don't take my word for it; Google the statistics for the rate of homicides committed by registered gun owners, responsible American citizens, versus the homicide rate by NON-registered gun owners, and see what you find out.

There's times when a gig is downtown somewhere in a big city, and the only place to park is in an alley. Here I am walking out of this gig with this Antique, and I'm by myself, and I just got paid in cash. I'm a responsible gun owner, registered to carry a concealed firearm, and I use discretion in such matters. The damn guitar is not for sale, and I ain't gonna give it to you, either!

On his education

When I started to get into the music business in my adult life, I took it upon myself to educate myself, with encyclopedias and dictionaries and almanacs. I had been wearing this Accutron on my watch for years, and I had no idea what a single thing in there did. At some point, I started to wonder, "How does this work?" I started to read about it; I sought to educate myself about this timepiece on my own.

So I got a combination of formal education when the school system was really good, and self-education when I perceived that the school system was bad. My education as a guitar player? I don't know. I leave that up to the listener, as to whether I am educated in my craft.

On recording

On my own albums, I never want to roll tape prior to nine o'clock at night. It's nuts. I'm a night-time person. I like doing a good take and going in the control room and hearing it. And back in the old days, I loved going outside, taking a walk, having a couple good tokes, drinking a beer and sitting around in the California night with Sam and Vassar, shooting the shit at two in the morning.

On his music

I'm not doing this so much for flattery as I am to offer people some escape from the bullshit of everyday living. I try to make it pleasant for my *own* ears first, which I don't think is egotistical, with the hopes of sharing it with somebody else.

I don't think any musician's capable of accessing every emotion and translating it to their playing, not that I know of. There are times when the two definitely connect, but there's other times that, to keep from embarrassing yourself, you play the only shit in a solo that you can play. And when you're in that moment, you're not thinking about a past lover as influence on this line coming up.

But other times, it seems as if I'm playing the tune for a friend that died.

On his resemblance to his father

I am more like my father than any of my brothers, probably by a country mile. He always paid his bills, and he paid 'em in cash. I did that up to the point where you couldn't do it anymore, where it's required that you carry around a piece of plastic so they can screw you over with finance charges. I don't know that my father ever had a credit card. He had a checking account. But I think he chose to pay his bills by cash whenever he could. Or he would do what I still do: put a cashier's check in the mail, so when they get it, they know they've got the money.

My father was a proponent of the right to fuck up. I am, too. I don't think it's fair to anybody in American society that we be so smothered with law breathing down our neck 24 hours a day . . . There's this giant force that wants to make sure we're all safe from the boogeyman. It keeps throwing law at us to make sure we

Herb Rice
(Courtesy Louise Rice)

live in this little bubble of safety. Which ain't never gonna happen!

I have a whole *lot* of resentments that my father had. I resent my Social Security number being used for anything whatsoever other than for when I start getting checks when I get old. Otherwise, I think it's an absolute *atrocity* that human beings should have numbers like that in some database for any fucker on this planet to wanna snoop around into.

On his occasional refusal to take encores

If I choose not to do an encore, it's not because I don't appreciate my audience. It has nothing to do with my audience. I'm always in the moment with that. 50% of the time, it's because my hands just won't move anymore. The other 50% of the time, it's a desire to NOT do an encore for the sake of doing an encore, and leave my audience with the memory of the last tune they heard . . . rather than go out and do an encore and deliver a sub-standard performance.

However, to counterbalance that, if everything is high-energy and the show has been good and I feel good, and I'm not exhausted, then it's not uncommon for me to respond to an encore and go out and play for another 15 minutes—three tunes, including maybe a long one.

I've never agreed that an encore should be part of a performance. It doesn't have to be. In the classical music world, an orchestra will get a standing ovation . . . a chamber ensemble will have people screaming for more. What the hell are they gonna do? They're not gonna play "Moon River" if they've just finished playing a Ravel symphony! The only thing the orchestra can do is take a bow.

On dealing with overeager fans

If I'm not feeling pressured, and if I have time to do my normal routine at a performance, then I am happy to talk to fans all day and all night. In general, I am very dedicated to my fans. They are the reason I do what I do.

But if I pull up to a gig and get out of my vehicle, and people are waiting, that pisses me off, terribly bad. I've been known to be extremely rude to people who I think are extremely rude to me, when the only thing they want is the autograph, and they want it *now,* and they could give a shit whether you have a few minutes to gather your thoughts. While you're trying to unload your instrument out of your vehicle,

somebody's handing you a pen and a CD. To me, that's just rude. I have my *own* autographs that I've gotten from my heroes. I would *never* catch them in a moment where I thought it was disturbing them to do that.

When I show up at a gig, the one thing I want to do is be alone with my band. I want to have time alone where I can warm up, and not necessarily have anybody else around to hear me playing the guitar. Sometimes when I'm warming up I sound like shit.

Even to this day, I hate situations where I'm surrounded by a whole bunch of people, unless it's at my discretion. I like my fans, and I like talking to people, but there's a time and a place for everything.

On dealing with people in general

Not that I put up a sign that says "Do Not Enter" or anything, but there's kind of an established policy around the house with people who know me. I think people can sense when you need time to yourself, and when you're ready to congregate with friends and family.

On tapers

We use discretion with allowing taping. Sometimes they're gonna do it anyway. You don't have control over that. What in the world is there to stop a sound guy from plugging a little tiny DAT machine or a CD recorder into the console?

That music doesn't deserve to be shared with anybody other than who was there and had direct eye contact with the event. So many gigs are full of mistakes. You get some asshole sending that shit out over a computer, and the person listening to it can only hear a little inkling of what was really going on. The vigil is gone. The crowd re-action is gone. The taped performance of the gig could have been vastly inferior to the sound reinforcement of the room. For that reason, I say artists have a right to re-sent bootlegging.

Every once in a while, I'm grateful it happens. Somebody will play a bit of a show we did somewhere, and it's so good, and the audio has captured it . . . but that's rare.

On his record collection

I'm still a vinyl fanatic to some degree, so I head to places that have good vinyl for sale. There's a used record store in Greens-boro; they've got gobs and gobs of vintage vinyl, and they take good care of it. I have quite a few early Oscar Peterson things I re-ally like and a lot of RCA Red Seal recordings.

So many things I have on CD sound better on vinyl. A couple of days ago I found a Wynton Marsalis album on Co-lumbia—I was flipping through a bin, and there it was: a pristine copy of *Marsalis Standard Time, Volume 1,* on vinyl. I've had the compact disc for over ten years.

There's no telling what I'm liable to come in the door with. Anything from atonal *avant garde* screaming horn players playing modern jazz to something as soft as Handel's *Water Music* or *Music for the Royal Fireworks* or Bach Partitas, or sonatas played by Heifetz . . . five minutes later it might be a Del McCoury album.

I consider music to be timeless. Some people are in a rush to get out there and hear the latest new thing that's stirring up a ruckus in the music world, and I'm the guy who thinks, "Well, if I don't hear it for five or six years, it's gonna be just as good then as it is now."

On listening

When I get in the mood, it sometimes lasts for weeks and weeks: the only thing I want to do is hear really good recorded music.

So much of musicianship actually in-volves *listening.* I put the emphasis on lis-tening to get inspiration. The ratio is differ-ent for some musicians. I'm probably 70% listening, 30% hands-on involvement my-self. John Hartford and I talked about this: *Where do you get ideas without listening?* I guess some people, if you locked 'em up in solitary confinement, could come out with some amazing music. Myself, I get inspira-tion listening to all kinds of music forms. I can't think of a single music form I haven't heard something out of to enjoy, and that includes opera and rap. I really love cham-ber music, and small-group modern jazz and bebop, and of course traditional blue-grass and folk music. Probably the music I listen to the least, because I think it's so mechanized and commercial, music made only for the cash register, is *country music from the last 25 or 30 years.*

On his stereo

There's a classification of people I think of as weird: people who buy elaborate sound systems to listen to the *system,* and not to the music. I'm a guy who listens to the music. If my ears perceive that I'm hearing the music with as much accuracy as the original artist intended, that's what I strive for.

Downstairs in my house, there's a larger room that's halfway underground. That's my main listening room. It's kind of acoustically dead, so it requires a lot to drive it up to control-room-standard listening level, right around 85–90 dB. That's the reason for the high power of the system: for clarity, because the room is so overstuffed with furniture and drapes.

Keeping an audio system up and running and well-tuned is kinda like having a Ferrari. It requires a little attention. The heart of my system is a Marantz Model 7 tube preamp from the late 1950s. I found it used in an audio store in Nashville. It's driving a pair of huge Marantz model 500 power amplifiers from 1971, in a balanced configuration. Each amp is driving just one speaker; they're over 1000 watts because they're driving 6 ohm loads. I've got a pair of Urei professional control room monitors with the original Altec 604 drivers. My analog stuff comes off a Ortofon MC30 phono cartridge and an old direct-drive turntable. I'm not one of the belt-drive fanatics. On the digital end, I have one of the newer Marantz models that also plays super-audio CDs. I run that into an Audio Research DAC 3 Mark II all-tube output stage digital-to-audio converter. I've got one of Sony's ES 2000 DAT machines, which I don't use much anymore because it's just as easy to record onto a CD as to DAT.

I think my entire system is cabled with Audio Quest cable. The guy who goes out and pays some enormous amount of money to run a cable from an amplifier to a speaker is out of his mind! I try to be practical with home audio. Some of the stuff I have is old, but it's very well cared for, and very well-tuned. In particular, I'm proud of the speaker system I bought out of a recording studio in Tampa, Florida. It's still a recording industry standard for accuracy in control rooms—the Urei 811s.

The newest toy I've got is a vacuum tube Stax headphone amplifier. I found one of their newer model vacuum tube headphone driver amps. It drives a pair of Stax electrostatic headphones. Boy, that's a really incredible listening experience. Sometimes I'll put them on to shield myself from the outside noise, as well as to shield the real word from my OWN noise. I've been known to play stuff so loud that the streetlights dim.

Years ago, I noticed that all good recording studio engineers play back at a fairly high level—not a level that's painful or damaging, but one that's fairly high for clarity and nuance. As time went on, I decided I wanted to have that at home. It's almost a never-ending process, to keep it all up and running. I don't profess to have golden ears or anything like that, but I've built a system based on practicality, and my desire to concentrate on the music, and not on the system.

On women in his past:

By nature, I don't kiss and tell. It's just one of those things.

(Photo courtesy of Louise Rice)

On losing Larry & Vassar:

I haven't come out of it yet, but I'm slowly getting there. Vassar and I were close for a long time. I don't know. I get the feeling that I was the one chosen to guide him through this process, because he knew he wasn't going to make it; he knew his chances weren't very good. It takes its toll. Of course, the next year, Larry got sick and died . . . and Pam's brother died about a month before Larry. Since Vassar got sick, life has been kind of rough.

I was holding Larry when he died. He'd been on life support and unconscious for well over three days. Most of the family was there, and Linda, his wife, was the one that had to make the decision. I was sitting on the bed with him when he took his last breath. That's not something you want to do every day.

I've got mixed feelings about what funerals represent in our culture. The older I get, the less importance I place on those

things. A lot of it is unnecessary ritual . . . especially the expense.

On faith and spirituality:

To me, God represents our universe and everything in it, and what people refer to as Jesus is just a culmination of the divine. That's about all I know about it. Spirituality, to me, is a very personal thing. So many people feel the necessity to congregate with their fellow beings in some form of organized worship, and look what's that done! Religious conflict is at the foundation of almost every war we've ever had.

I am not religious. I am not denominational. I do not subscribe to any form of organized religion. But am I a spiritual person? Yeah, you bet I am! I feel that connection with an infinite universe that did not start out of nothing. I never miss a day having coffee and talking to my Maker. That's part of the daily meditation I do every day, and I talk to the person I refer to as the Holy Creator. I have a deal with him: we don't get into serious conversation until we both agree that I've had enough coffee. And when that happens, we proceed with the conversation.

I actually say the same prayer . . . I guess it's a prayer, because it's a conversation with what I believe in as God: *"Dear Heavenly Father: I offer myself to Thee to build with me and to do with me as Thou wilt . . . Relieve me of the bondage of self, that I may better do Thy will. Take away my difficulties, that victory over them may bear witness to those I would help of Thy power, Thy love, and Thy way of life. And may I do*

Thy will always." I say it every day, whether I feel it or not.

On sobriety:

I have been sober since May 29, 2001. I wouldn't go so far as to say that my spiritual convictions are what keep me sober, because that wouldn't be true. What keeps me sober is that I don't want any alcohol to drink. I got tired of it. It was beginning to interfere with my music and my relationships with my peers. I got tired of being drunk, and I got tired of being alone.

But the reason I say it's not spirituality that keeps me sober is because if I wanted to indulge in alcohol, I'd get in my car and go up to the store and get myself a couple of six-packs of beer. I reserve the right to do it, but I just don't want it anymore. And no outside source of any kind tempts me to want to drink alcohol I don't want.

If I'm sad or angry, the first thing I think about is my days of trying to drink those things away, and how it only made it worse. Whatever problem or hardship might be happening, the alcohol always only made it worse. When you have a few glasses of wine, or a few shots of whiskey, or a few bottles of beer, there's that little timeframe when you feel like, "Who gives a shit? Let a nuclear bomb go off beside me and I could care less, because I feel good." But whatever goes up must come down.

The Tao of Tony

A healthy ego is one that you keep to yourself. I don't see myself as one iota egotistical. At the same time, I know what my musicianship is worth. I know that better than anybody else. When people would assume that I *don't* know that, they're wrong.

And I am aware of every note I miss. Every one of them.

Family, Friends & Fans

Tony called me downstairs to his dungeon one night to tell me something was in his fireplace. There, flapping around in the soot, was this little dove. I got a spare cage, removed the top, and he flapped inside. After a few days he seemed normal.

Tony loved that lil' guy so much. Every day he took him outside and sat the cage on the back of his pickup, so he could see the other doves. He really perked up for his outings. Tony can make a call just like a dove, so I think he thought Tony was a big dove, maybe his parent. We were waiting for his tail feathers to grow out so we could set him free. We waited six months or more and they never grew.

We went to bed one night and the bird seemed fine. When I got up that morning to go to work, he appeared to be sleeping in a nesting position. He was gone. I never like to give Tony bad news when he first wakes up, but I could not let him find Little Dove dead. He took it really hard.

When I came home and started burying him, Tony asked me why I had put him in a flower pot. That was also how I had buried Hootie, our cockatiel. I explained that after a year I would take the soil to a pretty place in the yard and plant an ornamental tree with them so they could go on living in another way for him to enjoy. He seemed pleased. He stayed and watched me place the rocks over the flowerpot tomb. We both had tears streaming down our faces. I often wonder what our neighbors think when they see us doing strange things like that. Two adults crying over a flower pot.

Pamela Hodges Rice, Tony's wife

(Photo by Pam Rice)

CARS & DRIVING

Mark Schatz:

Tony appreciates fine things. He likes a good guitar, nice threads, a good meal, a nice car . . .

Billy Wolf:

He knows about cars! It's another one of his hobbies. He has a fantastic brain.

Sam Bush:

When I moved to Louisville, I had my first car—it was a '62 Rambler station wagon, and we called it the Baja Buggy. The very first weekend I took that sucker up there to Louisville to play, before Tony joined the Bluegrass Alliance, I was at Ebo Walker's brother's house, it was parked in the street, and his neighbor backed out, didn't see my car, and creamed the driver's side. I don't think the door ever worked again. It had vacuum wipers. If you went up a hill, they would almost quit working. It was one of those "ya gotta put a quart of oil in at every fill-up cars." I bought it for $200 and was lucky to have it.

My first wife's dad helped us buy another car, so I sold the Baja Buggy to Tony. He just used it every weekend. After we'd get done playing Saturday night, he'd hop in his car, drive to Lexington and stay with Larry Sunday and Monday night, and come back Tuesday when we started playing again.

I always said, "Now, Tony, you got to put a quart of oil in that sucker every fill-up, and don't go over 55 or you're askin' for it!" I *never* had it over 55. Maybe he *did* keep the oil in it, but it just finally blew up on him going around New Circle Road in Lexington. I think he took the license plate off and left it on the side of the road, and that was it.

He really got into Chrysler LeBarons when he was living in Lexington playing with J.D. I guess later he started with the Lincolns. And now he's the Mustang Man.

Billy Wolf:

SpaceGrass was this Dodge Challenger he had, and of course he had a publishing company—well, it's hard to know who got named after what, but it was called SpaceGrass music. He's always been good with cars. We went down the main drag all hours of the night in that Challenger . . . A hundred miles an hour was *slow*. We used to *fly* in that thing! It was an automatic transmission, but he had a way of making it work like a clutchless stick.

Sam Bush:

We were in SpaceGrass, sitting on the Golden Gate Bridge in a traffic jam, and realized later that an earthquake had hit San Francisco while we were sitting on the bridge. We never felt it! We were going from Tony's pad over to the studio, and we got there, and Bill Wolf said, "Man, did you feel that earthquake? It was a big one!"

Todd Phillips:

We were kinda like brothers. If we weren't rehearsing, he'd pull up to my house every day about ten in the morning, and we'd either go down to the rollercoaster in Santa Cruz, or to Tower Records . . . I've even got pictures of him helping me pull a transmission out of a Dodge Dart. You've gotta see Tony under a 1966 Dodge Dart, pulling a transmission.

Tim O'Brien:

Another thing about him that amazed me: knowing that he played with Grisman; I thought of those guys as real sophisticates. When I first got to know Tony, I started thinking, "Geez, he drives a *Town Car?*" And then I realized he's more like Jimmy Martin, y'know? He's kinda like Larry Sparks or Jimmy Martin. He's a Southern Guy. He's one real true gentleman.

Peter Rowan:

In the whole time we've worked together, he flew one time: out to Wintergrass to play with the Grisman Quintet. Where a normal band might cover 2,000 miles in a weekend, flying here and flying there and driving there, Tony has to drive the whole thing. That's gotta be hard . . . fourteen, fifteen-hour drives. That's *work*. If we all decided to ride together, we could have a bus, and make it easy . . . But Tony wants to drive his car. He loves his car.

Pam Rice:

Tony doesn't like to fly, but he travels by car, fast. You learn to hold all your bodily functions till it's time for a gas stop. He drives a big black Mustang convertible with a dust cloud behind it . . . the 35th Anniversary model with Rausch conversion package and throttle body extension.

Billy Wolf:

I have to compute his mileage annually. We're talking between 50,000 and 80,000 miles a *year*. He's a million-miler behind the wheel. Several times over, probably.

I don't even *look* when he's driving. I'm thinking about something else. He's a rock. It's just like his rhythm guitar playing. It's just perfect, that's all.

Larry Keel:

He used to show up in a Mustang, but now it's some kind of truck, a Ford truck, I think.

(Photo by Pam Rice)

PHOTOGRAPHY

Mark Schatz:

Tony's a really fastidious, particular cat with everything that he does. The guitar, of course, is the main thing, but he's a big photography buff. His cameras are always in perfect shape, and he knows all the lenses.

Pam Rice:

Tony is one of the most amazing photographers. He does a lot of macro, a lot of wildlife shots . . . I like to do pen-and-ink drawings of old shacks, so he takes pictures of a lot of shacks. Someday he hopes to have a book out of his photography. Somebody who thinks Tony Rice was never in their neck of the woods is gonna be real surprised to see that he photographed some old building falling down next to their house with an old tractor under it.

We lost two of my favorite photos that he did in the flood. One was of burley tobacco, with an old barn. All the burley was leaning and coming up in a cone, and it looked like they were marching up a hill. The other was a white heron or an egret flying in the opposite direction of a rushing stream; that was amazing.

The one he did of the reproduction of the Statue of Liberty in Las Vegas is my current favorite. We spent a night in Vegas, and we didn't go into the casinos, but we rode up and down the Strip. I'd never seen it, but Tony went there a lot as a kid and camped out in the desert, because his dad owned land in Hot Springs, Nevada. When we were there, they'd just started to put up the Statue of Liberty. I drove the car, and Tony was hanging out the window.

Billy Wolf:

Anything he pursues, he pursues with excellence. He's a fantastic film-based photographer . . . If I could sneak him into digital photography, I think he would be a terror. But I don't think he likes computers. I don't think he likes the keyboard. He said, "This *double-click* and *single-click*." I said, "Tony, it's just like mashing a G-chord. Once you get it, it becomes instinctual."

And he knew all about the various California birds. I still have a couple of framed pictures of birds that he gave me in my office at home. And in Corte Madera, when he was with Leela, he had a bird he named Roscoe. It was a red cardinal that came and sat on the porch. He didn't have it in a cage or anything.

KEEPSAKES

Pam Rice:

Tony does this impersonation of a character based on all the turban-wearing men who work around the D.C. area in convenience stores. He would see one of them pretty often, and the guy would actually throw in this phrase—"one time"—at the end of every sentence.

Years ago Jewell worked at a North Carolina cable company. Tony would call her from Florida and leave messages like his cable was out all the time, speaking as that turbaned dude. He would say, "My cable is out, so can't you fix it *one time* . . ." Next message he left, he would be madder and add more, and end it the same way: *"one time!"* He would act like he was blaming them for all the problems in his life because the cable was out. "The cable is still not working and my uncle's heart attacked him, so will you come and fix the cable, please . . . *one time!"*

For Christmas that year, Jewell gave him a Colibri lighter engraved "ONE TIME," and he has carried it ever since. She has sent it back to the company numerous times for refurbishing. He took all of us to D.C. in 1987, and Jewell had never been there. She bought him a fake key that said "The Key to Happiness: Washington, D.C." He has carried it on his key ring for 21 years, and he will carry it to the grave and beyond if he can. Just like that old money clip. It was his first one; his first wife, Kate, gave it to him. It had a thunderbird on it, but it fell off. He has been given many clips since then, even gold ones, but he will only carry that old one Kate gave him.

CLOTHING

Peter Rowan:

I'll say something about Tony's dressing: it's completely different. Tony's dressing is more to the shape of his approach. He has a very straight line; it sets the guitar off . . . he wears these boots with a pointed toe, and his fingertips are kind of like those points, too. That ensemble is really reflective of the classicality of his stage presence. It's all balanced. Those tapering fingers, and the tie creates a line that crosses over the guitar neck, and the shape of the guitar body is soft and feminine, and he's a black silhouette. It's cool.

(Courtesy Mike Kelly)

Ronnie Rice:

Tony would be in a suit on his *boat.* I'm serious!

Pam Rice:

If he finds a shirt he likes a lot he goes back and buys six or ten of them. He has a tie collection that would blow your mind. If he really likes a necktie, he buys two, just alike. His reasoning behind duplication: if something happens to one, he has an exact spare. I indulge him in the quirk, but draw the line on a duplicate of me.

Mike Auldridge:

I'm from a family of nine kids, so I was washing and ironing my own clothes since I was eight or nine. When I got married, my wife had never ironed a shirt for me. One time Tony stayed here, and he came downstairs with a shirt in his hand, and he said to Lisa, "What are the chances of gettin' you to iron this for me?" She just looked at him and said, "Maybe *Mike* will iron it for you, but *I* don't iron clothes!"

My style is a little more on the cowboy side, and his is a little more on the New York Dude side. We were both very fastidious dressers.

Pam Rice:

Tony's zip boot is a Stacy Adams. Mostly he wears Lucchese, a cowboy-type boot; those are his favorites. He gets most of his boots and leather coats from Purgason's Leather Products in Greensboro.

Sharon Gilchrist:

It's kind of bizarre, working with Peter and Tony in the same band and trying to come up with any cohesive dress style. Peter's coming from left field, and Tony's wearing suits that are super-stylized, in perfect condition . . . I think it's a reflection of the way he does *everything*. It's in perfect condition, perfectly ironed—I don't know *how* he does that.

Pam Rice:
Our friend, Karen French, knitted him this beautiful long scarf way back in the 1990s. He has dragged it, like Linus, winter through summer. I asked him why in the world he packed the scarf in the car in summer. He said, "If I want to let the top of the car down at night, I can wrap it around my neck and keep my hair from blowing back in my face." Well, that makes sense, since his hair is a couple of feet long. He added, "If someone else is driving, and I get sleepy, I use it for my pillow in the back seat." That makes sense also, since he is skinny enough to fold up in the back seat of the Cobra and sleep!

Mark Johnson:
Tony turned me onto Rush Limbaugh. I'm the one who turned him onto the Rush Limbaugh ties—I bought him one for Christmas. He went out and bought 30 of them or something. You remember when everyone was showing up with the Rush Limbaugh ties? We would sit there and laugh and laugh, and then Bill Emerson got in on it, too.

John Cowan:
[horrified] He likes *Rush Limbaugh?!* How could he love John Coltrane *and* Rush Limbaugh?

Pam Rice:
Every one of Tony's stage ties has a mate. Back in 1993, I sent an emergency Tuscarora funeral care package to our friend Derek Lowry when the mother of Ray Littleturtle, a Lumbee tribal council representative, passed away. [The Lumbee and Tuscarora are Native American tribes with members in North Carolina.] Tuscarora traditionalist guys were dropping everything to get "back home" for her service. Derek said they were scrambling to find proper neckties for everyone to wear. I told him to stop looking; I would FedEx enough ties to cover it. I sent 52 of Tony's retired stage ties by overnight. Of course, they all had mates. Derek passed them out like hot coffee as each guy arrived. He said they all loved them.

PRACTICING & PERFECTION

Jerry Douglas:
He chewed his cuticles and kept his nails short. He played all the time. His schedule was to wake up around 5:00 P.M. and go to bed around 6:00 A.M., and if he was awake he had a guitar in his hands. His calluses were tough.

Harry Sparks (Louisville-based luthier and friend of Tony's):
Tony was tenacious in his zeal to become a real great guitar player. He worked as hard as anybody I've ever seen. And his mentor, to my understanding, was always

Clarence. Any time he talked about guitar playing, he talked about Clarence. He loved Doc and Chet and all these other founders of early guitar lead work, but he really loved Clarence White's playing and tried to emulate his style, to my knowledge. He just worked and worked and worked, and he never lost interest or showed a sign of despair.

Bill Amatneek:

Every time I'd go to Tony's house—Tee is certainly one of the greatest pickers I've ever played with—he would come to the door with a guitar strapped on. Call him on the phone, he'd be picking while he talked to you. Sit down at home with him for a conversation, and he'd strap on the Martin and start playing. He was constantly with the guitar.

Pam Rice:

He experiments on the guitar all the time. Our niece Tina [Wyatt's daughter] was here, and she said, "Why do they always practice? They're already so *good.*" I said, "Honey, he's not practicing, he's *experimenting.*" Only yesterday he found a transition chord between two notes that couldn't be connected. He was tickled to death! He's always experimenting, and that's how he got where he is.

Hal Poindexter:

If Tony misses a lick, he won't sleep for a couple of weeks. I've been around him all my life. I just know that. He's too tough on himself. Music is supposed to be fun, not taken as seriously as some people take it. If Tony messes up, he's hard to live with.

Ronnie Rice:

Tony's maybe a little bit TOO precise . . . I mean, for me, anyway.

ANIMALS

Pam Rice:

The way Tony is, the dogs and birds come first in the house. It can be hard.

Hootie was a cockatiel we took in because our friend Mark Cresenzo was unable to keep him at home. He came to our house already knowing how to whistle "Jesu, Joy of Man's Desiring." He could also whistle "Dixie." I started whistling "Saint Louis Blues" to him in E-flat. He learned it quickly. Over time he composed his own tunes by taking the notes of all three songs and making his own music. One day Tony played a piece of music on the guitar. It was very complex. He told me it was the one Hootie had "written," translated into a guitar piece. I dared him to record it, put it out and give writer's credit to a cockatiel named Hootie.

We have two standard poodles—one is Zorro David. I call him "Zorro" and Tony calls him "David." Yes, we have a dog named David, and we have a bird named Dinah, just like in the song! ["Me and My Guitar," written by James Taylor and covered by Tony on his 1986 recording of the same name.] The pregnant poodle is Xo'i, pronounced like Zoë. Everything functions around the dogs. Right now, we only have two, but that's because our other black standard poodle, Django, came down with cancer.

These dogs are marsh hunters. They're so intelligent. If you're down, they'll put their arms around your neck like a little child. We all sleep on the bed together, and sometimes Tony's been on the road and he comes home and gets in bed, and the big heavy dogs are all curled around him, and he'll say, "Oh, this feels so good, to have my dogs on me!" If he gets sick, they wrap around him like grapevines.

Django was named after Django Reinhardt. We had him for many years. He was very vicious. He frequently knocked out windows. He actually jumped through one during the recording of *River Suite for Two Guitars*. He saw something in the front yard he didn't like, and he sailed right through the glass in the front door and scared John Carlini to death.

Django was a standard poodle rescue. Standard poodles can be very high-maintenance dogs, very expensive. They're not like other dogs, where you can just put 'em outside or leave them in the house. They have to have babysitters. Three of our dogs have been from the poodle rescue. You practically have to go through an FBI check. But we would never skimp on anything. Those dogs are gonna eat whether we do or not.

We just went through a real long battle with Django, and then we lost him to cancer. We could not watch that dog suffer any longer.

Tony and TIpper in California, early '80s.
(Photo courtesy of Louise Rice)

And then we lost Tipper and Pokey. Tipper is the little red dog in the photo gallery at www.tonyrice.com. The one who looks like Gizmo from *The Gremlins* is Pokey. Tipper was 18 and Pokey was 17 when they died. They were totally dependent on me or Tony to do everything for them; they were both blind and deaf. We couldn't go through it again. We couldn't lose Django and then, two weeks later, lose Tipper. So we made the decision . . . it was very hard.

We held the dogs. We put them between us, and our friend Dr. Harrell put them to sleep. I didn't know you could put a dog to sleep that quickly. Then we had them cremated. A little part of the ashes will go in the D-28.

E-mail dated January 24, 2002: I wish I had a witness for the way Tony is acting over this pregnant dog. It is worse than any TV scenario ever written for the overreaction of an expectant father. He has two vets on call. Thank goodness they are friends. He had to drive somewhere a few hours away today. He called the vets to let them know he was leaving the house. The due date is not till Tuesday, but if Xo'i so much as pants a little, he thinks it's time. He grilled me to make sure I could handle it alone while he was gone. I finally told him I really could handle the birth of puppies. I am so afraid he will not let any of them leave the house after they are six weeks old. I already feel like I am living with Noah in the Ark! Bad thing is, this Ark won't float.

(Courtesy Tony Rice)

E-mail dated January 28, 2002: Still waiting. Wish I had a camera for early morning sleeping arrangement. Tony and Xo'i were cutting some zzzzzs. Tony on his back. Xo'i managed to prop her puppy-filled belly over his knee, making easy leverage for herself. Her rear leg was over his thigh. David was stretched the length of his other leg and all three were dead to this world.

I have never seen any woman get this level of attention for a birth. Jewell keeps calling, and Tony is pacing the floor. David is barking at Xo'i. I'm typing to my friend with the blow-by-blow description. Xo'i is posed with her front legs crossed, looking at the rest of us like she is Marilyn and we are the Munsters. Today's script from AS THE WATER BOILS . . .

E-mail dated January 31, 2002: Birth announcement is in guest book. Be first to comment. 6:30 A.M. to 6:00 P.M. First five hand-delivered by me. Third was breech. Last two a big surprise. Colors appear to be two white, two champagne and four black; maybe one of them is chocolate . . . I need a transfusion. Tony is beside himself with joy.

Post on tonyrice.com dated February 1, 2002: Mr. & Mrs. Tony Rice are proud to announce the Birth of 8 healthy standard poodle babies. Born from 6:30 A.M. till 6:00 P.M. today, 01-31-02. Mother Xo'i is fine . . . 2 little girls, 6 big boys . . . You can see pic. of Xo'i and me in photo gallery. My cousin, Jewell Penn, purchased the father, Sir Foldger de "Decca," 3 years ago for the sole purpose of continuing our "FAMILY BLOODLINE". This latest addition brings our house total to 10 Standard Poodles & 4 Cockatiels. ^^^^T.Bone

E-mail dated February 2, 2002: I can't believe how they grow. There really is a change from each hour to the next. Tony is so funny. We are getting the biggest kick out of watching him watch the puppies. He never goes over 20 minutes without doing a head count. The first time he did this he found an extra black puppy. He read the mothers sometimes lay on the babies and kill them, so that's his fear. He gets up in the night and checks on them if there is any whining from the closet.

Our black male standard (neutered) is the most paranoid. All night long, he jumps on and off the bed to check the pups. Sometimes the bed really rocks, because he and Tony are jumping on and off the bed, checking puppies.

Richard Bennett:

I haven't been to Tony's house since he got the new pack, seven or eight of 'em; he keeps me updated on every movement. He wants me to come over, but he says he can't have any company right now.

Pam Rice:

E-mail dated September 1, 2007: Hello, we are fine but really sad around here. Xo'i is most likely going to pass away soon from the same illness that took Django and Hartford. It was very difficult for Tony to leave today, he kept returning to tell her goodbye. He so fears one day she will pass away without being here and being able to tell her goodbye. He and I are very set in our belief that we should be there holding our loved ones when they pass over, whether it be two-leggeds, four-leggeds or winged beings. I had to be honest with him and tell him, should she start to suffer when he was on tour, I would have to put her to sleep rather than see her suffer

Tipper and Tony. (Courtesy of Louise Rice)

waiting for his return. I also told him that I would not admit to him she had passed if he was on tour. I never admit to bad things happening when he is away because I fear him driving and being burdened with sad or bad news.

You remember how he was over her when she was pregnant, always freaking over the slightest thing, calling the vet almost nightly, especially the last week of the pregnancy . . . I bet he hasn't missed a day since those puppies were born, telling her what a good brave momma dog she was.

Richard Bennett:

I just recently filled in for Tony this past year, up in Hazard, Kentucky. That's when he lost his dog. I think I was one of the first people he called to tell about it, and that he needed some help.

SPIRITUALITY

Pam Rice:

First thing that happens is Tony gets up, and makes himself coffee, and goes into the room with the birds. He'll have his coffee and do his meditation. He has this piece of art a guy did of Vassar's fiddle. He looks at Vassar's fiddle and says his prayers to his Creator. He's not disturbed during that time. He always told me, "When you redo this room, don't move the photograph of Vassar's violin, because I've gotten into the habit of meditating on it."

FOOD

Darol Anger:

Tony was discovering San Francisco and food; he went to Fisherman's Wharf five nights in a row and he discovered sourdough bread. You eat bread with your food, if you're from the South. We went to a Chinese restaurant and Tony said, "Hey, wouldn't it be great to have a big loaf of sourdough bread with this Chinese food?" Richard Greene said, "You idiot. You can't eat *bread* with Chinese food." Everybody just kinda sat there going *"Uhhh, uhhhh . . ."*

And J.D. finally spoke up very softly: "Well, I'll go along with Tony on that. I like bread."

Pam Rice:

Tony will drink three chocolate malts with his meal at Applebee's.

Sharon Gilchrist:

I think it was a big old pot roast dinner I saw him eat while we were recording our album. We were staying at a hotel that had an IHOP on the bottom floor. Yeah. *Pot roast.* This meat-and-three, huge dinner. I was surprised.

There's this infamous deli tray backstage that belongs to Tony. And he's pretty pissed if it's not there. For somebody you think might not even TOUCH the deli tray, it's one of the first things he'll talk about: *Where's the deli tray?*

Pam Rice:

In our fridge, you will always find Hellman's mayonnaise, Tropicana Homestyle orange juice, and professional film (can't get anything in the door shelves because the film lives there.) We have a black leather side-by-side unit. His coffee beans are in the freezer. I get only one shelf for food. The rest of the freezer is filled to the brim with Millstone Java or Columbian Supremo beans.

Our house smells like a coffee factory. He grinds his beans and uses a manual Melitta cone/pot rig. He is paranoid about his coffee beans and can consume coffee way beyond the lethal dosage for human consumption.

HEALTH

Billy Wolf:

With Tony not drinking, he's pretty healthy. I wish he wouldn't smoke. He's not overweight; I bet his blood pressure's okay. I'm sure his cholesterol is fine. He's got some physical ailments—this arthritis and so forth . . .

Gary Oelze:

Once, when Tony was staying with me, I sent him to MY doctor. He had the flu or something. Next time I saw him, my doctor said, "Jesus Christ, that guy's no bigger than a *bird.*"

Richard Bennett:

Tony's such a fragile person . . . I don't understand how the hell he keeps going like he does. This summer, we were together at Pigeon Forge, TN, and I went to visit him in his room. He just didn't eat anything for, like, an entire *day*. He doesn't weigh nothin'. He tells me he's in good health, so I guess he is.

Ronnie Rice:

Several of Dad's brothers were skinny. B.J. was like a toothpick, and Uncle Eugene was kinda thin like Dad, 140 lbs. or less. Tony was a good weight when he was with Kate; he ate good meals. He wasn't overweight, and he wasn't underweight. After that, he lost a lot of weight. And there was a point in time with Pam where he was getting kinda pudgy. Now I guess he's back to being skinny.

NOCTURNAL LIFESTYLE

Gary Oelze:

Tony don't sleep. I have a little library of my favorite books, and he got into all my Lincoln books. I'd wake up every morning, and he'd be sitting there reading; he hadn't even gone to bed.

Richard Bennett:

Tony's the vampire driver. He sits behind the wheel of a car and drives all night. I worry about him out there driving by himself. I call him sometimes when I know he's traveling, and try to keep him awake. Sometimes he'll call me at whatever damn hours of the morning, just to chit-chat.

CHARACTER

Mike Marshall:

He's got a tremendous intuitive sense about art, and about honesty and goodness and *right*. That super-high Southern gentleman moral thing. The same thing Sam Bush has. When something's right, it's just *right*.

Pam Rice:

It's really nice to have a husband other people respect. He does have very fine integrity. Tony Rice would not cheat anybody. He's the type of person, if he goes to the store and gets back too much money, he's gonna tell the clerk right then. He's very honest in that way. He would never cheat his fellow man.

Not to say that he hasn't told me some tales and got caught, because he has. But I'm his wife. The rest of the time, he's just a little pain in the rear, just like everybody else's husband!

Sharon Gilchrist:

He's one of the sweetest and most respectful musicians I've seen around. He doesn't talk that much shit about people. He keeps things pretty clean that way.

FUNERALS

Pam Rice:

Though Tony is weird about the formal funeral process, he will be by your side until you take your last breath, if he can. Funerals are really hard on him. I guess once someone passes over into the arms of God, Tony doesn't feel comfortable with the other formalities . . . and Southern culture, especially here where we live, is filled with certain protocol. I used to insist he attend every funeral, especially if it was one of his relatives. But it was like pulling eyeteeth to get him there.

Perhaps if a funeral was a celebration of one's life, as some are, he might find it something he could get become accustomed to attending, but it is too often just a bunch of grieving people gathered in one place, and he has great difficulty dealing with it. Crowds are also not his forte. Since we moved back to North Carolina, the funerals have been so numerous. It seems the more he loved a person, the more difficult it is for him to see them lying in a coffin.

Post on tonyrice.com dated September 17, 2006:
Tony's Maternal grandmother, Luna Strader Poindexter, passed away last evening. Tony's mother, Louise Rice, was the eldest of her 15 children. Arrangements are incomplete at this time. We will update here as soon as they are known.

Post on tonyrice.com dated September 25, 2006:
I would like to share with Tony's fans some words that Rev. Doss spoke to us at Tony's Grandma's graveside. He remarked that, "In this area, there were many families noted to be great hunters, and their descendants had carried guns out into the world. But Grandma's descendants had gone out into the world carrying guitars."

LIFE WITH PAM

Darol Anger:

I think Tony thrives in a kind of volatile relationship with just about anybody. I think he just needs the energy. He needs a dramatic connection to do what he needs to do.

Pam Rice:

No man could put up with me but Tony. I might say, "I'm gonna run to the store. I'll be right back." And I'll start looking at something, or I'll see someone I know, and I have no concept of time. But Tony doesn't worry, because he knows how I am. He knows I've always been that way. He knows I'm not up to anything. That would drive some other guy crazy.

Pam and Tony Rice.
(Courtesy Pam Rice)

It's not ideal. There are times I thought, "I cannot stay with him for *one more minute.*" There are times I prayed to God . . . I would say, "I give up! This is a mess, I can't put it back together. If you want us together, then YOU put it back together!" And there were times we stayed together for the sake of the dogs, because we weren't going to divide them. That's why I say that our house is a big doghouse. They are the nucleus of it.

Usually, if you're in a house with someone for a long time, and there's no conversation, people become uncomfortable. Some guy I was with before Tony may have thought I was being secretive or angry. But I draw away and communicate with myself, and Tony does the same thing.

I'm so proud of what he does. I think in terms of a planetary contribution: What are you gonna do when you're here to pay your dues, for the space you took up, the air you breathe? Tony can make the contribution for me. As long as I keep him healthy, keep his nest going, try to provide an environment to nurture him, then he can go out and make the contribution.

FANS & FAME

Mike Marshall:

He's really kind of a recluse. His makeup is just hyper-sensitive. He shuts it down in whatever ways he needs, to feel comfortable.

He was always a little skittish and super-shy, and he had fears about going into places . . . he just wanted to live in his circle of homeboys, and wasn't comfortable around all folks in all situations. He had this face he could put on, but it was clearly a face. I felt it was a real rite of passage when I was accepted into this inner circle of folks who were part of this sort of *brotherhood* he helped create. It became a kind of refuge for him, a safety zone. All of us felt we were kind of helping, in a way, to take care of him, and help him through these places that were scary for him.

Sharon Gilchrist:

He drives in after soundcheck, warms up for about an hour, is totally professional, cordial, fun to be around, funny . . . always cracking a joke, somewhere in there . . . He gets paid, and as soon as the gig is over, he's out of there, and drives on to the next town. He's just trying to save every second he can, away from crowds and stage . . . Just trying to keep to himself as much as he can.

Part of it has to be the way people *are* about Tony. They treat him like a god. He's this guy who cultivated this *sound* that people are still trying to replicate, and they worship him for doing it. I think it's a little hard to deal with. Tony also told me he doesn't like to talk about music very much. He gets so many crazy guitar players just staring at him, ogling him, after the shows . . . really intense, obsessive, guitar players who practice probably ten hours a day to sound like Tony, and they show up and they're just *gaga*. They want to ask him every question they can.

Frank Poindexter:

He tells me, "I go into hibernation sometimes, and I don't even wanna look at that phone, or do nothin'." And if he's in that mode, you won't talk with him. You have to wait till his time, till *he* wants to talk.

HIDDEN TALENTS

Sam Bush:

We went to Savannah, Georgia, in the spring of 1970. And he knows about skimboards. Hell, he used to surf a little bit, I think. We got the plywood and he made a couple. We were out on Savannah Beach with a little tiny wave about four inches high. He'd do the Jerry Reed when he'd jump on the skimboard: *"Boogety boogety boogety boogety boogety!"*

Billy Wolf:

His brain is so sharp. Tony can do a Rubik's Cube brilliantly fast, unbelievably. When we were in California, he looked like one of those kids doing it.

He's taken the Accutron thing a little farther. I would have considered him a professional photographer, just like now, he could be a professional Accutron repairperson. He can strip down an Accutron and put it back together.

Sam Bush:

Curtis and his brother and his dad came over and we started jamming after a gig one night. Tony decided he was gonna play upright bass. And the guy knows his way around on the doghouse. We're playing along, and he's getting into that slapping—*doon, kadoonk, doon, kadoonk doonk, doonk, kadoonk doonk, doon, doon*—he was all over it. The next day his hands were so blistered and bloody; he could hardly hold a flatpick. He just about killed himself on that thing. He was having a big ole time, playing high up on the neck . . . he could play "Grandfather's Clock" like Tom Gray!

PRECISION & TIMEPIECES

Sharon Gilchrist:

Everything around him has such *precision.* He's so synchronized in every way. That was one of the conversations we had for a while. At one point I asked him if his interest in timepieces related directly to music, and it's directly related for him.

Billy Wolf:

I have an Accutron, one that he gave me years ago, and I wore it and wore it . . . it finally died, so he took it and rebuilt it. Now it's stopped. Very rare in his work. He's been calling lately, putting his mind to figuring out over the phone what's wrong with it. He keeps wanting *me* to work on it, and I tell him, "Tony, I can barely SEE the thing." He's got this incredible microscope. I think he's called every night now for the last three or four nights.

Ronnie Rice:

We don't talk about stuff. We sit there and listen to music all day long, but we don't make comments about what he does for a living. I respect that, because a personal visit would turn into work for him. We talk about electronics and jazz and basses and watches . . .

He is obsessed with those watches . . . Works on 'em all the time. I'm not sure when that stage will be over. It seems like he goes in little patterns, three, four, five years of this and that . . . You detox from one and pick up another, with total obsession. I think that's a Rice trait. Maybe you could call it a degree of accuracy. Dad's family was like that. They were perfectionists in what they did. His older sister, Gladys, and her husband both worked for Douglas Aircraft, and she wound up working on the lunar module for the first mission that went to the moon.

Peter Rowan:

I think Tony finds rejuvenation in his own way. Maybe staying up 24 hours and working on watches. He's bringing them to the gigs now and talking about them and going to the jewelers to find old Bulova parts. Well, the Dalai Lama is a watch freak, too! He also takes apart clocks and watches and things, puts them back together again.

FINANCES

Frank Poindexter:

Tony seems as though he's always carried his own load . . . he's never been one to call and ask for money. It seems like he handles things in cash. I've always thought that was a little strange. Why you would do that? I'm a little bit mystified about that.

Billy Wolf:

He was audited this past year for 2005, which was *brutal* on me. He's gonna get some money back, but what an *agony*. If he weren't my best friend, I would be telling him, "Take your taxes somewhere else." And he's in a very high-risk category for an audit—a musician who's paid in cash a lot. They *love* that. This was his second audit. He was audited in '94; he'll have a pass now for a while.

I think he's going to get a considerable adjustment in his favor because of a mistake I made that had to do with the way the accounting was done, and the fact that Tony pays musicians on the road and doesn't get receipts. The chances of him carrying a little pad and saying, "Now, you gotta sign right here . . ." I don't think we'll be seeing *that* happening in the near future.

THE MAN BEHIND THE CURTAIN

Ricky Skaggs:

Nobody gets really, really close to Tony. We're all friends and we all love him and everything, but . . . As close as him and Sam are, there is just a part of Tony's heart that Sam's never been into somehow.

Tim O'Brien:

He's kind of mysterious and sort of hard to get. He's always acted like an artist. Once you get on the inside, though, he's the most gentleman-like guy in the world. But I think he should have got a little bit of the scene of having management and a protective shell around him a little bit.

Doyle Lawson:

Tony is a bit of an introvert, but not around people he knows. He's not an outgoing person, but he's a good person.

Todd Phillips:

He's crusty on the outside and gooey on the inside. He's hard to get next to; it takes him a while to feel safe around somebody. But once he lets you in, he's like a real good friend. It takes a while. I don't know what it is. He needs to feel safe or secure enough to let you be his friend. And he's *real* sensitive. Emotions play a big part in everything. When things aren't quite right, whether it's musically, personally, emotionally—yeah, he can be real down.

Dave Talbot:

A lot of artists are tumultuous and a lot of artists have demons they wrestle with. I think for some reason that just goes hand-in-hand with a lot of artists. Not just musicians, but painters, writers . . . I think half of us are crazy. You're laying yourself bare all the time, you know?

Frank Poindexter:

Maybe I should show more of an interest in his happiness. But I feel like I'm prodding, in a way . . . I might do it in a way that I would be able to sense if he wanted to talk or not. Probably either this week or next, I'm gonna go up there and get together with him and his watches.

That's his newfound hobby, those Accutrons. And he's *learned* 'em. He can take 'em totally apart and put 'em back together again. He *loves it.* That's a getaway for him. He's

Tony and Frank Poindexter. (Courtesy Louise Rice)

got something to do when he's home. When you see everything real neat, and how much attention he pays to detail in things he has control over, he wants that to be as good as it can possibly be.

You know, one other reason I think I've never asked Tony, "Are ya happy?" is this: *What if he DOES spill it out?* What if he DOES tell me all his problems? Is that gonna help any? Would it help him for me to be a sounding board, because what am I gonna do, what can I do?

Ronnie Rice:

Is he happy? I don't know. That's a good question.

Mark Schatz:

Tony was never very vocal about his feelings. We really cared about each other. It was a complex relationship. It's hard to get close to Tony. I also have my own little cocoon I'm in. So we kind of did this little dance. We really loved and cared about each other, but he's a little oblique. He's not someone you just sit down and look into his eyes and have a heart-to-heart talk with.

Bryn Davies:

We have a great relationship; we're really close, very good friends. He's the guy I can call at 3:00 in the morning if I'm anxious or freaking out, and I do the same for him. We have that kind of relationship, even though we don't talk a lot when we're not on the road. I know that if I ever needed anything, he would be there for me in a second. He's that kind of guy. When he's your friend, he'll give you the shirt off his back.

Kari Estrin:

Tony is a man filled with love. He is a gracious, generous, warm-hearted, fun, kind human being.

John Cowan:

Our friendship has really started in the last ten years. He was always very kind, and he would say nice things about my singing, but to be quite honest, before we became friends, I was enough enamored as a fan that I was pretty nervous around him. Our friendship has been built around the foundation of twelve-step recovery. That's what has bonded us.

It's a curious friendship. I feel privileged in a way, because I don't think there's a lot of people, even guys he's played music with in his life, that he has some kind of gentle friendship with. The thing I DO feel from him, that I don't think many people get to experience because he's so guarded publicly, is his *heart.* When he tells me he loves and misses me, I really feel that from him.

On the Road
Part 7

North to Roanoke

July 2005: I'm packing, getting ready to head home the following morning, when Tony calls and says he wants to go for a drive. The day is glorious; there isn't a cloud in the sky. He arrives at the hotel in the Cobra convertible. Before we set off, he puts the top down.

He heads north over the state line and deep into Virginia, past tobacco barns and old farmhouses on rolling roads through beautiful green meadows. Tony is driving fast today, quite a few miles per hour over the posted speed limit, but not once does it seem excessive.

As he drives, we listen to a recording by the beautiful Brazilian jazz singer and pianist Eliane Elias, and he comments approvingly about the disc's pristine audio quality. His conversation is a fascinating discourse that jumps from credit card companies to his love of liberty, from coffee beans to his disdain for electronic tuners.

Suddenly we have arrived at our destination and he has parked the car and is getting out. I look at the map and see that we are in Rocky Mount; he has driven about 50 miles to get here. It seems a damn long way to travel just to eat at a Bojangles'. "But it seemed a shame to waste a beautiful day like this indoors," Tony says happily as he works over a drumstick.

When asked, he pulls the small softbound copy of the Declaration of Independence and the Constitution from his back pocket where he always keeps it. It is well-thumbed and stuffed with receipts from obscure little vinyl shops up and down the Eastern seaboard, and from bookstores. Tony is an avid reader. He never touches fiction, but his non-fiction interests are wildly diverse and include biographies of his musical heroes, particle physics, audio technology, photography, U.S. history, photography, the science of horology . . . Like his musical interests, they seem to be all over the map.

He talks about one of his favorite biographies, *The Unlocked Book* by Asia Booth Clarke. "It's the most magnificent piece of writing I've ever read in my life," he says. "A very small book about her relationship with her brother, John Wilkes, and her childhood memories. She had so much personal stuff in there that she entrusted the manuscript to somebody to be released after her death, with the stipulation that there were no living characters that could be hurt. I have a lot of respect for her ability to write such a magnificent work and then never see it be released in her lifetime."

The conversation turns to his own biography, and the interviews and anecdotes that have been collected for it. He is perplexed over some of the comments shared by his closest friends. "I'm not saying this in a negative light; I don't take it in one," he says. "But they paint a picture of me as somebody that's hard to get to know. I would think that any of them know that if they needed to call me any time out of a 24-hour period and talk about matters of the heart, they could do it. And I don't know how to put those two things together. That's their perception, but it's mysterious to me on a real, real deep level."

He mentions a comment made by Unit bassist Bryn Davies, who said in her interview that she knew she would always be able to count on Tony for anything in a crunch, no matter what time of day or night. He was just that kind of friend, she attested. "That description of who I am is remarkably the way I see myself," Tony says simply, as he finishes his meal. "And on the same theme, there's a song by Bob Dylan I want you to hear."

The sun is still high and bright in the summer sky. In the car, he puts on the Dylan CD and cues it to "Restless Farewell." We listen in appreciative silence as we roll out of Roanoke. Nothing much has happened today. It has been a perfect day, and nothing much has happened at all. The magic of this adventure had nothing to do with the destination. As we head south, it becomes clear that it was all about the journey.

On the road, July 2005. (Photo by Caroline Wright)

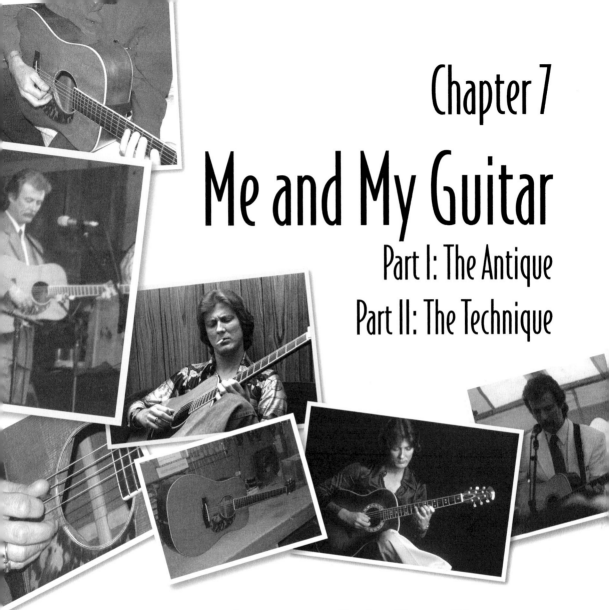

Chapter 7
Me and My Guitar
Part I: The Antique
Part II: The Technique

GARCIA: Tony gets a better tone, actually, than Clarence did.
GRISMAN: I know he's stronger.
GARCIA: *(to Tony)* You get a better sound.
TONY: Boy, I don't know . . . I appreciate it.
GARCIA: Well, I tell ya, I heard Clarence play a lot, Tony. Yeah, I
                listened to him a *lot*.

Dialogue from the sessions that would, in 2000, be released as *The Pizza Tapes;* recorded by Jerry Garcia, David Grisman, and Tony Rice in February 1993

It ain't the car, it's the driver.

Brian Fesler, Minnesota banjoist

Chapter 7: Introduction

Serial number 58957, Martin D-28 Herringbone.

Built in 1935. Formerly owned by Clarence White. Enlarged soundhole, many dings and divots, considerable playwear. Brazilian rosewood. The most valuable acoustic guitar on the planet. Described as the "Holy Grail." Not for sale . . .

Tony Rice's guitar, which he fondly calls "The Antique" (or sometimes the Herringbone, or simply the 'Bone) seems to possess as much mystique as the man himself. The smallest details of its legend are often debated by his fans. There is disagreement over how Clarence came to own it, how Joe Miller of Los Angeles came to have it in his possession, and even how much Tony paid Miller for the instrument. But its pedigree is unquestionable, and its influence on modern bluegrass music, and even acoustic guitar design, is undeniable. It is, as Tony says, "a ragged-out old guitar" with a blank Gretsch fingerboard and non-original pickguard, bridge and selected braces. It has been filled with sand, used as an ashtray, shot with pellet guns, lost in airports, floated in floodwaters, and it's arguably the most copied acoustic guitar in the world.

Considering the collective impact Clarence and Tony have had on the direction of bluegrass guitar, it's not surprising that the instrument they both played has become a legend on its own. The Antique has been studied in microscopic detail by everyone from fans to luthiers to journalists. In his definitive article on the Antique ["58957: Tony Rice and His Holy Grail Martin," from *Fretboard Journal*, Spring 2007], Art Dudley says:

> For the most part, every Martin dreadnought is impressive in some way. But 58957 is on another plane. It's not the loudest D-28 around—although it does have a wider dynamic range than most—nor does it have the deepest of lows or the highest of highs, but it is the most expressive. It sings with a voice that simply can't be ignored.

The sound that Tony has made with the Antique is the ultimate source of its mystique. And that sound comes from the man, not the instrument. Proof of this may be found in the legendary Rice tracks that were actually recorded with other guitars, including an Ovation round-backed guitar that Tony acquired in the late 1970s, as part of an endorsement deal with the company. For one reason or another, Rice decided to play that Ovation on the title track to *Manzanita*, and on other recordings throughout his career—including every song but one on Tony's favorite of his records, *Backwaters*.

During his years in California, Tony struck up a relationship with Richard Hoover of Santa Cruz Guitar Company, which led to the creation of a Tony Rice model with the same big soundhole and other appointments as the Antique. Yet the Rice models have never been intended as copies of the old Martin. Rice believes in them enough to make them his only signature model, and has played them extensively on the road and on recordings.

Still, there is a profound connection between Tony and his old Herringbone that has become almost symbiotic. The connection seems to grow stronger with time. After playing a Santa Cruz exclusively onstage for a number of years, Tony decided recently to take the Antique out on the road again. He says simply that it is now "a part of me" and is not for sale.

And that is as it should be. The Antique seems to be exactly where it belongs: on the lap and in the hands of a man who knows how to coax the very sweetest voice from its old wood and steel wires. The legend endures.

Great American Music Hall, San Francisco, CA
(Photo by Jon Sievert)

Pt. I: The Antique

It's not so loud, but the tone can't be matched. Tony pulls the tone out of it better than anyone can. It's a part of him.

Clay Jones, guitarist, Tony Rice protégé

In His Own Words: Tony's Story

My first guitar was either a '59 or '60 D-18. My father bought it in Los Angeles, brand-new at Wallich's Music City for around $250 or $300. That was a lot of money back then. He wasn't willing to scrimp on anything like that. He plunked on it for a few days and then finally I was in my bedroom one night getting ready to go to sleep. Larry and I had bunk beds and I slept on the top. In comes my father with this D-18 and says, "I'm gonna give this to you." So that was it.

It was a piece of shit for a D-18, too. Worst-sounding D-18 I have heard, except for the one Clarence had, which was a little worse. My father bought it for himself, but he gave it to me. I was about eight or nine. It was too big. There was not much of an awareness back then of vintage instruments being superior. If he had been aware that older, well-taken-care-of ones were much, much better, that's what he would have bought. But back then, it was just taken for granted: if it was marked D-18 and it was new, then it was the best. That guitar was brand-new and it sounded

absolutely horrible. I don't know of its final demise.

I had to have a really good guitar then, so my father took me to a pawn shop in Ocala, FL and bought a beat-up 1957 D-28 for me that was structurally perfect and all original. I mean, boy, was it ever original! I was with my father, and at the beginning, the pawnbroker presented himself as a typical con artist. But my father started talking to him, and getting him down on the price for the guitar, which was about vintage market price at the time; maybe about $400 or $500 in 1969 . . . a beat-up D-28 in good condition. I remember my father telling the guy, "I want you to hear this boy play this thing!" So I played a couple of tunes. The pawnbroker liked it so much that he sold my father the guitar for some ridiculously low amount.

It was the exception, rather than the rule, for a late 1950s dreadnought. Most of them were horrible. Most of them are *still* horrible. But once in a while, one of them rolls out of that factory that for some unexplained reason is the exception rather than the rule. This D-28 would have to be one of them.

I ended up trading that guitar with Clayton Hambrick, who played with Grass Menagerie. Somehow Clayton had just gotten Hylo Brown's old 1948 D-28, which was the one with the big pickguard he played all those years. There was something about that guitar I really liked a lot, so we ended up doing a trade. Clayton did that for me as a favor because he knew I liked it. I played that '48 all the way up until March of '75 when I got the Antique.

Most people think I cut the New South album with the Antique, but I didn't. It was cut with Hylo Brown's '48 and with Hugh Sturgill's D-35.

Somewhere along the line, I put a big Martin decal on the upper bout of Hylo's guitar. I think Mike Longworth gave me three of those promotional decals out at Winfield in '72 or '73. I thought, what in the hell am I gonna do with this? Put it on my car? I thought, "No, I'm gonna stick it on the side of this guitar right here." It's almost a logical place to put 'em, as it turns out. I wish I had one on the Herringbone.

The '48 sounded like a Herringbone, but it wasn't, and it was original. It was one of those rare good ones from the late '40s. It wasn't loud or deep, but the timbre was so good. I recorded *California Autumn* and the Japanese record for Sab with that guitar, too. After I bought the Antique, I held on to the '48 and rarely played it. When I was with the New South, there was another guy who used to

Hylo Brown's (and later Tony's) 1948 D-28.
(Courtesy Art Dudley)

play at the Sheraton Inn, and he wanted it so bad he could taste it. By then, I had the Herringbone so I sold the '48 to him.

Most of the straight-ahead bluegrass stuff Clarence did with the Kentucky Colonels was more rhythm than lead, and he

The Kentucky Colonels, circa 1963: Leroy Mack, Bobby Slone, Billy Ray Lathum, Clarence White with the Antique. Bandmember Roland White was in the Army at the time. (Courtesy John DelGatto)

always had two guitars with him when I saw them. If Clarence had to play lead, he would usually grab his D-18, but sometimes he played it on the Herringbone. He played a lot of great bluegrass guitar solos on this -28 right here.

The way I heard it, Roland and Clarence White and Billy Ray Lathum were looking for a guitar, and they went to the only guitar shop in the area, the original McCabe's in Los Angeles. Between the three of them, they had enough money to get it. They actually paid 35 bucks for it. The funny part about that was when they got it home, Eric, their dad, was pissed off at 'em. He said, "What in the hell have you got here? I hope you guys didn't pay any money for this!"

I don't know how he found this out, but Bobby Slone told me a girl who had been crippled with polio traded it in at McCabe's for a brand-new one, and that she was a student at one of the colleges in Long Beach.

They found somebody to put the fingerboard on at another music store. They didn't care what it was, just as long as it was a fingerboard that would allow Clarence to play. And it's still the same fingerboard that's on there now, a Gretsch. It never had any inlays. It was a blank, probably slated to have the little half-moon shaped inlays that go in Gretsches. It didn't have any frets in it either. Back then, this thing had action about an inch high. It was ragged-out, boy.

It was like something out of a fairy tale that I would own it. I played a long shot,

and the long shot—a one in a gazillion—came through.

Bobby Slone and I were talking one night in Kentucky about the old guitar, out of the blue. I said, "God, I wish I knew where that Herringbone was. I don't know if *anybody* knows where it is." And Bobby said, "I know where it is." And then he told me the story of how Clarence ended up letting a guy named Joe Miller have it. So I said, "I wonder how somebody would go about getting ahold of Joe Miller?" Bobby said, "The only thing I know about him is that his father owned a chain of real high-class liquor stores in Pasadena, CA." Joe was one of the college students out there in the early sixties who fell in love with the folk and bluegrass music movement, and befriended the Kentucky Colonels.

There are at least three stories about how Joe Miller ended up with the guitar. Story No. 1 involved Clarence and Suzie, his wife. They met through Suzie's aunt Jean, who was married to Bobby Slone. When Bobby was playing with the Kentucky Colonels in California, Suzie came out to visit, met Clarence and they fell in love. They got married but needed money to get an apartment and go on their honeymoon. Clarence supposedly went to Joe Miller—he was a rich guy and a fan—and said, "Joe, loan me some money. I'll leave you this D-28 as collateral."

In Story No. 2, Roland said Clarence sold that herringbone to Joe because Clarence was going to work with Ricky Nelson. Don Rich had offered to sell Clarence his Telecaster and an amp, and Clarence wanted it so bad that he just sold the Martin to Joe Miller so that he could buy the Telly, which Marty Stuart has now.

Another story is that the Colonels wanted to do a tour back East in 1964, but the tour needed some support money and a backer. The tour lost money, and Clarence didn't have the money to pay Joe Miller back. Clarence was starting to play electric guitar at the time, so he gave Joe the old guitar as collateral.

In the meantime, I guess a couple of other guys in the band had really pissed off Joe Miller, and just to be vindictive, Joe would never let Clarence have the guitar back. It had to have been principle, more than anything else, because Joe never touted the fact that he had the guitar. As far as I know, he didn't know how to play it.

I just played a hunch that maybe Joe Miller would know who I was, and maybe he'd be willing to let it go to me, as an innocent bystander. That was the long shot I played.

What was amazing was that I got on the phone in Kentucky, called information for Pasadena, CA, and had 'em look up Miller's Liquors. There was a whole bunch of 'em. They said, "Which one do you want?" I said, "Oh, it doesn't matter. Any of 'em in Pasadena." So they gave me a number. I called and said, "I'm trying to find Joe Miller. Do I have the right place of business?" The guy said, "Yeah, you do. Joe's not here, but he'll be back in a couple hours." When I called back, Joe was there. He was a real nice guy. I said, "Joe, you don't know me, this is Tony Rice, I play bluegrass." And he said, "Oh, no, I know

who you are, very well." I said, "Do you have Clarence's guitar?" He says, "Yeah, I do; I've had it for years." I said, "Would you consider selling it?" And he said, "To you, I would." Then we started talking about money.

Joe Miller said, "To be honest, I feel like it would be fair if I have the instrument appraised before I sell it to you." I thought, "Well, that's the end of that. He's gonna take it to somebody that's gonna tell him it's worth some outrageous amount of money that me or nobody else could afford." He called back the next day, and said he had taken the guitar to a guy named Russ Miller—no relation—who Clarence used to have work on it. He said, "I don't know if you want to pay this much or not, but Russ said that if it was in real good shape, it would be worth maybe $600 or $700. But in the shape it's in, it would only be worth maybe $400 or $500 at the most." I said, "Well, I'm certainly willing to split the difference with you. I'll give you 550 bucks for it." Joe said, "Yeah, you got a deal. Come out and get it." So the next day I flew out and got it.

It was arranged that I would meet Joe Miller at the Sheraton Hotel at the LA airport, and he would bring the guitar to my room and I would put $550 in cash in his hand. Which I did, and I got a receipt. After I got the receipt, the ONLY thing I wanted to do was to get the hell out of there with that guitar. No disrespect to Joe Miller—I will be indebted to him for as long as I live. But you think about it, $550 for an instrument of this historical magnitude is laughably low.

This thing started as just idle curiosity about the guitar. *No more than three days from then, I actually owned it.*

It was under Joe Miller's bed for nine years. When I got it, the strings had a thick coating of green stuff on 'em. Grisman had picked me up over at the airport. He was doing this Warner Brothers session for Kate and Anna McGarrigle. I tagged along with him and was out in the hall trying to play this thing with the same green strings on it. You could barely play it because the action was so high, but it sounded so good, even then. The producer came out in the hall and heard me playing it, and said, "Hey, get in here, we need you on this tune!" So I ended up playing the Antique on a couple of tunes or so for Kate and Anna McGarrigle that day.

Coming back, I had to change planes in Dallas. I checked the guitar to Dallas, so that I could pick it up at the baggage claim there and make sure it got back on the plane

to Kentucky with me, rather than leave the responsibility to the airline to make sure that it made the switch.

Two weeks after I got it back to Lexington, I drove it down to Randy Wood. Randy re-set the neck and planed the fingerboard, re-fretted it, re-bound it, put a new bridge on it, and did a bunch of stuff to get it to where it would look and play good.

There were five original tuners on the guitar. Clarence had Klusons, the close-backed style. Later, Frank Ford put the third string tuner on there. He happened to have a copy, when Richard Johnson was at Gryphon String Instruments down in Palo Alto. And about six months ago, the sixth string tuner finally gave way, so Snuffy Smith and I constructed a Grover out of three different gears for it. So the sixth is half-original and all the rest of them but the third are originals.

The guitar didn't have the original

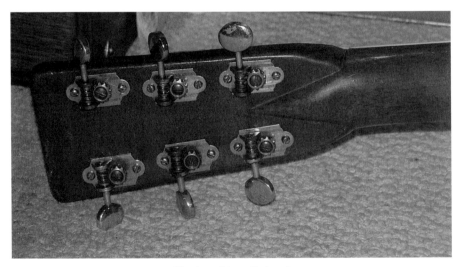

(Courtesy of Jason Burleson)

pickguard. If you look at old photos of the Kentucky Colonels, you don't see a pickguard on it. When Clarence had it, it had a piece of clear plastic in the shape of a pickguard. He had Ross Miller or somebody cut out a regular-style Martin pickguard later on. But these guitars didn't have tortoise pickguards originally. By 1935, Martin had started putting on a nitro celluloid pickguard.

In '85, when the Unit went to Japan, a guy backstage handed me this pickguard in a pack. It was real nice. He couldn't speak English, but he said, "Mr. Rice, a gift for you." I looked at that pickguard and I thought, "Man, this son of a bitch is GOING on this guitar. I don't care how original it looks."

The neck on this guitar is a curiosity, because it's apparently not a D-28 neck. More than likely, it's out of a '32 or '33 OM. It's '32 or '33 OM specs and there was no headstock name in those years. OMs had extremely low-profile necks, and all those -28s had big thick necks. The scale length is the same, but it had a shorter heel, so that would indicate it was from an OM. The arrow is real big too, which is also typical of OMs. By '34 they had shrunk 'em down in size, but that arrow is real big there, way up, and wide and black.

Martins from this era had "C.F. Martin & Co, Nazareth, PA" stamped on the back of the peghead. This one used to have it on there, but somebody has sanded it out. You can see the image of it but it's not very plain.

The bridge is a conversion. Mike Longworth sent me three of the original bridges,

and the saddle angle was wrong. They always *have* been, on Martins. Then I took it over to Hideo Kamimoto in Oakland, who used to do exquisite work on this Herringbone. Hideo took the saddle out and filled it in, and cut the slot at the right angle so that it would note right on the bass and treble. Then he put it back in. It still has the same saddle he put in. The nut is also the same one Hideo put in. He used bone I picked up in a pet store.

The sound hole was cut out before Clarence got it. If anything, I think enlarging the hole makes the sound worse. It definitely ain't the reason it sounds better. Besides, whatever has been cut away has been made up for where the fingerboard sticks out over the sound hole. The fingerboard is one fret longer than standard. So the overall volume is probably still the same.

It had a brace where somebody had cut out a big giant notch to mount a D'Armond pickup. It kept sagging, and finally about a year and a half ago, I told Snuffy, "This is not getting any better." Because the body was caving in through all those years, it just kept sinking and sinking. So Snuffy added a brace that was brand-new old stock slated for a '41 D-18. He glued some of the braces back from the flood, but they're all original. He re-glued the back braces that were most affected by the flood. The top braces are all original except for the top plate brace.

When the flood hit my house in Florida, I got out in my boat with my dog. Then I paid a guy $40 and he went over to my house and got the guitar. It was soaked, warped and the braces were loose. It was totally submerged for a couple of hours—there wasn't a dry spot on that guitar anywhere. Harry Sparks helped dry it out. It reached a point where it was sagging real bad and sounding thin; there were rattles in it. I had Snuffy go through it one day, and the braces in the damn guitar were just totally loose. Snuffy absolutely brought that guitar back to life.

I knew whatever warps were in it could be fixed and eventually it would dry out and recover. And I started thinking, "Damn, Clarence White filled it up with wet sand and it survived that, and being shot at, then he ran over it with a car and busted it all to hell. If it could survive all *that* . . ."

I thought it sounded better after the flood when Snuffy restored it. I probably started playing it before I should have, but it started getting better and better. It's sounding better now than it ever has. Today it's in good shape. It notes really good, all the way up to the 20th fret, boy, it's on the money. That is the best-sounding D-28 I've ever heard by *far*. It's got a sound all its own—there ain't nothing even close. I tell people it's like Vassar Clements's fiddle—there ain't no other fiddle sounds like that, and nobody knows why. I don't think even the most sophisticated in the scientific community could figure out why.

Richard Hoover told me one time that when Martin guitars were constructed, the way they put those things together, all the bodies would end up having a natural torque all their own. From how they've been glued together, they're really different. The most logical explanation would be

that this particular guitar had that magical amount of torque in the right places to give it that tone. It has such a sound all its own. It doesn't have a Lester Flatt-Jimmy Martin traditional dreadnought sound. It's a different sound, as magical as Heifetz's Stradivarius. It's tone, combined with charisma. It's very *charismatic,* if that's the right word.

Most of 'em, when you get up around the 8th–12th fret area, you gotta beat the hell out of 'em, but with this one, you just gotta barely touch it. Somebody recently called it "reserve power." It's got a lot of reserve. I have two rattlesnake rattles down in the body of the guitar for tone. One wasn't enough . . . Over the years, it's been used and abused. At one point, Clarence shot a pellet gun at it, put a hole in the top and the back . . . Another time, he filled it with wet sand at the beach. He didn't know what he had. It's just a ragged-out old guitar. It's still around, though—it'll outlive me, probably.

I don't know what will happen to it after I'm gone. I don't have a written will, but I've told my lawyer what I'd like to see happen, in the event of my death, is for the guitar to go to Billy Wolf. Billy would know who its next logical owner should be. Probably Wyatt, but I don't know.

I have played other guitars, even on record. I played a Santa Cruz on several songs on *Mar West* and I also used an Ovation on the tune "Manzanita," on two cuts on *Hot Dawg,* several from *Mar West* and every tune on *Backwaters* except one, "Common Ground." That's my D-28—you'd have to be an idiot not to hear that.

Tony and his Ovation in February 1978.
(Photo by Jon Sievert)

People have asked me how I got a tone so similar to the Martin's from those guitars. No matter what instrument we pick up, no matter how good, bad or indifferent, we're going to naturally gravitate to that sweet spot with the right hand, and find out what's going to give us what we're looking for. It's a subconscious thing. An instrument will take on the character of the person that plays it.

My relationship with Santa Cruz Guitar company came about when I was playing with Grisman. Darol Anger, Todd, and I went to a party one night and Richard Hoover and Bruce Ross from Santa Cruz Guitars were there. Darol said, "Hey, I want you to look at this guitar. This guy has made about two or three of them, and they're really good. And he would really like to make one for you."

I got to talking to Dick Hoover, and he asked me, "What do you want?" I said, "Well, I'd like to have a herringbone, trimmed up like this." So they made one and gave it to me. I played it for a while, but I didn't

keep it that long. I sold it because it just wasn't the one. The company and I both knew that it was time to move onward and upward.

Over the years, there's been a number of Tony Rice Santa Cruz models. They just keep cranking 'em out. As fast as I want changes done, they'll do it. The latest one is a monster. It has braces in different spots, basically Martin-style braces but it's lighter and scale lengths are getting shorter. Braces are being sprung in there so that they can be light. But under pressure, it limits the amount the top can actually come up. I call it a prosthesis guitar . . . I can't handle that 25¼" tension anymore. It's getting harder and harder on my hands.

I have talked to Chris Martin, president of Martin guitars, about a Tony Rice model. I told him, "You know, if you ever want to do one, I don't see any reason why it couldn't be worked out." He said, "Well, what about the thing with Dick?" [referring to Tony's endorsement of the Santa Cruz Tony Rice signature guitar] I said, "You know what? Richard Hoover and the Santa Cruz Guitar Company is no threat to Martin Guitars." People are playing guitars other than Martins now because Martin ain't made a decent guitar since 1955! They just haven't. That's reality.

I played a Tony Rice model Santa Cruz prototype from 2000–2005. It was so good I just kept playing it. And then in December of '05 I sold the Cruz to a guy in Milwaukee. For five years, the old D-28 stayed over in Snuffy's vault, and rarely would I take it out. I was over there one night playing it and all of a sudden it was almost like the instrument spoke and said, "Hey! What about me?" I thought, come rain, hail, sleet or snow, I'm gonna take it home and start playing it, and I did. It's like I got a connection with this instrument that's almost psychic.

There's no money in this world that can replace this guitar. None. It's a classic situation of something that's worth what somebody is willing to pay for it. Bill Monroe's mandolin just sold for $1.6 million. I'm sure that when Earl Scruggs passes on into another life, his banjo will be a similar commodity. And if I had to guess, I'd say my old D-28 is much more a conversation piece than either of the aforementioned instruments.

But what's its worth? The answer to that question is totally subjective. This is a 1935 D-28 made by Martin, and as good as it sounds, and as good as it plays, it is not nearly a collector-quality instrument by definition. So there's your subjectivity right there. But this guitar is part of me, and it ain't for sale.

The thing is, I'm so eager to have kids and guitar aficionados play it. I don't think I've ever turned anybody down that asked me if they could hold it or play it. I wouldn't deprive anybody of the pleasure. That would be stupid. But I use discretion. It takes me about three seconds to size somebody up to see if they're a threat.

The first case I used for the guitar was a Mark Leaf I got from Harry Sparks. In fact, Harry loaned me the Mark Leaf he

kept his D-45 in, and I flew the case to California when I went out there, just to fly the guitar back in. Then Harry bought me one. That was the case I used for many years until I started using the Anvil-style Viking. Then Ray Jones of Flight Line Cases from Danville, VA drastically improved on *that* design, so I used his Anvil case for years.

But I couldn't carry that Anvil case anymore with this tendonitis. I just got to where I couldn't deal with it. When I recorded with Bryan Sutton a couple years ago, he had one of these carbon-fiber Accord cases, and I said, "Man, I gotta have one!" They're made over in Croatia, and they're real expensive. They're made of a carbon-fiber-graphite composite used in the aircraft industry.

They were really hard to find at the time, but my friend in Atlanta, Bobby Fowler, found two of them in Santa Monica, and he bought both of 'em and gave one to me as a gift. So I ended up with one of them. It's the best case ever made. My Accord case is dark blue. It fits fine both in the backseat of the Mustang and behind the seats of my truck.

Snuffy Smith has done a *remarkable* job of keeping the old guitar up and running. It's a continuous process, like with a Guarnerius or Stradivarius. They've gotta be overhauled occasionally. And after every two dates or so it's gotta be in for a pit stop.

When it's at Snuffy's place in King, North Carolina, it stays in an old bank vault that's constantly kept at 70 degrees and 60% humidity, with a backup generator that cuts on if the power goes off. And if anybody's got any ideas about stealing it, they better bring something close to a nuclear bomb to get it out. They'd have to have a few keys and know a few combinations to get it, but even to get that far, they'd have to go through an enormous collection of high-powered weapons.

And then if they got out the door with it, through a one-in-a-million miracle, what would they do with it? Sell it? As if I wouldn't find it? Their only other option would be to take it home and not let anybody else on the planet know that they've got it! It'd be like stealing Bill Monroe's mandolin.

The Antique on Snuffy Smith's workbench,
King, NC.
(Photo courtesy Jason Burleson)

Pt. 1: The Antique

It was the most awesome sound I had ever heard. It made me want to learn how to play music.

Shawn Lane, multi-instrumentalist and vocalist with Blue Highway

Family, Friends & Fans

Sam Bush:

At the time he was in Bluegrass Alliance, Tony was playing a D-28, but it certainly wasn't the one he owns now. He might have already had a Gretsch fingerboard put on it like the one on Clarence's guitar, but the neck was too big for him. It didn't have any fret markers and I remember it was a bound fingerboard. He did it because of the Gretsch fingerboard on Clarence's guitar. He was that far into Clarence.

He took it to a guy named Fred Couch who was a violin repairman in Louisville. Fred was a real nice guy who used to work on mine and Lonnie's fiddles, but he didn't work that much on guitars. Tony had Fred cut down the neck so much the entire thing was the width of five strings. Tony was just mortified when he saw this thing. We went over to get it and the strings were so close together it was like a toy instrument or something. I think he ended up selling that guitar.

I believe he got another D-28 then that was probably the one he was playing in that Camp Springs video. When he first got it, it had kind of an oversized pickguard on it, and the story was that it had belonged to Hylo Brown.

J.D. Crowe:

See, Bobby [Slone] told me where that guitar was. And Bobby told Tony, and Tony got to thinking about it being Clarence's, and we knew he liked Clarence's picking . . . We thought he ought to have that guitar if he could get it.

Bobby Slone:

Tony brought it up once and I said, "Well, I know where that guitar is." Joe Miller's dad owned a chain of liquor stores out in Pasadena. But when he went with the Byrds, Clarence needed a little extra cash, and he knew he wouldn't need that acoustic guitar, so he kind of pawned it to Joe for a little money. Clarence came by and saw me in Lexington when he quit the Byrds. I said, "What about that old guitar?" He said, "Well, I tried to pick it up, but Joe said he was going to keep it. He said it was just the principle of it." It had been so long since he had tried to pay it back.

Clarence thought the guitar was an old Ditson. There was a little girl who had it. Clarence said she was in a wheelchair. She played it a lot. And her dad had done something to the guitar. They split the hole, so he just cut it out to make it even.

David Grier:

Roland said that in the '60s, he and Clarence would blow cigarette smoke into their instruments! Just chain-smoke two, three, four cigarettes, whatever, and blow the smoke all in the guitar and hold their hand over it so when they went out onstage with the lights, and they hit that chord, all the smoke would come out. That was cool back then, I guess.

Bobby Slone:

Joe Miller let a violin maker put a finish on it. When Tony come back with the guitar, that thing was all shiny.

J.D. Crowe:

It looked like a new one.

Hugh Sturgill:

Here's the story. When Clarence White and the Colonels were playing bluegrass, they didn't make much money. They were poverty-row. It was a hard go. There was a guy that owned a liquor store in California, and when they'd run short of money, they'd go by and borrow some money from him. Sometimes they could pay it back, and sometimes they couldn't, but he was kinda their sponsor. He kept them going.

Things got really bad when they were gonna break up, and Clarence went to the guy, and said, "Look, we're just not making it. I'm starving to death. I've got another job; I'm gonna try this rock gig with the Byrds. But I need some money to buy equipment and do some stuff. I don't have any credit. I'm gonna leave this old Martin, because I ain't gonna be playing acoustic with this band; I'm gonna be playing electric." I think he borrowed $700 and left the guitar.

Well, a year and a half or so later, after his big success with the Byrds, and having made a lot of money, he dropped into the liquor store to redeem that guitar. The guy said, "Hell, no, I ain't gonna let you have it back! I kept you alive for ten years, and when you hit success and things started going good, I don't see you for a year and a half. Is that any way to treat a friend?" And about two months later, Clarence was hit and killed by a car.

The guy felt terrible about it. Bobby got him in touch with Tony. And he sold that guitar to Tony Rice for $700.

David Grisman:

I was with him the day he got that guitar. He flew into Los Angeles to get it, and we hooked up, and we went over to Buell Neidlinger's house with Richard Greene, and played some tunes. Tony had never met Buell before. We played "Rawhide" and after that was over, Buell said, "Man, that's heart attack music!" The first day—the first jam session with that guitar. You can imagine what it sounded like! I was real happy for him. I think he got it for $600.

Bill Amatneek:

In the spring of 1977 Tony and I drove down to Santa Cruz to pick up the first Tony Rice Model guitar from the Santa Cruz guitar company run by Richard Hoover and Bruce Ross . . . [Note: Tony remembers this happening in 1979, but Richard Hoover confirms that the first prototype was built for Tony in late 1977.] When we got back to Tony's home in Kentfield, Tony started playing the new guitar. And right away he heard something wrong. "It don't sound right. It don't feel right," he kept saying. "Something's off." It sounded right to me.

So he took out a yardstick and measured the string length from nut to bridge on the Clarence White Martin, and then he measured it on the Tony Rice model. The string length was 1/8" longer on the Santa Cruz than on the Martin. Tony could feel the 1/8" and the string tension that it added. He could hear the tonal difference. [From *Acoustic Stories,* p. 67.]

Richard Hoover (founder/president of the Santa Cruz Guitar Company):

It's always interesting—is that the right word?—or amusing or aggravating to me that people consider the Tony Rice model a copy of his old Herringbone. He already has the old Herringbone. He was looking for something that had a more contemporary voice, a better midrange and treble for single-line leads and jazz phrasings. I consider it kind of a Trojan Horse into the realm of New Acoustic Music—we wanted it to be in a familiar package, and for Tony that was very important, because he's downright superstitious about some of the appointments and looks of his old Herringbone. But we wanted to have some real innovations within that familiar package. There's a lot about the Santa Cruz Tony Rice Model that's very, very different than a pre-war Martin dreadnought.

Probably one of the most important features that Tony wanted to duplicate was the enlarged sound hole. Researching the acoustic physics of duplicating the enlarged sound hole turned out to be really fortuitous for what we were trying to achieve. Enlarging the aperture on a resonating chamber raises the fundamental pitch, thereby giving the big, huge, boomy, bassy dreadnoughts better midrange and treble response.

(Courtesy of Jason Burleson)

Mike Longworth (former employee and late historian of Martin guitars):

The guitar itself has spawned a legend of its own. All this stuff about modifying the sound hole to get more sound is probably baloney. My understanding from Roland White is that the sound hole was eaten up so bad that it was enlarged to make it round again. Nevertheless people believe the big sound hole makes a difference, and manufacturers offer this feature to satisfy that belief.

It is a wonderful guitar, but personally I don't assign any superiority of sound to the enlarged hole. When I talked to Tony about it he seemed to share this opinion. My feeling is that it is simply a superior guitar. Perhaps it is because superior musicians have played it? I have a theory—only a theory—that there is some intangible effect a superior player can impart to an instrument. I have noticed there are others who can make my guitar or my banjo sound better than when I play it myself. There may be some form of attack or vibration one person gets and another doesn't manage. Just think . . . why should it be that Earl Scruggs happens to have the best banjo? Why would Bill Monroe have the best mandolin? Does some of this effect linger in the instrument? Do certain vibrations in the musician make an instrument vibrate in the same way?

Shawn Lane:

He singlehandedly made Martin Herringbones cost as much as they do today just because he plays one.

Bill Amatneek:

It was a good guitar, but it wasn't a great one. Rice can make a Harmony sound good. In fact, it was only nominally a Martin. Roy Noble, who made two other guitars for Clarence, had done extensive work on it, including replacing the entire fingerboard with one he got from a Gretsch. It was already pretty beat up. Clarence used a number of other guitars on his recordings, including the Nobles and a D-18. The David Grisman Quintet was put together in 1975; Clarence had only been about two years in the grave and I doubt that his guitar was a holy relic yet. Martin's Clarence White reissue is only a so-so guitar—at least that's true of the two I've played—but the Santa Cruz versions, which have been modified more to Tony's liking, are far superior.

Richard Hoover:

This is tricky . . . The old Martin D-28 became the inspiration for Santa Cruz Guitar Company to build the Tony Rice model, which inspired Collings to make their Clarence White model, which then came around full circle to inspire Martin to copy *our* copy of an old Martin (the Martin HD-28 LSV, and Grand Marquis LSH).

There are people who, of course, deify that instrument as the end-all, be-all of acoustic flat top guitars. And it is a neat old instrument in many regards, but it's limited in the same way a lot of the pre-war Herringbones are limited. That particular one sounds really good for my taste. I once had the great luck of playing three at a time, Tony's included, and found his to be the most lively, and interestingly, the lightest of the three. It still had that characteristic scalloped brace, advanced X, and big airspace, and it could almost be described as a bit tubby and woofy. Tony is able to move his attack with his pick closer to the bridge in getting some brightness of tone and more clarity. It's the kind of guitar that's delightful for a bluegrass player and probably a bit abhorrent to a jazz player because it's so predominant in the bass. It's been played an awful lot; the wood is really, really aged, and both of those things are great contributors to a neat sound.

Imagine a graphic equalizer with the sliders. . . . Advancing the X's is just like pushing the bass sliders up. By moving the X forward toward the sound hole, you're bringing the lower legs up, giving more flexibility to the lower bout. And bass responds better to flexibility where treble responds better to stiffness. So you're loosening up the lower bout and boosting the bass response. There's an idea that it increases volume, but really that's the phenomenon of the human ear being able to accept bass more readily than the higher ranges. The whole guitar *sounds* louder, but really all that's happening is the bass is louder. Same with scalloped bracing—there's a lot of ad copy about richer, fuller sound, and that's cute but it's not true. All scalloping does, again, is increase bass response. It has the illusion of being a louder guitar because the bass is more prominent.

Bill Amatneek:
I turned to him and asked, "Aren't you concerned about flooding here?" Tony said, "No way, Wild Bill. It would take a once-in-a-century flood to come up to the house." [From *Acoustic Stories,* p. 69.]

Mark Johnson:
It was the storm of the century. I thought, "Oh my God, I gotta go down and get Louise." I knew Crystal River was going to be flooding. I couldn't see anybody over at Louise's house, and I was closer to cutting across the road to get to Tony's, but the current was coming across the road waist-high. I had my waders and was walking through it, and I kept running into people that were getting stuck in cars and kind of floating, so I was helping them back. One guy got sucked through a culvert and pipe about a hundred yards away and popped out right by Tony's house.

I tried to get to Louise's and said, "Screw this, I'm going to get my John boat." Then I drove down to Larry's house, and said, "We got to get to Tony's; we gotta get the guitar."

We got out into Crystal Bay, crawled along the edge of the Bay over to Tony's house, and we tied off to his doorknob. We went in there and there was maybe ten inches to a foot of water in the room. And nothing had been taken care of. There was a huge LP collection that was 13 feet wide, a lot of hand-signed things from Ornette Coleman, just amazing stuff. We started getting albums off the upper level, got the Grammy, found the cameras—they were soaked. Larry and I were running around, just grabbing things. We didn't know where Tony was. We looked all over the place for the guitar and the guitar was not there.

The thing that broke my heart . . . We opened this one room and there were stacks of one-of-a-kind, two-track recordings on reels, just *mountains* of them, lying on the floor. That much of the lower part of the house got flooded. We saved all that stuff. We grabbed everything we could and got it into the boat. Over the next couple days, we started getting it into a storage facility.

Most of the LPs that got soaked ended up in my house in Dunellon. The mold was so bad. Tony would come to the house, and we would get these big garbage bags and just peel, just try to save the LP itself and peel all the covers away and throw them into the garbage bags. Just mountains of stuff.

Tony was renting a home on a little spit of land out behind Brown's Fish House, next to Knox Bait House. That's the only two-story building there, and that's where he ultimately wound up spending the flood. What we found out later that day was that Tony had gotten himself over to Knox Bait House and found a shrimper guy and paid him $40 to wade over, pick the guitar up. It had been sitting on the bed in the back bedroom, the guest bedroom, and the water had gotten that high, to the base of the bed, and actually got into the guitar and shifted the block a little bit.

Harry Sparks:

(Courtesy of Jason Burleson)

I said, "Well, I'll just rent a car and I'll come see you and we'll all decide what to do about it. The worst thing that can happen to that guitar is if it dries out fast. Keep it in the case with the lid shut; don't let it dry out, please."

So we drove up there and looked at it. I said, "This is gonna be a couple weeks' process, and Tony, if you don't do this real carefully, you're gonna have an awful lot of damage to this guitar. Stuff it full of wet paper towels, just damp, not soaking wet, and put 'em inside the guitar so that it dries very gradually. The outside has finish on it and the inside doesn't, and if we don't do this, the outside can't dry and the inside will dry too fast; it's going to differentially dry out and end up cracking all to pieces."

We made it dry out very gradually, but it still did end up developing a couple cracks over time.

Snuffy Smith (North Carolina instrument repairman/banjoist and friend of Tony's):

I saw the guitar right after the flood. There was a benefit over in Greensboro for Tony, and I was there. He was playing it, and at the time, it was still pretty much intact inside, but over time, the braces exhibit what I call "feathering." The end of the brace will start creeping up just a little bit. And with playing and vibration and time, it will start working itself completely loose.

At one point, you could hold the guitar up and tap the back and it would just go "bl-du-luddle-luddle." The braces were just flopping around in there. I re-glued every brace in the back of that thing. Evidently, the way the water got into it, it sat in the inside of the guitar, but it didn't get up to the top; just got the back of the guitar.

I had to clean it up because there was a lot of trash in there, grit and grime and that kind of stuff. And if you get something underneath the brace when you glue it, and it holds it up off the surface, you're doing a bad thing. So I had to clean the old glue out under everything. Of course, the sound hole is so big you can stick your arm in up to your elbow. But I did one brace at a time and locked them into place with little threaded machinist's jacks you can screw and tighten.

John McGann (Massachusetts multi-instrumentalist and composer):

I think the guitar itself is less important than the hands and mind behind it. Witness the fact that Tony sometimes recorded with an Ovation—can anybody guess what tracks? It all sounds like Tony. He could play a Volkswagen and sound good.

Bill Amatneek:

He used the Ovation sometimes on recordings during my era. Engineers liked it because of the even frequency response across the fingerboard. I think that's why Tony liked it too. No booming bass to contend with at the recording console. I used to joke with him that the instrument had been made without ever touching human hands: they sprayed the bottom of the guitar into the bottom of the case, sprayed the top of the guitar into the top of the case, and then slammed the thing shut. It was difficult for me to see or appreciate his loving an antique, classic Martin guitar, and loving a modern, somewhat plastic, even-sounding Ovation.

David Grier:

You can pick up a guitar and sound one way, and pick up another . . . and pretty much sound the same way. That's what happens when you reach a certain level and you've got your own voice on your instrument. The guitar is a tool to get out whatever you feel, whatever you want to say to someone else. A lot of people miss that. People come up to me all the time with abalone and inlay and their names and everything all over their guitars, and they say, "Whaddaya think of that?" And I say, "Hey, man . . . I don't like it." They paid a lot of money for it and wonder, "Why don't you like it?" It's a tool! A carpenter doesn't put rhinestones in his hammer handle. I like the beat-up guitar. It shows, *yeah, somebody liked this enough to play it.*

Look at how he *uses* that hammer. Look at how he uses that guitar. It's a craft; it's something you work at, and you get better, and you learn little secrets, little things, that maybe aren't that important till you put 50 of those little things together, and next thing you know, you have a style.

Harry Sparks:

I shoot shotguns and rifles as a hobby and I'm real serious about it. We've got a saying in the shooting world: "It ain't always the gun." You can hand a piece of junk to a lot of shooters and they'll just drill the center of the target, and everybody says, "Wow, what a gun." If I were playing that guitar, no one would notice. And I think yes, it's a fine, fine, fine guitar, but . . . I mean, it's the man shooting the gun. He could make a Washburn sound like a million dollars.

Snuffy Smith:

It's almost like it's part of him. He knew about the guitar from way back when Clarence had it, and when he got to buy it, it was like he just bought the Holy Grail. And he's had that kind of respect for it ever since. And the more time that goes by, the more endearing it is to him because he's had it so long. I'm sure it's like picking up an old friend. It feels right. And I'm sure that's what it means to him with the guitar, because he always talks about it with great reverence. He just really respects the guitar . . .

He's told me repeatedly over time, "If somebody comes in and you trust 'em, let 'em play the guitar." I've had the vault open and guys walk in the door and see that guitar and just freeze like a bird dog. They can't hardly talk. I let some of those guys play it and it just means the *world* to them to get to do that. It has so much history that everybody who plays guitar knows about it. It kinda means something to me, too, with some young guy who knows the guitar but has never even seen it in real life, to let him pick on it a little bit. And everybody to a man that I've let hold it or play it has handled it with reverence.

Jeff Phillips (songwriter; fan):

I'm just a fan of his. After finding his *Acoustics* CD in a little shop, I couldn't believe his mastery of the guitar. I was then amazed to find he was touring the DC area and went to see him at the Birchmere. After the show, I went backstage to say hello. Everyone had cleared out and it was just Tony, his guitar and a six-pack of beer on ice—and me. He was incredibly gracious. I nervously told him I also pick, and he offered his guitar to me to "strum a couple tunes." I didn't even lay a hand on that old Martin, but the offer was genuine—and it says everything about him. To me, it was as if the world's best photographer had offered me his camera to shoot some pictures.

Randy Hudson (mandolinist; fan):

One of the coolest festival workshops I have ever attended was back in '85 or '86 with Tony at Grass Valley, California. What was supposed to be a one-hour discussion on musicianship or something turned into a totally memorable experience when, at one point, Tony passed his guitar (THE guitar) around the circle of 15–20 folks who had shown up for the workshop so we could FEEL it. And he talked for over two hours. What a *real* guy.

Sharon Gilchrist:

When Tony and David Grisman put out the *Tone Poems* album, they performed in Nashville at 328 Performance Hall. George Gruhn was there emceeing, and it was really an interesting show, definitely for music lovers. It was kinda slow-paced, because George would tell the story behind every instrument . . . and then Tony and David would play whatever the instruments were, then the tune they'd recorded on them, or maybe something else.

The Antique.
(Photo by Tim Stafford)

I hadn't heard Tony for a while at that point, maybe since '94. There was an intermission at some point, and they went back on, and started going through the second set the same way . . . It was awfully cool, and the playing sounded really good, but something wasn't hitting me. I could not put my finger on it.

Then George Gruhn introduced the Clarence White guitar. Tony picked it up and strummed it into the mic . . . and got a standing ovation. It was like, *Oh! That's Tony Rice. That's what I was missing all night.* I swear, from that moment on, everything was different. It was amazing. That guitar is so much a part of him and the way he plays. It was phenomenal.

Kyle Estep (guitarist and Rice protégé):

I want to play his Martin just once before I die.

Bill Monroe plays the Antique, February 7, 1977.
(Photo by Jon Sievert)

He is living his breaks and not recreating something someone else has done in the past. He plays from his heart right through his fingers, not letting his head get in the way.

Tim Austin, bluegrass guitarist

He took the basics of Clarence White's style and followed them in directions White hadn't taken, suggesting new ways of approaching lead guitar solo work in bluegrass.

Neil Rosenberg, bluegrass historian

I think Tony is about one of the slickest guys I've ever seen play. He doesn't even look like he's moving. Where are all these notes coming from?

Terry Clements, lead guitarist for Gordon Lightfoot, from "Terry Clements in the Lead" by Ben Elder, *Acoustic Guitar,* **January 2000**

Part II: The Technique

A Study

By Tim Stafford

What exactly is he doing there?

Countless guitarists and fans have breathlessly waited to *see* Tony Rice play after hearing his records, because of the impossible technique he seems to invoke at will— the extraordinary timing, tone and power . . . The inevitable response to a live Rice performance is one of wide-eyed wonder.

"I think Tony is a great example of the triumph of will over body," says Darol Anger. "He's got one of the strongest wills of anybody I know, and he forces his body to do what nobody should really be able to do. He's not a strong guy—his hands are fairly delicate. But there's a lot of precision there. It's just amazing that he's been able to do this for as long as he has, and along the way, achieved something that is just *incredible*. It's obvious from the way people think about him. Nobody ever saw anything like that before, that concentration. He was the first person I heard that, when he strummed across all six strings, it sounded like one string. Everything he did was *crystallized,* like a diamond."

"There's a major, major serious thing going on when you hear Tony hit a guitar string, tone-wise," offers Dave Talbot. "I think a big part of it is he's hearing it in his head before he even hits the thing. I think you can't play with a great amount of tone unless your ears hear tone to start with, or you hear it inside your head. And then, of course, there's the emotional part, which really adds life to the note. There are people who play that don't seem to have any connections between their emotions and their playing. Their playing sounds like one of those player pianos with a paper roll in it. It's great, but there's no life to it. Tony is the opposite: he has an extremely emotion-filled value in everything that he plays, note-wise and/or rhythmically."

In his insightful article on Tony's playing ("Flatpicker Extraordinaire," *Acoustic Guitar,* June 2007, #174, p. 50), guitarist Scott Nygaard says much the same thing:

> One reason that alternating picking has become popular is that the metronome-like back and forth of the picking hand provides an easy way for the player to keep time. But Rice's time originates with his left hand—in the notes he wants to play. Which means that Rice's melodic and harmonic ideas come first, and the technique he uses to play them follow after. How much more musical can you get than that?

But what actually is going on when Tony puts pick to string? What causes such outpourings of emotion, admiration, laughter, and even disbelief? Is it his right-hand technique? The left? Is it his legendary 1935 Martin D-28, which once belonged to Clarence White and which he affectionately calls "The Antique"? Is the secret in his picks or the strings he uses?

The Strings

Tony has used a variety of different strings over the years, all standard medium-gauge sets. He says he started out with Martin. "I would alternate between Martin bronze, and there was a Martin string back then called 'Monel.' They haven't made them in 35 years."

Then he saw an ad for Vinci strings and was intrigued. "I was always looking for a string that sounded better than the norm, a little less bright than a Martin, D'Addario, D'Arco or something like that. So I started using Tom Vinci's strings and fell in love with them right away because they were brass. I had never seen any brass strings before."

Many bluegrass guitarists remember the Tony Rice Vinci ads from Bluegrass Unlimited magazines in the 1980s: "Tony Rice uses Vinci Strings exclusively . . ." The company had a distinguished pedigree; Thomas Vinci's father Amelio had invented the first automated string-winding machine in 1953. Its logo: *We taught the world how to make strings.*

But soon Rice had to switch allegiances. "When Tom Vinci went out of business, I called Teddy Krauss over at D'Aquisto and said, 'Teddy, are you back and running?' He told me he bought all of Tom's machinery. I said, 'Well, can you make me some steel strings? I can't buy any good ones.' He said, 'Oh, yeah, I can make 'em.' So he made me six sets and sent 'em to me. The first set I put on was almost like heaven. I thought, *Wow! Here it is; this is the sound.* But there ain't many people that use them any more. Sam (Bush) uses 'em and so does (Norman) Blake. Other than that, I don't know anybody."

To Rice, D'Aquisto steel strings actually reveal the sound of the guitar: "It's like you hear more of the wood and less of the strings," he says. "You put that bright bronze or whatever on there and you hear that New Age sort of *ringing* thing that goes on forever." New ads for the strings show Tony cradling The Antique under a heading that says *If you played like Tony Rice and you had the most famous Martin D-28 around, what strings would you use? There really is a difference.* "D'Aquisto strings are absolutely incredible," Tony testifies.

And perhaps they are. But do they really make Tony Rice sound like he does? Probably not, especially considering he's used at least three different brands over his nearly-40-year career.

The Picks

Probably mainly because of Tony Rice, the favorite choice of picks for modern bluegrass guitarists are those made of "tortoiseshell," actually shell from the endangered Hawksbill turtle. According to Tony, his inspiration for using these picks came from Clarence White. "I had always used tortoise picks because Clarence did," Rice says. "Clarence used to get these shell picks from McCabe's and they were called D'Andrea. They were real tortoise picks, and they sounded good and never broke. You couldn't hardly wear 'em out. Clarence called 'em 'turtle back.' That was the name everybody used back then. There was no such term as 'tortoiseshell.'"

Tortoiseshell picks have unusual properties that make them ideal for use as guitar plectrums. For one, they are incredibly stiff and maintain their stiffness even when cut exceedingly thin. When played for some time on an acoustic guitar, the edge wears down, giving the tone a slight scratchy edge. This combination of factors makes them powerfully useful in the guitarist's quest for perfect tone and attack. Tortoiseshell is the Holy Grail in the quest for a better plectrum.

Tony's picks are rounded on the corners, with "enough of a point you get good tone from them"—and he says he's always used something like this shape, which is similar to the old D'Andrea "turtle back" picks. He uses all the corners on both sides, which essentially provides him with six points to use and wear. He usually gets a whole year's use out of one medium-sized triangular pick, and if they wear too much, he will "hit 'em with a piece of 1000-grit sandpaper or something."

These days he uses shell procured for him by a friend from Alaska. "This guy has been doing some roadie stuff for me and Peter (Rowan), lives in Alaska, and he gets turtles that wash up on the shore there. He has a bunch of it and he rolled it out and cut it for me. And then I made my picks out of some of the tortoise I got."

A tortoiseshell pick makes a certain *click* against a string, and there's no doubt that at least some small part of Tony's signature tone consists of that sound. But can it account for the timing, power, emotion, attack, intonation or expressiveness of Tony's playing?

The Hands

If you want to find the *real* Holy Grail, the secret of the sound Tony Rice gets with an acoustic guitar—indeed, any acoustic guitar he plays—you must examine his hands closely, especially his right. Why? His left hand is a model of precision with no extraneous movement, fingers held closely to the fingerboard, while his left thumb grips the back of the instrument's neck nearly *perpendicularly*—a technique similar to that used by jazz and classical guitarists.

Tony's long-time engineer and friend Billy Wolf believes Tony's left hand is key to his tone. "Part of how he gets the tone out of the instrument is because his left hand is so physically strong . . . He's holding those strings down and they're not gonna buzz. He gets that big round tone out of all six of the strings. Really, the only other guy that gets close is Wyatt.

"He doesn't put his hand around the neck the way a lot of people do; he puts his hand and thumb behind the neck most of the time. And it's all leverage. That squeeze between the fingers and the thumb is *serious*. He puts a lot of pressure on, so that he can play—And some of it is his refusal to electrify, so live, he has to play hard and loud.

"His grip on the guitar is not as hard as the average guitar player, but it's very hard for the way he plays, which is almost like a classical or jazz guitarist. But he's doing

The right hand . . . (Photo by Tim Stafford)

it on a flat-top, in that style. If you can envision, he doesn't squeeze from the palm quite so much, in other words, have the neck cradled in his left hand, so you have this tremendous leverage when you do that . . . Thumb pressure is key," concludes Wolf.

But as important as his left hand is, the real secret of Tony's sound is contained in his right. Todd Phillips had years to examine that hand close-up. "His right hand is a mechanism . . . it's like he's hinged at the elbow and wrist, and his thumb and forefinger are also hinged," Phillips says. "I've never seen anybody push down with their thumb, and then push back *up* with his first finger! When you start looking at it, and let your mind soak it up half-speed . . . to me, it's the way those mechanisms are hinged and work; he can use his wrist for rhythm, but then he can also crosspick with the first finger and thumb, like a whole 'nother element. And it's real strong, real definite; there's nothing wishy-washy about it."

David Grisman says, "Tony's got a very unusual mechanism with his thumb; he seems to have uncanny control. It's almost like his thumb is double-jointed or something."

Billy Wolf has seen Tony's right thumb up close as much as anyone. "A good comparison would be Doc Watson," Wolf observes. "Doc uses his whole arm, and pretty much generates an up-down swing with his arm, whereas Tony uses his first finger and thumb, a lot closer to Clarence White-style—a lot of double-downs and double-ups. He holds the pick pretty tight.

In interviews for this book, Tony said the 2007 article Scott Nygaard wrote about his playing style for *Acoustic Guitar* magazine proved what he had suspected for years: he plays almost everything *backwards* from what's considered standard technique. Where others would start with a downstroke, he starts with an upstroke, and vice-versa. But as Nygaard demonstrates with tablature for Tony's version of "Billy in the Lowground," Rice doesn't always play "backwards."

According to Nygaard, there never seems to be a rule for when Tony uses a downstroke or upstroke. He may use several consecutive downs in an arpeggio, followed by an alternating section, followed by several ups—it is all driven by efficiency, and it is not random, but systematic. In general, he will play consecutive downstrokes on strings downwardly (towards the pickguard) adjacent to each other and consecutive upstrokes on strings upwardly adjacent, if efficiency calls for it.

This method has been called "sweep picking" in rock guitar circles for years. In his thoughts on Tony's technique from the liner notes for *58957: The Bluegrass Guitar Collection,* Ron Block says: "When I started reading instructional books by electric guitar players they were all talking about *sweep picking* and I thought, 'Tony Rice has been doing that for years.'"

But Rice learned this—subconsciously and even organically—over years of simply *doing* it, and he admits he is unable to quantify or qualify his own technique. "I can't do the norm at any given time. I can't do a pattern of anything—it's always gonna be different. It's hard to describe, and it makes it even more different to analyze because if I play a kickoff to 'Blue Railroad Train,' and I play the notes the same way, the pick strokes are always gonna be different."

The Tuning

Of all the things Tony does well, tuning may be the skill that is most often overlooked. His guitar always seems to be precisely and completely in tune, and tales of his ability to tune it in seconds, just before going onstage, are the stuff of legend. Rice doesn't use any modern devices like electronic tuners—he simply hits a tuning fork and places it against the bridge of his guitar and *listens.*

"Yeah, it's the A note right there—the 7th fret harmonic of the 4th string," he says, as he demonstrates his method on his guitar. "The harmonic is also a 440 third, so I just synch that up with the fourth note in the scale or the fourth string. And that's the string for reference—the fourth—because it has more tension on it than any other string of the set. So when you have that synched up with A on your fourth—" here, he hits the harmonic, then the fork—"then you've got your best source. Because they all note off up the neck. What I do is tune it so those notes are in tune." Here, he plays G-D-A-E. "Which is like a mandolin or fiddle: if you have the G note in tune, then your A and then the E, you've got the best compromise between the E, D, and G chords."

It's the "compromise" between actually playing chords and notes, and having strings in tune open, that makes Rice disdain the use of electronic tuners. "Them things are useless, man. I mean, what are you gonna do? Use an electronic tuner so that you have every string in tune open? Well, then, what's gonna happen when you make a chord? And what if you happen to be somebody with strong hands and you press a little bit harder than the next guy?"

Like many guitarists, Tony compensates the tuning of his second or B string, because he realizes it will not sound in tune if tuned perfectly open. "A piano does not mathematically compute if you keep going up without tempering the third interval. It's the Pythagorean Wolf. If you hit middle C on a piano and keep going up and down in octaves, to make 'em right, you have got to compensate for that third note."

However he does it, Tony just sounds more *in tune* when he plays, and it makes a big difference in the way people perceive his music.

Manzanita Band (Photo by Jon Sievert)

On the Road
Part 8

Off the Road, in the Dungeon

Tony Rice has just come off the long road after another thousand-mile weekend.

It was filled with a lot of solitary late-night hours in a fast car on dangerous roads, a weekend of too much coffee and not enough sleep. The motel room beds had lumps in all the wrong places. The outdoor venues were sometimes unpleasantly hot, or wet, or windy; the stages too dark or not dark enough. The sound systems were sometimes badly configured and inadequate. And there was a never-ending stream of fans, each with a CD to sign and a story to tell.

Yet he managed, over the course of a couple of days, to gracefully wing his way through a few hot 45-minute sets with his old buddies in the Unit. When any of them are asked, they say he's on fire these days. Every performance seemed a distillation of his finest musical moments.

An intense weekend, but pretty ordinary, as they go. Still . . . Tony Rice has barely been home for an hour, and he is already sitting in front of his microscope, his body taut and motionless, peering intently into the belly of an Accutron.

What *is* it that Tony Rice finds comforting about working on these old timepieces?

What would compel him to come off the long road from a thousand-mile weekend, after all that craziness and adrenaline and exposure, to sit in front of that microscope, perfectly motionless, gripping a pair of precision Swiss tweezers in one hand and a movement in the other, to stare, practically without blinking or breathing, at a tiny little tuning fork, for 24 hours at a stretch, sometimes?

What would compel him to do that?

When you walk into Tony's listening room, the half-underground basement room where he spends most of his hours at home, you immediately notice the timepieces. One of the first things you see is a big digital atomic clock with glowing letters. Several times a day, it aligns itself with the U.S. Naval Observatory Master Clocks in Colorado Springs and Washington, D.C. There are a couple of dozen watches in various stages of restoration, some sitting in double-sided heavy-duty aluminum travel cases and some on the table by his microscope. He always has an Accutron or two close by; they're as ubiquitous as his '35 D-28.

The world's first electronic wristwatches, Accutrons were made by the Bulova Company from the 1950s to 1977. Put them to your ear and you can hear the 360-hertz tuning forks humming inside. Swiss engineer Max Hetzel's idea was to make a transistor-based watch that would keep accurate time within two seconds to the day. In 1964, an Accutron was chosen for inclusion in a 5,000-year time capsule on the grounds of the New York World Fair as an example of one of the most innovative objects invented during the previous two and a half decades. Tony shares all this information as he focuses. One begins to wonder if he might not be obsessed with time. That would explain his extraordinary rhythm, right?

But it goes deeper than that. Tony's playing is like the Accutrons: vintage, trend-setting, anything but sloppy, immaculate in appointment and attention to detail. Everything he does is about *precision*. At least that's been his mantra, what he's striven for—it's what he seeks in his music (both what he plays, and what he listens to), his stereo, his watches, his clothing, his automobiles, his guitars.

"Elvis Presley wore an Astronaut Accutron," he says as he calibrates the tuning fork's frequency. "This is exactly like the one Elvis wore. This is from 1966; the first ones went into production in 1960. I've got all the parts for a total mint-condition restoration. It's just taken so much time and frustration." He does not know how many hours he's devoted to it already. "This one, I've spent two or three days on the movement alone. When I get done with it, it will look like the day it left the jeweler. You have to have the stillness of a brain surgeon to work on the Accutron. That's the reason not many people do it anymore."

It's the *stillness* he likes, he says, tapping the place on his narrow chest above his heart; the stillness he finds comforting. Working on these old timepieces requires him to be absolutely still in his core, so recently filled to overflowing with the weekend's chaos of music and money and rain and strangers and miles.

As he adjusts the microscope and takes another look at the old timepiece, his dogs settle in at his feet, as if they know they're in for a long evening. The miles slip away. He becomes lost in the quiet rhythm of his task, absorbed in his own wonder at the tiny, perfect universe under the lens.

After another thousand-mile weekend, Tony Rice is finally still inside.

Restless Farewell
Bob Dylan

Oh all the money that in my whole life I did spend,
Be it mine right or wrongfully,
I let it slip gladly past the hands of my friends
To tie up the time most forcefully.
But the bottles are done,
We've killed each one
And the table's full and overflowed.
And the corner sign
Says it's closing time,
So I'll bid farewell and be down the road.

Oh ev'ry girl that ever I've touched,
I did not do it harmfully.
And ev'ry girl that ever I've hurt,
I did not do it knowin'ly.
But to remain as friends and make amends
You need the time and stay behind.
And since my feet are now fast
And point away from the past,
I'll bid farewell and be down the line.

Oh ev'ry foe that ever I faced,
The cause was there before we came.
And ev'ry cause that ever I fought,
I fought it full without regret or shame.
But the dark does die
As the curtain is drawn and somebody's eyes
Must meet the dawn.
And if I see the day
I'd only have to stay,
So I'll bid farewell in the night and be gone.

Oh, ev'ry thought that's strung a knot in my mind,
I might go insane if it couldn't be sprung.
But it's not to stand naked under unknown' eyes,
It's for myself and my friends my stories are sung.
But the time ain't tall,
Yet on time you depend and no word is possessed
By no special friend.
And though the line is cut,
It ain't quite the end,
I'll just bid farewell till we meet again.

Oh a false clock tries to tick out my time
To disgrace, distract, and bother me.
And the dirt of gossip blows into my face,
And the dust of rumors covers me.
But if the arrow is straight
And the point is slick,
It can pierce through dust no matter how thick.
So I'll make my stand
And remain as I am
And bid farewell and not give a damn.

Cast of Characters

Burch, Curtis .... Guitarist who took Tony's place in Bluegrass Alliance in 1971; original guitarist with New Grass Revival

Burgess, Cole .... Saxophonist who played on Tony's *Me and My Guitar* project

Burleson, Jason .... North Carolina multi-instrumentalist; member of the group Blue Highway and Rice protégé

Bush, Sam .... Legendary mandolinist/singer, bandmate and confidant of Tony; founder of New Grass Revival

Campbell, Rick .... Tony Rice fan

Carlini, John .... Guitarist and mentor of Tony's

Carpenter, Fred .... Original violinist with the Tony Rice Unit

Carroll, Joe .... Original bassist with David Grisman Quintet

Carroll, Jon .... Pianist with Mary Chapin Carpenter; appeared on *Native American* and Rice Brothers records

Case, Keith .... Tony's booking agent since the 1980s

Cash, John Carter .... Son of music legend Johnny Cash; executive producer of new Tim Cowling film on Tony

Chapin Carpenter, Mary .... Washington, D.C. singer/songwriter and Tony protégé who achieved commercial success in the late '80s and early '90s

Chiavola, Kathy .... Nashville-based singer who sang on several cuts on *Me and My Guitar*

Chipoletti, Marilee .... Employee at Keith Case & Associates since 1997 and Tony's main contact/agent in the office

Clements, Vassar .... Legendary fiddler; one of Tony's greatest inspirations and dearest friends; died of lung cancer in 2005 (1928–2005)

Coltrane, John .... Legendary jazz saxophonist who inspired Tony and many of the musicians in David Grisman's circle (1926–1967)

Compton, Mike .... Mandolinist/vocalist with Nashville Bluegrass Band; protégé of Bill Monroe's

Cowan, John .... Bassist/singer with New Grass Revival; Tony's close friend and confidant in recovery

Cowling, Tim .... Documentary filmmaker; as of 2008, is working on a film about Tony and the Antique

Crary, Dan .... Legendary flatpick guitarist; replaced by Tony Rice in the Bluegrass Alliance in 1970

Crowe, J.D. .... Legendary banjoist & New South bandleader; hired Tony in 1970 with the New South; Tony's inspiration and collaborator

Davies, Bryn .... Bassist with Peter Rowan & Tony Rice from 1999–2007; bassist with Tony Rice Unit; formerly married to mandolinist Billy Bright

Davis, Brad .... Texas guitarist and Tony protégé

Davis, Miles .... Legendary creator of "cool jazz" and one of Tony's biggest inspirations (1926–1991)

Dilling, Steve .... Banjoist with IIIrd Tyme Out and observer of Bluegrass Album Band Tours in the 1980s

Douglas, Jerry "Flux" .... Ground-breaking resonator guitarist and collaborator of Rice's since 1975

Duffey, John .... Original mandolinist with the Seldom Scene (1934–1996)

Duncan, Stuart .... World-class fiddler; played on the Tony Rice Unit's first show

Edwards, Tommy .... Guitarist and acquaintance of Tony's in the late '60s and early '70s

Eldridge, Ben .... Banjoist with the Seldom Scene

Emerson, Bill .... Banjoist who replaced Eddie Adcock in the Country Gentlemen

Estep, Kyle .... Michigan guitarist and Tony Rice protégé

Estrin, Kari	Manager of the Tony Rice Unit in the early years
Evans, Bill	Legendary jazz pianist and inspiration to Tony (1929–1980)
Fesler, Brian	Minnesota-based banjoist; formerly played with the Lonesome River Band and Dusty Miller
Fike, Raymond	Tony Rice fan
Fleck, Béla	Ground-breaking banjoist and frequent Rice collaborator
Freeland, Dick	Owner of Rebel Records in the 1970s
Freeman, Kate	Tony's first wife (1972–79)
Fowler, Bobby	Friend of Tony's from Atlanta, GA
Garcia, Jerry	Founder of the Grateful Dead; recorded with Tony and David Grisman on *The Pizza Tapes* (1942–1995)
Gaudreau, Jimmy	Veteran mandolinist/vocalist and member of the Tony Rice Unit from 1985 until the mid-'90s
Gilchrist, Sharon	New Mexico-based mandolinist; played with Peter Rowan and Tony Rice from 2005–2007
Gillette, Steve	Singer/songwriter; wrote "Darcy Farrow" and "Grapes on the Vine," which Tony recorded
Gomez, Eddie	Noted jazz bassist who played on Grisman's *Hot Dawg* record with Tony
Gosdin, Vern	Country music star and early member of the Golden State Boys (1934–2009)
Grappelli, Stéphane	Legendary French jazz violinist; recorded with Tony and David Grisman (1908–1997)
Graves, Burkett "Josh"	Dobro® player with Flatt and Scruggs
Gray, Tom	Original bassist with the "classic" Country Gentlemen and the Seldom Scene
Greene, Richard	Violinist and associate/inspiration of Tony's and David Grisman's
Grier, David	Guitarist; son of banjoist Lamar Grier
Grisman, David	Visionary mandolinist and father of "Dawg" music
Gruhn, George	Nashville instrument collector and appraiser
Hale, Robert	West Virginia guitarist; played with J.D. Crowe and the New South
Hambrick, Clayton	Member of the band Grass Menagerie; sold Hylo Brown's 1948 D-28 Martin to Tony
Hamilton, Doc	Texas banjo/fiddler who played with Tony and Larry in Texas in late 1960s
Hamm, Steve	Original engineer for Rounder 0044
Haney, Aubrey	Nashville session fiddler/mandolinist
Haney, Carlton	Legendary festival promoter; founder of the Camp Springs event where Tony met Sam Bush
Haney, Dr. David	Guitarist and historian; teaches class on bluegrass music at Appalachian State University
Harkey, Milton	North Carolina promoter who named the Bluegrass Album Band; organized tours in the '80s
Harris, Emmylou	Legendary country & bluegrass singer; Tony worked for her briefly in the 1980s
Harrison, Mark	Tony Rice fan
Hartford, John	Legendary banjoist/singer/songwriter; Tony's good friend (1937–2001)
Heifetz, Jascha	Legendary classical violinist; one of Tony's favorite artists (1901–1987)
Hicks, Bobby	Legendary fiddler on the Bluegrass Album series
Higbie, Barbara	Bay area musician, Windham Hill recording artist and wife of Darol Anger in the 1970s and '80s

Hillman, Chris	Original member of The Byrds and a childhood friend of Tony & Larry; collaborated with them and banjoist Herb Pedersen on three recordings as Rice, Rice, Hillman & Pedersen
Hoover, Richard	Founder and President of the Santa Cruz Guitar Company
Hudson, Randy	California mandolinist; fan
Hughes, Donna	North Carolina singer/songwriter; Tony produced her first Rounder album in 2005
Hurst, Jim	Kentucky guitarist
Ickes, Rob	Resonator guitarist and frequent collaborator of Tony's
Irwin, Ken	One of the founders of Rounder Records
Jasper, Floyd	Dobro player who played with Rice brothers in Texas in the late 1960s
Jennings, John	D.C.-area guitarist; played on *Native American*
Johnson, Courtney	Original banjoist with the New Grass Revival (1939–1996)
Johnson, Dexter	Bay area instrument retailer and associate of David Grisman who provided many of the instruments Grisman and Tony used on *Tone Poems*
Johnson, Mark	Florida clawhammer banjoist and Rice family friend
Jones, Cecil	Engineer and owner of Lemco Studios where Tony recorded *Guitar* in 1974
Jones, Clay	North Carolina guitarist and Tony protégé; played with Mountain Heart
Kamimoto, Hideo	Oakland, CA-based master instrument technician; created a saddle and nut that are still in the Antique
Kaparakis, John	D.C.-area musician and close friend of Clarence White; instrumental in the meeting between Tony and Sam Bush
Kaukonen, Jorma	Original guitarist/vocalist with Jefferson Airplane; now runs a guitar camp in Southern Ohio called Fur Peace Ranch where Tony has performed
Keel, Larry	Guitarist and jam grass bandleader
Keith, Bill	Ground-breaking banjoist and early collaborator with Rice
Kopelson, Danny	Well-known jazz engineer who mixed *Backwaters*
Krauss, Alison	Legendary singer/fiddler who was profoundly influenced by Tony's music
Kuehl, Tom	Guitarist with the Golden State Boys, and with the Bluegrass Ramblers, 1962
Lacroix, Janelle	Tony's first kiss, 1957
Lane, Shawn	Multi-instrumentalist and vocalist with Blue Highway; formerly with Doyle Lawson & Quicksilver and Ricky Skaggs and Kentucky Thunder
Lathum, Billy Ray	Original banjoist with the Kentucky Colonels
Lawrence, Jack	Guitarist and sideman with Doc Watson; acquaintance of Tony's from the late 1960s
Lawson, Doyle	Legendary mandolinist/vocalist/bandleader of Quicksilver; collaborated with Tony on the *Bluegrass Album* series
Leadbetter, Phil	Resonator guitarist who played for a number of years with J.D. Crowe and the New South
Leaf, Mark	Instrument case designer and builder
Lee, Albert	British guitar legend; played and recorded with Tony and Emmylou Harris in the 1980s
Legere, Ray	Canadian mandolinist/fiddler who played shows with the Tony Rice Unit in 1988
Leighton, Marion	One of the founders of Rounder Records
Lightfoot, Gordon	Legendary Canadian singer/songwriter; Tony's favorite composer
Longworth, Mike	Former employee and historian of Martin guitars (1939–2003)
Mack, Leroy	Occasional resonator guitarist with the Kentucky Colonels

Magruder, Robbie	Drummer performed on *Native American*
Marsalis, Branford	Jazz clarinetist and inspiration of Tony's
Marshall, Mike	Florida mandolinist/Tony protégé; member of David Grisman Quintet and Ook 'n' Em; Tony's close friend
Martin, Jimmy	Hall of Fame guitarist/vocalist/bandleader; bluegrass music's greatest rhythm guitarist (1927–2005)
Massenburg, George	Legendary engineer who mixed Tony's California Autumn record
McCoury, Del	Legendary vocalist/bandleader/guitarist; member of the Golden State Boys in the 1960s
McElroy, Bill	Engineer at Bias Studios in Springfield, VA; mixed Rounder 0044
McGann, John	Massachusetts multi-instrumentalist and composer
McGarrigle, Anna & Kate	Canadian folksingers whose 1975 Warner Bros. album was the first to feature Tony playing the Antique. Kate (1946–2010)
McReynolds, Jesse	Legendary mandolinist/singer and co-founder with his brother Jim of the bluegrass band Jim and Jesse. Developed "cross-picking" mandolin technique. Composed "Stoney Creek."
Miller, Joe	Liquor store owner who accepted Clarence White's 1935 D-28 on pawn in 1966 and sold it to Tony in 1975
Miller, Russ	Los Angeles instrument dealer and appraiser; appraised the Antique in 1975 for $400 or $500
Monroe, Bill	Legendary mandolinist/vocalist/bandleader; "Father of Bluegrass Music" (1911–1996)
Neidlinger, Buell	L.A. session bassist and Rice confidant and mentor
Newton, Mark	Virginia singer and guitarist; has worked with Tony Rice Unit
Nichtern, David	Producer and author of "Plastic Banana" on Tony's first Rounder solo project
Nowlin, Bill	One of the founders of Rounder Records
Nygaard, Scott	California guitarist and writer
O'Brien, Tim	Multi-instrumentalist/singer/songwriter and co-founder of group Hot Rize; Grammy-winning solo artist
O'Connor, Mark	Seattle violinist/multi-instrumentalist who took Tony's place in the David Grisman Quintet
Oelze, Gary	Proprietor of the Birchmere in Alexandria, VA; Tony's good friend, and manager for a time in the 1980s
Oelze, Linda	Wife of Gary Oelze
Ørsted Pedersen, Niels Henning	Danish jazz bassist who Tony at one time claimed was his favorite musician (1946–2005)
Owens, Andy	Banjoist with the Haphazards
Parker, Charlie "Bird"	Legendary saxophonist, composer and co-founder of bebop jazz (1920–1955)
Parmley, Don	Third banjo player with the Golden State Boys; later founder of The Bluegrass Cardinals
Peck, Karen	Gospel singer from Georgia; Tony produced two of her recordings
Pedersen, Herb	Banjoist who collaborated with Tony, Larry Rice, and Chris Hillman on a series of records from 1997 to 2001
Peerce, Lonnie	Founder and bandleader of Bluegrass Alliance
Penn, Jewell	Tony's cousin and close friend
Peterson, Oscar	Legendary Canadian jazz pianist and one of Tony's biggest inspirations (1925–2007)

Petrucelli, Rico .... Bassist who performed on *Native American*
Phillips, Jeff .... Maryland songwriter; fan
Phillips, Todd .... Original second mandolinist and later bassist with the David Grisman Quintet
Poindexter Cox, Alice .... Tony's maternal aunt
Poindexter Perry, Angela .... Tony's maternal aunt
Poindexter, Clarence .... Tony's maternal uncle
Poindexter, Doris .... Tony's maternal aunt (deceased)
Poindexter, Floyd .... Tony's maternal uncle; one of the original Golden State Boys
Poindexter, Frank .... Tony's maternal uncle; resonator guitarist and picking partner of Tony's
Poindexter, Hardin Jr. "Hal" .... Tony's maternal uncle; also called "Uncle Junior" by family members; (mother's brother); guitarist who influenced Tony's rhythm playing
Poindexter Smith, Joyce .... Wife of Tony's Uncle Junior, Hal Poindexter
Poindexter, Harden William .... Tony's maternal grandfather
Poindexter, Leon .... Tony's maternal uncle; one of the original Golden State Boys
Poindexter, Luna Bell .... Tony's maternal grandmother (d. Sept. 16, 2006)
Poindexter Davis, Linda .... Tony's maternal aunt
Poindexter Tilley, Mary .... Tony's maternal aunt
Poindexter Roach, Nell .... Tony's maternal aunt
Poindexter Sanders, Pam .... Wife of Tony's uncle, Frank Poindexter
Poindexter, Walter .... Tony's maternal uncle (deceased)
Poindexter Barrow Faber, Betty ... Tony's aunt; moved to California with Rices in 1954
Poindexter Rice, Dorothy Louise . Tony's mother, known to family & friends as "Aunt Lou;" born 10/17/29 in Ruffin, NC
Poindexter Scott, Maggie .... Tony's maternal aunt; mother of Jewell Penn
Poindexter Doyle, Susan .... Tony's maternal aunt
Poss, Barry .... Founder of Sugar Hill Records
Ramsey, Aaron .... Mandolinist with Mountain Heart
Ratliff, Audey .... Tennessee mandolinist and luthier
Reed Hubbard, Jerry .... Legendary guitarist/songwriter; one of Tony's main inspirations (1937–2008)
Reinhardt, Django .... Legendary Gypsy jazz guitarist (1910–1953)
Reischman, John .... Original mandolinist with the Tony Rice Unit
Reno, Don .... Legendary bluegrass banjoist; one of the first lead flat-top guitarists in bluegrass; featured Tony on his *Family and Friends* record which appeared in 1988. (1927–1984)
Rice, B.J. .... Tony's paternal uncle
Rice, David Anthony "Tony" .... Born June 8, 1951 in Danville, VA
Rice, Diane .... Wyatt Rice's wife
Rice, Dossie .... Tony's paternal grandmother ("Mom Rice")
Rice, Eugene .... Tony's paternal uncle
Rice, Gabriel Pinkney .... Tony's paternal grandfather
Rice, Gladys .... Tony's paternal aunt
Rice, Herbert Hoover "Herb" ...... Tony's father (born 4/12/29; died 11/20/83)
Rice, Julia .... Tony's paternal aunt
Rice, Larry Prentis .... Tony's oldest brother (born 4/24/49; died 5/13/06)
Rice, Lillian .... Tony's paternal aunt
Rice, Pamela Hodges .... Tony's third wife (1989–present)
Rice, Ronald Dean .... Tony's middle brother, born 2/22/55
Rice, Wyatt Lynn .... Tony's youngest brother, born 1/06/65

Ronstadt, Linda .... Legendary pop vocalist and admirer of Tony's music

Rosenberg, Neil .... Bluegrass historian; published *Bluegrass: A History,* the definitive history of the genre, in 1985

Ross, Bruce .... Co-founder of Santa Cruz Guitar Company

Rowan, Peter .... Legendary singer/songwriter and former protégé of Bill Monroe; began performing with Tony in 1998

Russell, Leon .... Southern Rock singer/musician; New Grass Revival toured as his backup band for a time in the 1970s

Santamaria, Mongo .... Cuban percussionist whose "Afro Blue" inspired the structure of "Manzanita" (1917–2003)

Satyendra, Leela .... Tony's second wife (1980–84)

Sawtelle, Charles .... Guitarist with the group Hot Rize; before his death in 1999, Sawtelle also collaborated with Peter Rowan (1947–1999)

Schatz, Mark .... Bassist with the Tony Rice Unit, 1985–90; appeared on several Rice records

Scruggs, Earl .... Legendary banjoist; creator of modern bluegrass banjo style

Seviert, Jon .... Photographer who often shot the David Grisman Quintet

Shelor, Sammy .... Banjoist with the Lonesome River Band

Shelton, James Alan .... Veteran lead guitarist with Ralph Stanley's Clinch Mtn. Boys

Shoemaker, Bob .... Engineer at Arch Street Studios in the late 1970s and '80s

Shuffler, George .... Co-developer of the "crosspick" guitar style; played with the Stanley Brothers in the '50s and '60s

Shuping, Garland .... Banjoist and acquaintance of Tony's in the late 1960s; later played with Bluegrass Alliance

Simpkins, Rickie .... Fiddler/mandolinisit who joined the Tony Rice Unit in 1988

Simpkins, Ronnie .... Bassist joined Tony Rice Unit in 1990; brother of Rickie; now with the Seldom Scene

Skaggs, Ricky .... Legendary multi-instrumentalist and singer; collaborator with Rice since 1975, later a major country music star

Slone, Bobby .... Bassist/fiddler and bandmate of Tony's in the New South, 1971–75

Smith, Arthur .... Tony's art teacher in Crystal River, FL introduces Tony to the music of Gordon Lightfoot in 1968

Smith, Kenny (1) .... Virginia guitarist and Tony protégé

Smith, Kenny (2) .... Leader of Louisville, KY band Buster Brown in the '70s

Smith, Ma .... Tony's Uncle Junior's wife's mother, at whose home he progressed greatly on the guitar in the late 1960s

Smith, Snuffy .... Repairman and banjoist from North Carolina; does all work on the Antique

Sparks, Harry .... Louisville, Kentucky-based luthier and friend of Tony's

Stafford, Tim .... Guitarist, member of Blue Highway, co-author of Tony Rice biography

Starling, John .... Original guitarist and lead singer with the Seldom Scene; U.S. Army surgeon

Stern, Arthur .... Archivist of the David Grisman Quintet

Sturgill, Hugh .... Manager of J.D. Crowe and the New South during the Rice years

Surratt, Tim .... Bassist/multi-instrumentalist/singer who played with the group "Balsam Range" and also toured with the Tony Rice Unit in 2008

Sutton, Bryan .... Guitarist who took Tony's place on Béla Fleck's Bluegrass Sessions tour in 2007

Talbot, Dave .... Canadian banjoist; J.D. Crowe protégé

Tate, Fran .... Engineer at Track Studios in Silver Spring, MD for *California Autumn*

Dogs

Asti Spumante	Champagne-colored female from Zoi's litter, given to Jewell Penn
Buddy	Small Jack Russell terrier rescued by Pam's late brother, Dale
Django	Purebred standard poodle; a rescue dog; died in 2000 of lymphoma at 6½
Dragon Crowe	"Dragon Rain Crowe," black standard poodle from Zoi's litter, named for J.D. Crowe
Enzo Ferrari	White standard poodle from Zoi's litter, given to India Rice
Feather	"Alison Little Feather Spirit," white standard poodle from Zoi's litter, named for Alison Krauss and Pam's friend
Marquis	Black standard poodle from Zoi's litter; died in 2008; named for Marks Schatz, O'Connor, and Johnson, and Tony's friend and physician Mark Cresenzo
Pokey	Tony's Chihuahua-Yorkshire terrier mix dog; died in 2000 at age 17½
Ranzo Béla	"Ranzo Béla," black standard poodle from Zoi's litter named for Béla Fleck and Tony's friend Randy Cresenzo
Sam	"Samurai Lanikai," black standard poodle from Zoi's litter, named for Sam Bush and Charles Sawtelle (whose ashes are scattered off Lanikai Beach in Hawaii)
Tipper	Tony's Pomeranian mix dog, died in 2000 at age 18
Vassar	White standard poodle from Zoi's litter, named for Vassar Clements
Xo'i, Zoi	White standard poodle, mother of eight pups, died of lymphoma in 2008
Zorro David	Black standard poodle; "alpha male" of Rice poodle herd; a rescue dog. Named for Grisman.

Birds

Dinah	Tony's cockatiel
Hootie	Muscially gifted cockatiel given to the Rices by Mark Cresenzo; died of fright during a hurricane
Lonzo	Tony's cockatiel
Lucille	Tony's cockatiel
Roscoe	Tony's cockatiel

Milestones

A timeline of the life and career of Tony Rice

4/12/29	Herbert Hoover Rice is born in Gaston County, NC to Dossie "Mom" Rice and Gabriel Pinkney Rice; he is the youngest of a family of children that will number four boys (one who dies before reaching adulthood) and six girls.
10/17/29	Dorothy Louise Poindexter is born in Ruffin, NC to Harden William Poindexter and Luna Bell Poindexter; she is the oldest of fifteen children.
Before Oct. 1945	Louise, 14, goes to work at Dan River Mill, taking a room in a Schoolfield home owned by Mom & Pop Rice. There she meets Herb Rice, employed at Covington's and Sam's Hardware in Danville. Schoolfield was a mill village for workers at Dan River's Schoolfield mills.
Dec. 24, 1947	Herbert Hoover Rice and Dorothy Louise Poindexter are married.
1947–48	Herb & Louise Rice move from Herb's parents' home to their own small place in Ruffin, NC (it has no electricity or running water). Mom Rice moves with them.
February 1949	Frank Poindexter (Tony's youngest Poindexter uncle) is born.
April 24, 1949	Larry Prentis Rice is born.
June 8, 1951	**David Anthony Rice is born in Danville, VA.**
1951	The *SS United States,* which Herb Rice helped build, is launched. At 53,329 gross tons, she was, at the time, the largest ocean liner built entirely in the United States and is still the fastest liner ever constructed. Cost to build: $78 million.
1953	Herb Rice and Hal "Junior" Poindexter work in a little band in Newport News called the Blue Steel Boys, Herb on mandolin, Junior on guitar.
October 1954	Herb and Louise Rice and their family leave Newport News, VA, where Herb has been working in the shipyards, and move to California.
February 22, 1955	Ronald Dean Rice is born in Lynwood, CA, in the vicinity of Los Angeles.
1955	Herb and Louise Rice purchase home in Artesia, CA.
1956–57	One of Tony's earliest musical memories: playing a guitar with teeth broken off a giant novelty comb he found around the house.
1957	Tony's first kiss, age 6, from classmate Janelle LaCroix.
1957	Tony's maternal grandparents, Lula Bell and Harden Poindexter, Sr., move to Pelham, NC with their children remaining at home, settling in the house they'll live in for the rest of their lives.
1960	Golden State Boys are formed. The first members are Herb Rice on mandolin, Leon Poindexter on bass, Hal Poindexter on guitar, with Floyd Poindexter sitting in occasionally. Lee Casteen on banjo joins almost immediately thereafter. The name comes from Louise Rice, who sees it on a carton of Golden State milk.
1959	1935 D-28 Martin (Serial No. 58957) is sold to McCabe's Guitar Shop in Los Angeles, CA, reportedly by a young woman with polio who attends UCLA.
Nov. 26, 1959	The Rice family is in a bad car accident; all members of the family are injured except Tony.

May 1960 .... Hal "Junior" Poindexter and his wife, Joyce and son, Randy move to California; they live with the Rices for a little while and then find their own place.

1959–60 .... Tony, age eight or nine, receives his first guitar: a brand-new D-18 purchased for $250–$300 by Herb Rice for himself, and then given to Tony.

August 1960 .... Walter Poindexter arrives in California and begins playing banjo with the Golden State Boys.

1960 .... Clarence and Roland White, accompanied by banjoist Billy Ray Lathum, purchase 1935 Martin D-28 Serial No. 58957 at McCabe's Music Shop for $35.

1960 .... Tony meets Clarence White for the first time at the Town Hall Party in Compton, CA. Clarence and his brother, Roland, are regulars on the popular radio show with their band, the Country Boys. Tony, at the time, has just made his debut appearance on the program, singing "Under Your Spell Again," a Buck Owens tune.

1961 .... Don Parmley joins the Golden State Boys, replacing Walter Poindexter, who returns to the East Coast. He will remain with the band for the next four years or so.

1961–62 .... Golden State Boys record their first single: "Always Dreaming" by Hal "Junior" Poindexter and "Wicked Woman" by Don Parmley.

1962 .... The Haphazards are formed: Larry Rice on mandolin, Tony on guitar, Andy Evans on banjo, and Butch (surname unknown) on bass.

1963 .... Hal "Junior" Poindexter leaves the Golden State Boys over a now-forgotten disagreement. When he returns to the band, after about a month, Don Parmley has taken over as bandleader.

1963 .... Herb Rice forms his second band in L.A. with partner Tom Kuehl, called Tom and Herb and the Bluegrass Ramblers, with Mel Durham on bass and banjoist Ronnie LeGrand. Per Tony, who says he was 12 or 13 at the time, they played more for a hobby than anything else.

1963–64 .... The Haphazards appear every Friday night on Country Music Time, a television show on KCOP Channel 13. Tony often sees Clarence White at shows.

Jan. or Feb. 1964 .... Del McCoury quits Bill Monroe's Blue Grass Boys, leaves his Pennsylvania home, moves to California with Billy Baker and joins the Golden State Boys.

1964 .... Vern Gosdin replaces Herb Rice in the Golden State Boys.

1964 .... Eric White, brother of Clarence & Roland, joins the Golden State Boys as a bass player.

1964 .... Larry Rice, still in high school, plays with the Golden State Boys for about a year.

January 6, 1965 .... Wyatt Lynn Rice is born in Long Beach, CA.

April 1965 .... The Rice family leaves California and moves to Florida. They live with Leon Poindexter in Safety Harbor for a week or so, then rent a house in the same town. Tony finishes last two months of eighth grade in Safety Harbor.

Summer 1965 .... Rices move to Clearwater, FL.

1965 .... Frank Poindexter at 16 moves to Florida with his brother, Leon.

End of summer '65 .... The Rices move to Dunellen, FL where Tony enters high school; per Ronnie, this is where Tony, Herb, and Frank play frequently at the Wander Inn.

1965 or '66 .... Herb Rice purchases Tony's second guitar, a D-18, in Florida.

1966	Tony starts smoking cigarettes.
1966	Clarence White pawns his 1935 D-28 Martin (SN 58957) to Joe Miller of Miller Liquors in Pasadena, CA.
Fall 1966	The Rice family moves to Donaldsonville, GA; Tony becomes reacquainted with family's bluegrass albums, especially the first Jimmy Martin album with J.D. Crowe.
1967–68	The Rices move to Rosenberg, a suburb of Houston, TX, where Tony repeats his sophomore year of high school. It is the last year of high school he will complete.
1967	Frank Poindexter leaves Florida, returns to North Carolina, and takes a job at a steel company in Greensboro.
Early '68	The Rices move to Crystal River, FL, and Tony enrolls in his junior year of high school. Tony leaves home and goes out on his own, staying with different friends and relatives.
1969	Tony befriends an art teacher named Arthur Smith, who introduces him to the music of Gordon Lightfoot, via Lightfoot's first United Artists album. He also tries a Martin model 00-17 guitar owned by a friend, Leroy Arnold, and is astonished by how easy it plays. These events renew his interest in guitar.
1969	Herb Rice purchases Tony's third guitar, a 1957 D-28, from a pawnshop in Ocala, FL for $400–$500.
Early 1969	Tony quits school. He is 18, in his junior year of high school, and living with various relatives; his parents have separated.
1969	Tony moves in with Frank near his dad's, and works for three months as a pipefitter's assistant at Schlitz Brewery in Winston-Salem, a job Herb arranged for him.
1969	Tony tries unsuccessfully to enlist in the Navy in Roanoke; he fails the exam because he is color-blind.
Early '69—Summer '70	Tony alternately lives in Pelham with the Poindexters; with Uncle Junior and his wife Joyce in Reidsville; and with the Smiths, Joyce's family, outside Reidsville. For "quite a few months," he stays with the Smiths, working constantly on his technique, playing the '57 D-28; it is a very significant period for his playing.
Late 1969—early 1970	Tony, Frank, and Bobby Atkins, a banjo player & former Blue Grass Boy, joined by Kemp Atkins on bass, perform as the Appalachian Music Makers on *The Stone & Atkins Show* and at various dates in North Carolina & Virginia. Atkins says they were together around eight months.
1970	Tony works at Matkins Plumbing, Heating & Air Conditioning in Reidsville, NC, building and installing ductwork.
Early 1970	Tony records a single with Bobby Atkins and Frank: "Mary's Gone" on side A and "Farmer Man" on side B, both written by Frank Poindexter.
Spring 1970	Tony and Frank Poindexter record with Bobby Atkins; cuts from this session will be released on Old Homestead as *'68 Sessions* in 1981. Tony plays upright bass on most of the tracks in the sessions. Other personnel on the recording included Marshall Honeycut on snare drums, and Shirley Tucker and Rita Williams on vocals.
1970	Tony records soundtrack for *Preacherman*, a rather racy B-movie from Troma Entertainment, with Frank Poindexter, Bobby Atkins, Kemp Atkins, Shirley Tucker, Rita Williams, and Cub McGee.

June 1970	Tony goes to Myrtle Beach for a short vacation with Frank Poindexter when they meet Pam Sanders, who eventually marries Frank.
Labor Day Weekend 1970	Tony moves to Louisville, KY to join the Bluegrass Alliance after meeting Sam Bush at Camp Springs, a Reidsville, NC festival run by Carleton Haney.
1970	Tony loses his virginity, at age 19.
1970	Tony is drafted by the Army while living in Louisville; is classified 4-F because he is colorblind.
1970–71	Louise and Herb Rice reconcile and move to Mooresville, NC.
1971	Tony meets Kate Freeman (a Philadelphia native who works at the University of Kentucky in Louisville) at a club he's playing at called the Storefront Congregation.
1971	Tony trades '57 D-28 with Clayton Hambrick for an older D-28 that once belonged to Hylo Brown.
1971	Tony meets Eddie Adcock at Bean Blossom, IN; the two plus Jimmy Gaudreau sing together and talk about forming a group.
August 1971	Tony meets with Jimmy Gaudreau and Eddie Adcock at Renfro Valley, KY; decides to join them and form a new band, II Generation.
1971	Tony meets with J.D. Crowe at Gettysburg, PA; Crowe asks him to join the New South.
Labor Day Weekend 1971	Tony plays his final show with the Bluegrass Alliance and his first with J.D. Crowe and the New South, at Camp Springs Bluegrass Festival near Reidsville, NC. This is documented in the film *Bluegrass Country Soul*, which was shot at the festival.
1971–72	Herb, Louise, Ronnie and Wyatt live in Poquoson, VA; Herb works at a nuclear power plant in Surrey, VA and also at Busch Gardens, at the Budweiser Brewery, in Williamsburg.
1972	Tony marries Kate Freeman at a Lexington church, attended by Larry Rice and his wife, and Bobby Slone and his wife.
1973	Tony records his first solo album for Saburo Watanabe and Red Clay Records (*Got Me a Martin Guitar*, Red Clay 103, released 1974). The album is released in 1974 as *Guitar* in the U.S. on King Records (KB 529) and re-released by Rebel records.
1973	Tony records *Bluegrass Evolution* (not its original title) with the New South (other members are Larry Rice, J.D. Crowe, and Bobby Slone) and Nashville studio musicians Hal Rugg, Pig Robbins, Ray Eddington, Buddy Harmon, Kenny Malone, Dennis Digby; the album is more country than bluegrass.
July 14, 1973	Clarence White dies after being hit by a drunken driver while loading equipment onto a van in Palmdale, CA.
Early 1974	Larry Rice leaves the New South to join Dickie Betts' band on tour; he is replaced by Sam Bush for a few weeks, then by Ricky Skaggs, who agrees to join temporarily. Skaggs agrees to stay when he and Tony convince J.D. to unplug and undrum the band.
1974	*Got Me a Martin Guitar* is released in Japan.
1974	*Got Me a Martin Guitar* released in the U.S. on King Bluegrass as *Guitar*.
1974	Tony records *California Autumn* for Rebel Records.

1974–75	When lead singer John Starling can't make it, Tony sits in with the Seldom Scene a few times at the Red Fox in Bethesda, MD, where they have a regular weekly gig. "Tony knew all of our songs and could sing John's part . . . plus he put wonderful guitar solos in everything he did."
Dec. '74–Jan.'75	The New South moves from the Holiday Inn to the Sheraton Hotel in Lexington.
January 3, 1975	The New South records Rounder 0044 at Track Studios, Silver Spring, MD. The project is engineered by Steve Hamm and produced by Crowe; with J.D. Crowe, banjo, baritone vocal, guitar; Tony Rice, guitar, lead vocal; Ricky Skaggs, mandolin, fiddle, viola, tenor vocal; Bobby Slone, bass; Jerry Douglas, Dobro®; unidentified session musicians on drums and piano.
1975	Tony and Kate visit Frank & Pam Poindexter, who are living in a mobile home; Louise and Wyatt are also living with them at the time. Tony presents Wyatt with a D-18, a gift.
1975	*California Autumn* is released.
1975	Louise and Herb Rice are remarried; they move to Crystal River, FL. Herb lives here until his death in 1983; Louise lives there until the flood in 1993.
Early March 1975	Tony meets David Grisman during a recording session for *Something Auld, Something Newgrass, Something Borrowed, Something Bluegrass,* Bill Keith's first album for Rounder Records.
March 6, 1975	Tony flies to L.A. and purchases the Clarence White 1935 herringbone Martin D-28 for $550 from Joe Miller of Miller Liquors.
March 6, 1975	Tony records with 58957 for the first time, at a session for Kate & Anna McGarrigle.
May 1975	Jerry Douglas begins to play with the New South.
1975	Tony records tracks for John Starling's first solo project, *Long Time Gone,* at ITI Studio, located in a barge in Baltimore Harbor. It is produced by Lowell George, with guests Emmylou Harris (harmony vocals), Ricky Skaggs (vocals, fiddle, mandolin), Paul Craft (vocals, guitar, rhythm guitar), Fayssoux Starling (vocals), John Duffey (vocals), Buddy Emmons (steel guitar), Sam Bush (mandolin), Larry Rice (mandolin), Mike Auldridge (resonator guitar), John Cowan (bass), Tom Gray (bass), Ben Eldridge (banjo), etc.
August 1975	Tony seriously considers joining the Seldom Scene.
August 1975	Tony gives his notice to the New South.
August 30, 1975	Tony and the New South record *Holiday in Japan* at Kubo Hall, Tokyo, Japan. Tony plays guitar and bass on this recording.
Labor Day 1975	Tony plays his final show with New South in Osaka.
October 1975	Tony moves to California with Kate and begins rehearsing with David Grisman and other musicians to develop David's vision for Dawg, his new form of acoustic music.
Fall/Winter 1975	Tony teaches guitar in Richard Keldsen's San Francisco Fifth String music store (Keldsen now owns Saga Instruments). Rowan & Grisman are regulars; Paul's Saloon, which hosts many national touring bands, including J.D. Crowe and the New South, is right next door.
Late 1975	Rounder 0044 (the eponymous recording by J.D. Crowe & the New South, also known as *Old Home Place* for its first track) is released.

Jan. 31, 1976	The first gig of the David Grisman Quintet, in Bolinas, CA; band consists of Tony, Grisman, Todd Phillips on second mandolin, Darol Anger, and jazz bassist Joe Carroll.
1976	*The David Grisman Rounder Album* is released.
1976	Tony tours Japan with Grisman in a tour set up by Hiroshi Asata.
1976	Recording sessions for *Tony Rice* (Rounder 0085).
Spring 1977	Drives to Santa Cruz with Bill Amatneek to pick up the first Tony Rice Model guitar from the Santa Cruz guitar company run by Richard Hoover and Bruce Ross. [Note: Tony remembers this happening in 1979, but Richard Hoover confirms that the first prototype was built for Tony in late 1977.]
July 1977	Tony tours Europe with Bill Keith's Bicentennial Bluegrass Band: Keith, Darol Anger, David Grisman, and Bill Amatneek; plays festivals at Gerte, Courville, and Nyon. During the tour, the band meets musician Barbara Higbie, a student at the Sorbonne; she will eventually marry Darol Anger.
1977	*Tony Rice* is released.
September 1977	First sessions for *Manzanita* are recorded with Grisman, Bill Amatneek, and Darol Anger. Tony will end up discarding tracks recorded at these sessions.
Nov. 30, 1977	The first David Grisman Quintet album is released on Kaleidoscope.
1978	Tony records *Hot Dawg* with Grisman. The album has many players; Tony is the only musician beside Grisman who appears on all cuts.
Jan. & Feb. 1978	Recording sessions for *Manzanita*.
Summer 1978	Tony records music for the film, *King of the Gypsies*, with Stéphane Grappelli and David Grisman.
August 1978	Mike Marshall comes from Florida to visit Tony in California for a week. The Quintet is knocked out by his talent.
Oct. or Nov. '78	Mike Marshall leaves Florida and moves in with Tony, whose marriage to Kate Freeman is floundering. Mike moves out after a couple months.
Early 1979	Recording sessions for *Acoustics*. Tony uses his first Santa Cruz prototype on a couple tracks.
Spring 1979	Tony tours the East Coast with the David Grisman Quintet.
April 16–17, 1979	Tony meets Leela Satyendra in New York at the Bottom Line; an unknown Pierre Bensusan opens the show.
1979	*Hot Dawg* is released.
1979	*Manzanita* is released, the first album billed as "The Tony Rice Unit."
1979	*Acoustics*, by the Tony Rice Unit, is released on Kaleidoscope; Tony's first acoustic jazz album under his own name.
1979	Tony ends his marriage with Kate Freeman.
July 1979	Tony records *Roses in the Snow* at the home of Emmylou Harris, while she is pregnant with daughter Meghann; Ricky Skaggs is impetus behind Rice's participation.
1979	Tony records *Skaggs & Rice* with Ricky Skaggs.
Summer 1979	Tony turns down opportunity to tour with Stéphane Grappelli and David Grisman.
Labor Day 1979	Tony plays last date with Grisman as a band member.

Fall 1979	Live performance of *Manzanita* material by Tony, Ricky Skaggs, Jerry Douglas, Todd Phillips, and Sam Bush at the Great American Music Hall in San Francisco, CA. Performance is an opening set for The Whites.
1979	Tony leaves the David Grisman Quintet; is replaced by Mark O'Connor.
March 1980	*Roses in the Snow* is released.
1980	*Skaggs & Rice* (Sugar Hill 3711) is released.
1980	Tony records *The Bluegrass Album* with Doyle Lawson, J.D. Crowe, Bobby Hicks, and Todd Phillips. It sells so well that five more are recorded.
Sep. 28, 1980	Tony marries Leela Satyendra.
1980	*Mar West* (Rounder 0125) released.
1980	Tony assembles the Tony Rice Unit, a performing band.
1981	Tony records *Still Inside*.
1981	*Still Inside* (Rounder 0150), by the Tony Rice Unit, is released.
1981	*The Bluegrass Album* (Rounder 0140), by the Bluegrass Album Band, is released.
1981	Cuts from Tony's early recording sessions with Bobby Atkins and Frank Poindexter are released on Old Homestead as *The '68 Sessions,* though the tracks were recorded sometime in 1970.
Oct. 25, 1981	The Bluegrass Album Band performs live for the first time at Great American Music Hall.
1981	*Bluegrass Album, Vol. 2* is recorded.
Early 1982	Tony begins his association with Kari Estrin.
Early 1982	First East Coast tour of the Tony Rice Unit.
March 1982	Tony records *Backwaters*.
1982	*Bluegrass Album, Vol. 2* (Rounder 0164) is released.
1982	*Backwaters* (Rounder 0167) is released.
1982	Tony records *Church Street Blues*.
1982	*Bluegrass—The World's Greatest Show* (SH 2201) is recorded live at Lisner Auditorium, George Washington University, D.C. with material from the Classic Country Gentlemen, the (almost) classic New South (with Tony Rice), the classic Scene, the new Scene, the new Gents. The New South's performance of "Fireball" wins the '83 Grammy for Best Country Instrumental Performance.
1982–83	Tony records his first audio instruction tape for Jane & Happy Traum & Homespun Records.
Early 1983	Sessions for *Cold on the Shoulder.*
1983	*The Bluegrass Album, Vol. 3: California Connection* is released on Rounder; this is Jerry Douglas' first appearance in the series.
1983	The New South (Ricky Skaggs, Jerry Douglas, Tony Rice, J.D. Crowe, and Todd Phillips) wins Grammy for Best Country Instrumental Performance for "Fireball."
1983	*Church Street Blues* released on Sugar Hill.
November 20, 1983	Herbert Hoover Rice loses his life in a house fire.
November 1983	Tony goes on ten-day East Coast tour with Bluegrass Album Band (first gig 11/24/83 at the Myrtle Beach festival).

December 1983	*Double Time,* a collection of Béla Fleck's acoustic duets, is recorded in California and Tennessee; Tony appears on the album's third cut, "Double Play," recorded at His Master's Wheels, the same San Francisco studio at which *Hot Dawg* was recorded.
March 1984	Tony records tracks for Mike Marshall's *Gator Strut* at Mobius Music in San Francisco.
1984	Tony starts recording *Me and My Guitar* with "Early Morning Rain," a throwaway track from the sessions for Volume 4 of the *Bluegrass Album.* Doyle Lawson plays mandolin on this track.
1984	Tony records instructional video, "An Intimate Lesson with Tony Rice," for Homespun Tapes; it contains several tunes that appeared on *Church Street Blues.*
1984	*The Bluegrass Album, Vol. 4* (Rounder 0210) is released.
1984	Tony records with Don Reno (*Family & Friends,* released 1988).
1984	*Cold on the Shoulder* (Rounder 0183) is released.
1984	Tony attends his first AA meeting in San Francisco.
1984	Tony ends his marriage with Leela Satyendra.
1984	Kari Estrin takes over management and bookings for Tony.
June 1985	Tony puts deposit and rent down on house in Crystal River, FL.
July 1985	Tony leaves California for good; settles in Crystal River, FL.
1985	Jimmy Gaudreau (mid-1985) and Mark Schatz join the Tony Rice Unit.
1985	Tony completes recording *Me and My Guitar* ("Early Morning Rain" and "Fine as Fine Can Be" were recorded at an earlier session in 1984).
1985	Tony replaces pick guard on the Antique with a tortoiseshell guard given to him by a fan after a show in Japan.
1985	Tony attends Rounder's 15th anniversary party in Cambridge, MA, and jams with Norman Blake; they will go on to make *Blake & Rice* and *Blake & Rice 2.*
1986	First sessions for *Tony Rice Plays & Sings Bluegrass.*
1986	Tony does shows in Worcester, MA; Billy Wolf says his voice is "clear as a bell."
1986	Tony records *Home of the Red Fox* with Bill Emerson.
1986	*The Bluegrass Compact Disc* (Rounder CD-11502), a compilation of tracks from the Bluegrass Album Band recordings, is released.
Late '85, early '86	Tony goes to France and Germany with the Tony Rice Unit (Mark Schatz, Wyatt Rice, Jimmy Gaudreau, and Jerry Douglas) and Billy Wolf.
Late '85, early '86	Tony befriends Mary Chapin Carpenter, an aspiring singer/songwriter and a regular at the Birchmere.
11/10/86	Appears at the Seldom Scene's sold-out 15th Anniversary Celebration at Kennedy Center with special guests Charlie Waller, Emmylou Harris, Linda Ronstadt, Sharon White, Ricky Skaggs, etc.
March 1987	The Rice Brothers begin to record their first album at Bias Studios in Springfield, VA.
1987	*The Bluegrass Compact Disc, Vol. II* (Rounder CD-11516) is released, a second compilation of tracks from the Bluegrass Album Band recordings.
1987	Tony records *Home Is Where the Heart Is* with David Grisman.

1987	*Me and My Guitar* (Rounder 0201) is released.
1987	*Mar West* and *Still Inside* combined and released as *Devlin*.
March 1987	Tony, Larry, Wyatt, and Ron begin recording *Rice Brothers* at Bias Studios.
Summer 1987	Tony does last Worcester shows, which Billy Wolf has on tape; this is when he first began noticing trouble with Tony's voice.
September 30, 1987	Tony reconnects with Pamela Hodges, whose families knew each other when he was a child.
October 1987	Tony starts talking regularly on the phone with Pamela.
1988	*Native American* (Rounder 0248) is released.
1988	Fiddler Ray Legere plays shows with the Tony Rice Unit; Alison Krauss also plays fiddle on a number of shows.
May 1, 1988	Tony plays the first MerleFest in a stunning performance with Sam Bush, Jerry Douglas, Béla Fleck, John Cowan, and Mark O'Connor.
1988	Rickie Simpkins joins the Tony Rice Unit in Norfolk, VA.
1988	Béla Fleck's *Drive* (Rounder 0255) is released; Tony is guest musician.
August 8, 1989	Tony marries Pamela Hodges in Chatham, VA, the County Seat of Pittsylvania County.
1988	David Grisman's *Home Is Where the Heart Is* is released on Rounder; Tony is guest artist.
1989	Mike Auldridge's *Treasures Untold* (SH-3780) is released on Sugar Hill; Tony is guest artist.
1989	*The Bluegrass Album, Vol. 5: Sweet Sunny South* (Rounder 0240) is released; Vassar Clements appears for the first time in the series, playing twin fiddles with Bobby Hicks.
1989	*Blake & Rice* (Rounder 0233) is released.
1989	*The Rice Brothers* (Rounder 0256) is released; "Grapes from the Vine" becomes the first song to top *Bluegrass Unlimited*'s National Bluegrass Survey chart.
October 1989	Tony has surgery for deviated septum; John Starling does the procedure in Fredericksburg, VA.
1990	*Blake & Rice 2* (Rounder 0266) is released.
1990	Tony appears numerous times on *American Music Shop* with Mark O'Connor, J.D. Crowe, Vassar Clements, Jerry Douglas, David Grisman, etc.
1990	Tony gets a DUI in Dayton, OH and is retrieved from jail by Red Allen, who knows local law enforcement.
September 1990	The Bluegrass Album Band wins IBMA award for Instrumental Group of the Year at the first IBMA Awards show in Owensboro, KY; they perform "Blue Ridge Cabin Home" at the show, after an introduction by Vince Gill.
1990	Tony wins the first IBMA award for Instrumental Performer of the Year—Guitar. He has been nominated in this category every year since, and has won it again in 1991, 1994, 1996, 1997, and 2007.
1991	The Tony Rice Unit wins IBMA award for Instrumental Group of the Year.

1991 .... *Norman Blake & Tony Rice 2* is named Instrumental Recording of the Year at IBMA Awards.

1992 .... Tony records second *Rice Brothers* album with Larry, Ronnie and Wyatt.

1992 .... Footage that will become *Tony Rice: The Video Collection* (Vestapol 13058) is recorded, a compilation from three separate sets at the 1992 Merle Watson Memorial Festival in Wilkesboro, NC. Sam Bush, Jerry Douglas, Mark O'Connor, Mark Schatz, Béla Fleck, Ricky Skaggs, David Grisman, Pete Wernick, Rickie Simpkins, Del McCoury, and the Tony Rice Unit (Jimmy Gaudreau, Rickie and Ronnie Simpkins, and Wyatt Rice all perform with Tony.)

1992 .... *Twilight Motel* (VAN-79465) by Alison Brown is released on Vanguard; Tony is guest artist.

1992 .... Tony writes his last instrumental, "Wacahoota Station," for Alison Krauss & Union Station (who have never recorded it). He names it after an old railroad depot in the middle of nowhere, between Gainesville, FL and the Gulf of Mexico.

Feb. 4 & 5, 1993 .... Tony jams with David Grisman and Jerry Garcia in an informal session at Grisman's Dawg Studios, Mill Valley, CA. The recording disappears, rumored to have been stolen from Grisman's kitchen counter by a pizza delivery boy. It will be released in April 2000 as *The Pizza Tapes*.

1993 .... First sessions for *Unit of Measure*.

Mar. 13, 1993 .... Tony loses his home in Crystal River, FL, to floodwaters after a severe tropical storm.

April 25, 1993 .... A flood relief benefit concert for Tony is held in Greensboro, NC.

1993 .... *Tony Rice Plays and Sings Bluegrass* (Rounder 0253) is released.

January 1994 .... *Tony Rice Plays and Sings Bluegrass* is nominated for a Grammy for Bluegrass Album of the Year, competing against *Stuart Duncan*—Stuart Duncan; *Blue Diamond*—The Johnson Mountain Boys; *Waitin' for the Hard Times to Go*—The Nashville Bluegrass Band; *Saturday Night (& Sunday Morning)*—Ralph Stanley. The Nashville Bluegrass Band wins.

August 27, 1994 .... Tony sings onstage for the last time at a New South reunion [per Jimmy Gaudreau] or at a reunion of the Bluegrass Album Band [per Rice expert Allen Tolbert, who believes it happened on 8/27/94] or at a Unit gig [per Tony himself] at Gettysburg Bluegrass Festival.

1994 .... *The Rice Brothers 2* (Rounder 0286) is released.

May 24, 1994 .... Dan Crary's *Jammed If I Do* is released on Sugar Hill; Tony is guest artist.

June 7, 1994 .... *Tone Poems*, with David Grisman and Tony Rice, is released on Acoustic Disc.

1994 .... Ronnie Bowman's *Cold Virginia Night* is released; Tony plays rhythm guitar on recording. The title cut wins IBMA Song of the Year in 1995.

1994 .... Béla Fleck's *Tales from the Acoustic Planet* (WB-45854) is released on Warner Brothers; Tony is guest artist.

1995 .... The Tony Rice Unit wins its second IBMA award for Instrumental Group of the Year.

1995 .... *Tony Rice and John Carlini: River Suite for Two Guitars* (Sugar Hill 3837) is released.

1995	Tony is audited for tax year 1994.
1995	Jimmy Gaudreau leaves the Tony Rice Unit to found Chesapeake.
1995	Kathy Chiavola's *The Harvest* is released; Tony is guest artist.
Early 1996	Records *Out of the Woodwork* with brother Larry, Chris Hillman, and Herb Pedersen at Nashville's Nightingale Studios.
1996	*The Bluegrass Album, Vol. 6: Bluegrass Instrumentals* (Rounder 0330) is released.
1996	*Tony Rice Sings Gordon Lightfoot* (Rounder 0370), a compilation, is released.
1996	The Tony Rice Unit disbands.
1996	Second sessions for *Unit of Measure*.
1997	Pam Rice has heart surgery.
May 14, 1997	Tony has a major car accident a quarter mile from his home when he swerves to miss a deer. He is badly injured.
June 3, 1997	Richard Bennett's *Walking Down the Line* is released on Rebel Records; Tony is guest artist.
1997	*Out of the Woodwork,* the first recording by Rice, Rice, Hillman & Pedersen, is released.
1997	*The Bluegrass Album, Vol. 6: Bluegrass Instrumentals* (Rounder 0330) wins IBMA award for Instrumental Album of the Year.
Late '97–early '98	Tony begins working regularly with Peter Rowan.
January 1, 1999	Tony records *Live at the Ram's Head* with Dan Tyminski and the Unit. Sadly, this recording has never been released.
January 22, 1999	Béla Fleck's *The Bluegrass Sessions: Tales from the Acoustic Planet, Vol. 2* (WB-47332) is released on Warner Brothers; Tony is guest artist.
Spring 1999	First tour with Peter Rowan.
1999	*Rice, Rice, Hillman & Pedersen* (Rounder 610405) the second album from Tony, Larry, Chris, and Herb, is released.
1999	Final sessions for *Unit of Measure*.
August 18, 1999	Tony, intoxicated, drives his car into a ditch outside his Uncle Junior's house and gets stuck. When a policeman arrives on the scene, he asks Tony, "Are you drinking?" Tony's response: "Are you buyin'?" He is arrested and charged with unsafe movement and DWI.
April 25, 2000	*The Pizza Tapes* (ACD-41) is released on Acoustic Disc.
November 7, 2000	The Tony Rice Unit's *Unit of Measure* (Rounder 610405) is released; it is the only recording featuring the working unit of Gaudreau, Schatz, Wyatt Rice, Rickie Simpkins, and Tony.
January 2001	Tim Stafford begins work on a Tony Rice biography
May 29, 2001	Tony quits drinking.
June 2001	Tony's first show after he quits drinking, with the Rice Brothers & Vassar Clements at the Florida Folk Festival.
October 13, 2001	www.tonyrice.com, Tony's official website, is launched; site is designed and maintained by Christian Marks of Magic Bus Internet Solutions & Software Design.

October 30, 2001	*Runnin' Wild*, the third and final recording from Rice, Rice, Hillman & Pedersen, is released.
Late Fall 2001	Mini-tour with Darol Anger, Mike Marshall, and Todd Phillips.
April 30, 2002	*The Tony Rice Guitar Method* instructional video (DVD) is released on Homespun Tapes.
January 2003	Tony Rice Unit reunites as an instrumental ensemble, with Tony, Wyatt, Rickie and Ronnie Simpkins.
January 20, 2003	Tony's uncle, Walter Poindexter (banjo player and original member of the Golden State Boys) loses his life in a house fire. At the time, he resides in the same housing complex as Louise Rice.
February 2003	Gladys Rice (sister of Herb Rice) passes away at a nursing home in Beverly Hills, FL. She is the last surviving Rice sibling.
June 14, 2003	*Bluegrass Journey*, the documentary about bluegrass music, has its world premiere at the Maui Film Festival in Maui, HI; the film features Tony playing "Shenandoah."
June/July 2003	Caroline Wright visits Tony at his North Carolina home, and travels with him to the B.B. King Blues Club in New York City and to Grey Fox Bluegrass Festival in Ancramdale, NY. While they are traveling, Caroline interviews Tony about his life.
October 2003	A clip from the 1975 KETV (Kentucky PBS) video of the New South is played onstage at the IBMA Awards in Louisville, KY while a reunion configuration of the classic Old South (including Tony) performs "Old Home Place"; Ricky Skaggs sings lead.
2003	*58957: The Bluegrass Guitar Collection* (Rounder 611622), a compilation, is released.
April 21, 2004	Tony appears on CMT's 2004 *Flameworthy Awards* program, guest of Alison Krauss & Union Station; other guests include Stuart Duncan and Sam Bush. They played "Sawing on the Strings," written by Lewis Compton in 1953. Krauss later says that performing with Tony was her favorite part of the show.
September 28, 2004	*You Were There for Me* from Tony Rice and Peter Rowan is released on Rounder Records.
November 23, 2004	*An Intimate Lesson with Tony Rice*, instructional video from Homespun Tapes released on DVD.
Jan. 6–10, 2005	Tony goes on four-day Jam Cruise 3 to the Bahamas with Rowan, Bryn Davies, Sharon Gilchrist (performing with the band for the first time; they actually meet onstage as they're launching into their first show). The cruise also features acts like Karl Denson's Tiny Universe, STS9, Galactic, Umphrey's McGee, Les Claypool's Frog Brigade and 20 other bands and DJs.
June 2005	Tony records "The Cruel War" with Dolly Parton, to be released on *Those Were the Days* on Sugar Hill.
June/July 2005	Caroline Wright visits Tony in North Carolina to wrap up interviews; she also stays at the home of Louise Rice, Tony's mother, for four days and interviews her as well. Caroline accompanies Tony on trips to Harrodsburg, KY (for the Terrapin Farm Bluegrass Festival) and Nashville, TN

May 2005	Tony plays "Sawing on the Strings" on televised episode of the *Grand Ole Opry* with Alison Krauss & Union Station and Sierra Hull; backs up Alison Krauss on "Freeborn Man" on an untelevised segment.
October 2005	Peter Rowan & Tony Rice perform at Warren Hellman's Hardly Strictly Bluegrass Festival at Golden Gate Park in San Francisco, CA, with Bryn Bright and Sharon Gilchrist.
Late Winter 2005	Sharon Gilchrist is invited to join Rowan & Rice.
Dec. 10 & 11, 2005	Tony records with Vassar Clements at Randy Woods' shop; it is one of Vassar's final performances and will be released on CD in 2006 as *Vassar Clements, Tony Rice and the Low Country All-Star Band*. A benefit for Larry Rice will be held within a few days of these sessions.
February 2006	*Tony Rice Master Class: Up Close and Personal with a Guitar Great,* a DVD, is released by Homespun.
2006	Tony starts recording new CD with Peter Rowan, Bryn Davies, & Sharon Gilchrist.
May 13, 2006	At age 57, Tony's brother, Larry Prentis Rice, passes away. He is a victim of mesothelioma, asbestos-related cancer.
Summer 2006	Tony tours *Manzanita* on selected dates with Sam Bush, Jerry Douglas, Dan Tyminski, Barry Bales.
2007	Luna Bell Poindexter, Tony's maternal grandmother, passes away.
January 15, 2007	Bryn Davies leaves the Rowan & Rice Quartet to tour with Patty Griffin.
January 23, 2007	*Quartet* with Tony, Peter Rowan, Bryn Davies, & Sharon Gilchrist is released on Rounder.
Spring 2007	Tony appears on Alison Krauss' *Hundred Miles Or More* for Rounder Records.
Apr. 21–May 20, 2007	Tony tours with Alison Krauss & Union Station.
July 2007	Sharon Gilchrist announces that she is leaving the Rowan & Rice Quartet; she performs in her last show with the band a month later.
November 2007	Tony records four tracks for a new recording with Richard Bennett at Wyatt's studio.
December 2007	Tony is wounded in his left hand when a neighbor's small dogs get into his yard when his poodles are outside; Tony reaches into the fray to save the terriers and is bitten several times. He receives multiple lacerations, a fracture of his thumb joint, and two fractured bones in his wrist. His old Accutron, which flies off his wrist during the incident, is found a few hours later, unharmed.
2007	Tony is audited for tax year 2005 by the IRS. This is his second audit (the first was for tax year '94, and resulted in a refund for Tony.)
January 4, 2008	Homespun Video releases *Peter Rowan & Tony Rice Teach Songs, Guitar and Musicianship.*
April 12, 2008	Tony plays first show with Mountain Heart at the Paramount Center in Bristol, TN.
May 24, 2008	First appearance by Josh Williams with the Tony Rice Unit at the Acoustic Café in Hayden, AL.
October 3, 2008	Tony plays the Grand Ole Opry with Mountain Heart, performing "Freeborn Man" and "Blue Ridge Cabin Home."

August 5, 2008 .... Tony's vocal compilation *Night Flyer: The Singer-Songwriter Collection* is released on Rounder. It includes a "broad selection of the music icon's engaging vocal tunes taken from several of his albums—as well as three previously unreleased tracks." One of the unreleased tracks is Tom Waits' "Pony," the last vocal Tony ever recorded. Featured and accompanying musicians on this collection include Larry Atamanuik, Cole Burgess, Sam Bush, Kathy Chiavola, Vassar Clements, Jerry Douglas, Béla Fleck, Jimmy Gaudreau, Todd Phillips, Wyatt Rice, Mark Schatz, and Bill Wolf.

July 24, 2008 .... First vocal Tony Rice Unit show in many years, with Josh Williams & Bryn Davies handling vocal chores at Georgia Mountain Fair in Hiawassee, GA.

November 11, 2008 .... The DVD for Alison Krauss' *Hundred Miles or More* for Rounder Records is released, with Tony on two cuts.

TONY RICE DISCOGRAPHY

SOLO AND UNIT

1. Tony Rice, *Guitar* (King Bluegrass 529; Rebel 1582), 1974.
2. Tony Rice, *Got Me a Martin Guitar* (Same tracks as *Guitar*) (Red Clay 103, Japanese Release), 1974.
3. Tony Rice, *California Autumn* (Rebel 1549), 1975.
4. Tony Rice, *Tony Rice & Guitar* (Same tracks as *California Autumn*) (Seven Seas GXF6021, Japanese Release), 1975.
5. Tony Rice, *Tony Rice* (Rounder 0085), 1977.
6. The Tony Rice Unit, *Manzanita* (Rounder 0092), 1979.
7. The Tony Rice Unit, *Acoustics* (Kaleidoscope F10; Rounder 0317), 1979.
8. The Tony Rice Unit, *Mar West* (Rounder 0125), 1980.
9. The Tony Rice Unit, *Still Inside* (Rounder 0150), 1981.
10. The Tony Rice Unit, *Backwaters* (Rounder 0167), 1983.
11. Tony Rice, *Church Street Blues* (Sugar Hill 3732), 1983.
12. Tony Rice, *Cold on the Shoulder* (Rounder 0183), 1984.
13. Tony Rice, *Me & My Guitar* (Rounder 0201), 1986.
14. Tony Rice, *Native American* (Rounder 0248), 1988.
15. Tony Rice, *Plays and Sings Bluegrass* (Rounder 0253), also listed by a couple of obscure retailers as *Bluegrass Man* (Identified by Rounder numbers 358250 & 97843 and UPC number 0011661025325, the UPC number corresponds with *Plays and Sings Bluegrass*; however, neither Rounder number appears in the Rounder catalog), 1993.
16. Tony Rice, *Crossings* (Mountain Home 105), 1994.
17. The Tony Rice Unit, *Unit of Measure* (Rounder 610405), 2000.
18. The Tony Rice Unit, *Acoustic Swing* (Same tracks as *Acoustics*) (Vivid Sound 153, Japanese Release), 2002.
19. The Tony Rice Unit, *Mar West* (Vivid Sound 140, Japanese Release), 2003.

DUET

20. Ricky Skaggs & Tony Rice, *Take Me Home Tonight in a Song* (Sugar Hill), 1978.
21. Ricky Skaggs & Tony Rice, *Skaggs & Rice* (Sugar Hill 3711), 1980.
22. Norman Blake & Tony Rice, *Blake & Rice* (Rounder 0233), 1987.
23. Norman Blake & Tony Rice, *Norman Blake & Tony Rice 2* (Rounder 0266), 1990.
24. Tony Rice and John Carlini, *River Suite for Two Guitars* (Sugar Hill 3837), 1995.
25. Peter Rowan and Tony Rice, *You Were There for Me* (Rounder 0441), 2004.
26. Vassar Clements, Tony Rice and the Low Country All-Star Band (Flatt Mountain, FMR 001), 2006.
27. Peter Rowan and Tony Rice, *Quartet* (Rounder 0579), 2007.

COMPILATIONS

28. The Tony Rice Unit, *Devlin* (Rounder 11531), 1987.
29. Tony Rice, Sings *Gordon Lightfoot* (Rounder 0370), 1996.
30. Tony Rice, *58957: The Bluegrass Guitar Collection* (Rounder 11622), 2003.
31. Tony Rice, *Night Flyer: The Singer-Songwriter Collection* (Rounder 11619), 2008.

HOMESPUN INSTRUCTIONAL

32. Tony Rice, *An Intimate Lesson with Tony Rice, 1984* (DVD), 2008.
33. Tony Rice, *Teaches Bluegrass Guitar,* 1996.
34. Tony Rice, *Teaches New Acoustic Guitar* (6 Cassettes), 1999.

35. Tony Rice, *Tony's Choice*, 2000.
36. Tony Rice, *Tony Rice Guitar Method*, [2 DVD set], 2002.
37. Tony Rice, *New Acoustic Guitar* (6 CDs), 2003.
38. Tony Rice, Tony Rice Master Class, [DVD, music, tab], 2006.
39. Various Artists, *Great Guitar Lessons: Bluegrass Flatpicking* (DVD), 2006.
40. *Peter Rowan and Tony Rice Teach Songs, Guitar and Musicianship* (DVD), 2008.

BROTHERS & OTHERS

41. Larry Rice, *Mr. Poverty* (King Bluegrass 543), 1975.
42. Bobby Atkins, Frank Poindexter, and Tony Rice, *1968 Session* (Old Homestead OHCS 126), 1981.
43. Larry Rice, *Hurricanes and Daydreams* (Rebel 1646), 1986.
44. Larry Rice, *Time Machine* (Have not confirmed TR's participation) (Rebel 1656), 1987.
45. Larry Rice, *Artesia* (Rebel 1666), 1988.
46. The Rice Brothers, *The Rice Brothers* (Rounder 0256), 1989.
47. The Rice Brothers, *The Rice Brothers 2* (Rounder 0286), 1994.
48. Larry Rice, *Notions and Novelties* (Rebel 1734), 1996.
49. Tony Rice, Larry Rice, Chris Hillman, Herb Pedersen, *Out of the Woodwork* (Rounder 390), 1997.
50. Rice, Rice, Hillman & Pedersen, *Rice, Rice, Hillman & Pedersen* (Rounder 610450), 1999.
51. Rice, Rice, Hillman & Pedersen, *Running Wild* (Rounder 610483), 2001.
52. Larry Rice, *Clouds Over Carolina* (Rebel 1801), 2005.

J.D. CROWE & THE NEW SOUTH

53. J.D. Crowe and the New South (with Tony and Larry Rice, J.D., Bobby Slone), 45 rpm single; A side, "Come on Down to My World"; B side, "The Leaves That Are Green." (self-produced), 1973.
54. J.D. Crowe & the New South, *J.D. Crowe & the New South* (Rounder 0044), 1975 [CD, 1986; also released on Cracker Barrel Old Country Store® Heritage Music Collection, 2002].
55. J.D. Crowe & the New South, *New South Live* (Trio 6326), 1975.
56. J.D. Crowe & the New South, *Holiday in Japan* (Towa 106-S), 1976.
57. J.D. Crowe & the New South, *New South Live Volume II: Includes Hot Picker Tony Rice* (Towa 106-S), 1976.
58. J.D. Crowe & the New South, *J.D. Crowe & the New South* (Early New South LP later released on CD as *Bluegrass Evolution,* not the same as the legendary Rounder 0044) (Starday 489; Gusto 0010), 1977.
59. J.D. Crowe & the New South, *Bluegrass Evolution* (Starday 489), 1997.

THE BLUEGRASS ALBUM BAND

60. The Bluegrass Album Band, *The Bluegrass Album* (Rounder 0140), 1981.
61. The Bluegrass Album Band, *The Bluegrass Album, Vol. 2* (Rounder 0164), 1982.
62. The Bluegrass Album Band, *The Bluegrass Album, Vol. 3: California Connection* (Rounder 0180), 1983.
63. The Bluegrass Album Band, *The Bluegrass Album, Vol. 4* (Rounder 0210), 1985.
64. The Bluegrass Album Band, *The Bluegrass Compact Disc* (Rounder 11502), 1986.
65. The Bluegrass Album Band, *The Bluegrass Compact Disc, Vol. 2* (Rounder 11516), 1987.
66. The Bluegrass Album Band, *The Bluegrass Album, Vol. 5: Sweet Sunny South* (Rounder 0240), 1989.
67. The Bluegrass Album Band, *The Bluegrass Album, Vol. 6: Bluegrass Instrumentals* (Rounder 0330), 1996.
68. The Bluegrass Album Band, *The Songs of Flatt & Scruggs* (Easydisc 7002), 2002.
69. The Bluegrass Album Band, *Down the Road: Bluegrass Songs of Flatt and Scruggs* (Rounder 0345), 2002.
70. The Bluegrass Album Band, *The Songs of Bill Monroe* (Easydisc 7003), 2002.
71. The Bluegrass Album Band, *Lonesome Moonlight: Bluegrass Songs of Bill Monroe* (Rounder 0346), 2002.

WITH GRISMAN & OTHER MANDOLIN PICKERS

72. David Grisman, *The David Grisman Rounder Album* (Rounder 0069), 1976.
73. The David Grisman Quintet, *The David Grisman Quintet* (Kaleidoscope F5; Pastels 2016; Rhino 71468), 1977.
74. The David Grisman Quintet, *The David Grisman Quintet* (RCA RVP-6237, Japanese Release), 1977.
75. David Grisman, *Hot Dawg* (Horizon 731; Mobile Fidelity 506; A&M 75021-3292-2), 1979.
76. David Grisman, *Mondo Mando* (Warner Brothers 56963; Zebra/MCA 42248), 1981.
77. David Grisman, *Dawg Jazz/Dawg Grass* (Warner Brothers 9238041), 1983.
78. Mike Marshall, *Gator Strut* (Rounder 0208), 1987.
79. David Grisman, *Home Is Where the Heart Is* (Rounder 0251/0252), 1988.
80. David Grisman, *The David Grisman Rounder Compact Disc* (Rounder 0069), 1993.
81. Tony Rice & David Grisman, *Tone Poems* (Acoustic Disc 10), 1994.
82. The David Grisman Quintet, *DGQ-20* (Acoustic Disc 20), 1996.
83. Radim Zenkl, *Strings & Wings* (Shanachie 5021), 1996.
84. Jack Tottle, *The Bluegrass Sound* (Copper Creek CCCD 0165), 1998.
85. Jerry Garcia, David Grisman, Tony Rice, *The Pizza Tapes* (Acoustic Disc 41), 2000.
86. Alan Bibey, *In the Blue Room* (Sugar Hill 3910), 2000.
87. Jimmy Gaudreau, *In Good Company* (CMH 8983), 2006.
88. Sierra Hull, *Secrets* (Rounder 11661), 2008.

WITH BANJO PICKERS

89. Bill Keith, *Something Auld, Something Newgrass, Something Borrowed, Something Bluegrass* (Rounder 0084), 1976.
90. Tony Trischka, *Banjoland* (Rounder 0087), 1977.
91. Tony Trischka, *Robot Plane Flies Over Arkansas* (Rounder 0171), 1983.
92. Béla Fleck, *Double Time* (Rounder 0181), 1984.
93. Tony Trischka, *Hill Country* (Rounder 0203), 1985.
94. Tony Trischka, *Dust on the Needle* (Rounder 11508), 1987.
95. Don Reno, *Family and Friends* (Kaleidoscope F 34), 1988.
96. Béla Fleck, *Drive* (Rounder 0255), 1988.
97. Bill Emerson, *Home of the Red Fox* (Rebel 1651), 1990.
98. Bill Emerson, *Gold Plated Banjo* (Rebel 1671), 1990.
99. Bill Emerson, *Reunion* (Webco 140), 1991.
100. Alison Brown, *Twilight Motel* (Vanguard 79465), 1992.
101. John McEuen, *String Wizards 2* (Vanguard 79468), 1993.
102. Emerson and Tayor, *Appaloosa* (Webco 0146), 1994.
103. Mark Johnson & the Rice Brothers & Friends, *Clawgrass* (Bangtown 1), 1994.
104. Béla Fleck, *Tales from the Acoustic Planet* (Warner Brothers 45854), 1995.
105. Bill Emerson, *Banjo Man* (Webco 151), 1996.
106. Mark Johnson & Clawgrass, *Bridging the Gap* (Pinecastle 1069), 1997.
107. Sammy Shelor, *Leading Roll* (Sugar Hill 3865), 1997.
108. Béla Fleck, *Bluegrass Sessions: Tales from the Acoustic Planet, Vol. 2* (Warner Brothers 47332), 1999.
109. Alison Brown, *Fair Weather* (Compass 4292), 2000.
110. Steve Huber, *Pullin' Time* (Strictly Country 41), 2002.
111. Alison Brown, *Best of the Vanguard Years* (Vanguard 79709), 2002.
112. Tony Trischka, *Double Banjo Bluegrass Spectacular* (Rounder 116610548), 2007.
113. *Bill Emerson and the Sweet Dixie Band* (Rebel 111823), 2007.

WITH FIDDLERS, DOBROISTS & BASSISTS

114. Richard Greene, *Duets* (Rounder 0075), 1977.
115. Mark O'Connor, *Markology* (Rounder 0090), 1978.
116. Mark O'Connor, *On the Rampage* (Rounder 0118), 1979.
117. Richard Greene, *Ramblin'* (Rounder 0110; Vivid Sound 154, Japanese Release), 1979.
118. Darol Anger, *Fiddlistics* (Kaleidoscope F8), 1979.
119. Jerry Douglas, *Fluxology* (Rounder 0093), 1979.
120. Todd Phillips, *Released* (Varrick 011), 1984.
121. Mark O'Connor, *Retrospective* (Rounder 11507), 1987.
122. Jerry Douglas, *Everything Is Gonna Work out Fine* (Rounder 11535), 1987.
123. Mike Auldridge, *Treasures Untold* (Sugar Hill 3780), 1990.
124. Rickie Simpkins, *Dancing on the Fingerboard* (Pinecastle 1063), 1997.
125. Rickie Simpkins, *Don't Fret It* (Doobie Shea 2006), 2002.
126. Aubrey Haynie, *The Bluegrass Fiddle Album* (Sugar Hill 3957), 2003.
127. Hunter Berry, *Wow Baby!* (Upper Management Music, UMM 7002-20-60-001), 2007.
128. Jerry Douglas, *Glide* (Koch 4553), 2008.

WITH OTHER GUITARISTS, VOCALISTS, SONGWRITERS & GROUPS

129. Bobby Atkins and Frank Poindexter, 45 rpm single; A side, "Mary's Gone," B side, "Rambling Man"; Tony remembers B side as "D.J.'s Theme," (Time 1001), 1970.
130. Dan Crary, *Bluegrass Guitar* (TR penned liner notes) (American Heritage AH 401-27), 1970. [re-released in 1992 on Sugar Hill 3806].
131. Hugh Sturgill, 45 rpm single; A side, "River Movin' On," (McKee Records), date unknown.
132. Kate & Anna McGarrigle, *Kate & Anna McGarrigle* (Warner Brothers 9362; Hannibal 4401), 1975.
133. John Starling, *Long Time Gone* (Sugar Hill 3714) 1977 [re-released on CD with bonus cuts, 1990].
134. Eric Thompson, *Bluegrass Guitar* (Kicking Mule 215), 1979.
135. Ricky Skaggs, *Sweet Temptation* (Sugar Hill 3706), 1979.
136. Jon Sholle, *Catfish for Supper* (Rounder 3026), 1979 [re-released on CD, 1996].
137. Emmylou Harris, *Roses in the Snow* (Warner Brothers/Reprise 3422), 1980.
138. Buck White & Down Home Folks, *More Pretty Girls than One* (Sugar Hill 3710), 1980.
139. Emmylou Harris, *Evangeline* (Reprise 3508), 1981.
140. Kate Wolf, *Close to You* (Kaleidoscope 15; Rhino 71482), 1981.
141. Kate Wolf, *Gold in California, Vols. 1 & 2: A Retrospective of Recordings* (Kaleidoscope 3001), 1986.
142. Kate Wolf, *Gold in California: A Retrospective of Recordings* (Rhino 71485), 1986.
143. Mary-Chapin Carpenter, *Hometown Girl* (Columbia 40758), 1987.
144. The Seldom Scene, *15th Anniversary Celebration* (Sugar Hill 2202), 1988.
145. Lou Reid, *When It Rains* (Sugar Hill 3788), 1991.
146. Jim & Jesse, *Music Among Friends* (Rounder 0279), 1991.
147. Michelle Shocked, *Arkansas Traveler* (TR thanked in liner notes) (Mercury 512101), 1991.
148. Dan Crary, *Jammed If I Do* (Sugar Hill/Koch 3824), 1994.
149. Ronnie Bowman, *Cold Virginia Night* (Rebel 1704), 1994.
150. Chesapeake—*Rising Tide* (Sugar Hill 3827), 1994.
151. Ralph Stanley & Joe Isaacs, *A Gospel Gathering* (Freeland 642), 1995.
152. John Bowman, *Footprints of Faith* (TR, associate producer) (Mountain Home 106) 1995.
153. The Isaacs, *Carry Me* (Horizon 107), 1995.
154. David Johnson, *Wooden Offerings* (TR penned liner notes) (Mountain Home 66), 1995.
155. Claire Lynch, *Moonlighter* (TR penned liner notes) (Rounder 0355), 1995.
156. Karen Peck & New River, *Unlimited* (Horizon 68), 1995.

157. Mo Canada, *Stoney Lonesome* (Mo Music 033), 1995.
158. Kathy Chiavola, *The Harvest* (Demon 779; KCP 1002), 1995.
159. Ric-o-chet, *Carolina Memories* (TR-Prod., mixing) (Rebel 1722), 1995.
160. Jeanette Williams, *Dreams Come True* (Flyin' Cloud FC 025), 1995.
161. Emmylou Harris, *Portraits* (Warner Archives 45308), 1996.
162. Richard Bennett, *Walking Down the Line* (Rebel 1738), 1997.
163. Karen Peck & New River, *Makin' a Difference* (Horizon 651), 1997.
164. Mark Newton, *Living a Dream* (Rebel 1744), 1998.
165. Tony McManus, *Pourquois Quebec* (TR identified in credits by some sources, have not confirmed nature of TR's participation, if any) (Greentrax 151), 1998.
166. Ronnie Bowman, *The Man I'm Tryin' to Be* (Sugar Hill 3880), 1998.
167. Ricky Skaggs, *Highway 40 Blues* (Greatest Hits, TR on "Sweet Temptation") (Platinum Disc 1770), 1999.
168. Karen Peck & New River, *Southern Gospel* (Horizon 740), 1999.
169. Eddie from Ohio, *Looking out the Fishbowl* (Virginia Soul 6), 1999.
170. Dan Tyminski, *Carry Me Across the Mountain* (Doobie Shea 2002), 2000 [re-released on Rounder 0537, 2003].
171. Mark Newton, *Follow Me Back to the Fold* (Rebel 1764), 2000.
172. Kate Wolf, *Weaver of Visions: The Kate Wolf Anthology* (Rhino 75596), 2000.
173. Eric Thompson, *Thompson's Real: Bluegrass Instrumentals with Guitar* (CD reissue/repackage of Kicking Mule 215) (Herringbone 101), 2000.
174. Ricky Skaggs, *Highway 40 Blues* (Greatest Hits, TR on "Sweet Temptation") (Slightly different packaging from Platinum Disc 1770) (Sony Music Special Products 1785; Platinum Disc 17852), 2001.
175. Emmylou Harris, *Anthology: The Warner/Reprise Years* (Rhino 76705), 2001.
176. Peter Rowan & Don Edwards, *High Lonesome Cowboy* (Shanachie 6058), 2002.
177. Nitty Gritty Dirt Band, et al., *Will the Circle Be Unbroken, Vol. 3* (Capitol 40177), 2002.
178. Emmylou Harris, *Roses in the Snow* (Expanded) (Rhino 78140), 2002.
179. Billy & Bryn Bright, *Billy & Bryn Bright* (Blue Corn Music 201), 2002.
180. The Isaacs, *Christmas Spirit* [TR—producer and guitar] (Horizon 854), 2002.
181. Jim Lauderdale, *The Hummingbirds* (Dualtone 1121), 2002.
182. Ronnie Bowman, *Starting Over* (Sugar Hill 3933), 2002.
183. Norman Blake, *Old Ties* (Rounder 611583), 2002.
184. Nitty Gritty Dirt Band, et al., *Will the Circle Be Unbroken, The Trilogy* (Capitol 91400), 2003.
185. Nitty Gritty Dirt Band, *Dirt on the Strings: The Instrumental Collection* (S&P 716), 2004.
186. Jonathan Elias, *American River* (Decca 2978), 2004.
187. Dolly Parton, *Those Were the Days* (Sugar Hill 4007), 2005 [Sanctuary 410, 2005; Liberty 3501422, 2006].
188. John Carlini, *Game's Afoot* (TR penned liner notes) (FGM 110), 2005.
189. Emmylou Harris, *The Very Best of Emmylou Harris: Heartaches & Highways* (Rhino 73123), 2005.
190. Mo Canada, *Grassoline* (FGM 121), 2006.
191. Doc and Merle Watson, *Black Mountain Rag* (Rounder 11620), 2006.
192. Bryan Sutton, *Not Too Far from the Tree* (Sugar Hill 4001), 2006.
193. Emmylou Harris, *Songbird: Rare Tracks & Forgotten Gems* (Rhino 74744), 2007.
194. Donna Hughes, *Gaining Wisdom* (TR produced album in addition to playing) (Rounder 0554), 2007.
195. Alison Krauss, *A Hundred Miles or More: A Collection* (Rounder 0555), 2007.
196. Balsam Range, *Marching Home* (Mountain Home 1142), 2007.
197. Jeanette Williams, *Thank You for Caring* (Blue Circle Records BCR 007), 2008.
198. Alison Krauss, *Essential Alison Krauss* (Rounder 06552; Decca 6106552), 2009.
199. Assembly of Dust, *Some Assembly Required* (Rock Ridge Music 61236), 2009.
200. Josh Williams, *Down Home* (Pinecastle 1173), 2010.

COMPILATIONS AND VARIOUS ARTISTS

201. *O Fino Do Country* (TR on "Some Old Day" by J.D. Crowe & the New South) (Band 33074, Brazilian Release), 1980.
202. *New Acoustic Music Sampler* (Rounder AN-02; Rykodisc 20002), 1984.
203. *Rounder Folk* (Rounder/Rykodisc 20018), 1986.
204. *Bluegrass: The World's Greatest Show* (Sugar Hill 2201), 1987.
205. *Rounder Bluegrass, Vol. 1* (Rounder 11511), 1987.
206. *Rounder Bluegrass, Vol. 2* (Rounder 11512), 1987.
207. *Rounder Guitar* (Rounder 11541), 1988.
208. *Every Time I Feel the Spirit: The Best of Sugar Hill Gospel, Vol. 1* (Sugar Hill 9102; SH-CD 9102, 1993), 1988.
209. *Way Down Deep in My Soul: The Best of Sugar Hill Gospel, Vol. 2* (Sugar Hill 9103; SH-CD 9103, 1993), 1988.
210. *The Bluegrass Suspects* (Kaleidoscope 37), 1990.
211. *Bluegrass Class of 1990* (Rounder AN-07) 1990.
212. *Guitar Player Presents: Legends of Guitar: Country, Vol. 2* (Rhino 70723), 1991.
213. *Stained Glass Hour: Bluegrass and Old-Timey Gospel Music* (Rounder 11563), 1991.
214. *Rounder Fiddle* (Rounder 11565), 1992
215. *Son of Rounder Banjo* (Rounder 1158), 1992.
216. *Jubilation! Great Gospel Performances, Vol. 3: Country Gospel* (Rhino 70290), 1992.
217. *Blue Ribbon Bluegrass* (Rounder CD-AN-11), 1993.
218. *Acoustic Disc: 100% Handmade Music* (Acoustic Disc 8), 1993.
219. *Sugar Plums: Holiday Treats from Sugar Hill* (Sugar Hill 3796), 1993.
220. *Roundup Records CD Sampler, Summer 1994* (Rounder), 1994.
221. *Acoustic Disc: 100% Handmade Music, Vol. II* (Acoustic Disc 16), 1995.
222. *Must Be Santa! The Rounder Christmas Album* (Rounder 3118; Polygram 528438), 1995.
223. *Hills of Home: 25 Years of Folk Music on Rounder Records* (Rounder AN-16/17), 1995.
224. *Hand Picked: 25 Years of Bluegrass on Rounder Records* (Rounder AN-22), 1995.
225. *Top of the Hill Bluegrass* (Sugar Hill 9201), 1995.
226. *Appalachian Stomp: Bluegrass Classics* (Rhino 71870), 1995.
227. *The Real Music Box: 25 Years of Rounder Records* (Rounder 618525), 1995.
228. *Rounder Bluegrass Guitar* (Rounder 11576), 1996.
229. *Blue Ribbon Guitar* (Easydisc 7006), 1996.
230. *Blue Ribbon Fiddle* (Easydisc 7004), 1996.
231. *25 Years of Strictly Country Magazine* (TR on Steve Huber's "Wait Until Tomorrow") (Strictly Country 45), 1996.
232. *Rebel Records: 35 Years of the Best in Bluegrass* (Rebel 4000), 1996.
233. *Smoky Mountain Memories: Acoustic Hymns* (Dollywood 641), 1997.
234. *Legacy: A Tribute to the First Generation of Bluegrass* (Sugar Hill 9202), 1997.
235. *Acoustic Disc: 100% Handmade Music, Vol. III* (Acoustic Disc 24), 1997.
236. *Mystery Train: Classic Railroad Songs, Vol. 2* (Rounder 1129), 1997.
237. *Blue Ridge Mountain Banjo* (Pinecastle 1070), 1997.
238. *Acoustic Holidays* (Easydisc 367068), 1998.
239. *Bluegrass Breakdown: 14 Instrumentals* (Easydisc 9014), 1998.
240. *Bluegrass Essentials* (Hip-O 40102), 1998.
241. *Appalachian Stomp: More Bluegrass Classics* (Rhino 75720), 1999.
242. *Sacred Voices: An A Cappella Gospel Collection* (Sugar Hill 3898), 1999.

243. *Choice Picks: Celebrating the 10th Annual International Bluegrass Music Awards* (Sugar Hill 7000), 2000.
244. *Bluegrass Essentials, Vol. 2* (Hip-O 64682; Polygram 564682), 2000.
245. *Newgrass: Modern Bluegrass* (K-Tel 4427), 2000.
246. *True Bluegrass* (Rounder 611615), 2001.
247. *Bluegrass Mountain Style* (Rounder 611616), 2001.
248. *Roots Music: An American Journey* (Rounder 610501), 2001.
249. *National Geographic: Destination Appalachia* (Sugo 102), 2001.
250. *The Rough Guide to Bluegrass* (World Music Network 1059), 2001.
251. *Cool, Blue and Lonesome: Bluegrass for the Broken-Hearted* (Sugar Hill 3944), 2002.
252. *Mother Queen of My Heart: A Collection of Songs Inspired by Mom* (Sugar Hill 3948), 2002.
253. *Best of Acoustic Swing: As Time Goes By* (Includes "Mar West" and "Neon Tetra" by the Tony Rice Unit) (Vivid Sound 157, Japanese Release), 2002.
254. *O Christmas Tree! A Bluegrass Collection for the Holidays* (Rounder 610513), 2002.
255. *Bluegrass Goes to Town: Pop Songs Bluegrass Style* (Rounder 610511), 2002.
256. *Time-Life's Treasury of Bluegrass* (Time Life 18701), 2002.
257. *Acoustic Disc: 100% Handmade Music, Vol. VI* (Acoustic Disc 48), 2002.
258. *American Lullaby: Folk, Country, Gospel & Old-Timey Bedtime Songs* (Ellipsis Arts 4294), 2003.
259. *Merlefest Live: The 15th Anniversary Jam* (Merlefest 6893), 2003.
260. *White Dove: The Bluegrass Gospel Collection* (Rounder 610523), 2003. *Blue Grass Roots* (Etown 0539), 2003.
261. *The Old Home Place: Bluegrass and Old Time Mountain Music* (Rounder 610514), 2003.
262. *Winter's Eve: Acoustic Music for the Winter Season* (Compass 4349), 2003.
263. *Lonesome Valley: Classic American Bluegrass, Appalachian and Old Timey Country* (TR on "Little Cabin Home on the Hill" from Ricky Skaggs' *Sweet Temptation*) (Manteca 030), 2003.
264. *All Songs Considered: 4 CD Collection* (NPR National Public Radio 29), 2004.
265. *Merlefest Live! The Best of 2003* (Merlefest 79766), 2004.
266. *Best of King & Starday Bluegrass* (King 952), 2004.
267. *Bluegrass All-Stars: Sixteen Grand Slams from Sugar Hill* (Sugar Hill 3982), 2004.
268. *100% Handmade Music* (Acoustic Disc 56), 2004.
269. *Bluegrass Express* (Rounder 1159), 2004.
270. *Windham Hill America* (Windham Hill 60132), 2004.
271. *Bluegrass Hits: Twenty Timeless Favorites from Yesterday and Today* (Rounder 0659), 2005.
272. *Flatpicking 1999* (Flatpicking Guitar Magazine 103), 2005.
273. *Flatpicking 2000* (Flatpicking Guitar Magazine 103), 2005.
274. *Strings and Things: The Best in Bluegrass, Vol. I* (Dualtone 1208), 2005.
275. *Tone Poets* (Acoustic Disc 62), 2005.
276. *Blockbuster Bluegrass* (Copper Creek, 6002), 2006.
277. *Celebration of Life: Musicians Against Childhood Cancer* (Skaggs Family 09001), 2006.
278. *Sugar Hill Records: A Retrospective* (Sugar Hill 3999), 2006.
279. *Voice of the Spirit, Gospel of the South* (Dualtone Music Group 01228), 2006.
280. *Ricky Skaggs, The Best of Ricky Skaggs* (Sugar Hill Americana Master Series 4045), 2008.
281. Various Artists, *Jazz Manouche, Vol. 4* (Wagram), 2008 [David Grisman Quintet's cut of "Minor Swing"].
282. Various Artists, *My Favorite Martin: Legendary Guitarists Playing Legendary Guitars* (Solid Air 2083), 2008. [Tony's version of "Danny Boy"]
283. Various Artists, *Bluegrass Roots* (Etown 0539), 2010.

VIDEO

284. *J.D. Crowe and the New South Live on KET* (Kentucky Public Television), 1993.
285. *Tony Rice, The Video Collection* (Vestapol 13058), 2001.
286. *Legends of Flatpicking Guitar* (Vestapol 13005), 2001.
287. Various Artists, *Bluegrass Journey: A Documentary* (Blue Stores 1), 2005.
288. Various Artists, *Bluegrass Country Soul* (Time Life 19264), 2006.
289. Various Artists, *Larry Keel: Beautiful Thing* (Beach Movie LLC TLEC9W37), 2008.
290. Alison, Krauss, *A Hundred Miles or More: Live from the Tracking Room* (Rounder DVD 610625), 2008.

MOVIES AND SOUNDTRACKS

291. *Preacherman,* 1971; re-released by Troma Entertainment, Inc., 1996. TR played on the movie soundtrack.
292. *Eat My Dust,* 1976, New World Pictures; re-released by Buena Vista Home Entertainment, 2007. TR played on the movie soundtrack.
293. *King of the Gypsies,* 1978; re-released by Paramount, 1998; re-released by Legend Films, 2008. TR played on the movie soundtrack.

Many thanks to Chuck Emory for his invaluable assistance compiling this discography.

Tony reviews Chuck's discography with pleasure, July 2005.
(Photo by Caroline Wright)

SELECT BIBLIOGRAPHY

BOOKS

Amatneek, Bill. *Acoustic Stories: Playing Bass with Peter, Paul & Mary, Jerry Garcia, and Bill Monroe, and Eighteen Other Unamplified Tales.* Vineyards Press, 2003.

Anthony, Ted. *Chasing the Rising Sun: The Journey of an American Song.* Simon & Schuster, 2007.

Bacon, Tony. *The Ultimate Guitar Book.* Alfred A. Knopf, 1997.

Barenberg, Russ. *Teach Yourself Bluegrass Guitar.* Oak Publications, 2000.

Bell, Madison Smartt. *Anything Goes.* Pantheon Books, 2002.

Birosik, Patti Jean. *The New Age Music Guide: Profiles and Recordings of 500 Top New Age Musicians.* Collier Books, 1989.

Black, Bob, and Neil Rosenberg. *Come Hither to Go Yonder: Playing Bluegrass with Bill Monroe.* University of Illinois Press, 2005.

Boak, Dick, Steve Miller, and C.F. Martin IV. *Martin Guitar Masterpieces: A Showcase of Artists' Editions, Limited Editions, and Custom Guitars.* Bulfinch Press, 2003.

Bogdanov, Vladimir, Chris Woodstra, and Stephen Thomas Erlewine. *All Music Guide to Country: The Definitive Guide to Country Music.* Backbeat Books, 2003

Brackett, Nathan and Christian Hoard. *The New Rolling Stone Album Guide: Completely Revised and Updated 4th Edition.* Simon and Schuster, 2004

Byworth, Tony, Ed. *The Billboard Illustrated Encyclopedia of Country Music.* Billboard Books, 2007.

Cantwell, Robert. *Bluegrass Breakdown: The Making of the Old Southern Sound.* University of Illinois Press, 2003.

Carr, Joe. *Getting Into Country Guitar.* Mel Bay Publications, 2004.

Carr, Joe. *School of Country Guitar: Adv. Rhythm, Steel Bends.* Mel Bay Publications, 2008.

Carlin, Richard. *Country Music: A Biographical Dictionary.* Taylor & Francis, 2003.

Cochran, Mickey. *Guitar Crosspicking Technique.* Mel Bay Publications, 2002.

Coelho, Victor. *The Cambridge Companion to the Guitar.* Cambridge University Press, 2003.

Cohen, Norm, and David Cohen. *Long Steel Rail: The Railroad in American Folksong.* 2nd Edition, University of Illinois Press, 2000.

Cohen, Ronald D. *Folk Music: The Basics.* CRC Press, 2006.

Cross, Dan, and Douglas Lichterman. *The About.com Guide to Acoustic Guitar: Step-by-Step Instruction to Start Playing Today.* Adams Media, 2006.

Davis, Brad. *Tony Rice Style Guitar Solos.* Musician's Workshop, 1998.

Davis, Brad. *Flatpicking the Blues.* Mel Bay Publications, 2006.

Davis, Elizabeth A. *A Basic Music Library: Essential Scores and Sound Recordings.* Music Library Association, ALA Editions, 1997.

Dorian, Frederick, Simon Broughton, Mark Ellingham, James McConnachie, Richard Trillo, and Orla Duane. *World Music: The Rough Guide.* Rough Guides, 2000.

Edwards, Bill. *Fretboard Logic III Applications: Creative and Analytical.* Bill Edwards Publishing Corp.; 4th edition, 2004.

Erlewine, Michael, with contributors Michael Erlewine, Vladimir Bogdanov, and Chris Woodstra. *All Music Guide to Country: The Experts' Guide to the Best Recordings in Country Music.* Hal Leonard Corporation, 1997.

Erbsen, Wayne. *Old Time Gospel Songbook.* Mel Bay Publications, 1993.

Erbsen, Wayne. *Rural Roots of Bluegrass: Songs, Stories & History.* Native Ground Books & Music, 2003.

Erbsen, Wayne. *Backpocket Bluegrass Song Book: Words and Music to 40 Classic Bluegrass Tunes.* Native Ground Books & Music, 2008.

Evans, Bill. *Banjo for Dummies.* John Wiley and Sons, 2007.

Evans, C. Wyatt. *The Legend of John Wilkes Booth: Myth, Memory, and a Mummy.* University Press of Kansas, 2004.

Fleischhauer, Carl and Neil V. Rosenberg. *Bluegrass Odyssey.* University of Illinois Press, 2001.

Flora, Joseph M., Lucinda Hardwick MacKethan, and Todd W. Taylor. *The Companion to Southern Literature: Themes, Genres, Places, People, Movements, and Motifs.* LSU Press, 2002.

Gale Group. *Bibliographic Guide to Music.* G K Hall, 2001.

Garcia, Jerry, and John Newton. *Jerry Garcia's Amazing Grace.* HarperCollins, 2002.

Gelo, Dan. *Fiddle Tunes & Irish Music for Guitar.* Mel Bay Publications, 1997.

Gerken. Teja, Richard Johnston, Frank Ford, and Michael John Simmons. *Acoustic Guitar: An Historical Look at the Composition, Construction, and Evolution of One of the World's Most Beloved Instruments.* Hal Leonard Corporation, 2005.

Goldsmith, Thomas, ed. *The Bluegrass Reader.* University of Illinois Press, 2006.

Griffin, Sid, Eric Thompson, and Eric Andrew Thompson. *Bluegrass Guitar: Know the Players, Play the Music.* Hal Leonard Corporation, 2006

Grisman, David and Tony Rice. *Mel Bay Tone Poems for Mandolin.* Mel Bay Publications, 1996.

Hamburger, David. *The Acoustic Guitar Method: Learn to Play Using the Techniques and Songs of American Roots Music.* Hal Leonard Corporation, 2002.

Hatlo, Jim. *Hot Licks: Today's Top Guitar Players Present the Fundamentals of Speed and Accuracy.* Guitar Player Magazine, Hal Leonard Corporation, 1989.

Hunter, Dave. *Play Acoustic: The Complete Guide to Mastering Acoustic Guitar Styles.* Hal Leonard Corporation, 2005.

Jackson, Blair. *Garcia: An American Life.* Penguin Non-Classics, 2000.

Judd, Naomi, and Bud Schaetzle. *Love Can Build a Bridge.* Random House, Inc., 1994.

Kaufman, Steve. *You Can Teach Yourself Flatpicking Guitar.* Mel Bay Publications, 1994.

Kaufman, Steve. *Mel Bay Complete Flatpicking Guitar Book.* Mel Bay Publications, 2004.

Kaufman, Steve. *Championship Flatpicking Guitar.* Mel Bay Publications, 2004.

Kingsbury, Paul, Laura Garrard, Daniel Cooper, John Rumble, *The Encyclopedia of Country Music: The Ultimate Guide to the Music.* Country Music Hall of Fame & Museum, Nashville, Tenn. (Published by Sourcebooks, Inc.), 2004.

Kitts, Jeff, Guitar World Magazine, and Brad Tolinski. *Guitar World Presents the 100 Greatest Guitarists of All Time: From the Pages of Guitar World Magazine.* Hal Leonard Corporation, 2002.

Kleber, John E. *The Encyclopedia of Louisville.* University Press of Kentucky, 2001.

Knight, David. *Swimming in Circles.* Sorry Ma Publishing, 2003.

Kochman, Marilyn, ed. *The Big Book of Bluegrass.* William Morrow & Co., 1984.

Ledgin, Stephanie P. *Homegrown Music: Discovering Bluegrass.* Greenwood Publishing Group, 2004.

Lee, Guy. *How to Make a Living Teaching Guitar (and Other Musical Instruments): And Other Musical Instruments.* Guytar Publishing, 2004.

Lichtenstein Creative Media. *Music and the Mind.* Lichtenstein Creative Media, 2002.

Lord, Tom. *The Jazz Discography.* Lord Music Reference, 1997.

Lundy, Ronni. *Shuck Beans, Stack Cakes, and Honest Fried Chicken: The Heart and Soul of Southern Country Kitchens.* Grove Atlantic Press, 1994.

Malone, Bill C. *Country Music, U.S.A.* University of Texas Press, 1985.

Malone, Bill C. *Don't Get Above Your Raisin': Country Music and the Southern Working Class.* University of Illinois Press, 2002.

Malone, Bill C., and David Stricklin. *Southern Music/American Music.* 2nd Edition, University Press of Kentucky, 2003.

Marshall, Mike. *The Mike Marshall Collection: Music for Mandolin, Fiddle and Guitar.* Mel Bay Publications, 2000.

Marshall, Wolf. *Stuff! Good Guitar Players Should Know: An A–Z Guide to Getting Better.* Hal Leonard Corporation, 2008.

Matteson, Jr., Richard. *Bluegrass Picker's Tune Book.* Mel Bay Publications, 2006.

McGuire, Jim. *Nashville Portraits: Legends of Country Music.* The Lyons Press, 2007.

Noad, Frederick. *The Complete Idiot's Guide to Playing Guitar.* Alpha; 2 Pap/Cdr edition, 2001.

O'Connor, Mark. *Flatpicking Guitar Masterpieces: Acoustic Guitar CD Songbook.* Hal Leonard Corp, 2000.

Peterson, Oscar. *A Jazz Odyssey: My Life in Jazz.* Continuum International Publishing Group, 2006.

Phillips, Mark and Jon Chappell, *Guitar for Dummies.* For Dummies Press, 2005.

The Purchaser's Guide to the Music Industries. Music Trades Corp., 1996.

Randall, Alice, Carter Little, Courtney Little, and George Jones. *My Country Roots: The Ultimate MP3 Guide to America's Original Outsider Music.* Thomas Nelson Inc, 2006.

Rehder, John B. *Appalachian Folkways.* JHU Press, 2004.

Rice, Tony. *Tony's Choice: Licks, Kickoffs and Solos.* Hal Leonard Corp, 2000.

Rice, Tony. *Tony Rice Teaches Bluegrass Guitar: A Master Picker Analyzes His Pioneering Licks and Solos.* Homespun Listen and Learn Series, 2008.

Rodgers, Jeffrey Pepper. *Rock Troubadours: Conversations on the Art and Craft of Songwriting.* Hal Leonard Corporation, 2000.

Patricia Romanowski, *New Rolling Stone Encyclopedia of Rock & Roll: Completely Revised and Updated.* Fireside; Revised edition, 1995.

Rosenberg, Neil V., and Charles K. Wolfe. *The Music of Bill Monroe.* University of Illinois Press, 2007.

Rosenberg, Neil. *Bluegrass: A History.* University of Illinois Press, 1985 (20th Anniversary Edition, 2005).

Sandberg, Larry. *Acoustic Guitar Styles: For Beginning and Intermediate Guitarists.* Routledge, 2002.

Scully, Michael F. *The Never-Ending Revival: Rounder Records and the Folk Alliance.* University of Illinois Press, 2008.

Smith, Richard D. *Bluegrass: An Informal Guide.* A Capella Books, 1995.

St. John, Allen. *Clapton's Guitar: Watching Wayne Henderson Build the Perfect Instrument.* Free Press, 2005.

Stambler, Irwin, and Grelun Landon. *Country Music: The Encyclopedia.* Macmillan, 2000.

Stimpson, Michael. *The Guitar: A Guide for Students and Teachers.* Oxford University Press, 1988.

String Letter Publishing. *Vintage Guitars: The Instruments, the Players, the Music.* String Letter Publishing, Hal Leonard Corporation, 2001.

Taylor, Joe. *The World's Thinnest Fat Man: Stories.* Swallow's Tale Press at Livingston Press, The University of West Alabama, 2005.

Thompson, Eric. *Bluegrass Flatpicking & Crosspicking Guitar.* Mel Bay Publications, 2003.

Thompson, Justin. *Mel Bay Presents The Tony Rice Unit: Acoustics, Transcribed by Justin Thompson.* Mel Bay Publications, 1999.

Tichi. Cecelia. *High Lonesome: The American Culture of Country Music.* UNC Press, 1996.

Tichi, Cecelia. *Reading Country Music: Steel Guitars, Opry Stars, and Honky-Tonk Bars.* Duke University Press, 1998.

Trager, Oliver. *Keys to the Rain: The Definitive Bob Dylan Encyclopedia.* Billboard Books, 2004.

Trager, Oliver. *The American Book of the Dead: The Definitive Grateful Dead Encyclopedia.* Simon and Schuster, 1997.

Tribe, Ivan M. *Country: A Regional Exploration.* Greenwood Publishing Group, 2006.

Verheyen, Carl. *Studio City: Professional Session Recording for Guitarists.* Hal Leonard Corporation, 2001

Watson, Doc, and Steve Kaufman. *The Legacy of Doc Watson.* Mel Bay Publications, 1999.

Weissman, Dick. *Which Side are You On?: An Inside History of the Folk Music Revival in America.* Continuum International Publishing Group, 2005.

Weissman, Dick. *Songwriting: The Words, the Music and the Money.* Hal Leonard Corporation, 2001.

Willis, Barry. America's *Music: Bluegrass : A History of Bluegrass Music in the Words of Its Pioneers.* Pine Valley Music, 1997.

Wolfe, Charles K. *Kentucky Country: Folk and Country Music of Kentucky.* University Press of Kentucky, 1996.

Wolff, Kurt, and Orla Duane. *Country Music: The Rough Guide.* Rough Guides, 2000.

ARTICLES

"J.D. Crowe and the New South, an Interview by Fred Bartenstein," Fred Bartenstein, *Muleskinner News* (July 1973).

" J.D. Crowe & The New South," Mary Jane Bolle, *Bluegrass Unlimited* (February 1974).

"Strings and Things: A Word About Strings from Tony Rice," Tony Rice, *Bluegrass Unlimited* (June 1975).

"Tony Rice: East Meets West," Jack Tottle, *Bluegrass Unlimited* (October 1977).

"Tony Rice: Guitarist in Overdrive," Mark Hunter, *Frets* (April 1980).

"A Conversation with J.D. Crowe," Marty Godbey, *Bluegrass Unlimited* (July 1981).

"J.D. Crowe, Back-Forty Fugitive," W. H. Ward, *Appalachian Journal: A Regional Studies Review* 8, no. 2 (Winter 1981), pp. 155–159.

"Would You Play 'Ground Speed'?" Eddie Cummins, *Bluegrass Unlimited* 20, no. 8 (February 1986).

"The Truth About Clarence's D-28." *Frets* (July 1986), p. 51.

"Tony Rice: Getting the Most out of Acoustics," Jas Obrecht, *Guitar Player* 21 (May 1987), p. 14.

"Tony Rice: Artist at a Crossroads," Mark Hanson, *Frets* (September 1987).

"Tony Rice: A Distinct Talent," Logan Neill, *Bluegrass Unlimited* (August 1989).

"The Talented J.D. Crowe"; "Food for Thought from J.D. Crowe," Joe Ross, *Bluegrass Unlimited* 25: 5 (November 1990).

"The techniques and inspirations behind the trailblazing guitar of Tony Rice," David McCarty, *Acoustic Guitar,* No. 21 (November/December 1993).

"Equipment Picks from Tony Rice," David McCarty, *Acoustic Guitar,* No. 21, (November/December 1993).

"David Grisman & Tony Rice," Tom Stern, *Bluegrass Unlimited* (July 1994).

"J.D. Crowe," Douglas Fulmer, *Bluegrass Unlimited* (April 1995).

"The Very Versatile Tony Rice," Nancy Cardwell, *Bluegrass Now* (January 1997).

"Tony Rice's Banjo Roll," Tony Rice, *Guitar Player* 30: 6 (June 1996), p. 135.

"Tony Rice, Flatpicking Master," Bryan Kimsey, *Flatpicking Guitar Magazine* (November/December 1998).

"Béla Fleck: Bluegrass Journeys into Uncharted Territory," Caroline Wright, *Bluegrass Now* (April 2001).

"Peter Rowan: Living in a Musical Moment," Caroline Wright, *Bluegrass Now* (January 2002).

"Where are the Female Tony Rices?" Elena Corey, *Bluegrass Unlimited* (February 2002).

"Offstage with Tony Rice," Caroline Wright, *Bluegrass Now* (April 2002).

"Measure for Measure: Flatpicker Tony Rice Looks Back on his Long Career at the Top of the Newgrass Heap," Craig Havighurst, *Acoustic Guitar* No. 114 (June 2002).

"A Day in the Life of the World's Best Guitarist," Caroline Wright, *Listener Magazine* (July/August 2002).

"How to Raise a Great Musician, Part II," (interview with Louise Rice) Caroline Wright, *Bluegrass Now* (July 2002).

"His First Love, The Guitar—Tony Rice," Geoffrey Himes, *Bluegrass Unlimited* (October 2002).

"The Magic of Vassar Clements," Caroline Wright, *Bluegrass Now* (April 2004).

"J.D. Crowe: Shining Bright and Clear," Caroline Wright, *Bluegrass Now* (July 2004).

"Bluegrass and Beyond: Tony Rice Reveals His Secrets to Fiery Flatpicking," Andy Ellis, *Guitar Player* 39: 1 (January 2005), p. 96.

"58957: Tony Rice and His Holy Grail Martin," Art Dudley, *The Fretboard Journal* (Spring 2007).

"Flatpicker Extraordinaire," Scott Nygaard, *Acoustic Guitar* (June 2007).

"Tony Rice—Going with the Flow," Caroline Wright, *Bluegrass Unlimited* (June 2007).

"Dawg Days: The First David Grisman Quintet," *The Fretboard Journal* (Summer 2007).

"Mike Compton: Carrying the Torch," John Bridgland, *Bluegrass Unlimited* (September 2008).

REVIEWS

"J.D. Crowe and The New South," George B. McCeney, *Bluegrass Unlimited* (November 1975).

"Manzanita," Rich Kienzle, *Country Music* 8 (March 1980), p. 48.

"Skaggs and Rice," Rich Kienzle, *Country Music* 9 (October 1980), p. 76.

"Mar West," Jas Obrecht, *Guitar Player* 14 (December 1980), p. 126.

"Mar West," Randy Savicky, *Down Beat* 48 (June 1981), p. 44.

"Still Inside," Roy Blount, *Esquire* 97 (June 1982), p. 104.

"Backwaters," Michael Tearson, *Audio* 67 (November 1983), p. 104.

"Backwaters," Mike Joyce, *The Washington Post 106* (February 13, 1983), p. F11.

"Church Street Blues," Mark Greenburg, *Sing Out!* 30 (January–March 1984), p. 86.

"Church Street Blues," Dan Forte, *Guitar Player* 18 (April 1984), p. 120.

"Church Street Blues," Alanna Nash, *Stereo Review* 49 (April 1984), p. 90.

"Me and My Guitar," Robert E. Allen, *Country Music* (May–June 1987), p. 60.

"Me and My Guitar," Jon Sievert, *Guitar Player* 21 (May 1987), p. 149.

"Blake and Rice," Jon Sievert, *Guitar Player* 22 (February 1987), p. 168.

"Cold on the Shoulder," Norm Cohen, *Journal of American Folklore* 101 (January–March 1988), p. 71.

"Me and My Guitar," Norm Cohen, *Journal of American Folklore* 101 (January–March 1988), p. 71.

"Native American," Alanna Nash, *Stereo Review* 53 (December 1988), p. 130.

"Norman Blake and Tony Rice 2," Jon Sievert, *Guitar Player* 25: 3 (March 1991), p. 117.

"The Bluegrass Album, Volume Four," Norm Cohen, *Journal of American Folklore* 106 (Spring 1993), p. 197.

"Tone Poems," Chris Gill, *Guitar Player* 28: 9 (September 1994), p. 142.

"Plays and Sings Bluegrass," Alanna Nash, *Stereo Review* 59: 4 (April 1994), p. 93.

"Out of the Woodwork," Bob Cannon, *Entertainment Weekly* 363 (January 24, 1997), p. 69.

"The Pizza Tapes," Andy Ellis, *Guitar Player* 34: 8 (August 2000), p. 105.

"Running Wild," John Vasile, *Country Music* 219 (April–May 2002), p. 94.

"Running Wild," Mike Regenstreif, *Sing Out!* 46: 1 (Spring 2002), p. 148.

"The Tony Rice Guitar Method," Tom Druckenmiller, *Sing Out!* 46: 4 (Winter 2003), p. 168.

"Peter Rowan and Tony Rice: You Were There for Me," Art Thompson, *Guitar Player* 38: 12 (December 2004), p. S82.

"Peter Rowan and Tony Rice: You Were There for Me," John Lupton, *Sing Out!* 48: 4 (Winter 2004), p. 159.

"Peter Rowan and Tony Rice: Quartet," Stephanie P. Ledgin, *Sing Out!* 51: 2 (Summer 2007), p. 121.

"Vassar Clements, Tony Rice and the Low Country All-Star Band," Tom Druckenmiller, *Sing Out!* 50: 4 (Winter 2007), p. 160.

"Krauss Gives Bluegrass Hero His Voice Back," Ralph Berrier, Jr., *Roanoke VA Times* (May 19, 2007).

"Tony Rice Sings Again in New Compilation: Bluegrass Notes," Keith Lawrence, *Messenger-Inquirer* (Owensboro, KY) (August 1, 2008).

NEWSPAPER ARTICLES

"Tony Rice," Joe Sasfy, *Washington Post* (February 13, 1985), p. B10.

"Tony Rice Defies All Categories," *The Roanoke VA Times* (May 25, 1990).

"Tony Rice, Picking up the Tempo," Mike Joyce, *Washington Post* (January 3, 1991), p. C11.

"Fair-Weather Friends Musicians Rally to Tony Rice's Support After Disastrous Storm," Peter Khoury, *Greensboro News and Record* (April 23, 1993).

"Tony Rice harvests his bluegrass roots," Geoffrey Himes, *Washington Post* (December 10, 1993), p. WW22.

"Flat Out the Best, Guitarist Tony Rice Stays True to Bluegrass Roots," Michael Miller, *Columbia SC State* (December 12, 2002).

"Acoustic Freedom: David Grisman's Quintet Took the Stage in 1976, and Stringed Music Hasn't Been the Same Since," Mark Whittington, *San Jose Mercury News* (January 26, 2006).

"Alison Krauss Can't Believe She's Touring with Tony Rice," Wayne Bledsoe, *Knoxville News-Sentinel* (May 11, 2007).

"Singing Tony Rice's Praises," Ralph Berrier, Jr., *Roanoke VA Times* (May 18, 2007).

"Alison Krauss and Union Station in Guitar Heaven with Tony Rice," Dave McKenna, *Washington Post* (May 18, 2007), p. C10.

"Creative Sponsorship Helps Team: Bluegrass Music Legend Tony Rice Donates Items to Raise Funds," Charity Apple, *Burlington, NC Times-News* (June 8, 2007).

"Peter Rowan and Tony Rice Work Well—and Closely—Together," Walter Tunis, *Lexington Herald-Leader* (Lexington, KY) (January 17, 2008).

THESES AND DISSERTATIONS

Reed Jones, "The Bluegrass Album: Changing a Music's History by Revisiting It." BA History Thesis (Eastern Mennonite University, Harrisonburg, VA), 2006.

ACKNOWLEDGEMENTS

A special thanks to my Heavenly Father, the Holy Creator, for giving me this life, and this gift to share with people; and thanks to every living thing in the Universe.

Thanks to Billy Wolf, my closest friend and confidant on this planet, and to Caroline Wright and Tim Stafford for their years of hard work on this remarkable book. And my gratitude to Gordon Lightfoot; to my former bosses, J.D. Crowe and David Grisman; and to John Carlini, Richard Greene, and Buell Neidlinger, guys from the early Dawg era who were responsible for pulling me out of the bluegrass mold and allowing me to expand my musicianship to where I never dreamed it could be.

To Dr. Mark Cresenzo from one of his most frustrating patients: thank you for being my dear friend. My sincere gratitude to Wade Smith, my attorney and friend, for getting me out of a few jams along the way; to the staffs of Rounder Records and Keith Case & Associates for all their hard work on my behalf over the years; and to Peter Rowan, a special thanks for being my working partner in crime for the past decade—our collaboration could be a book in and of itself!

I'd like to thank my immediate family and my animals for their unconditional love, and a special thanks to my wife, Pam, for the life we've shared for the past 21 years. I wish I could thank all of my friends, fans, and fellow musicians individually, but there isn't enough time or ink on the planet for that. There are others I may have forgotten to include here, but they know who they are. And to those I have trespassed against, I beg your forgiveness; to those who have trespassed against me, I love you.

I wish to express my appreciation and love for my late brother Larry, and to other beloved friends who have passed on: Vassar Clements, John Hartford, John Duffey, Jimmy Martin . . . and to my little dog Tipper, and other animals who have been dear to me and now are gone: if there is really a place in God's kingdom where we'll all be reunited, I hope they'll be the first old friends I see when I get there.

Last but not least, a very special thank you to all the members of the Tony Rice Unit, past and present. Your contributions to that rhythm section speak for themselves.

Tony Rice

First, I must thank the world's greatest acoustic flatpick guitarist, Tony Rice, for his willingness to do this book and his gracious patience with me as it turned into a decade-long quest interrupted by my own career and projects—I count you one of my true friends; Caroline Wright for her patience, hard work and true writing talent over these last seven years or so; Bobby Starnes and Johnny Burton for the friendship and for believing in this project and Word of Mouth Press. Also many thanks to those who either read the manuscript and/or offered suggestions and help: Brian Abrams, Fred Bartenstein, Ron Block, Jason Burleson, J.D. Crowe, John Delgatto, Jon Fox, Frank Godbey, Steve Gulley, David Haney, Rob Ickes, Ken Irwin, Carolyn Larkins,

Dan Miller, Senor McGuire, Chip Petree, Frank Poindexter, Ronnie and Wyatt Rice, Linda Rice, Kim Roulias, Scarlett Smith, Harry Sparks, Trish Stafford, Connie Starnes, Arthur Stern, Dana Thorin, Allen Tolbert, Jack Tottle, and Jon Weisberger, among many others. Thanks to the hundreds of folks who graciously agreed to be interviewed either in person, via phone, or by email survey. And thanks to Ricky Skaggs for agreeing to write the introduction. Special thanks to my Mom, Bernice Stafford, and my sisters Colleen and Carla, and all the guys in Blue Highway. Love ya all . . .

Tim Stafford

So many people have been part of the journey that ends with this book. My love and gratitude to the Rice women, Aunt Lou and Miss Pamela, both of whom contributed to this project in innumerable ways, and to Jewell Penn and India Rice for their kindness. Love and appreciation to my Adirondack clan and all the Gardiner women, especially my hero, Trish, my sister Nancy and my late mother Carol Rumpf; to my children, my father and my husband for living with this project for so many years; to dear friends Keith Cabiles, Art Dudley, Sally Yong, Wendy Thatcher, Mike Kear, Bonnie Chappell, Linda & Chris Ostrom, and especially and forever Billy Mack. *Mahalo nui loa* to my Bluegrass Hawai`i `ohana, especially René & Teresa Berthiaume, Jeb Wiemer, Bob and Mary Schornstheimer, Neal Snyder, Dr. Lisa Gomes, Scott Rhode, Evelyn Greene, Janet & Harley Eblen, Sam Hayakawa, Doug Toews, and the Saloon Pilots: Kilin Reece, Lesley Kline, Paul Sato, Alex Morrison, and Bill Griffin. Thanks also to Allen Tolbert, the sweetest guy on the planet; to Señor Tomas Texino and to Ron Block for listening; to Georgia Getz for laughter; to Rob & Lisa McCoury and Ronnie & Garnet Bowman for their hospitality; to Donna Hughes, Wayne and Deb Bledsoe, Mary Doub, Dan Hays, Nancy Cardwell, Ken Irwin, Bill Nowlin, Sharon Watts, Pete & Kitsy Kuykendall, and Keith Case for their friendship and interest in this project. Many thanks to Johnny Burton, Bobby Starnes, and Scarlett Smith at Word of Mouth Press; and to my co-writer Tim Stafford, one of the finest and most talented men who ever brandished a pick or a pen.

Finally, my love and gratitude to Tony Rice. Thanks for letting me ride shotgun.

Caroline Wright

Tony, Tim, and Caroline would like to thank the following people who helped make this book possible: Jason Burleson and Allen Tolbert for reading the manuscript at various times and making invaluable suggestions and contributions; Chuck Emory for his discography, which we used as a model for the one which appears in this book; Masahiko Abe, Darol Anger, Bobby Atkins, Mike Auldridge, John Carlini, Dix Bruce, Jason Burleson, John Delgatto, Steve Dilling, Art Dudley, Nancy Gatling, Frank & Marty Godbey, Laurie Hills, Mark Johnson, Steve Johnson, Donn Jones, Mike Kelly, Lee Kotick, Ken Landreth, Barry Lane, Mike Lane, Mike Marshall, Jim McGuire, Terry McManus, Akira Otsuka, Louise Rice, Pam & India Rice, Tony Rice,

Jon Sievert, Tim Talley, Phil Zimmerman, and other photographers and friends who shared their photos and stories, whether they found their way into the book or not; Rounder Records, Keith Case & Associates, and IBMA; Christian & Laura Marks at Magic Bus.com, and all of the interviewees who gave of their time willingly and freely, including Brandon Lee Adams, Bill Amatneek, Darol Anger, Bobby Atkins, Mike Auldridge, Mike Auman, Tim Austin, Jeff Autry, Barry Bales, Russ Barenberg, Fred Bartenstein, Richard Bennett, Alan Bibey, Benny Birchfield, Ron Block, Sam Bush, Rick Campbell, John Carlini, Fred Carpenter, Jon Carroll, Keith Case, Mary Chapin Carpenter, Kathy Chiavola, John Cowan, Dan Crary, J.D. Crowe, Bryn Davies, Brad Davis, Steve Dilling, Jerry Douglas, Tommy Edwards, Ben Eldridge, Chris Eldridge, Bill Emerson, Kyle Estep, Kari Estrin, Brian Fesler, Raymond Fike, Béla Fleck, Jimmy Gaudreau, Sharon Gilchrist, Tom Gray, Richard Greene, David Grier, David Grisman, Robert Hale, Doc Hamilton, David Haney, Emmylou Harris, Mark Harrison, Barbara Higbie, Chris Hillman, Richard Hoover, Randy Hudson, Donna Hughes, Jim Hurst, Ken Irwin, John Jennings, Mark Johnson, Clay Jones, John Kaparakis, Jorma Kaukonen, Larry Keel, Bill Keith, Kent Kessinger, Alison Krauss, Shawn Lane, Jack Lawrence, Doyle Lawson, Phil Leadbetter, Gordon Lightfoot, Mike Longworth, Leroy Mack, Mike Marshall, Jimmy Martin, Del McCoury, John McGann, Tim O'Brien, Mark O'Connor, Gary Oelze, Don Parmley, Herb Pedersen, Jeff Phillips, Todd Phillips, Frank Poindexter, Hal "Junior" Poindexter, John Reischman, Larry Rice, Louise Rice, Pam Rice, Ron Rice, Wyatt Rice, Linda Ronstadt, Peter Rowan, Mark Schatz, Sammy Shelor, James Alan Shelton, Jon Sievert, Rickie Simpkins, Ronnie Simpkins, Ricky Skaggs, Bobby Slone, Kenny Smith, Snuffy Smith, Harry Sparks, John Starling, Arthur Stern, Hugh "Turtle" Sturgill, Bryan Sutton, Dave Talbot, Alan Tolbert, Jack Tottle, Happy Traum, Jeff Troxel, Dan Tyminski, Saburo Watanabe, Jeff White, Billy Wolf; and all the hundreds of people who have donated encouragement, photos, anecdotes, advice and support—we can't thank you enough.

Tony at Grey Fox Bluegrass Festival,
Ancramdale, NY, 2003.
(Photo by Caroline Wright)